NO FAMINE IN THE LAND

Studies in honor of

John L. McKenzie

To Charles and Ju
With love
John L. McGee
Feb. 14, 1978

NO FAMINE IN THE LAND
Studies in honor of
John L. McKenzie

Edited by
JAMES W. FLANAGAN
ANITA WEISBROD ROBINSON

Published by
SCHOLARS PRESS
for
The Institute for Antiquity
and Christianity — Claremont

Distributed by

SCHOLARS PRESS

University of Montana

Missoula, Montana 5980l

NO FAMINE IN THE LAND

Studies in honor of
John L. McKenzie

Edited by
James W. Flanagan
Anita Weisbrod Robinson

Copyright © 1975
by
The Institute for Antiquity
and Christianity — Claremont

Library of Congress Cataloging in Publication Data

No famine in the land.
"A bibliography of the books, articles, and reviews
of John L. McKenzie, by Donald H. Wimmer": p.
Includes bibliographical references and index.
CONTENTS: Munson, T. N. Biographical sketch of John
L. McKenzie. — Robinson, A. W. Letters from Life. —
Freedman, D. N. The Aaronic benediction (Numbers 6:24-
26). [etc.]
1. Theology — Addresses, essays, lectures.
2. McKenzie, John L. 3. McKenzie, John L. — Biblio-
graphy. I. McKenzie, John L. II. Flanagan, James W.
III. Robinson, Anita Weisbrod. IV. Institute for
Antiquity and Christianity.
BR50.N55   230   75-33108
ISBN   0-89130-051-1

PRINTED IN THE UNITED STATES OF AMERICA
1 2 3 4 5 6
Printing Department
University of Montana
Missoula, Montana 5980l

Editorial Note

> "Listen," says the Lord, "the days are coming when I will send a famine to the land; not a famine of bread, not of thirst for water, but of hearing the word of the Lord."
>
> Amos 8:11

> I may have failed, but I tried, God knows, to give not description but explanation; to show people how to find in their own experience elements of meaning, how these elements can be assembled into ancient modes of meaning, why in antiquity the elements were assembled in this manner.
>
> John L. McKenzie, 1975

If there is ever to be a famine of hearing the word of the Lord, it will not be during the lifetime of John L. McKenzie. He has lived with the conviction that the word's freedom is to be enjoyed by everyone, and he has spent his life as scholar, teacher, churchman and author making it accessible to those who seek it. The purpose of this volume is to recall and record the impact of McKenzie's writings on the various worlds in which he lived. We are pleased that the publication of this book coincides with his sixty-fifth birthday and that it is presented to him at the lllth national meeting of the Society of Biblical Literature — which recognized his contribution to the scholarly community in 1967 by electing him President. He has been the only Roman Catholic to enjoy this honor.

Contributors were asked to respond to McKenzie's work where it intersects theirs. Thus the range of topics treated in this volume illustrates his own breadth of interests, embracing scripture, theology and contemporary religious thought. In this way the volume mirrors not only his gentle friendship in which the contributors share, but also his own provision that there be no famine in the land.

We are grateful to all those who have cooperated in the publication of this volume. In addition to the essayists, we are indebted to Rev. William LeSaint, S.J., for the anecdotes from his years of close association with John L. McKenzie which have enlivened the photographic section. We also wish to express appreciation to The Institute for Antiquity and Christianity for sponsorship, to Robert W. Funk, Director of Scholars Press, for patient guidance throughout the enterprise, to the Department of Theology of DePaul University, McKenzie's present academic home, to Maureen Holub for help at an early stage, and to Sharleen Martenas and Mary McMahon for their invaluable assistance in preparing the indices.

July, 1975   J. W. F.
                                                                  A. W. R.

Abbreviations

AASOR	Annual of the American Schools of Oriental Research
AB	Anchor Bible
ACW	Ancient Christian Writers
Adv haer	Irenaeus, *Adversus Haereses*
AER	*American Ecclesiastical Review*
ALBO	*Analecta lovaniensia biblica et orientalia*
AnBib	Analecta biblica
ANET	J. B. Pritchard (ed.), *Ancient Near Eastern Texts*
AnOr	Analecta orientalia
Ant	Josephus, *Antiquities*
1-2 Apol	Justin Martyr, 1 Apology, 2 Apology
ArOr	*Archiv orientální*
ASNU	Acta seminarii neotestamentici upsaliensis
ATD	Das Alte Testament Deutsch
ATR	*Anglican Theological Review*
BASOR	*Bulletin of the American Schools of Oriental Research*
BBB	Bonner biblische Beiträge
BH	Biblia Hebraica
BHS	Biblia Hebraica Stuttgartensia
Bib	*Biblica*
Bib Today	*Bible Today*
BJRL	*Bulletin of the John Rylands Library*
BLeb	*Bibel und Leben*
BR	*Biblical Research*
BWANT	Beiträge zur Wissenschaft vom Alten und Neuen Testament
BZ	*Biblische Zeitschrift*
BZAW	Beihefte zur ZAW
CAH	*Cambridge Ancient History*
Cath World	*Catholic World*

CBQ	*Catholic Biblical Quarterly*
CDigest	*Catholic Digest*
Class Bul	*Classical Bulletin*
1-2 Clem	1-2 Clement
CMind	*Catholic Mind*
Comm	*Commonweal*
CrossCurr	*Cross Currents*
Diogn	Diognetus
DJD	Discoveries in the Judean Desert of Jordan
EB	*Enchiridion Biblicum*
EvT	*Evangelische Theologie*
ExpT	*Expository Times*
FRLANT	Forschungen zur Religion und Literatur des Alten und Neuen Testaments
GKC	*Gesenius' Hebrew Grammar*, ed. E. Kautzsch, tr. A. E. Cowley
Heaut	Terentius, *Heautontimorumenos*
HNT	Handbuch zum Neuen Testament
HPR	*Homelitic and Pastoral Review*
HTR	*Harvard Theological Review*
Ign Eph	Ignatius, Letter to the Ephesians
Ign Magn	Ignatius, Letter to the Magnesians
Ign Pol	Ignatius, Letter to Polycarp
Ign Rom	Ignatius, Letter to the Romans
Ign Smyrn	Ignatius, Letter to the Smyrnaeans
Ign Trall	Ignatius, Letter to the Trallians
Int	*Interpretation*
JAAR	*Journal of the American Academy of Religion*
JBC	R. E. Brown et al. (eds.), *The Jerome Biblical Commentary*
JBL	*Journal of Biblical Literature*
JES	*Journal of Ecumenical Studies*
JesuitEdQ	*Jesuit Educational Quarterly*
JPS	Jewish Publication Society
JR	*Journal of Religion*
JTS	*Journal of Theological Studies*
LCL	Loeb Classical Library
LD	Lectio divina

LXX	Septuagint
ModSch	*Modern Schoolman*
MT	Masoretic Text
MTZ	*Münchener theologische Zeitschrift*
Mur	Wadi Murabba'at text Pesher (commentary)
NAB	*New American Bible*
NCE	M. R. P. McGuire et al. (eds)., *New Catholic Encyclopedia*
NCEA Bul	*National Catholic Educational Association Bulletin*
NEB	*New English Bible*
NovT	*Novum Testamentum*
NovTSup	Novum Testamentum, Supplements
NTA	*New Testament Abstracts*
NTAbh	Neutestamentliche Abhandlungen
NTS	*New Testament Studies*
Or	*Orientalia*
OTS	*Oudtestamentische Studiën*
Pol Phil	Polycarp to the Philippians
1QIsa$^{a, b}$	First or second copy of Isaiah from Qumran Cave 1
3Q15	Copper Scroll from Qumran Cave 3
4QJer^{b}	Second copy of Jeremiah from Qumran Cave 4
4QSam$^{a, b}$	First or second copy of Samuel from Qumran Cave 4
RB	*Revue biblique*
RhM	*Rheinisches Museum für Philologie*
RSV	*Revised Standard Version*
SB	Sources bibliques
SBJ	*La sainte bible de Jérusalem*
SBT	Studies in Biblical Theology
SC	Sources chrétiennes
Scr	*Scripture*
SJT	*Scottish Journal of Theology*
SNTSMS	Society for New Testament Study Monograph Series
Spir Life	*Spiritual Life*
ST	*Studia theologica*

StAnth	*St. Anthony Messenger*
TD	*Theology Digest*
TDNT	G. Kittel and G. Friedrich (eds.), *Theological Dictionary of the New Testament*
TLZ	*Theologische Literaturzeitung*
TQ	*Theologische Quartalschrift*
TS	*Theological Studies*
TZ	*Theologische Zeitschrift*
VC	*Vigiliae christianae*
VS	Verbum salutis
VT	*Vetus Testamentum*
VTSup	Vetus Testamentum, Supplements
WMANT	Wissenschaftliche Monographien zum Alten und Neuen Testament
ZAW	*Zeitschrift für die alttestamentliche Wissenschaft*
ZDPV	*Zeitschrift des deutschen Palästrina-Vereins*
ZNW	*Zeitschrift für die neutestamentliche Wissenschaft*
ZST	*Zeitschrift für Systematische Theologie*
ZTK	*Zeitschrift für Theologie und Kirche*

Contents

xi

John L. McKenzie

Thomas N. Munson

A Biographical Sketch of John L. McKenzie

Brazil, Indiana, located about twenty-five miles from Terre Haute, is still a small town, and it was smaller yet when John Lawrence McKenzie was born there on October 9, 1910. Many would still consider Vigo County to be the "boonies," notwithstanding the metropolis-like air that threatens Terre Haute now that it cradles a flourishing Indiana State. Like so many other towns that have been revived by the influx of students, Terre Haute has lost some of its somnolent ways, and reactions to the new ways of life are mixed. But the McKenzies who are still there: John's mother, sister Peg, and brother Jimmy and family, are, like John himself, both independent and resilient people. Having moved to Terre Haute when John was young, and moved much about it since then, the McKenzies have never lost the uncomplicated ways and hardheaded realism of the smalltown Hoosier. Terre Haute, John used to say in one of his bursts of phrase-making, did not have a depression; it was one. The Irish — Mrs. McKenzie was a Daly — who came to work on the railroad watched their livelihood dribble away. Life was hard, to be battled with a courage that bordered on stoicism. The discerning eye could mark this past in the six McKenzie children, of whom John was the eldest. No one knew that sister Betty had terminal cancer until she was rushed hemorrhaging to the hospital. When she died, a sensitive outsider could detect in her family an unsentimental loyalty that was coupled with an astounding objectivity. How many people can coldly assess the pros and cons of a brother or sister while still remaining loyal and charitable?

Harry McKenzie did not work for the railroad; no use looking there for John's lifelong passion for trains. Even when he was very small, his mother reports, he was forever running to the other side of town to see the trains. His colleagues and students at West Baden, he confided to me in later years, supposed that behind the closed door of his room sat a McKenzie endlessly poring over his books. Little did they know how often a railroad timetable

1

sat on his lap and exercised his memory. Anyone who has traveled with him can vouch for this confidence. "The main line of the Santa Fe," he assured me as we journeyed out West. "As you know, it runs neither through Atchison nor Topeka nor Santa Fe." "Certainly you know why it is called La Junta?" I recall a memorable drive from Phoenix to Tucson, when I was urged to speed up so that through the window of the car the perennial enthusiast might take a snapshot of a Southern Pacific locomotive.

Because the young Jack had become interested in the Jesuits, the family sacrificed and sent him off to high school at St. Mary's, Kansas, where the Missouri Province of the Society conducted a boarding school. Initially, the Jesuits did not realize that they had a kind of prodigy on their hands, a young man gifted with total recall who at home used to sprawl on the living room floor to read. Nor did John realize that he would later return, long after the depression had forced the institution's closing, to spend four years "in the middle of nowhere: nowhere being Topeka, twenty-eight miles away" studying theology and grasshoppers. Appropriately, the institution has now been given — should I say back? — to the Indians.

In 1928, after graduating from high school, John McKenzie joined the Chicago Province of the Society of Jesus, which had recently established a novitiate at Milford, Ohio. With those of us, his students and friends who later experienced the same regime, there has been little conversation about the everyday life of the Jesuit novice and scholastic. More important to him were the people, each great in his own way, whose gifts left a lasting impression: Fr. Francis P. Kemper, his master of novices, who combined profound insight with childlike simplicity; Fr. William J. Young, his prescient dean of the juniorate, who in later years was still talking about the stellar class of McKenzie, et al. to whom he wisely gave free rein to read and enjoy the Latin and Greek classics; Fr. Francis X. McMenamy, the invincible instructor of the final year of Jesuit training, whose uncompromising asceticism shaped a generation of Jesuits. To him John pays the highest compliment of a stylized imitation and quotation: a slight nod forward with a gesture of removing one's glasses, accompanied by the paternal "My dear Father . . . as Father General says . . . ."

One advantage which some of us who have come after him believe that Mr. McKenzie, S.J., did not fully appreciate was that at an early stage in his Jesuit career he was destined to study scripture. Granted that this did not mean that he, like several of his students, went off at an early age to work at Johns Hopkins with William Foxwell Albright; still, he had more than an inkling of his future, which meant that he could seek direction in reading and begin to tackle the required languages. It meant, too, that because he was destined to go to Rome for five years for the doctorate in Scripture after the normal Jesuit course, he escaped to theology after one year of college teaching. The usual was a three-year period following the completion of the course in philosophy. At one time, high school teaching was *de rigeur*. Without it, one had not really had the course. At any rate, that one year, at St. John's College in Toledo, gained John McKenzie one of his closest friends. Among his students was Dan Herr, of *The Critic* and Thomas More Association.

The evidence suggests that Mr. McKenzie did well as a philosopher at St. Louis and at West Baden, where the Chicago Province opened its own scholasticate in 1934. Indeed, how could he have failed to do well with his photographic memory? Those were the days when, with few exceptions, Jesuits were vying with one another to prove themselves better Thomists: more willing to embrace the twenty-four theses that presumably were the distilled essence of Thomism, more skillful in proposing subtle distinctions, more astute in savaging adversaries whose greatest sin, as we now see it, was that they were not Thomists and did not appreciate the explanatory range of Aristotelian hylomorphism. Today, for sure, John McKenzie pretends to share the non-metaphysical mentality of the biblical writers. He says nothing of the early book reviews and articles he contributed to *Modern Schoolman*, which in his day was edited largely by the Jesuit students of St. Louis University. No one, of course, who knows him accuses John of being close-minded. Nonetheless, out of concern for his philosophical image, I once ventured to chide him about the dustiness of some of his views. I was properly silenced by the remark that the discussions of our colleagues scarcely encouraged him to update himself.

John McKenzie was ordained a priest in 1939. He duly returned to St. Mary's to complete his theology, and then spent his final year of Jesuit training at St. Stanislaus Tertianship in Cleveland. With the outbreak of World War II, it became evident that Jesuits destined for studies in Rome would have to find an alternative. And so Father McKenzie and the other "biennists" were sent to Weston College in Massachusetts to work for doctorates in theology. Not many who know what John has accomplished realize that his professional studies in scripture were limited to one year. For the Chicago Province was opening a theologate at West Baden and Fr. McKenzie was needed to teach. With dissertation undone he left Weston, thereby entering the ranks of the self-made man. Most of us stand in admiration of the accomplishment in the light of the preparation.

Regrettably, there are some professionals who disdain the self-educated, and others whose seven or eight years of leisurely preparation has ill-equipped them for anything but elitist communication. John McKenzie has never thought that an understanding of scripture was for the privileged few.

In due time the dissertation was completed and the degree of doctor of sacred theology was conferred on John McKenzie by the "prestigious" Weston College. Not that it was easy to complete that task. For most of us, getting up new courses is a prodigious effort. Besides, even though he was free from the intellectual and artistic distractions of city life while "down on the farm" (West Baden, adjacent to French Lick, Indiana, was a spa, from which one had to flee a good sixty miles to enjoy the culture of Evansville or Louisville), Fr. McKenzie undertook the job of book review editor for the *Catholic Biblical Quarterly*. It was a convenient way of getting books when the scriptural cut of the budgetary pie was thin. Summers were never entirely free. To escape the humidity of southern Indiana, one had to give retreats, conduct institutes for sisters, or teach theology in a college. In those early years, too, John wrote straight theological stuff, for instance his articles on Theodore of Mopsuestia. No doubt it was these that led John Courtney Murray at one time to reply that Fr. McKenzie was then the best theologian he knew of in the States.

It was in 1945 that I first came in contact with John McKenzie. Aside from being a rather formidable presence, he was an unknown quantity to us philosophers until Februeary 1946 when he was finally admitted to his vows as a fully-formed Jesuit. The feast traditionally provided an occasion for a roasting job, and McKenzie's students played it for all its worth. The gestures, the quips that spared neither house nor inmates: they had it all down cold, except, to be sure, the wit behind these sallies that kept us all — or at least some of us — from taking ourselves too seriously. It was a talent that I came to know better later, particularly as his student from '53-'55. Those were still the days when the laugh was more spontaneous than the bite, and I was unaware of these "shafts of wit" ("What did I say?") as a salutary letting off of steam.

Nowadays we can only regard those nineteen years at West Baden — affectionately known as Tombstone, the dead center of Indiana — as productive McKenzie years, even though he referred to the domed structure that housed us as the bushel under which he hid his light. Its very isolation was likely to turn even the most unwilling student into a scholar for sheer lack of anything else to do. For John the years provided a remedy for the missed opportunities. Always a voracious reader, he maintained a furious pace, churning out even more professional papers, reviews and journal articles. In my time he availed himself of the genius of a student who had returned from Johns Hopkins with the doctorate in Semitics. And then his first book appeared, *The Two-Edged Sword*, still regarded by many as his finest work. It was duly acclaimed by the critics. Written in the easy, jovial, McKenzie style, the book was intended for non-professionals, though its scholarship shone through to rejoice the scholarly reader. The work was a spiritual study of the OT: sensitive, delicately balanced, applauded by both Catholics and Protestants alike. It was a fillip to the self-made man, though some of his seminary colleagues protested that its popularity owed as much to the publicist activities of its author as to the merits of the book itself. For from that time — until many years later when some of us convinced him that he was spreading himself too thin — the scholarly recluse became the much-sought-after lecturer who could never say no to any group of concerned listeners. Genial, witty, trenchant: the lecturer mirrored his book, which he later admitted came at the right moment. It filled a vacuum and thereafter rode the crest of the swelling scriptural movement.

The guest lecturer, to be sure, cuts a figure different from the workaday professor. How did Fr. McKenzie strike the seminarians who shared his bucolic lot? For many, he was the bluff, preoccupied man who might or might not grunt a return to the passing "Good morning." Not one to suffer fools gladly, he was the examiner who delighted in skewering the over-confident, particularly the artful memorizer who encountered no difficulties with theses. By comparison with the professors of dogma, he could appear less serious because of his casual manner: an impression abetted by the off-the-top-of-the-head character of his lectures, which prompted students to grade his performance any place between brilliant and zilch. Never an athlete — he claims that in his seminary days he played a mean game of Jesuit-style handball by using his bulk to advantage — he was regularly invited by the bridge addicts to add to a challenging evening of fun. Yet frankly, there were those who were put off by the independent and undemonstrative ways of the smalltown Hoosier. He seemed unsympathetic toward those less gifted than himself; and often his barbs which were intended to stimulate — like asking his students, whose average age was thirty, what they had accomplished — caused wounds that began to suppurate. Unfortunately, there are always those who do not penetrate façades to the sense of things.

For there was method in the McKenzie madness. Surely one can disagree with the teaching technique; but he must fit it into a context of, and hence estimate it as a reaction to, spoonfeeding. Perhaps our empty seminaries have put an end to the argument whether the purpose of the seminary is to train priests or scholars. The McKenzie stance needs no elaboration. Because he, too, had been subjected to "the course": a bizarre clutter of courses designed by Rome for youngsters who purportedly learned nothing if they were not in class — and we must pity the professors who, because orthodoxy was at a premium, perforce taught at a level where all could assimilate the truth — the McKenzie students, primarily those with intellectual initiative and sensitivity, would be treated to a breath of fresh air. If the students read, then this teacher responded to their interest and the class was a delight. But if student interest flagged, oftentimes because of the burden of the above-mentioned bevy of courses, then the method was counterproductive. Personally, having taught in a seminary myself, I am more tolerant of the drawbacks of this whole procedure. I taught the "minor disciplines" in a Jesuit seminary — although scripture was not minor, its dosage was minimal — so I am better placed to understand the McKenzie frustrations.

I noted above that people were most important to John McKenzie; one has to grasp this fact if he is to understand why this scholar has popularized his work. Undoubtedly many Jesuits would demur. Victims of the McKenzie wit, they would still classify him as a nettle and insist that my picture is a failure to present "warts and all." They are put off by the reserve of the "smalltown boy," who is still surprisingly reticent in a group until he feels at home. Distance has always borne opposing interpretations. Yet John McKenzie has been shaped by the Jesuits since he was in his early teens. If anything, the traditions of the Missouri and Chicago Provinces would have encouraged his reserve, fostered a withdrawal from emotional involvement with others, and placed a development of the social graces low on the hierarchy of values.

Systems of education may shape but they rarely transform a nature. And so, paradoxically, it was the "distant" McKenzie who made his way backstage after the show — both in the seminary and at Loyola — to congratulate the actors. In my fourth year of theology John had his gall-bladder operation. He came home gaunt and weak. Yet there he was on Christmas morning, clad in pajamas and bathrobe, in the theologians' recreation room celebrating his return with the people for whom he really cared. I must admit, that episode gave me an insight into John McKenzie that the years have only deepened. Others, too, sense the loyalty that is so much a part of his character. At Loyola, the troubled leadership of the

AAUP chapter turned to him for guidance and support. Is it surprising that he was the only clergyman invited to, and asked to address, the organizational meeting of the Association of Catholic Laymen? "I can say honestly and gratefully," Fr. Bill LeSaint wrote me, "that I have never had a better friend, in or out of the Society." I know the feeling; for during my last hospital sojourn, it was John McKenzie who came every night that he was not teaching. "Of such services," he remarks in the preface to his recent book, "is the fabric of life woven, and we too often forget it." This author means it when he presents his work "to my friends with deep gratitude."

I once remarked to a friend that there were many battles that we who came after did not have to fight because of John McKenzie. For all of the Order's scholarly traditions, the Jesuits of the American provinces were peculiarly unproductive. O yes, one could point to a Macelwane, the geophysicist, or a Garraghan, the historian; but these were notable exceptions. An enlightened prefect of studies in the Chicago Province foresaw the need for Ph.D.'s, but even his vision was limited to their prestige value. Fortunately, this man was given a free hand. In spite of the clamor for men to feed the institutional expansion after World War II, a determined provincial sent a generous number of capable men for higher degrees. The S.J. no longer supplied for "all lesser degrees." But the colleges were not similarly enlightened — or perhaps it was the men themselves. Ph.D.'s in philosophy, economics and the like filled out their extracurricular schedules as dorm prefects and counselors. One's contribution to a university was usually measured in terms of retreats given, convents served, confessions heard and, disproportionately, PR flimflam. Perhaps there were a few who actually sacrificed scholarly ambitions for dry-as-dust administrative positions. But most who had so sacrificed never really exhibited what it was that they had sacrificed. Hence, more likely than not, they were victims of the Jesuit syndrome. Having been pressured all their lives — sanctions hung over one's head like the sword of Damocles until one's final vows — they finally found themselves free, compelled to move on their own initiative. For this the life of sanctions had unfitted them, so why not, with the Ph.D. ticket, get on the power train?

If this picture seems overdrawn, then one should ask himself in all honesty about the Jesuits vis-à-vis the more formidable boat-rockers like Teilhard de Chardin, Karl Rahner, Henri de Lubac, John Courtney Murray and to mention two who do not pretend to scholarship, Archbishop Roberts and Dan Berrigan. At the time that we were theologians, we could surmise some of the obstacles in the McKenzie path;

the others lay outside our ken, or were to surface only later. But given his
effort to instill in us by precept and example the self-discipline of
scholarship — in this he was seconded by the above-mentioned Fr. Bill
LeSaint — we recognized that following in his footsteps inevitably
entailed tilts with the establishment. Apparently scholarship demanded
exceptions, and these seemed to be reserved for those in positions of
authority. A car at West Baden was a necessity, not a luxury. But the house
cars were not for an individual's use on a lecture tour (McKenzie arrived
several hours late in Hamilton, Ohio, because the train was late).
Secretaries or their electronic replacements were too expensive for the
ordinary Jesuit. Then there was the annual hassle over books, which were
not a personal possession and hence could not be marked. Everyone knows
that the "regular order" of a religious house operates against those with
different requirements. The person who works best at night or needs
uninterrupted stretches of time is unlikely to rise at 5:00 A.M. or attend
community exercises. Rooms were never soundproof, so the midafternoon
typist was soon admonished for violating the silence of siesta. Indeed, this
was the cardinal sin committed by John McKenzie. His nineteen years at
West Baden ended abruptly because he placed too high a price on his
scholarship. He could not afford the daily two hours of his neighbor's
snooze. I suppose what bothered John most — he certainly was not
depressed about leaving Tombstone — was that the superior who decided
in favor of regular order was one of his former pupils. In this case — he was
soon to learn in how many others — he had failed.

It is probably as true of John McKenzie as of anyone else that he did not
win many battles, which is why his detractors insist that his book on
authority is simply the product of "personal problems." Yet when one looks
at the beleaguered position of authority today and counts the number of
Jesuits, priests and scholastics, with doctorates who have left the Society, it
becomes plain that McKenzie has won a war that he tried to prevent. I am
told that the academic horrors of the past are impossible in today's Society.
That McKenzie's war against ecclesiastical bullies has been won is more
problematical, although a healthy fear of the press seems to have achieved
results where an appeal to principle has not. It may prove significant to
some that at the very time that his "attack on authority" was being
published, he was giving authority more than its due behind the scenes. I
know; I lived with him then at the University of Chicago.

Jesuit law required the examination of all manuscripts by two censors,
whose reach, by the way, extended beyond the canonical "freedom from
error" to the judgment of a work in the light of the Society's reputation.

John McKenzie, like John Courtney Murray, had the distinction of an additional Roman censor, thanks to the worries of the then Apostolic Delegate, who later presided less harmfully over the Vatican Bank. The work was approved by these men on the condition that some of its teeth be extracted. Yet because its topic was sensitive, the book was censored once again and finally cleared for publication. Then one day — John was already correcting page proofs — a letter arrived from his provincial stating that Fr. Arrupe, the Jesuit General, was concerned and requested still another censorial reading. Understandably, when I listen to a recitation of the book's inadequacies, I wonder whether the critic knows how much was deleted in successive readings, and whether he himself would have submitted to this kind of emasculation.

At first Loyola University, Chicago, was a relief for John, even though his appointment was to history, not to theology. The chairman of theology was an unforgiving former student. John likes Chicago: its libraries, its opera, its restaurants, even its golf courses. Besides, he was not totally dependent upon house cars. His students, unlike the seminarians, signed up because they wanted to take his courses, which in itself was a good shot in the arm. Most of them read and challenged, which he liked, although not all were pleased by those off-the-top-of-the-head lectures. No doubt they felt that they should not have to draw him out. Still, it is a tribute to the man that he numbers many friends among his former students. Their loyalty is repaid in kind.

The exposure of Chicago no doubt convinced John that theology was too serious a business to be left to the professionals. His contacts with the lay faculty opened him further to their spiritual and intellectual hungers. He responded to a plea from a group of archdiocesan chancery officials to teach them scripture once a week. From his students he learned of the disruption of their lives caused by the draft, which led him to delve more deeply into the grounds for pacifism in the sacred writings. There was the perennial problem of academic freedom, which he met for the first time in all of its concrete urgency. Should I say that from this period he became more fully aware of his mission? Unlike most scholars, John has never really written just for his peers. He has always tried to spread the good news, which I translate into an increasing awareness that he ought to help people free themselves: intellectually, morally, spiritually, socially, politically. Is not such a task religion *par excellence*, the ultimate task of deconditioning? And upon whom does this burden rest more heavily than the priest and interpreter of the Sacred Books?

His former student, Loyola's academic vice-president, who had brought him there found that he was incapable of delivering some of the promised goods. The lone "faculty secretary" for the North Shore campus needed nine months to return a twenty-page manuscript. Office space was at a premium. This time, however, the provincial, a West Baden former colleague, saved the day by providing these amenities for John at the Loyola University Press, paid for by the province out of the royalties that the McKenzie books accrued. The set-up was a bit inconvenient, but at least it provided one scholar with some of the perquisites of the administrator. Should one object that these are needless superfluities, let him try typing *The Dictionary of the Bible*. It was during this time that this six-year-long work was completed: surely the book that John hopes will be remembered as his finest scholarly contribution.

In September 1965 we left Loyola together for the University of Chicago: he, to be the first Roman Catholic Visiting Professor in the Divinity School; I, to work with Mircea Eliade on a cross-disciplinary fellowship. Four of us lived together at the Catholic Student Center. I was presented with the best opportunity to discover the man behind the books and battles, and thus came to know better the forthrightness and the foibles, but above all the loyalty of a solid friend.

Every career has its peaks and troughs. In retrospect, his decision to take a position at Notre Dame was a fateful one; the next five years were not easy. No "dark night" is all gloom, of course. Several new, wonderful friendships date from that time, and several old friends joined him at the university. "McKenzie Day" was inaugurated: tickets to a football game and "the works" for some of his longstanding associates. Academically, his productivity never lagged. He was, he said, the only faculty member who never complained about the lack of windows in his office; he had seen enough of the Indiana prairie. He bought himself a set of golf clubs; spent many a weekend in Chicago; and continued, a trait as yet unmentioned, his seemingly interminable auto excursions. I still recall a trip to a meeting in Washington, D. C. He arrived safely, only to learn that the meeting was scheduled for the following week. He must know all the landmarks along old Route 66 between Chicago and Los Angeles. The interest in trains is still there, but driving is his passion.

Undoubtedly Jesuit authorities never found John McKenzie an ideal subject. That natural independence always showed under the coating of docility. Eventually his hardheaded realism conflicted with a lip-service paid to obedience and poverty that appeared to him a not-so-subtle ruse for control. The apparent lack of seriousness about scholar-ship — incidentally, we might note that John's attitude has never been that all Jesuits should be scholars; he wished merely that those who were might not be penalized for their efforts — had already loosened the fabric of his Jesuit relations. In the Notre Dame years the issue of freedom — his own and that of others — presented itself in a very painful way. Finally, the fabric came undone and difficult decisions had to be made.

The keynote of the McKenzie character is loyalty; it would be preposterous to suppose its overnight evanescence. For the most part, Jesuit authorities left him alone; the rank and file often stopped in on football weekends before heading home. There were many things to upset. Former students without the prestige of his name lacked his leverage with superiors. At first their departure was only a trickle. The then Bishop Jim Shannon stopped by just to talk; he knew where he could find a measure of understanding. Dan Berrigan wrote for moral support: the ostracized speaking to the ostracized. It was typical of John that he wrote a strong letter to Rome deploring the failure of Jesuits to back their own. His column in *The Critic* became a voice for the timid and unheard. He used it to deflate the pretensions of Cardinal Carberry, not only because no other priest or bishop would risk trying to get through to him, but also, again characteristically, because the Cardinal had allegedly used his position to insult one of John's former students. Not even the Pope was spared. Annoyed at an address that once again blamed the lack of mortification of the laity for the dearth of religious and priestly vocations, John assailed the pomp and circumstance of the Roman Curia. "Come off it, Your Holiness," he wrote; and of course these were the words that a Chicago newspaper trumpeted in a headline. Understandably, the Jesuits found him an embarrassment.

And John knew it. He knew in theory that institutional loyalty is merely a way of talking; the practice is all the other way. Yet after all those years, even his own realism faltered. When he was toying with the idea of leaving the Society, a former student took him aside for a friendly lecture. A gesture of concern, no doubt, but with little understanding behind it. Later, when this man had himself become a pariah, he left the Society and the priesthood. John is not the type to remind him of the lecture. Still, the internal agonies and external battles were taking their toll. His tone became shrill. His sense of betrayal drenched his words in acid. The laugh disappeared from the wit and only the bite remained.

A new Jesuit provincial, a former student, asked to see him. When all the formalities were taken care of, the critical issue was finally broached. "What," came the pitiful question, "are you doing with your money?" So lightly was the tie of forty-some years undone. In reality, the subsequent correspondence with the Jesuit General over the un-Jesuitical blast at the Pope lacked the force of a denouement. Indeed, if after forty years one has not got "the spirit," it is better to leave.

For many Catholics leaving a religious order is only a step above leaving the priesthood. But their dismissal of him is no match for the McKenzie resilience. Bishop Cletus O'Donnell of Madison took him under his wing: undoubtedly an expression of his thanks to John for the scripture lessons in the Chicago chancery. What is more, not only had John been invited to the Madison installation, he parked with the archbishops! Ecclesiastically, at any rate, for the first time in his life John found himself truly free.

This new freedom has brought about a resurrection of the old McKenzie. The easy laugh, the sharp but not sardonic sense of humor: these have returned with a flowering of his innate independence. Suffering tempers the soul, and we are grateful for the new mellowness that graces him. He has the satisfaction that comes from being a priest by commitment, not because he can do nothing else and perforce must live off the church. To me it has been gratifying to hear people say how much they have gotten out of his book on the Roman Catholic Church or enjoyed *A Theology of the Old Testament*. The vintage McKenzie is in these books: a thorough grasp of the materials presented with clarity and verve.

The mellowing of McKenzie has been concomitant with his return to Chicago, where he has joined a group of exceptional colleagues at DePaul University. He has taken, with difficulty, to domestic chores, for which life in seminaries and religious houses has totally unfitted him. The first SOS to me was: "What does it mean to simmer?" He now knows that steaks are broiled on the top part of the broiling pan, tosses a mean salad, and has evidently reached the epitome of culinary art. "Why," he told me one day with obvious pride, "I'm even cooking two things at once."

In this biographical sketch it has clearly not been my intention to burden the reader with dates and places, with awards (the honorary doctorates from Bucknell and Rosary, the Cardinal Spellman theology award) and other signs of professional recognition (e.g., the first Catholic to be president of the Society for Biblical Literature). More important to us who acknowledge the external trappings is the man himself and the values that he has espoused. He is not a man to insist that all should share his commitments. But his life has been a testimonial to his belief that these committals deserve a rational and open-minded discussion.

Father John McKenzie is not, and never has been, a churchy priest. He has fond memories, to be sure, of the parish in Downey, California, where he helped out several summers. But one suspects from his conversation that the recollection is of the people he met, and of Pat, the pastor, and Dick Harnett, the assistant. "You were lucky," his brother George told him after his sister's funeral, "that Father Munson was there to direct things." The liturgical changes have passed him by; the mindless shifting of saints' feasts makes him grateful that he is not involved. Only occasionally does he rise to the bait. When I told him about the use of grape juice at Mass by alcoholic priests, he exclaimed: "They can't; it's invalid." Essentially, his priesthood lies deep in the man and his sense of mission. We should be grateful that he has tried in his way to share with us the bread of truth, and taken so deeply to heart the idea that the truth shall make us free.

ANITA WEISBROD ROBINSON

Letters From Life

April, 1929: Carissime McKenzie: Very nervous, jumps, moving always, head jerks, words jerky . . . . In Exercitium Modestiae he takes a complaining air . . . . In sweeping, should take more time, not bang broom about.

[Letter to Dan Herr, publisher of *The Critic*, in which McKenzie had a regular column for five years.] "Since your Ex-Jesuit McKenzie finds the Church so corrupt, *why the Hell doesn't he leave it*? Why does he write his rotten vicious stuff in *your rag*? Why do you print it? Why do you print that rag at all? You belong in jail with the publishers of *Screw* mag. for what you write and print is just as filthy. *We'll have to take action!*"

June, 1971: Dear Father McKenzie . . . Don't worry about sounding old and conservative. Nobody could doubt *your* guts and honesty. We have to call it like we see it no matter what's fashionable.

April, 1971: Lieber John: Der Herr Professor in Tübingen kann nicht anders, als dem Herrn Professor in Chicago sehr herzlich für die ausführliche Besprechuno seines Buches im NCR zu danken . . . . Und insofern lebt man von den Freuden, die sich ihrerseits mutig einsetzen. Und so möchte Ich Ihnen von Herzen danken für Ihr Engagement in dieser Sache welches der Kirche helfen kann, ihren Weg in dieser Frage zu finden.

November, 1971: Dear Father McKenzie:. . . I read your column in *The Critic* faithfully, and I read *Authority in the Church* with enormous gratitude. I am sorry that you have been ill and hope that you are feeling fine now. I am also sorry that you are growing a little bitter and discouraged; but so am I, and it is a comfort to know that I have company. Thank you for your truthfulness.

It would be not quite true to say that I have been as great a fan of McKenzie's correspondence as I have been of McKenzie; but it is an exaggeration I know he and, I trust, the reader will appreciate. In fact, it was tempting to write this contribution to his Festschrift entirely from quotations from letters, for in reading through them they almost began to take on a life of their own, much as Pirandello's Six Characters did. Any one who undertakes a serious and steady career in writing can anticipate receiving the standard fan and pan mail. The remarkable thing about the McKenzie correspondence, apart from its sheer abundance, is that it is the

15

only place where the many facets of the man can be seen. In the quotations which begin this article, one of the writers sees only the human frailties of a candidate for membership in the Society of Jesus; another is infuriated by his liberalism; another tells him not to be discouraged at being called a conservative; still another thanks him as a fellow theologian; and yet another commiserates with his disenchantment. I do not wish to belabor further this obvious point: that almost all of us see our fellow man only in the context of our first encounter with him. If the person is only one-dimensional, the failure to perceive is not too serious. But to know only one facet of a many-faceted person is scarcely better than not knowing him at all.

It is both McKenzie's greatest strength and his greatest weakness that he played a number of roles, each of which would have been enough by itself for most of his contemporaries. He was concerned with OT studies, NT studies, patrology, fundamental theology, and theological education. He lectured widely and produced dozens of articles and reviews in theological journals. He was a gadfly on the institutional church; he lectured and wrote on the peace movement. He was a teacher both in the seminary and in the university, and he played a large part in the ecumenical movement. With all this, he was a priest of the Roman Catholic Church — in the Society of Jesus from 1939 until 1970, and since then in the diocese of Madison, Wisconsin. In all, a splendid career, long and various, which has brought light and strength wherever it has turned. But this article is intended neither as a catalogue of McKenzie's achievements nor as a discussion of the pitfalls and problems of being a generalist in a world no longer suited to such an approach. Rather, it hopes to celebrate the man behind the roles: interesting and dull, funny and foolish, courageous and ordinary , serious and silly, hardy yet fragile — as indeed we all are.

In 1928 McKenzie graduated from high school at St. Mary's College, St. Mary's, Kansas, having led his class three out of four years. That fall, just short of his eighteenth birthday, he entered the Society of Jesus at Milford Novitiate, Milford, Ohio, the novitiate of the Chicago Province. An old friend and former colleague (Fr. William LeSaint, S.J.; taken from an interview given in the fall of 1974) recalls:

> I first learned there was a John McKenzie in September of 1928. I was a Junior at the time — two years of special study in the classics after the novitiate. And our professor of Greek told us in class one time, perhaps to inspire us to work a little harder, about the wonderful class of novices they had that year. The eight or ten men who came in September, 1928 were really brilliant young men. Maybe brilliant is too strong a word to use, but anyway, they were

exceptionally good students. This teacher had just come back from Oxford. He was full of the classics and so he just handed it to them. I heard of John McKenzie when he told us about this class and said that he had given them a Greek theme to write. They were to translate from Shakespeare's *Henry VIII* "Cromwell I charge thee, fling away ambition. By that sin fall the angels." He said that one of the novices made a beautiful use of the ethical dative and quoted McKenzie: "*aphiei moi tēn philotimian toutō gar tō hamartēmati hoi daimones peptōkasi.*" It was the "*moi*" that got him. To think that someone just out of high school had such a fine appreciation of the nuances of Greek composition and Greek poetry!

How typically McKenzian a picture we get: bright, competitive, alert, and with that special sensitivity to words that has always graced his work.

In 1940 McKenzie finished theology with the traditional two-hour examination on the entire seven years of philosophy and theology. Conducted in Latin (like all examinations), this could be terrifying, and it was the most searching exam of the whole course, for its outcome determined whether one became a Professed Father or a Spiritual Coadjutor. In that same year he also began tertianship or second novitiate at St. Stanislaus Novitiate in Cleveland. By all accounts, this was not one of McKenzie's happiest experiences. He likes to quote a classmate who described the year as "sanctity through piddling." Tertianship was built on the assumption that the Jesuit at this phase of his life would have been exposed to enough worldliness, pride, vanity, assorted concupiscences and lax observance of the Rule for some of the sheen to have worn off. It included a thirty-day retreat for the second time; the first was made in the novitiate. The tertians studied the Spiritual Exercises and were expected to prepare a manuscript which would equip them to give an eight-day retreat. There were classes in the Jesuit Constitutions and various frequent exhortations to repentance and a better life. On one such occasion McKenzie was given the following evaluation: "A trifle stubborn and wedded to his own opinion; at times critical of teachers and superiors; somewhat irascible and sullen; he has undoubted talent and gave more than ordinary satisfaction in his teaching work at West Baden during the Summer." I did not meet McKenzie until some twenty years later, when many of the sharp points had been smoothed and rounded out, but the description is still amusingly recognizable.

Although McKenzie's first book was published in 1956, it was not until after he moved to Loyola University of Chicago in 1960 that he began to acquire the large readership and voluminous correspondence which has continued to the present. What is intriguing about these letters is the remarkable cross-section of people and places they represent — and the folksy, sometimes brutally frank, and often affectionate tone that perfect strangers adopt in writing to McKenzie, obviously quite unconsciously.

In November of 1966 the following letter was addressed to a couple who were on the reception committee for a McKenzie lecture:

> This is an awfully impulsive thing which I am doing, but one can only attain a good by seeking! Someone, who knows of my admiration for Father McKenzie, gave me a clipping from the *Hartford Times*, and as I read that he was going to be so close to us I couldn't resist asking my superior if I could write to you about his visit. If I weren't cloistered I'd surely "manage" to get to him somehow. But, alas, that is out of the question and the only possibility is that he would be generous enough to come to us.
>
> Of course, this is probably out of the question — if I remember how such persons are sought after and their schedules arranged down to the minute. But perhaps you will be gracious enough to tell him that a group of cloistered Benedictines would love to see him — anytime — and rely so much on his lead in much of today's muddle . . .

Also in 1966 a fellow priest from the East coast wrote to McKenzie:

> Dear Father John,
> You may be surprised that I call you Fr. John. It seems that I have known you all my life as I read all my thoughts so wonderfully expressed in your books . . . . I wrote to you maybe five months ago . . . I wanted to meet you at Fordham U. in July, but I had you confused with another Fr. MacKenzie. You found time enough in your endless schedule to give me a little reply in a kind & humble way, which touched me deeply. I still want to see you and would love to talk with you.

Spread out on the desk front of me are fifteen letters (not a total but simply the point at which I stopped counting), all of which echo the sentiments of the following excerpt: "I look at this letter and wonder why I should write to you with such candor, and all I can say is your books and the tone of your articles inspire it." Of course, many of the letters addressed to McKenzie fall into the simple thank-you tradition. But what is interesting about them is the large number that present serious questions calling for an equally serious response. One letter is twenty-one pages long, another is scribbled on the sides of six envelopes because no more suitable stationery was available when the writer was inspired, still another is on a home-made card; some are typed, others are hand written; some are formal and correct, others casual and direct. Although many of the letters are favorable, a goodly number of them are not, and these range in tone from mild disagreement to open hostility. But the point common to all these missives, whether favorable or unfavorable, is that they were written as a personal and immediate response to something that McKenzie said or wrote and all of them received a personal and immediate reply.

Unfortunately, McKenzie rarely kept copies of his own letters to others. But perhaps that is not so surprising, coming from a man who doesn't even have copies of all the material he has published over the years. In 1968 McKenzie received a letter from Dan Berrigan, in response to which he wrote a letter to the Father General of the Society of Jesus. The vitality of the correspondence, the way in which it seems to capture both the men involved and the crisis to which each had addressed himself, is striking:

Friday, June 14

Dear Father John

I am writing you to ask if you would help, in contributing to our defense, for the Baltimore draft files burning.

I assure you I do not shrink at spending considerable time in prison if that contingency is inevitable. At the same time I think it would be irresponsible to go to prison without having tried to make a case. I am writing to you to ask whether you would help us develop the issue of primacy of conscience and peace-making tradition in the Catholic Church. I do not know if the issue can be clarified from Jesuit history, but perhaps that is unnecessary in any case.

Am also writing Fr. Bob Drinan of Boston College Law School to ask if he would drum up trade for us among Jesuit lawyers.

Another point of great import, if I may stress it, is approaching the Fr. General with your convictions and whatever determination you resolve on to help. He is under great pressure to dismiss me from the society — and while I do not think this will happen, a letter or statement from you (and others) will help.

I can only, at present, present my request to you in general terms. Undoubtedly at some point we will need recognized authorities in theology to testify that we come out of something more than a vacuum.

. . . I have a sinking feeling that this may be a last ditch chance for decent renewal — but if it is to come, in the Church or the Society, it will have to come through individuals. Such was the story in Germany in the 30's — which we seem cursed to repeat.

So I need your help — but so, I am convinced, does the Church. Would you give this serious thought, and let me know your reactions? . . .

Gratefully, fraternally,
Dan Berrigan, S.J.

July 10, 1968
Very Rev. Pedro Arrupe, S.J.
Borgo Santo Spirito 5
Casella Postale 9048
Rome 00100

Dear Father General,

P C.

It is with distress that I learn that the society has "officially washed its hands" of Father Daniel Berrigan, to use the phrase in which the information came to me. He receives neither censure nor support. I believe this demands serious thought, and I shall try to set forth my own reflections.

So many people in this country now agree that our war in Vietnam is a wicked thing that it is no longer an eccentric idea. It means nothing to say that the issue is controversial; most moral issues are controversial, but this does not keep Jesuits from reaching a decision. There has been no official direction concerning this question . . . . Father Berrigan has ample support for his position on the morality of the war, a position which I share . . . .

The question can concern only the means which Berrigan chose for his protest, not the protest itself. I did not choose and would not choose the means he chose; whether this indicates that he was imprudent or that I am a moral coward I would prefer not to discuss. He has evidently decided that the gravity of the question demands a direct challenge of the iniquitous civil authority. He did what he did in full knowledge that it was a symbolic act, and he is willing to face the consequences. The consequences now appear to be a prison sentence. There has always been room for such symbolic acts of protest; and it is hard to think of any one which was not as open to question as Berrigan's act is.

For the Society it is a question of whether the members have a right to express their moral convictions in extreme ways. Our Society has a long history of men who were entangled with civil authority. Many of them have been canonized or beatified, others are venerated. I do not know of any who were repudiated by the Society. It seems to me that the kind of surrender which the Society demands of its members implies a kind of support proportionate to such a total surrender, even if the members are wrong. The Society can be wrong too. Whether Berrigan is wrong, or to what degree, is a question which is not answered simply. If the Society repudiates one of "Ours" just because he has become embarrassing, I find that repulsive. I am not attempting to equate Berrigan to the martyrs; he would be the first to resent that. But I wonder whether the kind of "prudence" which repudiates him and his action would not have counseled Isaac Jogues to go along with the war practices of the Iroquois. Jogues might have lived longer if he had. I am convinced that future historians, when they investigate this sad episode in American history, will say that Berrigan represented the authentic traditions of the Society and that his superiors did not. Or perhaps I idealize these traditions.

Your Paternity may know that I have had my own problems with certain aspects of the moral quality of Jesuit government. I do not wish to discuss these; they are not relevant. I only want to say that these problems do not arise from any consciousness of moral superiority in me; God knows that I do not have and am not entitled to any such consciousness. It is just that there are some moral lapses so appalling that it takes no more than a very low level of moral sensitivity to recognize them. Let me mention the failure of the Society to support Teilhard de Chardin, Henri de Lubac, John Courtney Murray and Karl Rahner in their hours of trial. Let me ask what the Society thought it was saving by this cowardice, dignified by the name of obedience. When I entered the Society and during my early years I felt that I might have gained something by membership in a society which thought big and acted big. Perhaps it was never that big; it is clear that in my generation it has become petty. Whenever it gets a big man, it crucifies him and then honors his memory. As Jesus said of the Pharisees, it honors the prophets whom its ancestors stoned. Again I do not intend to assimilate Berrigan to the scholars named above. The only similarity is the refusal of the Society to support its members when they are trapped in either ecclesiastical or civil politics. Whatever be the merits of the case, such members are simply thrown to the wolves. If this is "paternal," I do not know what the word means; I can do nothing but pray to spared from such paternal interest. It could kill me. One might at least look for some primitive clan or tribal loyalty to a fellow clansman, who need his group most when he is in trouble.

This is written at too great length. Let me summarize by saying that if the Society repudiates Dan Berrigan, it will perform an act so contemptible that no decent person who hears of it can do anything but abhor it. And Dan Berrigan is too well known and too widely admired for any secrets to be kept. You can save some shreds of the honor of the Society, of which little seems to be left, by a public statement that without approving Dan Berrigan's action, you respect the sincerity of his moral convictions and that you support him in his effort to right a great wrong. I can make the same public statement, but I cannot speak for the Society. Do this, and comfort those who would still like to feel that the title of Jesuit confers honor on him who bears it.

With all good wishes and prayers,

> Sincerely yours in Xto
> (Signed)
> John L. McKenzie, S.J.

McKenzie's popular essays frequently elicited divergent responses. In the 11 June, 1971 issue of *Commonweal* he wrote a review of a recently published book by Louis Evely. The following excerpts are typical of the kinds of reactions McKenzie evoked:

> . . . the point of this letter is simply to point out that arguing that scholars knew all about Bultmann (obviously!) does not answer my question at all, which was

about the gap between such scholarly conversations and the ordinary Catholic
reading public who does read Evely. Also as you know very well the whole idea
of demythologizing is still considered a forbidden area in Catholic exegesis
generally, and heads of theologians; i.e. Germany, roll for using it. But, thanks
to your exceedingly bad-tempered article and ill-mannered reply, the gap has
been filled somewhat, and the *Commonweal* reading Catholic public has been
notified that there is such an idea floating around and maybe they will try to
find out something about it. They might even read your essay, although I
would advise them to read Bultmann, as the most reliable authority on what
Bultmann has to say.

Dear John L.:

    You know that I'm a long time fan of your Opera Minora such as your
Q.E.D. in *The Critic*. Well, I just read your piece on Louis Evely in
Commonweal and I just want to tell you that I think it superb. It's vintage
McKenzie: witty, incisive and casually wise.

    This article is as difficult to stop as it was to start, for once begun the
quotable quotes seem endless. The quality of John L. McKenzie which this
collection of comments is meant to suggest is best summed up in a present
McKenzie received several years ago. The accompanying letter reads:

You've a strange kind of "fan" in me: I've never met you, don't follow your
current writing too closely — yet I do think of you often — at Eucharist.
We've at least one mutual friend in common and also I've seen what your
writing does for many. Therefore, this rather simple and poor expression of joy
and appreciation. Thought this might be apt for the time of All Saints as we
celebrate who we are for, and with, others.

The present is a hand-made card and it proclaims:

                    the full measure of a man
                        is to be found . . .
                    not in the man himself —

                    but in the new colors and
                    textures that come alive
                    in other people
                    because of him.

Photos from Life

High School graduation,
St. Mary's Kansas, 1928.

"The regime out at St. Mary's was very rigid: regular hours, a lot of bell ringing, study hall, something on the order of the British Public School. Besides the regular courses at which he excelled, John did a lot of desultory reading. He read everything he could get his hands on; this helped to expand his wide knowledge of so many different things — history, geography, railroads, pirates, tours of the Scottish border. He's probably the only Scripture scholar who's an authority on the old 3 I league (Indiana, Illinois and Iowa minor professional baseball league)."

In 1930 McKenzie began the Juniorate, two years of classical studies, which then were Latin, Greek, English and history. He also became editor of *Ripples*, a student magazine, in which "he wrote editorial columns which were read with delight by everybody at Milford, faculty and students alike."

Milford, Ohio, 1931. L to R: George McKenzie, Mrs. McKenzie, John L. McKenzie and Betty McKenzie.

In 1932 McKenzie received a Litt. B. from Xavier University, of which Milford Novitiate was an extension. This happened to no other Junior but was granted McK. because he had read and written papers on a prodigious amount of Latin and Greek literature. "The Dean," McKenzie recalls, "omitted Ovid, Martial, Persius, Catullus, Aristophanes, and some tragedies from the reading." McKenzie's first printed article appeared a year later in the *Classical Bulletin*.

Milford Novitiate,
Milford, O., 1931.

In the fall of 1932 McKenzie began the normal three year philosophy course for Jesuits at St. Louis University. Most scholastics were expected to acquire a Master's degree in some subject other than philosophy to prepare for teaching; McK. obtained an M.A. in Greek. He also became a member of the editorial staff of *The Modern Schoolman*, then the student journal of philosophy it was founded to be.

Modern Schoolman Picnic at Corley Farm, St. Louis, 1934. L to R: McK., F. Mangan, W. LeSaint, F. Corley, F. Smith, J. McGrall, R. Finn.

In 1935 McKenzie was assigned to teach Latin and Greek at St. John's College in Toledo. "He was received with a great deal of appreciation by the students in his classes. As his one extra curricular activity he was in charge of the mission collection and he always boasted of the fact that the missionaries never had it so good as the year he was collecting money for them at St. John's."

St. John's College, Toledo, Ohio, 1936

St. John's College
Toledo, Ohio, 1936.

Beginning in 1936 McKenzie studied theology at St. Mary's College. He spent 5-6 p.m. every Sunday and Thursday, the seminary holidays, with Michael Gruenthaner and two or three students studying Hebrew and a few other Semitic languages. "In spite of the fact that he was working in this way he always had time to do a lot of other things: play bridge, shoot pool — he was a real pool shark — play ping pong — he was very clumsy at ping pong — play volley ball, and take long walks over the prairies. He was not always an indoor man; he liked a little exercise in those years. One time John and I were writing imaginary obituaries for ourselves and he said he'd begin his obituary with this remark: 'Father McKenzie was a man of few virtues, but he did work at the job he had to do.' "

St. Mary's College,
Kansas, 1938.

John L. McKenzie's First Mass, celebrated at St. Benedict's Church, Terre Haute, Ind., 6 June 1939. McKenzie is in the center of the third row; to the right are his sister Betty, his Mother Myra, Fr. Wm. Dehler, and his sister Peggy. His brother George is the altar boy standing in the middle on the left. The Bride is his niece Mary Ann McCauley.

In 1941 McKenzie conducted his first eight-day retreat; before he terminated this work about 1960 he lead a total of 26 such retreats. "I think I enjoyed a fair success, but I gave up the work because I became convinced that Ignatius Loyola meant the Spiritual Exercises to be made only at major critical points in one's life. In a well ordered life such crises should not arise annually."

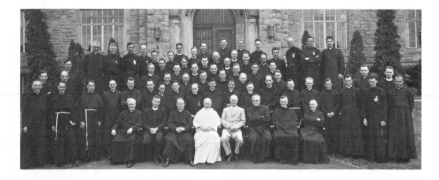

Catholic Biblical Summer School, Niagara University, N.Y., Aug. 16-25, 1946, at which W. F. Albright (front row center) lectured. McK. is in the 3rd row far left.

Catholic Biblical Association, Perryville, Mo., 1954. McKenzie is in the 4th row, far left. In 1951 McKenzie was elected book review editor of the *Catholic Biblical Quarterly*, a position which he held until the end of 1954. The *CBQ* reviewed only six books in the issue which preceded his appointment. But by the time he resigned the section had grown to the extent that no major book in Europe or the U.S.A. failed to reach the *CBQ* for review. In 1964 McKenzie was elected President of the Catholic Biblical Association.

Catholic Biblical Association, Niagara University, 1956. McKenzie is in the 3rd row, right of center.

McKenzie in his study at West Baden College in 1956.

"When I saw Magee (the Provincial Superior), he said, 'I do not know where to send you'; when I arrived at West Baden, Macke (Father Minister) said, 'I do not know where I can find a room for you'; when I saw Healy (Dean of Theology), he said, 'I do not know what you are going to teach.' This was an inauspicious beginning for a career of 18 years."

"He was a sparkling teacher, and he combined that wit with a professional knowledge of his field and also with a great gift for communication. I still hear former students who come in to visit quoting his bons mots. I think of John as being one of the great teachers we had at West Baden."

In 1958 McKenzie organized a colloquium on the city in the Ancient Near East at Loyola University of Chicago. Pictured above are some of the participants in the "Symposium on the City." From L to R: McKenzie, E. A. Speiser, G. Mendenhall, and L. Zabkar.

S. Sand.nel and J. L. McKenzie were two of the participants in "The John XXIII Memorial Lectures" presented by Saint Xavier College March 20-21, 1965.

McKenzie giving a lecture at Mundelein College, Chicago, 1966.

McKenzie standing outside the home in which he was born in Brazil, Indiana. 1967.

Officiating clergy at the wedding of Mr. & Mrs. J. M. Robinson at Bond Chapel, University of Chicago, 1971. L to R: Wm C. Robinson, N. Perrin, J. L. McKenzie.

"Uncle Jack" and his goddaughter
Rosemary in Claremont, Calif. 1974.

Photo from *Dubuque Telegraph-Herald*,
taken in the Summer of 1973 when
McKenzie lectured at Loras College.

McKenzie and J. M. Robinson on the beach at
Big Sur, Calif. 1971.

DAVID NOEL FREEDMAN

The Aaronic Benediction
(Numbers 6:24-26)

The Aaronic Benediction has come down to us through the traditions of early Israel. The setting (Num 6:22-23) explains both its preservation intact, and its function unchanged. It has the ultimate sanction of the deity, and was transmitted through Moses for use by Aaron and his priestly descendants in blessing the community of Israel. The poetic form and transparent simplicity of the piece have insured its faithful transmission through oral and written media, while its universal liturgical usefulness has guaranteed its persistence in the cult of Israel and its inheritors, the synagogue and the church.[1]

The soundness of the text has never been questioned seriously, nor can there be much doubt about the meaning or interpretation of the passage. Chief interest has lain in the word-associations, theological values, homiletical expansions and applications, as well as form-critical considerations. Little has been said about metrical pattern or structure, and apparently for a good reason. Nevertheless, just because the text is intact, and the meaning of the parts quite clear, it makes an ideal subject for metrical analysis. An inductive assembly and assessment of the data should provide us with a clear picture of this poem, the nature and relationship of its component parts, and its structure.[2]

In the following analysis, I will attempt to vocalize the text as it was spoken or chanted in the classic period of biblical Hebrew (around the 10th century B.C.). In this way it may be possible to fix the syllable count more accurately than if we simply followed the Massoretic vocalization. While the latter is generally satisfactory (and often we have no better information about pronunciation), and the results are comparable to those derived from more sophisticated methods of vocalization and syllable-counting, for a poem as brief and beautiful as this one, greater precision is both desirable and necessary.[3] It need not be added that in any metrical analysis the preserved text must be treated as given, and not subject to casual emendation, as otherwise the value of the exercise, which is to determine

35

meter inductively, is diminished to the extent of the alterations, and is in continuous danger of becoming a self-serving expression of scholarly ingenuity and expediency. The vocalization generally follows the MT, but where there is compelling evidence for an earlier and more correct pronunciation, that is given instead.

24)	y^ebārek^ekā yahweh	7	(a)	May Yahweh bless you
	w^eyišm^erekā	5	(b)	And may he keep you
25)	yā'ēr yahweh pānāw 'ēlekā	9	(c)	May Yahweh make his face shine upon you
	w^eyaḥunnekkā	5	(d)	And may he treat you graciously
26)	yiśśā' yahweh pānāw 'ēlekā	9	(e)	May Yahweh lift up his face upon you
	w^eyāśēm l^ekā šālōm	7	(f)	And may he grant you peace

a) That the first word (ybrkk) originally had five syllables (and even the vocalization of the MT supports this view) may be shown in the following manner. The original form of the Piel of the verb with the 2nd m. s. suffix was probably vocalized as follows: *yabarrikika. The reduction of the doubled middle consonant of the root does not affect the syllable count. The original vowel connecting the pronominal suffix to the verb was -u, -i, or -a, depending upon the mood of the verb. The Massoretic vocalization or indication by shewa is ambiguous: i.e., it could be interpreted as silent, though the vocal form is more likely. But the Massoretic pointing is not determinative in this case, since the spelling of the word with two kaph's shows that there must have been in intervening vowel. Otherwise the consonant would have been written only once. Therefore there can be no doubt that in classic usage, the expression had five syllables, not four.

b) According to Massoretic vocalization, the expression wīḥunnekkā has only four syllables; but this form reflects the elision of the yodh of the pronominal prefix, and the consequent reduction from an original five syllables. The classic reading would have been something like this: wayaḥunnikkā (the doubled kaph reflects the assimilation of the so-called energic nun at the end of the verbal component). That the five-syllable pronunciation persisted into late times is shown by the preservation of the yodh, which might otherwise have been dropped from the spelling once the consonant had been elided in pronunciation.

The metrical pattern of the poem may be described in the following way:

$$24) \quad 5 + 2 = 7 ; 5 ; 12$$
$$25) \quad 2 + 2 + 2 + 3 = 9 ; 5 ; 14$$
$$26) \quad 2 + 2 + 2 + 3 = 9 ; 3 + 2 + 2 = 7 ; 16$$

There may be a question about the vocalization of the pronominal suffix -kā. In very early times, as in very late times (i.e., the vocalization reflected in the MT), the pronunciation was -kā (or -ka), and at those times, the syllable would be counted. There was a period during which two forms were distinguished: the long form was spelled -kh and pronounced -kā; the short form was written -k and pronounced without the final vowel, e.g., -āk. In view of the fact that only the short form is preserved in the MT in this passage, the short pronunciation should be reckoned as a possibility if not a probability in this case. It is plausible that at some point in the transmission of the text, the short form and pronunciation prevailed.[4] Since the pronominal suffix occurs in each colon of the poem, each shoud then be reduced by one syllable, producing the following pattern:

24) $4 + 2 = 6 ; 4 ; 10$
25) $2 + 2 + 2 + 2 = 8 ; 4 ; 12$
26) $2 + 2 + 2 + 2 = 8 ; 3 + 1 + 2 = 6 ; 14$

The ratios and correlations among the cola are scarcely affected by the reduction, and the resulting patterns will be the same, or nearly so, whichever enumeration we adopt.

It will be observed immediately that in the form in which we have the blessing there is a stair-like progression from shorter to longer bicola: 10/12: 12/14: 14/16 (giving both shorter and longer syllable counts). Whether or not such a structure is considered symmetrical depends upon one's view of the term "symmetry"; but in any case, it is a balanced pattern, and was consciously constructed by the poet. Further examination exposes other possibilities in analysis and organization of the material, and these may turn out to be more artistically persuasive and satisfying. Thus, for example, there is a striking correlation between the first and last cola of the poem: they are exactly the same length, 6 or 7 syllables, and they form an excellent frame or envelope around the body of the poem:

ybrkk yhwh	May Yahweh bless you
wyśm lk šlwm	and grant you peace.

The association of "blessing" and "peace" is a frequent one in the hymnody of the Hebrew bible, so we may regard the collocation and separation as intentional on the part of the poet. Comparison with Ps 29:11 is instructive:[5]

yhwh ybrk 't-ʿmw bšlwm	May Yahweh bless his people with peace!

It may also be noted that one combination does not exclude others, and that the more skillful the poet, the more complex his structures, the more diverse his objectives, and the more subtle his connections. In this case, reading the poem consecutively makes perfectly good sense, but it is equally possible, and possibly more satisfying to recognize other arrangements of the parts.

Once the association of the opening and closing cola (*a* and *f*) is acknowledged, then it is a matter of sorting out and combining the remaining cola (*b,c,d,e*). Since *a* and *f* together make a bicolon of 14 syllables (12 on the short count), the remaining units can and should be combined to produce the same total: $5 + 9 = 14$, and $5 + 9 = 14$. The symmetry of the bicola is even more impressive if we adopt the lower numbers: (a $= 6 + f = 6$ for a total of 12; b $= 8 + c = 4$ for a total of 12; d $= 8 + e = 4$ for a total of 12).[6]

If we regard the combination of *a* and *f* as both plausible and logical, then we must consider the proper order of the remaining cola: *b,c,d,e*. The natural sequence is possible, to be sure, but the presence of the conjunction *waw* before *b* and *d* (as also before *f*) suggests that they should be balancing (i.e., second cola) rather than initiating elements; and that we must begin such combinations with the other heavier units, *c* and *e*. Following the initial leap from *a* to *f*, it would be natural to proceed then to *e*, rather than *b* or *c*; the contents of the blessing support this supposition: the raising of the face precedes its shining, i.e., it is only after the face is raised, that its beams can shine upon the worshipper, or to change the image back to the original idea behind the blessing: it is only after the sun has risen that it shines upon the world. If *e* follows *a-f*, then we have a choice between a simple retrogression, *e,d,c,b*, or a more serpentine arrangement, *e,b,c,d*. While the former is straight-backward, the latter seems to me slightly more artistic, and in keeping with the initial pattern: a-f, e-b, c-d. Structured in this fashion, the poem would read:

> May Yahweh bless you
> > and may he grant you peace!
> May Yahweh raise his face upon you
> > and may he protect you!
> May Yahweh make his face shine upon you
> > and may he be gracious to you!

These arrangements are not mutually exclusive; the poet has achieved multiple effects by using interchangeable parts. In each case, the verb and its pronominal complement (whether attached directly to the verb as a suffix or indirectly as a prepositional phrase) have five syllables: there are three cases with the pronominal suffix (*a, b, d*), and three with the prepositional phrase (*c, e, f*). Thus each unit has a verb of five syllables (with complement). There are also six nouns (each of two syllables) to go with the six verbs: *a* and *f* have one noun each, while *c* and *e* have two; *b* and *d* have none. Three of the nouns are subjects (Yahweh in every case: *a, c, e*); three are objects (*pānāw* twice, *c* and *e*; and *šalōm* once, *f*). Taking the bicola as units, in each pair we have two verbs and their complements, five syllables each, and two nouns, one subject and one object, two syllables each: making a total in all cases of 14 syllables. The parts are all metrically interchangeable, thus guaranteeing the symmetry of the poetic structure. For the pair, *a-f*, the two cola are evenly matched with verb and complement in each colon, and the subject noun in the first, and the object noun in the other; in the case of *eb* and *cd*, or *ed* and *cb* the nouns are bunched in the first unit, thus dividing the bicolon unevenly (the dividing point comes roughly at 2/3 and 1/3, and would be exactly there if we used the shorter count: 6/6 and 8/4; 8/4).

The content of the blessing has become so familiar through repetition in liturgical usage that its unusual character is hardly noticed. The emphasis on the "face" of Yahweh brings us back to the earliest period of Israelite religion, and ultimately to the experience of Moses himself. In the oldest references to the annual feasts, the obligation of all Israelites to present themselves before Yahweh three times a year is emphasized. Comparison of the relevant passages (Exod 23:14-17 and Exod 34:20-24) shows that the specific objective was "to see the face of Yahweh," although the Massoretes tried to avoid the plain statement by revocalizing the verbs.[7] If the Aaronic Blessing had its original setting in these annual feasts, then it expressed the confidence or hope that when the worshipers assembled in the sanctuary, Yahweh would raise his face as an act of grace, so that the rays of his countenance (like the sun in its splendor) would shine upon them.

I suggest that in the background of the Blessing lies the experience of Moses, recorded in the tradition, concerning the "face" of Yahweh, and the extended discussion or debate about whether Moses would be granted the beatific vision. There is a persistent tradition in the bible that human beings cannot see the face of God and survive the experience. It is not implied that the experience is impossible, only that it is likely to be fatal. Hence the wonder expressed when having seen the face of God, the beholder survives: e.g., Gen 32:31, "And Jacob called the name of the place, 'Peniel: for I have seen God face to face, and I have escaped with my life' " (cf. Judg 13:2-23). The same point is made in connection with Moses' request that he be allowed to see "the glory" of God (Exod 33:18, "And he said, 'Show me your glory' "). The response is that, "You cannot see my face, for human beings (*hā'ādām*) cannot see me and live" (Exod 33:20). A compromise solution is reached: "It shall be, when my glory passes by — I shall have set you in the cleft of the rock, and covered you with my hand until I pass by — then I will remove my hand, and you shall see my back, but my face shall not be seen" (Exod 33:22-23).

While this tradition reflects the deep concern to affirm that Moses saw the person of God, and at the same time deny that he saw the divine face, there is another tradition, which implies if it does not flatly assert that Moses was granted the beatific vision, and therefore that Moses was the exception to the rule: "And Yahweh would speak to Moses face to face, as a man talks to his companion" (Exod 33:11); "And there has not arisen a prophet in Israel like Moses whom Yahweh knew face to face" (Deut 34:10). While the verb "to see" is not used in these "face to face" confrontations, it must be assumed as the parallel passage in Gen 32:31 indicates (cf. Judg 13:22). Also pertinent is the account in Exod 34:27-35 of Moses' conferences with Yahweh (a parallel or complement to the story in Exod 24:12-18; note especially the 40 days and 40-nights). The glory of God is present at the mountain (Exod 24:16-17), and Moses spends the time at the top of the mountain in conference with the deity. When Moses comes down from the mountain to confer with Aaron and the others, they observe that his face is shining (Exod 34:29, 30, 35). After he speaks with the people he covers his face with a veil, but when he approaches the deity, he uncovers his face. The inference is that he sees the radiant face of God, and that his own face shines with the reflected glory of the divine countenance.

Moses' experience as the recipient and beneficiary of the beatific vision of God is clearly linked to his vocation as the unique prophet to whom Yahweh spoke directly, face to face, rather than in dreams as he does with other prophets.[8] The Aaronic Benediction seems to reflect the experience of Moses, and to express the hope that the worshiper may have a share in it, and see the refulgent glory of God's face. The general idea of sharing or democratizing the privileged experience of the Chosen One or Few is found, for example, in the story in Num 11:25-30, in which the spirit of God comes upon the 70 elders, and also moves the two men in the camp, Eldad and Medad, to prophesy. Far from being disturbed at this untoward development, Moses is quoted as saying on that occasion: "Would that all Yahweh's people were prophets, and that Yahweh might put his spirit upon them" (Num 11:29).

The conclusion is that the Aaronic Benediction is a product of that early period of Israel's history when the people went up three times a year to present themselves to Yahweh and "to see his face." The blessing itself, more specifically, is rooted in the experience of Moses, the unique prophet, who spoke to Yahweh face to face, and whose own face shone with the reflected glory of Yahweh's countenance. It expresses the confident hope that Yahweh will raise his face, and let it shine upon the worshipers gathered in his presence.

I further suggest that the poem — a gem of metrical symmetry and artistic simplicity — belongs to the same period, Phase I, as the Song of the Sea, Psalm 29, and the Song of Deborah. In style and manner, in the use of the divine name, it has the characteristic features of that period (12th century B.C.). With it, we may associate other poetic pieces, now scattered through the books of the Pentateuch, especially Numbers and Deuteronomy. We may speculate that at one time they formed part of Moses saga, an early poetic treatment of the life and achievement of Yahweh's first prophet, and leader of his people. On a provisional basis, we can identify the following items as belonging to the saga of Moses:

Numbers 10:35

qūmāh yahweh	$2 + 2 = 4$	Arise Yahweh
w^eyāpūṣū 'ōy^{e}bēkā	$4 + 4 = 8$	and let your enemies be scattered
w^eyānūsū m^{e}śan'ēkā	$4 + 4 = 8$	and let those who hate you flee
mippānēkā	$4 = 4$	from your presence

mśn'k. The original pronunciation was something like: *maśanni'ika*, which has five syllables. The contraction may have occurred at an early date, and would then have been available to the poet. In view of the regularity of the lines otherwise, and the close correlation between the second and third cola, the four-syllable count seems preferable.

Numbers 10:36

šūbāh yahweh	$2 + 2 = 4$	Return Yahweh
rīb^{e}bōt 'alpē yiśrā'ēl	$3 + 2 + 3 = 8$	Myriads of the troops of Israel

The second utterance relating to the ark seems to be truncated, and we would expect another 12-syllable bicolon to match the first. Since the second line as it stands is not entirely comprehensible, the missing parts may have fallen out at various points. The passage is to be compared with Ps 68:18 and Deut 33:2, and seems to combine the heavenly hosts of Yahweh (*rbbwt*) with the earthly armies of Israel.

šūbāh. The word is naturally interpreted as an imperative form of the root *šūb* I "turn, return." The root may be *šūb* II, a biform of *yšb*, with the meaning "rest, sit."[9] The pairing of *qūm* and *yšb* in a number of passages supports this interpretation.[10] As between *š^{e}bāh* and *šūbāh*, there is not a great deal to choose, and it may be that the original form was the former (from *yšb*). However, there is good reason to suppose otherwise, and to defend the MT in the reading *šūbāh*, since it corresponds exactly to *qūmāh*. In other words, the poet deliberately chose a rarer biform rather than a common form, in order to preserve a stylistic pattern (assonance and rhyme): the meaning is more likely to have been "rest" than "return," but it cannot be proved. A similar usage occurs in Ps 23:6, where *wšbty* (vocalized in the MT as *wešabtī*) must be rendered "and I will dwell."[11] The MT requires the derivation from the root *šub* rather than *yšb*, so in order to retain the rendering (which is not really in question), we must appeal to *šub* II as the root.

<u>Numbers 12:6-8:</u>

6)	*šimˤū - nā' debārāy*	$2 + 1 + 3 = 6$
	'im - yihyeh nebī'akem yahweh[a]	$1 + 2 + 4 + 2 = 9$
	bammar'āh 'ēlāw 'etwaddāˤ	$3 + 2 + 3 = 8$
	baḥalōm 'adabber - bō	$3 + 3 + 1 = 7$
7)	*lō'- kēn ˤabdî mōšeh*	$1 + 1 + 2 + 2 = 6$
	bekol - bētî ne'mān[b] *hū'*	$2 + 2 + 2 + 1 = 7$
8)	*peh 'el - peh 'adabber - bō*	$1 + 1 + 1 + 3 + 1 = 7$
	ūmar'eh[c] *welō' beḥīdōt*	$3 + 2 + 3 = 8$
	ūtemūnat yahweh yabbīṭ	$4 + 2 + 2 = 8$
	ūmaddūˤ[d] *lō' yerē'tem*	$3 + 1 + 3 = 7$
	ledabbēr beˤabdī bemōšeh	$3 + 3 + 3 = 9$

Listen intently to my words
If any of you is Yahweh's prophet
In a vision I may make myself known to him
In a dream I may speak with him.

Not so is Moses my servant
In my whole house, he is the most loyal

Mouth to mouth I speak with him
Not in a vision or in riddles
And the form of Yahweh he beholds.

And why were you not afraid
to speak against Moses my servant?

a) The sequence *nby'km yhwh* is peculiar, but no emendation is required. The broken construct chain is a recognized phenomenon in Hebrew poetry.[12] The terms *nby'* and *yhwh* form a natural construct chain: "the prophet of Yahweh." The pronominal suffix *-km* is connected more loosely but clearly refers back to the subject of *šm'w* (vs. 6) and ahead to the subject of *yr'tm* (vs. 8). The sense may be expressed as follows: "If there is among you a prophet of Yahweh," or more pointedly: "If either of you [Aaron and Miriam are the ostensible subjects] is or claims to be Yahweh's prophet [i.e., as a rival to Moses, who is], in a vision, I will [or may] make myself known to him, in a dream I will [or may] speak to him."

b) In the MT, the vocalization is *ne'emān*, three syllables. However, the compound shewa is secondary, and should not be counted.

c) *ūmar'eh* is ambiguous. Apparently the Massoretes wished to distinguish the word from *mar'āh* above (vs. 6), and there may be reason then to interpret this word as meaning "visible appearance" rather than "vision." If the latter is true, then the word should be taken as a parallel to *tmwnt* and analyzed as the direct object of *ybyt*: ". . . and the appearance and the actual form of Yahweh he observes." The phrase, *wl' bhydt*, however, must be taken with the verb *'dbr-bw*: "Mouth to mouth I speak with him, . . . and not in riddles." While in poetry there can be a great deal more flexibility in the order and arrangement of terms, there is a plausible alternative which does not require such adjustments. The term *mr'h* would be interpreted as equivalent to *bmr'h* above, and linked with *bhydt* and the expression *wl' b-* (the latter would apply to *mr'h* as well as *hydt*).[13] This arrangement, with the meaning: "And neither in visions nor in riddles," would correspond more closely to the pairing of equivalent terms in vs. 6: *bmr'h* and *bhlwm* // *mr'h* and *bhydt*. It may be added that there is important textual support for the reading *bmr'h* instead of *wmr'h* (vs. 8). If an error is involved (either way), it would be due to the confusion of bilabial sounds in the course of oral transmission, or dictation to scribes. In view of the occurrence of the preposition before the other three terms, it may well be original here; in that case, it would tip the scales in favor of our second interpretation. The metrical count would be not affected in any case.

d) The vocalization of *wmdw'* in the MT is *ūmaddūa'*, four syllables. However, the *patah* furtive is secondary and should not be included in the syllable count.

The opening unit, vs. 6, consists of two bicola with 15 syllables each, making a total of 30 syllables. It is balanced by another unit, including vss. 7 (6 + 7 = 13) and 8de (7 + 9 = 16), which also consists of a pair of bicola, with a total of 29 syllables. The latter (vss. 7 and 8de) serves as an envelope for a tricolon (8abc: $7 + 8 + 8 = 23$) which is the core of the poem, and expresses the main theme of the poet: Moses' unique status as Yahweh's prophet. The links and echoes of terms and forms confirm the analysis: thus 2nd m. pl. forms are used in 6ab and again in 8de (*šmᶜw* and *nby'km* in 6, and *yr'tm* in 8); 7a and 8e form an inclusion with the repetition of the terms *ᶜbdy* and *mōšeh*. Vs. 6cd finds an echo in 8ab (note the repetition of the expression *'dbr-bw*, and the association of *bmr'h* and *wmr'h*). The third colon of the tricolon (8abc) is expansionary and emphasizes the unique aspect of Moses' prophetic vocation: he alone sees the actual form, the person of Yahweh.

Numbers 21:17-18 — The Song of the Well

While there is no explicit connection with Moses, this bit of verse has an archaic ring to it and is linked by vocabulary with the Song of Deborah: note the terms *śārīm, nᵉdībē (hā) ᶜām*, and *mᵉḥōqēq* in the Song of the Well, and the corresponding terms in Judg 5:2, 9, 14, 15.

ᶜa͆lī bᵉ'ēr[a]	$2 + 1/2 = 3/4$
ᶜᵉnū lāh (a)[b]	$2 + 1/2 = 3/4$
bᵉ'ēr ḥᵃpārūhā śārīm[c]	$1/2 + 3/4 + 2 = 6/8$
kārūhā nᵉdībē (hā)ʸām[d]	$2/3 + 3 + 1/2 = 6/8$
bimḥōqēq[e]	$3/4$
bᵉmišᶜᵃnōtām[f]	5

"Spring up, O well!"
Sing to it.
Well which the princes dug
which the leaders of the people hollowed out
with their staff
with their sticks

a) *bᵉ'ēr*. The vocalization of the MT is artificial. The original form of the noun was *bi'ru*; with the loss of the case ending, it became *bi'r*, and then in due course, with the quiescence (or assimilation and later reduction of the doubled consonant) of the 'aleph, *bēr*. The MT *bᵉ'ēr* is a back-formation, designed to restore or preserve the 'aleph as a consonant.[14] The minimum count for the colon would be $2 + 1 = 3$.

b) The form *lāh* is pausal; the more original form would have been *laha* or *liha*, with an additional syllable. In my view, the treatment of the 3rd f. s. suffix would have been the same throughout the poem in all positions: the final *-a* would have been preserved as a long vowel *-ā* or dropped entirely. I assume that in the very early period of which we are speaking (12th-11th centuries), the longer form was more common, if not regular. During the same period (at least until the 10th century final vowels were not indicated in the spelling), there would have been no difference in the orthography. The minimum count for this colon would have been three syllables; more likely we should count four.

c) The minimum count would be $1 + 3 + 2 = 6$. The 3rd f. s. suffix should probably be counted, in which case the total would be 7.

d) Here the minimum count would be $2 + 3 + 1 = 6$. The definite article with ʿām probably should not be counted, since it is very rare in early Hebrew poetry; however, its occasional occurrence may be deliberate on the part of the poet, and care should be exercised in dealing with the phenomenon. Since the article is relatively rare in poetry in general, and is standard usage in prose, scribal inadvertence in copying (especially since little if any distinction was made in copying practice between prose and poetry) is to be expected, and there are doubtless many cases in which the article has been added in Hebrew poetry. At the same time the fact that the distinction has been preserved to a statistically significant extent (the use of the article is much more common in prose books of the bible, in contrast with its relative paucity in poetic books), suggests that its occasional presence in poetry may be deliberate and not accidental. Hence caution should be exercised in making a decision. It is important to note that the corresponding term śārīm is just as definite as hāʿām, but there would be no warrant for adding the article to the former word, though the *he* could be regarded as a double-duty particle.[15] It would be very difficult to make any distinction between the parallel terms on the basis of the presence or absence of the article. The minimum count is 6 syllables, but if we added the 3rd f. s. suffix to the verb, the total would be 7.

e) The minimum count, following the MT, would be 3. An earlier form of the expression would have had an additional syllable, i.e., bimaḥōqēq. The elision, which takes place in accordance with Massoretic rules, may have taken place at almost any time. Whether it was available to the poet, and whether he exercised his right to use it must remain matters of speculation. The syllable count must have been either 3 or 4.

f) The syllable count on the basis of the MT would be 5. It has been suggested that the final *mem* is enclitic rather than pronominal, but this would not affect the syllable count; in any case there is no reason to question the traditional analysis or interpretation. The antecedent is clearly understood as the plural nouns in the preceding cola (śrym, and ndybv hʿm). The suffix would then serve double duty with bmḥqq. The only remaining question is whether the noun is to be taken as plural (as vocalized by the MT), or singular as implied by the singular *mḥqq*. The preserved orthography would be equally valid for either form intò late post-Exilic times (only then would a *waw* have been inserted before the *taw* to signify the plural ending, and then not consistently in these suffixed forms). The singular form, if correct, would have been vocalized as follows: *bᵉmišᶜantām*, or four syllables against the MT five. The minimum count for the bicolon would be $3 + 4 = 7$. The vocalization of the MT gives us $3 + 5 = 8$, while the maximum possible would be $4 + 5 = 9$.

The minimum and maximum syllable counts for the four units are as follows:

1)	6 - 8	(7)
2)	6 - 8	(7)
3)	6 - 8	(7)
4)	7 - 9	(8)

I have indicated the most likely count in each case (the number in parentheses).

Numbers 21:27-29

This poem is a unique example of a non-Israelite composition of early date, and deserves detailed treatment beyond the limits of this paper. For the present see the studies of Paul Hanson and John Van Seters.[16] I hope to bring out a study of this work in the near future.

All together these poetic bits and pieces contribute significantly to the picture of the early period in the wilderness, and especially to the Moses tradition. The Aaronic Blessing fits with the other poems as an archaic composition. It has the characteristic features of Phase I poetry (12th century), and there are specific affinities with early poems like Psalm 29. Its central interest is in the "face of Yahweh" and the gracious, protective light which radiates from it. Just as in the oldest traditions of the annual festal pilgrimages, the Israelites are enjoined to present themyelves before Yahweh, and to see his face; so here the complementary benediction of the divine presence is offered: they will see his face, and his face will shine upon them. Behind it all are the traditions concerning Moses, and his unique status as the servant of God, who spoke with him, mouth to mouth, and saw him in person. The narrative in Exod 34:27-35 describes the specific effects of the face-to-face confrontation: the face of Moses shines with the reflected glory of Yahweh's radiant countenance, because Yahweh first raised his face, and graciously made it shine upon Moses.

1. The most recent study is by P. D. Miller, Jr., "The Blessing of God: An Interpretation of Numbers 6:22-27," *Int* 29 (1975) 240-51.

2. Ibid., esp. 243, n. 11: "It has been pointed out that there is no metrical symmetry to these lines." While the present study was planned and worked out before the appearance of Miller's article, a primary objective of it is to challenge the common opinion, and to show that there is metrical symmetry, and to explain its nature and structure.

3. I have discussed the theory and method of syllable-counting in a number of articles, and hope to give a comprehensive and detailed account in a proposed volume on Hebrew poetry. For the present, see my "Prolegomenon" to G. B. Gray, *The Forms of Hebrew Poetry* (reprint; New York: Ktav, 1972), vii-lvi; "Strophe and Meter in Exodus 15," *A Light Unto My Path: Old Testament Studies in Honor of Jacob M. Myers* (eds. H. N. Bream, R. D. Heim, and C. A. Moore; Philadelphia: Temple University, 1974) 163-202; "Acrostics and Metrics in Hebrew Poetry," *HTR* 65 (1972) 367-92; "The Refrain in David's Lament over Saul and Jonathan," *Ex Orbe Religionum: Studia Geo Widengren* (eds. C. J. Bleeker, S. G. F. Brandon, and M. Simon; Supplements to *Numen* 21-22; Leiden: Brill, 1972) vol. 1, 115-26.

4. See the discussion in F. M. Cross and D. N. Freedman, *Early Hebrew Orthography* (Philadelphia: American Oriental Society, 1952) 65-70.

5. See the study by D. N. Freedman and C. Frank-Hyland, "Psalm 29: A Structural Analysis," *HTR* 66 (1973) 237-56.

6. The same pattern appears in Exod 15:4 ($8 + 4 = 12$ syllables; $6 + 6 = 12$ syllables). Failure to observe this larger balance has led to unwarranted emendation of the first colon; see the discussion in "Strophe and Meter in Exodus 15," 179; see also "Prolegomenon," xxxiv-xxxvii.

7. In Exod 23:15 and 34:20 we read: *wᵉlō' - yērā'û pānay rēqām,* "And my face shall not be seen empty-handed." The meaning, however, must be: "They must not present themselves before me (i.e., see my face) empty-handed (i.e., without suitable offerings)." In Exod 23:17, the reading is: *yērā'ēh kol - zᵉkūrkā 'el pᵉnē hā'ādōn* "Every one of your males must appear (present himself) before the Lord." But Exod 34:23 has *'et - pᵉnē YHWH,* which makes the Niphal form of the verb more difficult to accommodate. The original meaning must have been: "Every male among you shall present himself before Yahweh (i.e., shall see the face of Yahweh)." The same interpretation must be given to Exod 34:24, *lērā'ōt et pᵉnē YHWH ᵉlōhēkā* "to see the face of your God" (reading the Qal inf. *lir'ōt* for the Niphal).

8. Num 12:6-8, a poetic piece, preserves the same tradition, but articulates it in slightly different terms: "Mouth to mouth, I speak with him / and the figure of Yahweh he beholds."

9. On the occurrence of this root, *šūb* II, see M. Dahood, *Psalms I* (AB 16; Garden City: Doubleday, 1966) 44, 148, 213; *Psalms II* (AB 17; Garden City: Doubleday, 1968) 69.

10. Cf. Ps 127:2, 139:2, Lam 3:63, Gen 27:19, Isa 52:2, Deut 6:7, 11:19.

11. See my forthcoming study of "Psalm 23" in the Festschrift in honor of Prof. George Cameron, University of Michigan.

12. See my article, "The Broken Construct Chain," *Bib* 53 (1972) 534-36. See the recent discussion of the entire unit by F. M. Cross, *Canaanite Myth and Hebrew Epic* (Cambridge: Harvard University, 1973) 203-4.

13. The same treatment was suggested by W. F. Albright (*Yahweh and the Gods of Canaan* [Garden City: Doubleday, 1968] 42) and has recently been seconded by E. F. Campbell ("Moses and the Foundations of Israel," *Int* 29 [1975] 146).

14. On this formation see GKC, §23f. But see also §93t.

15. On double-duty particles, see Dahood, *Psalms III* (AB 17A; Garden City: Doubleday, 1970) 437-39.

16. See the recent studies by P. Hanson, "The Song of Heshbon and David's *'Nir'*," *HTR* 61 (1968) 297-320, and J. Van Seters, "The Conquest of Sihon's Kingdom," *JBL* 91 (1972) 182-97. In my opinion the poem ends with vs. 29; the travelogue is resumed in vs. 30. It is instructive that neither Yahweh nor any other sanctioned name of the God of Israel appears in the poem, only Chemosh the god of Moab; the role assigned to Chemosh is very much like that assigned to Yahweh in Israelite poems. It seems clearly to be a non-Israelite composition, which makes it all the more interesting.

Elizabeth Bellefontaine

The Curses of Deuteronomy 27:
Their Relationship to the Prohibitives

Recent studies in the field of OT law have concentrated almost exclusively upon one or other of the series of laws designated by Alt as apodictic.[1] The results of these studies suggest that the apodictic law category is not formally homogeneous and that Alt's original division of the pentateuchal laws into just two categories is an oversimplification. The present article reviews two major works dealing with two subgroups of Alt's apodictic laws and proceeds to an investigation of a third subgroup.

The first serious attack upon Alt's form-critical classification was undertaken by Erhard Gerstenberger.[2] Since Gerstenberger's thesis is generally well-known, a detailed presentation need not be given here. Briefly, Gerstenberger confines Alt's term "apodictic" to the prohibitions and commands which refer to hypothetical future offenses and which lack all statement of a fixed legal consequence. These prohibitions and commands are described as non-conditional norms of everyday life, are usually formulated in the second person singular and appear mostly in negative form.[3] Their origin lies in the kinship ethos of the Semitic clans. Because of their predominately negative expression, Gerstenberger refers to them as "prohibitives." While the present writer does not accept all of Gerstenberger's conclusions, the term "prohibitive" will be used in this article with his definition.

Hermann Schulz accepted Gerstenberger's conclusions and proceeded to his own analysis of the biblical death laws characterized by the phrase *mōt yûmāt*.[4] The death laws along with the prohibitives and the curses of Deuteronomy 27 had all been subsumed by Alt under the category of apodictic law. Schulz questioned Alt's designation and proposed that the death laws constitute a separate law form.[5]

Schulz begins by a study of the three-fold prohibitive list in Exod 20:13-15 and finds a corresponding death law for each prohibitive: Exod 21:12; Lev 20:12 and Exod 21:16. The death sentence is imposed for crimes

49

forbidden by the prohibitives, and the prohibitives form the basic norms from which the death laws are derived. In each case the death law defines the corresponding prohibitive more precisely and brings it into the legal sphere. For example, the prohibitive, "You shall not kill" (Exod 20:13), is made legally more precise by the death law, "Whoever strikes a man so that he dies, shall be put to death" (Exod 21:12). Conversely, without reference to the prohibitive, the death law is not correctly understood.

An analysis of all the death laws reveals that each one is rooted in a corresponding prohibitive.[6] For some, the prohibitives have not been preserved, although without doubt they once existed and formed the basis for the existing laws.[7] These probable forms have been reconstructed by Schulz. In other cases the prohibitive has been assimilated to the death sentence so that the two now appear in a single statement.[8]

Schulz points out that the prohibitive constitutes a norm for action but does not suffice for judging concrete cases. The death law was the initial legal formulation which brought the prohibitive into the sphere of law. Therefore, a special legal relationship exists between the death law and the prohibitive norm. Furthermore, there is a traditio-historical relationship since the death laws reflect an advanced stage of development which required a more exact definition of the criminal act and a determined legal consequence.

These connections are sustained in later texts. Schulz finds that the death laws of Leviticus 20 are based upon the corresponding prohibitives of Leviticus 18 and 19 and that they represent a later stage of development than the participial death laws of the Book of the Covenant. The participles have given way to relative clauses, and every fundamental element of the death law has been expanded. Yet the legal relationship between prohibitive and death sentence endures. New emphasis is placed upon the relationship by adding to the death law a declarative statement which contains in part the formulation of the parallel prohibitive.[9]

Schulz insists that despite the legal connection the death law is not merely a derivative of the prohibitive. The latter establishes a fundamental order of life for the community. When this order is violated a new law is needed by which the violation can be recognized and a penalty imposed.[10] The death law is to be understood as an independent legal statement with a unique structure and origin. The origin is determined by an analysis of Gen 26:6-11. The incident described is typical rather than historical and leads Schulz to conclude that the tribal community was the situation in life of the death law.[11]

A further significant point made by Schulz concerns the community and its imposition of the death sentence. To deal with death law violations the assembly of the local community as a secular judgment community did not suffice. The community needed assurance of divine protection against possible disastrous effects released by the execution of a criminal. In cases concerning the death law it was necessary to convene the people as a cultic judicial community. Only such a sacred assembly could have jurisdiction over death law cases and be competent to pronounce the death penalty. [12]

Further details of Schulz's study of the death law need not be presented here. What is of significance are his conclusions that the death law is a distinct law form within Israelite legal tradition, that it has a special legal relationship to the prohibitives, and that the application of the death law could be made only in a sacral setting.

Schulz's conclusions prompt us to ask similar questions of the curses of Deuteronomy 27. Is a relationship such as that between death laws and prohibitives peculiar to these forms, or does a similar relationship exist between other law forms, specifically between the curses of Deuteronomy 27 and certain prohibitives? [13] It is the proposal of this paper that such a relationship does exist; that each curse had at one time a corresponding prohibitive norm from which it was derived and which it was designed to protect and define. Since all the curses relate to crimes committed in secret, it is this aspect of any corresponding prohibitive which will be noted.

The curse list of Deut 27:15-26 is recognized as very ancient, dating from the earliest period of Israel's history. [14] The last verse, however, cannot be considered as part of the original list. It is not directed, like the preceding curses, towards a definite violation of the divine will but refers back to Deut 17:3 and speaks of "the words of this law" in general. Furthermore, it departs from the positive formulation used throughout the list ("cursed be he who . . . ") and expresses itself negatively . ("cursed be who does not . . ."). The verse must be considered a later deuteronomic addition to the primitive list. [15]

The antiquity of the first curse is likewise questionable. In general the language reflects a late period. [16] The style of the verse differs from the usual curse formulation by the use of the relative construction instead of a participle after 'ārûr, "cursed be . . . . " [17] Therefore, despite attempts to reconstruct a simpler, original statement, [18] one hesitates to consider this verse as an element of the primitive list. It seems to have been composed later than the rest of the list and joined to it either before or after the list was placed in its present context. Nevertheless, the verse betrays the author's effort to compose a curse against idolatry in keeping with the viewpoint of the basic series, and so can be studied as an independent element of the present list.

After excising the definitely late phrases in the middle of the text (vs. 15) and the adjective "molten," there remains: "Cursed be the man who makes a graven image and sets it up in secret." The concluding phrase qualifies the first clause and brings it into harmony with the rest of the list. There is no prohibitive in the OT against the setting up of an image in secret. The general prohibition against images, however, is a basic tradition in Israel.[19] The prohibitive upon which the first clause of vs. 15 is based is Exod 20:4: *lō' ta'ăśeh lᵉkā pesel.* The correspondence is clear: *'arûr hā'îš 'ăšer ya'ăśeh pesel.* To this first clause was added the qualifying statement regarding the secrecy of the deed. The result is an imprecation against anyone who would make an image and erect it secretly. A development of the prohibitive norm has taken place. The curse has taken up the prohibited deed, under a certain aspect, an aspect which could not be reached by the ordinary process of law, and has given it new form by means of the curse formulation. Further, by placing it under the special jurisdiction of the divinity, it has established for the prohibited deed an inescapable consequence to be determined and executed by the deity. In this way, the prohibitive norm has been made legal: it has been given the only legal character possible under the aspect of secret violation. That this character is of a sacral-legal nature is evident from the curse formula itself, from the ritual ceremony which the series describes and possibly also from its situation in life in the covenant renewal ceremony.[20]

The same relationship to a basic prohibitive norm can be demonstrated for most of the curses in the original list, and it can be argued for the others. Deut 27:16 invokes a malediction upon one who treats with contempt, that is, dishonors (*qlh*) his father or his mother. The OT has preserved no negative statement corresponding to this curse. There is, however, the positively formulated precept of Exod 20:12 commanding the honoring (*kbd*) of mother and father, as well as Lev 19:3 which employs the verb *yr'*. There also exist the two death laws of Exod 21:17 and Lev 20:9 directed against those who curse (*qll*) mother or father. Several scholars have argued for an original negative form of the parents command in the decalogue which would have read: "Do not curse (*qll*) your mother or your father."[21] Schulz in particular argues for the existence of such an original prohibitive which would have formed the basis for the existing death laws, for Lev 19:3a, and perhaps also for Exod 20:12. The latter would either have been derived from the negative precept or have existed along with it.[22]

While such a reconstruction provides a correlative basis for the death laws, it fails to do so for the curse employing, as it does, a different verb.

This holds true even if one accepts *qll* as meaning not only verbal repudiation but any expression of repudiation.[23] While the curse is understood as meaning the exact opposite of the decalogue command,[24] it could not have been derived directly from it.

More acceptable is the proposal of an original negative formulation employing the verb *qlh* and reading: "*lō' taqle 'et-'ābīka we'et-'immeka*," "You shall not despise [treat with contempt, dishonor] your father or your mother."[25] The verb used here is broader in meaning than the more specific terms "curse" (Exod 21:17) and "strike" (Exod 21:15), and encompasses a wider range of actions relating to rejection of parental authority.[26] This original prohibition has not been preserved. Just as the positive command, "Honor your father and your mother," covers a broader sphere of action than the prohibitive against cursing and came to replace it, so too, it eventually displaced the negatively formulated precept against "dishonoring" parents. We may conclude, therefore, that a prohibitive correlative to the curse of Deut 27:16 originally existed and has been lost to the present text. The curse formula extends to all actions contrary to the original prohibitive and still covered by the positive precept of the decalogue when these are done in secret.

Deut 27:17 invokes a curse upon the man who removes his neighbor's landmark. The only prohibitive in the biblical legislation against the removal of a neighbor's landmark is found in Deut 19:14. Deut 27:17 takes up this prohibitive and places the action under a curse. The correspondence is clear: Deut 27:17: *'arûr massig gebûl rē'ēhû.* Deut 19:14: *lō' tassig gebûl rē'aka.* There is no secrecy clause, but the deed is obviously one which would not be done openly. Judging by other references to the landmark in the biblical text,[27] such tampering remained a problem in Israel. The removal of the landmark, especially in the early period, was seen not merely as a civil offence. Since the land belonged to Yahweh and was only given in fief to the people, transfer of land was not permissible. This is the meaning of Lev 25:23 which reflects Israel's earliest attitude towards the land.[28] Removal of a landmark involved the appropriation of land granted by Yahweh to another as an inheritance; it meant violating Yahweh's proprietorship. Hence, action contrary to the prohibitive of Deut 19:14 brought the deed into the sacral sphere. The malediction of Deut 27:17 is rooted in this prohibitive and brings it into the sacral-legal sphere for the punishment of violators.

The curse of Deut 27:18 is directed against one who "misleads a blind man on the road." There is no direct parallel to the curse among the biblical prohibitives. The only precept regulating conduct toward the blind is the second prohibition of Lev 19:14 forbidding the placing of a stumbling block before a blind man. The curse does not take up the forbidden deed as described. Nevertheless, while verbal parallelism is lacking, it is clear that the curse is similar in function and force to the prohibitive. Both the intent of the curse and the range of actions covered by it are inclusive of the action described in the prohibitive. To mislead a blind man would be to fail to lead him on a safe — and unobstructed — path and to deliberately direct him along an unsafe — perhaps obstructed — way. The curse of Deut 27:18 seems to have been phrased so as to take up not only the specific deed of Lev 19:14 but also all other similar acts of meanness against a blind man. The prohibitive, while being taken into the sacral-legal sphere, is expanded and interpreted in the broadest possible terms. Such a malediction would be necessary because the blind man would likely be unable to bear witness in court. Only the vengeance of God could reach the person who would take such unfair advantage of the handicapped.

The rights of other unfortunate members of society are safeguarded by the malediction of Deut 27:19: "Cursed be he who perverts the justice due to the sojourner, the fatherless, and the widow." The curse is rooted in the prohibitive of Deut 24:17 where the verbal parallels are very close. The word order is the same, but the perversion of justice toward the widow is defined precisely as taking the widow's garment in pledge.[29] The prohibitive states: "You shall not pervert the justice due to the stranger, to the fatherless, or take a widow's garment in pledge." Originally the widow was probably simply named along with the stranger and the orphan, as in the curse formula, and the expansion into a separate prohibitive sentence was the result of a later need for more exact definition of the deed. This supposition is strengthened by the omission in the prohibitive of the conjunctive *waw* before *yātôm* (orphan) which appears as it does in the three-fold series of Deut 27:19.

The linking of these three disinherited classes is a typical deuteronomic combination.[30] Yet the linking is not original with Deuteronomy since a similar grouping is found in the earlier tradition of Exod 22:20-23. The second verb of vs. 20a is an addition. So too is the motivating clause of vs. 20b, which is in the plural address and from which the plural has been transferred to vs. 21.[31] By excising these additions two short, terse prohibitives remain: "You shall not wrong a stranger. You shall not afflict any widow or orphan." These prohibitives along with Exod 23:9 (cf. also Lev 19:33-34) are part of the same tradition which is expressed in more legal terms in Deut 24:17. It is this latter prohibitive, in its original shorter form, which is taken up by Deut 27:19 and recast in the form of a curse bearing the consequence of divine vengeance.

The act of bestiality accursed by Deut 27:21 has a prohibitive correlative in Lev 18:23 and is placed under the sentence of death by Exod 22:18 and Lev 20:15. The verb used to describe the action is *škb* (to lie with) and designates sexual intercourse.[32] It is questionable, however, that the prohibitive of Lev 18:23 forms the basis for the curse. It belongs to a short, rather loosely unified list (Lev 18:18-23) dealing with unnatural sexual acts. It seems to have been composed expressly as an appendix to the preceding series of prohibitions on sexual relations within the family (Lev 18:7-17).[33] It bears the stamp of the priestly tradition and is more concerned with ritual cleanness than with the actual crime.[34] Beastiality was prohibited earlier than the time of the composition of this list, as is clear from the death law in the Book of the Covenant (Exod 22:18). In fact, the wording of the curse is more consonant with that of the death law than with the prohibitive of Lev 18:23.

The seriousness of this act seems to lie not merely in its unnaturalness but in its function as a cultic sexual practice. The three death laws of Exod 22:17-19 which include the death penalty for bestiality form a unit characterized by opposition to the service of gods other than Yahweh. The religious motivation behind the Israelite opposition to copulation with any kind of animal is clearer when considered in the light of the Hittite legislation on the topic. Hittite law forbids copulation with animals which are considered sacred — cows, dogs, swine — but allows it with mules and horses.[35] Neither the Assyrian law nor the Code of Hammurabi have anything to say on the matter which may suggest a tolerance of the practice. For the Israelites, the prohibition against bestiality must be understood as a protest against intercourse with animals as a cultic sexual act such as was practiced not only by the Hittites but also by the Canaanites for the purpose of promoting fertility by sympathetic magic.[36] These three death sentences of Exod 22:17-19 have as their cultic-legal principle the commandment to worship Yahweh alone. This must be seen as the prohibitive basis for the sacral-legal ritual invoking the vengeance of the deity upon one who copulates with any kind of beast. The curse of Deut 27:21 finds its prohibitive basis in Exod 20:2-3.

Deut 27:24 invokes a curse upon the man who slays his neighbor in secret. Without doubt such a man has violated the decalogue commandment: "Do not kill" (Exod 20:13). However, in describing the deeds, different verbs are employed. Whereas Exod 20:13 commands: *lō' tirṣaḥ*, the curse formula reads: *'arûr makkēh rē'ēhû*. The participle *makkēh* also occurs in the death sentence of Exod 21:12. Schulz has convincingly shown that this death law is based on the prohibitive of Exod 20:13, and that the participle of the death law more precisely defines the originally objectless prohibitive and brings it into the legal sphere.[37] If this is so, then the curse formula must also be rooted in the prohibitive of Exod 20:13. The distinction drawn in Exod 21:12-14 between intentional and unintentional killing underlines the essential link between the death law and the prohibitive of the decalogue. It also portrays the attempt to deal within the legal sphere with all violations of the decalogue commandment. However, neither of these provisions obtain when the crime is committed in secret and the criminal is left without fear of the death penalty and without need to flee to a city of refuge. That such a criminal, though undetected, might not go unpunished is the purpose of the curse of Deut 27:24. The action forbidden in Exod 20:13 is taken up by the curse and is more sharply defined by the specification that the crime is committed "against the neighbor" and "in secret." It also implies premeditation on the part of the killer. The imprecation of Deut 27:24 can, therefore, be viewed as the specific application of the more general prohibitve norm of the decalogue.

Deut 27:25 curses the man "who takes a bribe to slay an innocent person." It applies the prohibitve of Exod 23:8, "and you shall take no bribe" to a specific case: the successful hired assassin who has escaped suspicion. The incident is not simply a case of secret murder; that would be covered by vs. 24. The acceptance of the bribe is the sole motivation for the murderer's act for he holds no personal case against his victim.[38] Therefore he has no "right" — such as the law of vengeance might allow — to kill the designated person. In this view, the victim is "innocent." Thus, the weight of the curse rests upon the taking of the bribe for the purpose of assassination. The prohibitive foundation is not the prohibition against murder (Exod 20:13), but the prohibition against acceptance of bribes which leads to the violation of justice (Exod 23:8; cf. Deut 16:19).

The prohibitive foundations of the remaining three curses, Deut 27:20, 22 and 23, are not so clearly discernible. The incestuous behavior condemned by the curses is likewise forbidden by the prohibitions of Lev 18:8, 9 and 17, and is also linked with the death penalty in Lev 20:11, 17 and 14. Literal correspondence between the curses and the prohibitives is lacking. Whereas Lev 18:8, 9 and 17 use the phrase 'erwôt . . . lō' t^egallēh (you shall not uncover the nakedness of . . .), the curses are formualted 'ārûr šōkēb 'im (cursed be he who lies with . . .). The prohibitives belong to a series of sexual prohibitions (Lev 18:7-17) which are rooted in the earliest period of Israelite history but which are not now found in their original form.[39] The motivating clause attached to each prohibitive, as well as the repetition of the prohibitive in vss. 7 and 15 and the definition of "sister" in vs. 9, have been added secondarily to the prohibitives. The original complex consisted of a series of short, unqualified prohibitives: "You shall not uncover the nakedness of your mother. You shall not uncover the nakedness of your father's wife," and so forth.[40] While there is similarity of content with the curses, the lack of verbal correspondence suggests that we look elsewhere for the prohibitive basis of the curses.

In the series of death laws in Leviticus 20 we find a law which employs both the verb *škb* (lie with) and the expression "uncover the nakedness of": "The man who lies with his father's wife has uncovered his father's nakedness; both of them shall be put to death, their blood is upon them" (Lev 20:11). Lying with one's father's wife is deserving of the death penalty because one has violated the prohibitive, "You shall not uncover the nakedness of your father's wife; it is your father's nakedness" (Lev 18:8). The death law, while using the verb *škb* to express illicit sexual relations, has also incorporated the wording of the prohibitive and has used it to define the action for which the death penalty is imposed. In this way the crime of lying with one's father's wife receives precise legal definition as well as a determined legal consequence. The case is similar to the rest of the death laws in the series, Lev 20:11-21. While late revisions and expansions are evident, the predominant use throughout the list of the expressions "lie with" and "uncover the nakedness of" argues for an originally consistent unit which used these two expressions. We conclude, therefore, that the death laws of Leviticus 20 rest upon two sets of prohibitives: the preserved list in Leviticus 18 and another list, now lost, which employed the verb *škb* to express sexual intercourse. This lost list corresponded to the act mentioned in the principal clause of the death law, and was the crime for which the penalty was death.[41] We also accept that it is this ancient list of prohibitives, corresponding in form and content, that formed the basis for the curses of Deut 27:20, 22 and 23.

Without doubt, the curse list of Deuteronomy 27 is rooted in the legal traditions of early Israel. Every act which is made the object of a curse is condemned in one way or another elsewhere in the biblical tradition. In all cases a prohibitive foundation can be demonstrated for the accursed deed.

A further confirmation of the original rooting of the curses in definite corresponding prohibitives is provided by the intent of the curse ritual itself. The curse ceremony as described in Deuteronomy 27 consists in the pronouncement of the curses by the Levites and the corresponding response of affirmation by the community. The purpose of the ceremony extends beyond the desire that every criminal may receive his due. It reflects a genuine fear on the part of the community that one member may indeed commit a designated crime in secret and escape apprehension. In this event the whole community would be liable to the divine vengeance. Such a situation was the cause of Israel's defeat under Joshua because Achan had violated the prescriptions of the ban at Jericho (Joshua 7). Hence, in Deuteronomy 27 the imprecations uttered by the Levites, and totally assented to by the members of the assembly, were designed to invoke God's vengeance upon the guilty member alone and thereby to ensure the safety of the whole community.

The curse ritual as such does not necessarily promulgate new demands. The deeds mentioned were already known to the community as liable to the wrath of God. It was the possibility of their secret commission, of the criminal's eluding of justice and the consequent fearful results for the people, that prompted the community's solemn invocation of divine retribution upon the criminal. Each of these deeds, therefore, must have been previously prohibited and have been made the object of a curse only when the community was unable to punish the transgressor. However, insofar as the curses deal with the deeds under a new as-pect — secrecy — they can be considered as new demands. Moreover, belief in the power of the curse to effect vindication would have had a deterrent effect upon potential transgressors.[42] In the case of one who had already committed a crime and had escaped apprehension, participation in the liturgy would place him in the unenviable position of calling down divine judgment upon himself.[43]

It is the aspect of commission in secret that explains how a crime which is the object of a curse could be covered elsewhere by the death penalty (e.g., Deut 27:16, 20, 21, 23, 24). In the case of the death law, the crime is viewed as determinable and punishable within the judicial — albeit, the sacral-judicial — process. With regard to the curse, only the scrutiny of the deity could assure the execution of justice for secret crimes.

Despite its prohibitive basis, the curse, like the death law, is a unique law formulation within the legal history of Israel. The prohibitive, by its nature, is unconditional and does not envisage disobedience; hence, it has no adjoined legal consequence. In practice it is not operative within the legal sphere. The death law, as we have seen, makes its corresponding prohibitive legal by defining the act more precisely and by providing a definite legal penalty: death. In like manner, the curse brings into the legal sphere certain prohibitives whose violation in secret would escape the ordinary legal process. As previously noted, the "ordinary judicial process" with regard to the death law is the proceedings of the sacral-legal community. But even this sacral judicial assembly cannot adjudicate hidden crimes. The community, as sacral assembly, must solemnly invoke the action of the deity in such cases. The curse provides the prohibitives with the only punishment which can reach secret sins: the inescapable consequence of the vengeance of God. In the curse the prohibitive norm under the aspect of secret violation is made legal.

We may conclude, therefore, that there exists a special legal relationship between the prohibitive and the curse. The action forbidden by the prohibitive is taken up by the curse, usually under a new or more specific aspect, refashioned in sacral-legal terms, and presented in a new law form.

The above study of the biblical legal traditions indicates the importance of this literature for understanding the total life of the ancient Israelite community. John L. McKenzie, of course, has long recognized this importance and has documented it in many of his writings. I am pleased to take up one suggestion made by him[44] and to offer him this paper as response.

1. A. Alt, "Die Ursprünge des israelitischen Rechts," *Kleine Schriften zur Geschichte des Volkes Israels* (3 vols.; München: C. H. Beck'sche, 1953; 1959) I, 278-332.

2. *Wesen und Herkunft des "apodiktischen Rechts"* (WMANT 20; Neukirchen-Vluyn: Neukirchen Verlag, 1965).

3. Some positively formulated passages are considered original although in context they may be prohibitive. These include commands to refrain from some action (Exod 23:7a), and those which extend or define more precisely a prohibitive (Lev 19:10; Deut 23:19-20), as well as positive commands which have no negative counterpart such as the observance of the Sabbath and the honoring of parents (Exod 20:8, 12; also Lev 19:32). Gerstenberger, *Apodiktischen Rechts*, 43-49.

4. H. Schulz, *Das Todesrecht im Alten Testament. Studien zur Rechtsform der Mot-Jumat-Sätze* (BZAW 114; Berlin: Töpelmann, 1969). In general, Schulz accepts throughout his work the conclusions of Gerstenberger.

5. He likewise rejects the proposal that the death laws are more accurately defined as casuistic law. The proposal was made by H. Gese, "Beobachtungen zum Stil alttestamentlicher Rechtssätze," *TLZ* 85 (1960) 147-50; R. Kilian, "Apodiktischen und Kasuistisches Recht im Licht ägyptischer Analogien," *BZ* 7 (1963) 185-202.

6. Lev 24:15b is an old death sentence with Exod 22:28a as its prohibitive basis. Exod 21:15 is related to 21:12 and is similarly rooted in Exod 20:13. Exod 22:18-20 is a death sentence list connected with the cult.

7. Exod 21:17; 21:20; 31:14a.

8. Lev 27:29; Exod 21:18.

9. Schulz, *Das Todesrecht*, 46-51.

10. In Gen 26:6-11 and Lev 24:20-23 the OT has preserved some accounts of how the death laws came to be formed.

11. Schulz, *Das Todesrecht*, 95-113.

12. Schulz, *Das Todesrecht*, 113-29.

13. Another question, of course, which lies beyond the scope of this paper, is that of a possible relationship between the curses and the death laws. Schulz deals briefly with the question and concludes that they do not reveal any noticeable interdependence. Schulz, *Das Todesrecht*, 61-71; cf. 79-83.

14. G. von Rad (*Deuteronomy* [London: SCM, 1966] 167) describes the list as "the most ancient series of prohibitions preserved for us in the Old Testament." See also P. Buis, *Le Deutéronome* (VS: Ancien Testament, 4; Paris: Beauchesne, 1969) 371; H.-J. Krause, *Worship in Israel* (Richmond: John Knox, 1966) 141-44. For opinions which date the curses in the deuteronomic period, see E. Sellin and G. Fohrer, *Introduction to the Old Testament* (Nashville: Abingdon, 1968) 143; Schulz, *Das Todesrecht*, 81.

15. von Rad, *Deuteronomy*, 167.

16. J. Blenkinsopp, "Deuteronomy," *JBC* 6:65.

17. von Rad, *Deuteronomy*, 168.

18. Alt considered the relative clause as a modification of an original participle and reconstructed the statement to read: "Cursed be he who sets up an image in secret." Alt, "Die Ursprünge," 314. P. Buis proposes: "Cursed be the one who makes an idol and places it in a hiding-place." P. Buis et J. LeClerq, *Le Deutéronome* (SB; Paris: Librairie LeCoffre, 1963) 173-75.

19. Cf. Exod 20:4, 23; 34:17; Lev 19:4; 26:1; Deut 4:15-18, 23, 25; 5:8.

20. On the question of the situation in life see Alt, "Die Ursprünge," 322-28; Krause, *Worship*, 145.

21. von Rad, *Deuteronomy*, 58; J. J. Stamm and M. E. Andrew, *The Ten Commandments in Recent Research* (SBT 2/2; London: SCM, 1967) 96.

22. Schulz, *Das Todesrecht*, 52-55.

23. As suggested by A. Phillips, *Ancient Israel's Criminal Law* (New York: Schocken, 1970) 80.

24. S. R. Driver, *Deuteronomy* (Edinburgh: T. and T. Clark, 1960) 301.

25. E. Nielsen, *The Ten Commandments in New Perspective* (London: SCM, 1968) 84, 89.

26. The legal-historical narrative of Deut 21:18-21 provides a typical illustration of such repudiation.

27. Prov 22:28; 23:10; Job 24:2; Hos 5:10.

28. Alt, "Die Ursprünge," 327-28; G. von Rad, "The Promised Land and Yahweh's Land in the Hexateuch," *The Problem of the Hexateuch and Other Essays* (Edinburgh: Oliver and Boyd, 1966) 85.

29. Cf. Exod 22:26-27.

30. Deut 10:18 (the order is reversed); 14:29; 16:11, 14; 24:17, 19, 20, 21; 26:12, 13; 27:19. See also Jer 7:6; 22:3; Ps 94:6; 146:9; Mal 3:5; Ezek 22:7; Zech 7:10; Isa 1:17; 10:2; etc.

31. M. Noth, *Exodus* (London: SCM, 1962) 186; Gerstenberger, *Apodiktischen Rechts*, 82, note 1.

32. Cf. the list of laws with *škb* in Lev 20:11-13, 15-16, 18, 20.

33. K. Elliger ("Das Gesetze Leviticus 18," *ZAW* 67 [1955] 1-25) divides the lists thus: vss. 7-17a; vss. 1, 17b-23.

34. Cf. the references to defilement (vss. 20b, 23a) and the appended defining clauses, "it is wickedness" (vs. 17b), "it is an abomination" (vs. 22b), "it is perversion" (vs. 23b). In vs. 20 adultery is considered only as a ritual impurity. Cf. also vss. 19 and 23.

35. See Hittite Laws 187, 199 and 200 in *ANET* 196-97.

36. See G. R. Driver, *Canaanite Myths and Legends* (Edinburgh: T. and T. Clark, 1957) 107; J. Gray, *The Legacy of Canaan* (VTSup 7; 1965²) 81-82; H. Cazelles, *Etudes sur le Code d'Alliance* (Paris: Letouzey et Ané, 1946) 76.

37. Schulz, *Das Todesrecht*, 7-16. Cf. Num 35:6 which has developed from Exod 20:13 + 21:12: ". . . that the manslayer who kills a person may flee there."

38. This meaning is clearly presented in the translation of the *NEB* which reads: "A curse upon him who takes a reward to kill a man with whom he has no feud."

39. Elliger, "Leviticus 18," 2.

40. R. Kilian, *Literarkritische und Formgeschichtliche Untersuchung des Heiligkeitsgesetzes* (BBB 19; Bonn: Peter Hanstein, 1963) 26-27.

41. This is against Schulz who finds the prohibitive foundation for the death laws of Leviticus 20 in the prohibitives of Leviticus 18. He claims that originally the prohibitives had a different form, possibly: "You shall not lie with your father's wife," etc. The transformation from the original to the present form resulted from the influence of the declarative statement appended to each sentence (e.g., "it is your father's nakedness," vs. 8). Schulz's explanation presupposes a complex history: 1) an original primitive list which employed the term *škb*; 2) the subsequent addition of the declarative statement with the expression "it is the nakedness of"; 3) a still later stage in which the influence of the declarative statement caused the change from "You shall not lie with . . . " to "You shall not uncover the nakedness of . . . ." Schulz's argument is not convincing. His proposal would demand a long period of development and would militate against the antiquity of the present list. Moreover, in only three of the declarative sentences does the expression "uncover the nakedness of" appear (vss. 8, 10, 16). More often the reason given for the prohibitive is the proximity of consanguinity (vss. 7, 11, 12, 13, 14, 15; cf. 17b). It does not seem advisable, therefore, to suppose a more primitive list behind the core of prohibitives in Lev 18:7-17. See Schulz, *Das Todesrecht*, 46-51.

42. H. Cunliffe-Jones, *Deuteronomy* (London: SCM, 1964) 151.

43. A. Phillips, *Deuteronomy* (The Cambridge Bible Commentary; Cambridge: University, 1973) 181.

44. In his review of Schulz's work (*CBQ* 32 [1970] 307-08), McKenzie suggests that the study could open up other areas of investigation to the reader.

George E. Mendenhall

Samuel's "Broken *Rîb*": Deuteronomy 32

The historical nihilism characteristic of so much of biblical scholarship during the past century and still existing as a legacy from the 19th century has both stultified biblical scholarship and reinforced political tendencies that are extremely dangerous to civilization today. Lacking almost entirely any sense of historical perspective, especially with regard to the Early Iron Age ca. 1200-1000 B.C., biblical academia is seemingly incapable of realizing that we have in the biblical record an incredibly detailed mass of information about this period in Palestine in contrast to all other parts of the entire Mediterranean world.

To be sure, we are faced with the same problem (and even the methods) of Homeric scholarship, namely to distinguish between that which is really ancient, and that which derives from the reuse of old traditions for much later political purposes. But it does not seem to have gotten through to the world of biblical scholars that the early 19th century methods of "source analysis" of Homeric scholarship were given up decades ago. That is a matter of little importance in comparison with the virtual monopoly that has been obtained by those whose competence and academic output has only to do with literary forms and style. One is tempted to draw an analogy between the mainstream of modern biblical and religious scholars and those 15th century Byzantine monks who could find nothing valuable to do at the very time their whole world was tumbling down other than to gaze at their own navels. There can be little doubt that much of the current output of "biblical scholarship" in literary forms is nothing but navel-gazing, and has equal value to the world of humanity in serious trouble.

Fortunately, we do have in the biblical sources some very old materials that have been preserved with little change since they are in poetic form. A serious historical problem exists, however, in the identification and dating of those early sources, and even more serious is their interpretation and utilization for social and intellectual history. Albright's last attempt to date the old poetry on the basis of stylistic forms[1] is most unconvincing since it

63

presupposes exactly the same kind of "unilinear evolution" that he had resisted throughout his entire scholarly career, and relies entirely upon stylistic phenomena that could easily be nothing more than individual or local poetic preferences or habits. What we need instead is in the first place a serious linguistic history of that particular dialect (or collection of dialects) of Iron Age Canaanite that has far too long been termed "Hebrew." Secondly, we need a *responsible* correlation of ancient sources with ancient historical reality — an endeavor that biblical and theological scholars seem to avoid as the bubonic plague. There is good reason for this attitude, for there can be little doubt that authoritarian social structures must depend on some kind of "phony history," and scholars must produce it.

Nevertheless, the ancient poem of Deuteronomy 32 presents a most fascinating complex of problems that still have no satisfying solutions, but little seems to have been written about it since 1962. The primary problem in the historical utilization of this source is its dating. Since it is not possible in this short essay to produce all the technical customary "proofs" for dating that are currently fashionable in academic circles, I shall only concur in the conclusions of Eissfeldt and Albright that the poem belongs to the second half of the eleventh century B.C. It not only constitutes a most important witness to religious thought of that period, but also is a most important source for the entire prophetic proclamation of several centuries later.

Cornill's description of the poem as a "compendium of prophetic theology" is perfectly accurate, but it does not follow by any means that it is a product of the prophetic movement of the 9th to 7th centuries, as even Wright argued.[2] In fact, what little we know of the 9th century prophecy gives little indication of capability of such profound theology as that exhibited in Deuteronomy 32. We have no evidence until Amos that prophecy turned from its futile and even self-destructive political "activism" to a much more mature understanding both of the nature of the original Yahwist faith and the total predicament of civilization.

It is now generally conceded that the 8th century prophets represent a continuity of the old Mosaic Yahwism, a position that I think not only justified but essential to any rational understanding of ancient Israel's faith and history. Yet, at the same time, far too many scholars are suffering from the delusion that pre-monarchic Israel was "too primitive" to have any highly developed theology, or that we have no sources for describing that theology.

It is certainly true that Deuteronomy 32 has extremely close ties with especially the 7th-6th century prophecy. Virtually all the major themes of those prophets (including even the "remnant") have their antecedents in Deuteronomy 32. But, rather than concluding that the poem was their product, it would be much more rational to argue that Deuteronomy 32 was a major source, the "bible" so to speak, of the prophetic movement. In the first place, to dispose of Wright's dating of the poem to the 9th century (followed unthinkingly by Cross)[3] there can be no doubt that the poem is actually *quoted* in the 9th century prophetic charge to Jehu (2 Kgs 9:7; cf. Deut 32:43a) and therefore was already an authoritative ancient *source* even for the rather degenerate 9th century prophets, who seem to have been interested in little but politics. The close ties between the poem and the later prophets can best be understood as a part of the nostalgia for the past that characterizes so much of the history, culture, and thought of the 7th-6th centuries. It was a re-valuation of very old tradition, and the discovery that it had much to offer to a society on the verge of catastrophe. But as Jeremiah particularly illustrates, it was too little and too late to avert the impending doom. For it cannot at the present time be too strongly emphasized that if politics is the "art of the possible," it is public opinion that determines *what* is possible, and that public opinion is always religious: i.e., either the worship of Yahweh with its *necessary* ethical concerns, or the worship of Baal and Asherah — the symbols of power, wealth, (and, to be sure, sex.)

Perhaps the ideological arguments against an early date can be most easily dealt with — and disposed of. We have already mentioned the close ties to 8th-6th century prophecy and suggested a reason that fits well with everything else we know about that period. Much more important is the close tie between the content of Deuteronomy 32 and the covenant ideology of the Late Bronze Age, as it has been reconstructed by the present writer and others during the past twenty years. The traditional late dating of Deuteronomy 32 makes it possible for those who argue that the covenant form is late in Israelite thought, to ignore it and conclude that the covenant ideology either did not exist, or was merely a late theological formulation, especially connected with the deuteronomic work. As G. E. Wright has described fairly well, Deuteronomy 32 and the structure of the Late Bronze Age covenant ideology are inseparable, but he was led astray by traditional form-critical ideas about the *Sitz im Leben* (usually defined as cultic whenever we are dealing with biblical texts). If we should start instead with the question "when and where is it most likely that the structure of covenant thought would be used, in the context obviously of a catastrophic *defeat* by an unnamed enemy?" then there can be no possible alternative to that suggested by O. Eissfeldt and others. It is a prophetic response to the catastrophic defeat at Ebenezer and the destruction of Shiloh that must have seemed at the time to destroy all confidence in the religious ideology, its social organization, and its rudimentary institutions that were barely more than a century old at the time.

The poem cannot have originated at any time other than after the destruction of Shiloh and before the radical paganization of Yahwism that began early in David's reign and ran its natural course with the accession of Rehoboam and the consequent disidentification of the northern tribes from any further connection with the pagan Jerusalem regime. In other words, the poem must come from ca. 1050 B.C. to 1000 B.C. Any time after David's successes in war against the Philistines is reflected in Psalm 78, which is certainly a "theological answer" to Deuteronomy 32. But the conclusion that Deuteronomy 32 is a "broken" *rîb*, "that is, a specific cultic form adapted and expanded" by those "other themes," is a failure to understand historical reality when it is most vividly preserved for us. It is particularly weak when Wright tried to tie the "covenant lawsuit" to an alleged "covenant renewal" ceremony for which we have very little evidence other than Joshua 24 and Deuteronomy 27, both of which are either garbled by later tradition or have other historical contexts. The misunderstanding is compounded when it is combined with the "divine assembly" concept so popular at Harvard, which undoubtedly has clarified a few otherwise obscure passages of the Hebrew bible, most of which cluster about the period of Exile (Job, 2nd Isaiah, Genesis 1, etc.), but which has also been appealed to for explanation of many passages in the Hebrew bible where it is not relevant.

But if we delete from the discussion of Deuteronomy 32 the various themes currently fashionable among OT scholars, what have we left? In other words, the poem has nothing to do with the "divine assembly," covenant renewal, covenant "lawsuit" (whatever that may be), cultic confession and praise, and a host of other academic clichés that have been misused in order to escape historical reality.

Though it cannot now be proven, it is at least worthwhile to point out that further biblical research cannot merely assume that Deuteronomy 32 dates to the period of the divided monarchy. In the first place, there is absolutely nothing in the poem that presupposes even the existence of the monarchy. Secondly, though this cannot be used as proof at the present time, there is an impressive number of linguistic correlations in this text with the language and idioms of the syllabic texts from Byblos[4]; those correlations also cluster about Exodus 15, Judges 5, Deuteronomy 33, and

Genesis 49. It is partly for this reason that I cannot take seriously the various arguments from "form-criticism" that would assign a late date to this poem.

Most of the old poetry of the Pentateuch and other sources has as its theme the celebration of successes in an indubitably turbulent period all over the once "civilized" world. Deuteronomy 32, on the other hand, stands alone as a reaction to historical calamity, and therefore the usual stylistic and form-critical analyses are simply irrelevant. What we must deal with is not mere literary "form," but with the language and content — what does it say, and how does that content fit in with what we know of the theological history of OT thought? Though I should like to come back to this poem with a thorough linguistic and conceptual analysis, it does not seem probable in the near future. Perhaps others can be stimulated to do what is imperative at the present critical stage of OT history and theology.

Just a few characteristics of the poem must be pointed out. Eissfeldt has already pointed out very archaic features of the language, as has also Albright. But the theological concepts are equally archaic. Not only does the poem illustrate the most vivid structure of the Late Bronze Age covenants before the late baroque attempt on the part of the deuteronomist to revivify it, it also illustrates the stage of thought prior to the monarchic rewriting of history for political purposes. As is the case in all the archaic poetry, this poem knows nothing of Abraham and Isaac, nothing of "Israel in Egypt," nothing of the Exodus or even the so-called "Conquest," nothing even of any concept of "national state," much less the monarchy. Israel was "found" in a desert land, historically the truth, for the "mixed multitude" (Num 11:4) that escaped Egyptian servitude with Moses was not "Israel" until it was created (vs. 6) by an act of God,[5] and it was not a territorial state in contrast to the numerous political structures of·the time (vs. 8) until the paganization under the monarchy. In this regard there is a curious coincidence with the evidence from the Merneptah Stele that seems to have escaped attention, for in both very old sources political-territorial boundary lines had nothing to do with the character of the human "portion of Yahweh," or the nature of the religious community. It is indeed difficult to find or reconstruct any better description of the religious ideology of ancient Israel before the so-called "wise men" of the monarchy concocted a largely phony history for political purposes by attempting to combine certain elements of the Mosaic history with the dominant religious ideology of the pagan Bronze Age, namely the "divine charter" theology associated with the Abraham-Davidic tradition. It may be that the Bronze Age pagan ideology was right, but the record of the biblical history (or of more recent history) certainly does not justify that idea. For even the Christology of the NT constitutes the acceptance of the old pagan ideology that had been so dominant in Jewish tradition since David, and, separating it entirely from its original political function, assimilated it completely to the mainstream of the Mosaic — early Israelite theology of the kingdom (= rule) of God.

As a framework for further progress in understanding not only this particular poem, but also for the history of Israelite religion, I would offer the following suggestions and observations:

1. Historical context: over against Wright's vague 9th-7th centuries, Eissfeldt is surely correct (among others) in seeing the poem as a religious response to the destruction of Shiloh and the capture of the Ark of the Covenant. The event cannot but have called into question the entire viability of the still relatively new religious ideology of Yahwism as well as the social structure (the twelve tribe federation) that was entirely dependent upon, and the result of the former (cf. vs. 6). But the breakdown of the Yahwist theology in favor of older pagan gods (Josh 24:14-15), or perhaps new faddish cults (vs. 17?; cf. Judg 5:8; unfortunately both passages are obscure), cannot but have weakened the ability of the village populations to ward off the rapacious urban warlords. The entire structure of Judges emphasizes this point, but because it is so schematized and reduced to a formula, no one seems to have taken seriously the fact that in spite of the wooden Procrustes' bed of that history, it must well have been historically correct. At the same time, this evidence strongly reinforces the contention of those who maintain that the Mosaic Yahwism was a radically new religious ideology incompatible with the pre-Mosaic pagan cults; it also emphasizes strongly that the attraction of those pagan cults for the Israelite tribes is due to the fact that those cults must have been traditional and socially functional in local Palestinian society before the establishment of the federation. The fact that Yahwism was established and survived at all in the face of traditionally conservative village society is perhaps the greatest miracle of all those in the bible — but unnoticed and unappreciated because of modern pagan cults of nationalism and racism.

As a corollary, it almost inevitably follows that the author of Deuteronomy 32 is the prophet Samuel himself. The entire poem is not only a phrase-book for the later prophets, it *is* prophecy in every sense of the term. As a prophetic oracle there are virtually no remaining serious problems of form or content, and at the same time it illustrates for us the incredible potential of the early Yahwist movement in thought as well as the indubitable social achievement of unifying a very diverse population over an astoundingly large area with no centralized monopoly of force. Albright was certainly correct in emphasizing the enormous importance of the prophet Samuel during this transition period when the old institution of Ark and Tabernacle (and its priesthood) had been almost entirely discredited. Deuteronomy 32 points out in very vigorous terms that such social institutions and their fate are the consequence of covenant obedience or disobedience, not the *cause* either of covenant or of historical event. At any rate, the fates of Shiloh and the Ark had nothing to do with the continuing dominion of Yahweh — indeed they were *caused* by him for good reason. The same theme was repeatedly to become the basis for the *prediction* of destruction of Jerusalem and Samaria by the later prophets, though only Jeremiah specifically pointed to Shiloh as an early precedent.

2. *Sitz im Leben*: though I have not made any systematic search, I have a strong impression that this term is used only in regard to the (largely vain) search for the liturgical occasion or purpose of a rigid ritual form. If so, the term is absurd when scholars attempt to apply it to prophetic oracles. What is the *Sitz im Leben* of the oracle, also from Samuel, against Saul in 1 Sam 15:22? One can add Nathan's parable to David, Amos at Bethel, Jeremiah at the Temple (Jeremiah 7), and most of canonical prophecy. It is only the pagan Balaq who expected the pagan prophet Balaam to produce the proper oracle for a cultic occasion, though no doubt the equally pagan kings of Jerusalem and Samaria expected their court prophets to function in a similar fashion (cf. Micaiah and his non-colleagues). The mainstream of the biblical prophetic tradition had nothing necessarily to do with public office (as also at Mari), but rather with the message received by the prophet from Yahweh, almost always in connection with some concrete historical situation. "Cult prophets" certainly existed; some of the canonical prophets certainly were or may have been associated with them (Elisha), but to say that canonical prophecy is an *office* in OT tradition is just as absurd as it would be to argue that Jeremiah's cistern is evidence that Zedekiah's bureaucracy was short of office space, and Jeremiah was simply being treated like many a junior faculty member in many universities and colleges today.

Rather than searching for some cultic *Sitz im Leben* for the oracle of Deuteronomy 32, it would be much more appropriate to look for the historic *occasion* in which the oracle fits. This is given us at considerable length in 1 Samuel 7, especially vs. 3, and the rest of the chapter describes the consequences, both ritual and historical. The social occasion of Deuteronomy 32 is, then, the very understandable gathering of the survivors to consider what was the cause of the calamity, and what should be the future policy. I would guess that the oracle of Samuel was delivered at a time when the debacle was at least fresh in the memory of the tribal leaders, if not very shortly after the defeat itself. (It goes without saying that the existing context, 1 Sam 7:1-2, anticipates the subsequent history of the Ark, since that had been the major theme of the preceding sections, and therefore does not necessarily give the context of the events described in 7:3-4.) It is interesting to compare the pious clichés of 1 Sam 7:3-4 with the highly developed theology of Deuteronomy 32, even though there can be little doubt that they describe the same occasion.

3. Form: since Wright has already given a fairly adequate description of the coincidence between this poem and the covenant structure, we need not be further concerned with this topic here though many side comments could and should be added. The term Wright uses, following H. B. Huffman[6] (and for which I may myself be at least indirectly responsible) "covenant lawsuit" now seems peculiarly inappropriate, at least in application to this poem.

As I have maintained for at least two decades, this poem is probably the best indirect evidence we have for actual village court procedures in Palestine of the Early Iron Age. It is a form thus *transferred* (as is the covenant itself!) from normal political-legal procedures into the realm of religious and historical thought. But here Yahweh is *not* suing anyone for breach of covenant; instead the breach *had* taken place, the consequences *had* been suffered, and the issue is whether or not Yahweh would be a reliable refuge for the future. In this regard, the poem is remarkably reminiscent of the prophecies of the Exile, and to dismiss the assurances of Deut 32:36-43 as "generalized expressions of hope," as Wright did (p. 40), is to miss the point entirely. For the issue was precisely whether the nascent Yahwism with its highly developed theology was simply to give up in favor of the old Bronze Age worship of power symbols — the baals of the city states. A generation later this did happen, but in the meantime the Yahwist theology had become so well established that it never entirely died out, even though its later major spokesmen, the prophets, had no more chance of making themselves heard than Elmer Berger has in becoming president of the World Zionist Congress.

Contrary to the expectations of finding all kinds of mythological allusions that are admittedly characteristic of much of the old poetry of the Pentateuch, the poem is almost entirely historical in context except only for vss. 7-9. But except for the curious fragment of Gen 6:1-4, it would be difficult to find in the entire OT a more accurate description of the *historic* function of ancient mythology than the passage in question. To conclude, therefore, for a late date on the basis of what is not otherwise present is hardly an adequate scholarly method, particularly when the poem is without any real parallel other than elements that were taken up by later prophetic tradition.

Consequently, the appeal to heavens and earth have nothing to do with the "divine assembly" so popular in much later times. Instead these elements of the natural world are appealed to simply as witnesses who are expected to be active in the enforcement of the findings in a court of law. The modern legal concept of a "witness" is completely misleading and irrelevant to the social function of a witness in ancient village law courts. In the absence of governmental functionaries, those who have witnessed a legal action (or even a crime) are expected to be relied upon when a remedy is needed (cf. Ruth 4). In view of the fact that both blessings and curses are mediated largely through the natural world, there should be no difficulty in understanding the appeal to heavens and earth as witnesses in a *transferred* procedure in which I have a strong impression that Yahweh is the original defendant — in other words, Deuteronomy 32 is a prophetic theodicy long before that literary form existed. The calamity of the battle of Aphek-Ebenezer, particularly after the Ark had been brought into the battle scene, can only have led to the conclusion that Yahweh had let them down, and only a vigorous reversal of the roles of plaintiff and defendant could have been effective — as it evidently was, if the connection with 1 Samuel 7 is admitted, and as the historical evidence seems to confirm.

4. The prophetic prolegomenon: (vss. 2-3) this has absolutely no connection with the "wisdom literature" tradition as Wright correctly pointed out. Instead, it is very comprehensible in the context of a village society where there exists no monopoly of force, and where there can be only a hope that wise statements will be accepted and result in action appropriate to the situation. The optimism of vs. 2 can be of course, and has been, compared to Isa 55:10-11; but this passage should also be compared (or contrasted) to Isa 6:9-10. It is worthy of note that the optimistic expectations concerning the acceptance of the Divine Word coincide with the historical periods when "He sees that their power is gone. . . . "

The prophetic word, or oracle, is historically significant in two different ways: it is either accepted as policy by the religious community, or it is rejected and enforced by God Himself through the media of the natural world and the pagan nations. In this connection it is worth consideration that the verb forms in vs. 2 should be considered as jussives and are usually so translated; I would much prefer the term "optative" — a wish form, for the prophets were never in a position of social power that enabled them to command.

5. The early down-grading of Samuel: the curious inconsistencies in the narratives concerning Samuel that so exercised the ingenuity of an earlier generation of biblical scholars seem now comprehensible. For not only was Samuel notoriously in adamant opposition to the public demand for establishing a centralized monopoly of force, he also publicly rejected and renounced Saul and thereby doubtless contributed to the latter's tragic downfall. Since virtually all of our historical narratives were written during the period of the monarchy by scribes closely identified with the royal court, it is not to be expected that those scribes would be highly enthusiastic about prophetic king makers and breakers. The prophetic intervention in North Israelite politics certainly could have done nothing to alleviate the nervousness of the pagan Jerusalemite kings, particularly after Shemaiah effectively vetoed the royal stupidity of Rehoboam. For this reason, the "late source" is likely to be more historically accurate, though after nearly half a millennium, it is too far removed from the chronological scene of action to be satisfactory. The attribution of Deuteronomy 32 to Moses himself is sufficient evidence of the very deficient historical perspective of the late history-writers.

To sum up, Deuteronomy 32 is not a "lawsuit" at all. It is a prophetic oracle essentially concerned with the interpretation of history past, and appealing for public opinion that would make the future more palatable. It is not a "broken" *rîb*, for under the circumstances following the Philistine victory, the only possible and the only necessary course of action was a rejection of the pagan ideologies that disrupted the unity upon which the independence of the tribal villages was absolutely dependent, and a reaffirmation of the Yahwist theology.

Further, as Wright has well delineated, we have no more impressive illustration of the old covenant structure of thought than this poem, at least before Deuteronomy. To be sure, we do have bits and fragments of that old theology in the canonical prophets, especially the blessings and curses formula so well described by D. Hillers, but we need a similar study of the prophetic use of historical traditions particularly since the "historical prologue" is so important in OT theology as well as Late Bronze Age suzerainty treaties in contrast to those of the Iron Age. Wright is entirely correct in saying, " . . . there is no covenant without Credo, and no Law without Gospel" (p. 52, n. 55). Unfortunately, a political monopoly of force can easily get by for a time without gospel, and the obligations that stem from gospel are usually not at all those that a political monopoly of force can effectively enforce ("apodictic" law). The widely used term "covenant law" is a contradiction in itself, since law by definition refers properly to those social obligations enforced by social organization, while covenant obligations must underlie and even make possible social enforcement of law. Conversely, it is equally easy to construct "credo" without any obligations other than proper performance of rituals (Deuteronomy 26, a fairly late and degenerate reductionism). Virtually all the prophets have scathing denunciations of this theme, but even today dominant concepts of religion seem to include only those themes characteristic of any primitive culture: ritual reinforcement of existing social solidarities, "proper" linguistic behavior in dealing with religious themes, and observance of ritual tabus inherited from some obscure and often phony past history. This sort of fundamentalism is, and always has been, a great danger to the successful functioning of civilized society, for like primitive society in general, it has no concept of historical dynamics, of cause and effect relationships, and effectively prevents the development of a sound historical perspective, and often enough, the reinforcement of a tolerable public and private ethic as well.

The Early Iron Age must have been an extremely traumatic period for people all over the civilized world of the eastern Mediterranean, when social organizations of all kinds including empires were disintegrating, most of them to disappear forever. It may be true that the economy and social organization of early Israel appears "primitive," but it does not follow at all that the ideology of that society can be termed primitive. For there is no other period of history when the unique system of religious thought so characteristic of the bible could have originated, and to that system Deuteronomy 32 is an invaluable witness, emphasizing the principle that "what a man sows, that shall he also reap" (Deuteronomy 32; cf. 1 Sam 15:23b).

1. W. F. Albright, *Yahweh and the Gods of Canaan* (London: Athlone, 1968) 1-46.

2. G. E. Wright, "The Lawsuit of God: A Form-Critical Study of Deuteronomy 32," *Israel's Prophetic Heritage: Essays in Honor of James Muilenburg*, eds. B. W. Anderson and W. Harrelson (New York: Harper & Row, 1962) 26-67.

3. F. M. Cross, *Canaanite Myth and Hebrew Epic* (Cambridge: Harvard University, 1973) 264, n. 193.

4. On internal evidence I maintain that these texts cannot be much later than 2000 B.C. and could well be even earlier, or at least reflect an earlier stage of Northwest Semitic.

5.   Note the astonishing, and correct, statement in Deut 27:9. It includes, of course, the late anachronistic use of the term "all Israel," but it is certainly correct in its emphasis on the fact that "becoming the people of God" is a function of religious conversion.

6.   "The Covenant Lawsuit in the Prophets," *JBL* 78 (1959) 285-95.

JOSEPH BLENKINSOPP

The Quest of the Historical Saul

1

It may be idle to speculate what might have happened if some small circumstance in the past had been other than it was; if, for example, Alexander had not plunged into the icy water at Babylon (if indeed he did) or Julius Caesar had caught a chill and stayed home at the Ides of March. Yet I cannot resist the temptation of reflecting how different the history of Israel would have been if Saul had paused to take aim before trying to pin David to the wall with his spear. We may not have had the psalms of Saul or hosannas sung to the son of Saul, but there would have been no Davidic empire, no Davidic messiah and there may have been no pilgrims singing the songs of Zion as they went up to the city of the Great King. But Saul, already possessed by an evil spirit from Yahweh, missed; and from that point on his $b^e r\bar{a}k\bar{a}h$ drained away like blood from an open wound. Since it is generally the winning side that writes the history the consequence in this case is that it is now very difficult to assess Saul's achievement and to know what actually happened during his reign.

To begin with the sources contained in 1-2 Samuel, on which alone our knowledge of the historical Saul has to be based, they evince interest only in his call to the kingship, persecution of David and eventual defeat and death. This circumstance made it easier for the deuteronomist to ascribe to him a reign of only two years (1 Sam 13:1), whereas in effect it must have been considerably longer, perhaps twelve or even twenty years.[1] This is only one example of a highly tendentious historiographical tradition which developed at a fairly early date and has made it extremely difficult to reconstruct the vitally important half-century preceding the united monarchy. Thus it is hardly a coincidence that outside of Samuel, Chronicles, a few psalm titles and a passing reference to "Gibeah of Saul" in Isa 10:29, the Hebrew bible does not even mention his name. As late as the second century B.C. Jesus ben-Sirach studiously avoided his name at the point in his historical recital where we would naturally expect it. "Samuel," he tells us, "anointed *rulers* over his people" and "revealed to *the king* his death, in order to blot out the wickedness of the people" (46:13, 20).

Any attempt to understand Saul and the historical significance of his rule over the tribes must take full cognizance of this polemical and negative historiographical tradition. In the Samuel narratives themselves it will, for obvious reasons, be most apparent where Saul appears with either Samuel or David, given the fact of prophetic and Judahite opposition to Saul. Thus in one of the two versions of Saul's rejection by Samuel (1 Sam 15) we may note that the outcome is very different from the encounter of David with another prophet, Nathan. Both kings confess their fault, even in identical words ("I have sinned," 1 Sam 15:24; 2 Sam 12:13), but while David is pardoned Saul is not. The same bias finds less obvious expression in the designation of Saul as king in 1 Sam 10:20-24 where the technique used is the casting of lots, employed elsewhere in the OT for the discovery of a guilty party.[2] It will not be difficult to show that many of the other narratives have also been redacted to testify against Saul.

The main lines of this negative evaluation were already firmly and inalterably laid down in the deuteronomic historical work and can be traced fairly clearly in later retellings of the history. While he can praise his mental and moral qualities and speak of his death on the battlefield as a noble example of submission to fate in the Stoic manner, Josephus ascribes his fall to disobedience to the divine will revealed by a prophet. After his own manner, he adds a psychological note to his account of the change in Saul's fortunes (*metabolē*) and speaks of a strange, demoniacal disorder to which he was subject. This, he is careful to point out, had nothing to do with possession by the divine spirit since he was afflicted by it before his visit to the prophets at Naioth (1 Sam 19:22).[3] The author of *Liber Antiquitatum Biblicarum*, writing perhaps in the first century of the era, also adds his own embellishments: Saul spared Agag in the hope that he would reveal to him the whereabouts of hidden treasure and drove out the mediums and sorcerers not out of piety but vainglory. His opposition to David was, of course, occasioned by jealousy so that there was no wonder he came to such a bad end.[4] A consideration of the scattered references to Saul in the Talmuds, not all of which are hostile by any means, would take us even further from the biblical sources.[5] None of these contributes anything to our historical knowledge.

We have seen that in his "praise of famous men" Jesus ben-Sirach rather pointedly omits referring to Saul by name, and we can now add that in other retrospective surveys, usually of a liturgical nature, there is a marked tendency to cover the period immediately before the reign of David with a veil of silence.[6] Apart from relatively minor omissions — the stripping of the corpse of the dead king, the exposure of the body on the wall of Beth-shan and the cremation — the Chronicler stays fairly close to his source in Samuel. For him the story of Saul's downfall, with which he begins his history, serves to emphasize by contrast the status and religious achievements of David who, unlike his predecessor, kept the commandments and obeyed the voice of the prophet (1 Chronicles 10). While here again, therefore, the historian finds nothing of value to add to the Samuel narratives, the case is quite different with the genealogical table of Saul's family which is presented at 8:29-40 in association with a Gibeonite table and repeated at 9:35-44 as an introduction to the history of Saul's downfall. We shall return to this later.

Of prime importance for the evaluation of the Saul material in Samuel is the recognition that it falls within the deuteronomic history of Israel from Sinai (Horeb) to exile. This historical work, written from the perspective of national collapse and dispersion, quite naturally exhibits a starkly negative evaluation of the monarchy and it would be no surprise to find it concentrating its attack on the beginnings of the monarchy with Saul as it clearly does on the beginnings of the monarchy of the central and northern tribes with Jeroboam. Given the situation in which it was written, the purpose of the work was to provide a theologically convincing answer to the problem of destitution and abandonment by the covenant God. To this end the history from Moses to Jehoiachin is presented as one of recurrent sin and infidelity expressed primarily through disobedience to God's will revealed by the prophets. The work is presented schematically in discreet periods: the Mosaic age, the occupation of the land, the judges, the institution of the monarchy, the monarchic period.[7] With respect to the material in 1 Samuel this results in the following division: 1-7, Samuel, last of the judges; 8-12, institution of the monarchy; 13, beginnings of the monarchy with Saul. While it is true, as has been recognized by almost all the commentators, that the deuteronomic school added little of its own in 1-2 Samuel, we have to bear in mind that the selection and disposition of the material is also an important aspect of history writing. With this in mind we shall look briefly at the three sections.

From Samuel's valedictory in 1 Samuel 12 it is clear that at some point he was considered to be the last of a series of four "judges" or national saviors; and if we view the section 1 Samuel 1-7 as a whole we will see that it follows much the same pattern as the judge-narratives in the book of Judges: designation (from infancy, as with Samson), critical situation brought on by sin, redemptive action by success at arms.[8] This patterning is the result less of historical rewriting than skillful arrangement — and where necessary modification — of existing sources. These include an Ephraimite prophetic account of the origins and call of Samuel which, as we will go on to see, made use of a still earlier story about the conception and birth of Saul (1:1 - 4:1a); and a section of a Jerusalemite ark narrative which is continued in 2 Sam 6:2 (4:1b - 7:1). While the deuteronomist clearly regarded Samuel as a critically important figure he felt it possible to let the juxtaposition of these two narratives speak for itself without adding anything significant of his own. It is quite different, however, with the concluding account of Samuel's convocation of the tribes at Mizpah, the ensuing Philistine attack and miraculous deliverance (7:2-17). For here, as has long been recognized, there are unmistakeable signs of the deuteronomist's hand.[9] The outcome of this theological rewriting of history was to displace Saul from the list of charismatic warrior-saviors and put Samuel in his place; for we need hardly stress that the Philistines were not at that time subdued and that Saul rather than Samuel was responsible for their temporary discomfiting. Indeed, it could be plausibly argued that 7:2-17 is in effect a theologically inspired rewrite of the much earlier war-narrative in 13:2 - 14:46. In both cases there is a Philistine rout effected with extraordinary divine assistance (7:10; 14:15), a stone is set up (7:12;14:33) and an altar dedicated (7:17; 14:35), and the Philistines are pushed back into their own coastal region (7:14; 14:31, 46) after they had themselves taken the initiative. In this respect what the deuteronomist did, then, was to put his seal on a polemically inspired presentation of Samuel rather than Saul as the last of the charismatic warrior-saviors.

   In the account of the institution of monarchy (8-12) the deuteronomic historian has incorporated two early narratives dealing with the designation of Saul as *nāgîd* (9:1 - 10:16) and his calling up the tribal levy to save the Gileadites (11:1-15). These have been left practically untouched. The occasion of the transition to monarchy was the moral corruption of Samuel's sons in the judgeship (8:1-3), and this is described in typically deuteronomic fashion.[10] There follows the granting of the people's request for a king "like all the nations" (8:5 cf. Deut 17:14) and the recital by Samuel of the practice of kingship (*mišpāṭ hammelek*, vs. 11) which appears to be a tendentious variation on the rule for the kingship (*mišpāṭ hammᵉlukāh*) later to be written down by Samuel and laid in the sanctuary (10:25). It would be safe to suggest a connection between this and the copy of the law which, according to Deut 17:18-19, the king must keep by him.[11] As is generally recognized, the narrative-line in 8:4-22 is continued in the narrative of the tribal convocation at Mizpah in 10:17-27 and this again is continued in the valedictory address of Samuel to the people in ch. 12, presumably also at Mizpah. Whether this was a free composition of the deuteronomist or a reworking of earlier material cannot be decided for sure. What we do know is that in the deuteronomic history such addresses serve to mark the end of epochs, so that it is no surprise to find close parallelism between the final address of Joshua to *kol yiśrā'ēl* at Shechem (Joshua 24) and that of Samuel at Mizpah. [12] And for anyone familiar with the deuteronomic history as a whole it is entirely to be expected that Samuel end his harangue with the threat of exile for both people and king (vs. 25).

To the corpus of traditions dealing with the reign of Saul (in effect, as we have seen, almost exclusively with his rise to and fall from power) the deuteronomic author added little more than his characteristic introductory formula giving the name, age at accession and length of reign (13:1). Since Saul could not very well have been one year old at his accession and three at his death almost everyone in the modern period has turned to textual emendation for a solution, and very properly so. We must bear in mind, though, that according to the deuteronomic theory of divine retribution a short reign was fitting punishment for religious infidelity; hence the appropriately short reign accorded to Ishbaal (Ishbosheth) at 2 Sam 2:10, hence also the insoluble problem set by the early death of the good king Josiah. Having made this point, the author no doubt felt that the story which he inherited and which ends in defeat and death could be allowed to speak for itself. And since the obverse of divine retribution is divine ratification of success, it could move on, with somewhat unseemly haste, to deal with David and his rise to power.

The total effect of the deuteronomic version of the transition from the judgeship to the monarchy — especially in 7:2-17, 8:1-22, 10:17-27 and 12 — was then to glorify Samuel as "judge"[13] at the expense of Saul. It must be added, however, that the author's polemic is not against Saul himself but against the monarchy which he regarded as the architect of the nation's spiritual and political ruin. He did not therefore originate the negative historiographical tradition about Saul for it was already there in his sources. To these we must now turn.

It is no longer fashionable to look for the continuation of the early pentateuchal sources in 1-2 Samuel since this approach, which goes back to Eichhorn, seems to raise more problems than it solves. For the many who claimed to find fairly abundant evidence for E in these chapters the arguments tended to focus on "prophetic influence," with special reference to prophecy in the northern kingdom. [14] E, however, has turned out to be if not chimerical at least very hard to pin down. The situation therefore at once becomes simpler and more defensible if we are content to speak of a source or sources emanating from prophetic groups in the Ephraimite region who never reconciled themselves to the monarchy, attached closely as they were to the ancient traditions of the federation. That such existed from a very early period is beyond question. Apart from the many prophets who opposed and were persecuted by the Omrids, chief among whom were Elijah, Elisha and Micaiah,[15] both Hosea and Amos knew of prophetic predecessors who were not part of the state machinery, who denounced injustice and infidelity in high places and suffered for it.[16] Hosea himself was intransigently opposed to the monarchy and speaks of its institution as, so to speak, the "original sin" of Israel (8:4; 9:9, 15; 10:9). All of this is quite homologous with much of the pre-deuteronomic material in 1 Samuel which evinces open hostility to Saul and the monarchy in general. We shall take a brief look at the more important of these passages.

As it now stands, the opening pericope about Samuel at Shiloh concludes with an account of his prophetic call in the sanctuary (3:1 - 4:1a). Without claiming direct dependence on any specific call narrative in the canonical prophets,[17] we may simply acknowledge the structural homology and conclude that the intention was to present Samuel as one of them. If we go on to look more closely at the *incipit* and *excipit* of this narrative (3:1, 4; 3:21 - 4:1a) we may perhaps go further and suggest that the intention was to present the vision in the sanctuary as the beginning of classical prophecy, one of several attempts in the tradition to trace it back to its origins.[18] There is no explicit commission given in the call, but it is implied that Samuel communicate the verdict of judgment on the Shiloh priesthood, which he does. More or less parallel with this is the direct revelation of doom to Eli conveyed by an unnamed man of God (2:27-36). It seems entirely feasible to me that both of these judgment oracles should be read in the light of early prophetic denunciations of the shrine priesthoods. Hosea in particular has some hard things to say about the sacrificial cult as practiced in his day in the northern kingdom and in several places denounces the priesthood for neglect of the law and for venality, the point at issue here.[19] While agreeing that both of these judgment oracles have been edited by the deuteronomic author,[20] we should note that only at the end of the first (2:35-36) is the scope of the prediction widened to include Zadok and his line and the unhappy lot of the shrine priesthoods resulting from the deuteronomic reform (cf. Deut 18:6-8 and 2 Kgs 23:8-9). This has the distinct look of a deuteronomic addition to the original anti-Elide prophetic pronouncement.

The narrative in 4:1b - 7:1 which deals with the ark and says nothing of Samuel was often treated as Ephraimite by older commentators like Cornill and Nowack but is now generally regarded as of Jerusalemite provenance together with its continuation in 2 Sam 6:2.[21] The material in 7:2-17, 8, 10:17-27 and 12 which I have attributed to the deuteronomic school may have come originally from an Ephraimite prophetic source, but if so it has been so thoroughly reworked as to be no longer clearly recognizable. The story in 9:1 - 10:16 of Saul's search for the asses and eventual designation as military overlord by Samuel has nothing prophetic about it nor does Samuel appear in it as prophet, *pace* the glossator who identified him as such at 9:9.[22] This leaves us with the two versions of Saul's rejection (13:8-15a and 15) in both of which Samuel plays the decisive role. The reason given in the first is the usurpation by Saul of the role of sacrificer (which he performs anyway later on in the narrative without arousing comment) and, in the second, violation of the *herem* represented as disobedience to the divine will made known through the prophet. It seems to me that these two pericopes are not variants and need to be evaluated in quite different ways. The former aims at giving a particular theological coloring to the well attested fact that Saul succeeded in antagonizing both the prophetic and priestly groups within his jurisdiction.[23] In it Samuel appears not as one of the classical prophets, who did not claim the right to sacrifice, but rather like one of the older figures such as Elijah who appear in a prophetic and priestly role and as such stand closer to the archaic institutions of the tribal federation.[24] The latter also has to do with sacrifice, in that the best of the Amalekite flocks were, allegedly, spared the *herem* in order to be sacrificed to Yahweh (15:15). However, it looks as if the story has been composed as an illustration of the verse oracle (vss. 22-23) which contrasts sacrifice and obedience after the manner of Hosea (cf. Hos 6:6; 8:13; 9:4). In content and form, then, it reveals its origins in prophetic circles.[25]

From the moment that David appears on the scene the narratives dealing with his relations with Saul and his family (1 Samuel 16 - 2 Samuel 4) are written from a Judahite perspective and betray not unexpectedly the tendency to glorify David at the expense of Saul. The controlling theme is stated near the beginning (16:13b-14) and repeated at intervals throughout: that the spirit of Yahweh has now departed from Saul and come mightily upon his successor. We are not concerned here to trace this in detail through the various attempts of Saul to despatch his rival, his outbursts of insane jealousy and the measures taken by David himself to secure his ascendancy. While some historically reliable information can be sifted from this extended narrative (a good part of which comes to us in parallel versions) we must suspect bias against Saul in any passage where he and David appear together just as we must in those in which he and Samuel appear together. It is neither cynical nor hypercritical to note that in this as in other instances the winning side has written the history. If David, one of the supreme political opportunists of history, had failed in his ambition as he came close to doing, we may suppose that the story and the assessment of characters would have read very differently.

One further point calls for mention before we leave these Judahite traditions. The Jerusalemite ark story, which has been spliced into the narrative at two different points, has also been made to serve, albeit indirectly, the same polemical intent. The first section of the narrative ends with its deposition at Kiriath-jearim (2 Sam 7:1), the only city of the Gibeonite tetrapolis ascribed to Judah in the city lists (Josh 15:60) and with ethnic connections in Judah.[26] Since it is clear from the story to that point that the ark-God only settled where he chose to settle, we are in effect being told that it was due to divine providence that it abandoned Benjaminite territory to take up a permanent abode in Judah. This is only one of several indications in early Judahite traditions of a strong anti-Benjaminite bias, understandable in view of the early (and very obscure) history of this tribe and its rise to prominence under Saul.[27]

To summarize briefly what has been said so far: access to usable historical information about Saul and his reign has been rendered extraordinarily difficult by politically and theologically inspired polemic built into the primary sources; the most inclusive of these was the deuteronomic historical work which made use of an Ephraimite prophetic source which glorified Samuel and Jerusalemite sources which glorified David; while the bias in the deuteronomist's work and the Ephraimite source was mainly anti-monarchic, the Jerusalemite sources were directly anti-Saul and anti-Benjamin; the deuteronomist who, for the most part, allowed his sources to speak for themselves, set the seal on this negative historiographical interpretation which remained standard thereafter.

2

We must now go on to ask whether, in view of the situation described above, it is possible to recover anything of historical value about Saul and his reign. We will now try to answer this question in a mood of cautious optimism; for not only has our analysis left three important sources untouched by this polemic (i.e., those dealing with Saul's early successful period in 1 Sam 9:1 - 10:16, 11 and 13:2 - 14:52), but even in those passages which are heavily and overtly hostile to Saul it will be possible to find information serviceable to the historian. The three passages referred to must, however, have the first claim on our attention.

Though it records adverse opinion on Saul (at 10:11-13) the first of the sources in 1 Samuel which mentions him (9:1 - 10:16) itself betrays no prejudice against his person. It records how he was sent with a servant to recover the straying asses of his father and how, after a circuitous journey, he providentially encountered Samuel, was anointed by him as military overlord and sent on a further and final stretch of his itinerary ending at a place called Gibeah or the hill of Elohim (10:5, 10). While it is possible to read it as a consecutive narrative there are some problems which the commentators have not failed to note, e.g., that the city of Kish, the starting point of the itinerary, is not named (unusual in such narratives, cf. 1:1 and Judg 13:2)[28] as the city where the encounter with Samuel took place is not,[29] that Saul is sent out by his father and yet reports to an uncle of whom we have heard nothing to this point. These are only the more obvious ones. As for the journey, those more familiar with the habits of donkeys than most modern commentators have observed that these animals rarely if ever undertake such long trips on their own, a circumstance which, when taken with the baffling topographical references,[30] has given a widespread impression of a folkloristic or symbolic narrative.[31] This, of course, tells us very little unless we go on to say why such a genre was deemed appropriate at this point and what function it was meant to serve.

Rather than recite all the various attempts at analysis which have been made in recent years it may be more useful for the present purpose to limit ourselves to one observation. If the story had ended with the designation by Samuel of Saul as *nāgîd* difficulties like the ones alluded to could probably have been overlooked. Even if we chose to read it as a conflation of two traditions — one concerning the search for the lost asses the meaning of which is now opaque,[32] the other dealing with the recommendation of Saul by Samuel the seer to tribal representatives[33] and his designation as military overlord — we would still have to explain why the conflation took place. The main problem with the story as it now stands, ending as it does with the fulfillment of the threefold sign, is that it lacks its conclusion. For Samuel tells the young Saul that after the spirit of Yahweh comes mightily upon him he is to "do whatever your hand finds to do" (10:7), that is, perform a military exploit which will save his people; yet no such exploit follows.[34] Instead the narrative is, so to speak, sidetracked by another tradition concerning Saul's affinity with ecstatic "prophecy" and its practitioners among the "sons of the prophets" (10:9-13). Moreover, the fact that the possession of the spirit is made dependent on anointing by Samuel can hardly fail to raise suspicion, for šopᵉṭîm like Samson (and like Saul himself in 11:6) are possessed by the spirit in a quite spontaneous and unmediated way, anointing being for kings, especially usurpers, after the manner of Canaan.[35] It is at these points that the unitary character of the narrative begins to appear fragile. What at any rate is asserted in it, even if by different individuals or groups, is: that Saul came by the leadership in a providential manner; that he was accepted by tribal representatives and designated by Samuel; that he had affinities with ecstatic prophecy; and finally that he was to perform a decisive military exploit against Israel's enemies.

If Saul's hand did not find anything to do in this pericope it would be logical to look elsewhere for a military exploit. The editor who added the reference to a future meeting at Gilgal (10:8) was evidently thinking of the successful revolt against the Philistines described in 13:2-23; and if with the LXX we read Gibeah for Geba at 13:3 the case would be strengthened, for we find a reference to a Philistine nᵉṣîb at Gibeah in the narrative just considered (10:5). Yet we would have to conclude that this editorial linking of episodes was singularly inept since the Saul designated and anointed by Samuel was evidently a young man working for his father while the author of the *coup de main* against the Philistines was already king and old enough to have a son fighting at his side.[36] On balance it would seem better to turn to Saul's Ammonite campaign which follows immediately after the inserted Mizpah source (10:17-27) and in which also the spirit comes mightily upon him (11:6). We would not thereby be obliged to conclude to a historical sequence. As has already been hinted, it is much more likely that Saul, like such heroic predecessors as Samson, was directly inspired to military action and that therefore the anointing, if historical, followed rather than preceded such action.

It is reasonably clear, to begin with, that Samuel did not appear in the original form of this tradition since the reference to him in vs. 8 is clearly obtrusive and the conclusion (vss. 12-15) has the purpose of linking with the later source in 10:17-27 which we have already discussed. While it does not ensure historical reliability, the absence of Samuel or David in a Saul tradition certainly gives good ground for optimism, and in point of fact the mustering of the tribal levy by Saul on behalf of Jabesh-Gilead has good independent support. A quite independent if later source asserts that the Ammonite campaign was the occasion for the transition to monarchy (12:12) and there is sound evidence for a special bond between this city and

Saul's tribe. The Jabesh-Gileadites were the only ones who did not participate in the war of extermination against Benjamin (Judg 21:8); it was they who rescued Saul's remains, at considerable risk, from the wall of Beth-shan (1 Sam 31:11-13; cf. 2 Sam 21:12), and it has been correctly observed that David's overtures to the same city presuppose the existence of a treaty between it and Saul, one that David was seeking to renew.[37] Transjordanian Hebrews took part in the opening stages of the revolt against the Philistines instigated by Saul (1 Sam 13:7) and it was hardly by happenstance that Ishbaal continued to rule from Mahanaim, within the borders of Gilead. Gilead is listed first among the territories over which he reigned (2 Sam 2:9).[38]

Practically all commentators agree that this source represents Saul after the manner of Israel's charismatic war heroes.[39] Rather than repeat all the arguments which have been advanced in favor of this reading we shall limit ourselves to a comparison with the Jephthah narrative complex in Judg 10:17 - 12:7. Jephthah was a Gileadite who, after being banished by his tribe, became the redoubtable leader of a band of irregulars operating out of the small Aramaean state of Tob. Ammonite aggression against Gilead led to his recall and, after some hesitation, he was appointed as head and leader ($l^e ro'š$ $ûl^e q\bar{a}ṣîn$, 11:11) at the Gileadite sanctuary of Mizpah, though he agreed to assume this role only after the successful outcome of the campaign (vs. 9). After an unsuccessful attempt to negotiate with the Ammonites the spirit of Yahweh came upon him too (11:29; cf. 1 Sam 11:6), he passed through Gilead and Manasseh to raise the levy and made a vow to offer a human sacrifice in the event of a successful outcome. The narrative concludes with opposition and threats from Ephraim on the grounds that it had not been included in the levy and that the Gileadites had seceded from the Joseph tribes (12:1-4).

The affinity between these two traditions is certainly very persuasive and instructive. Both men are appointed military leaders over considerable opposition from their home towns (Judg 11:2-3, 7; 1 Sam 10:11-12, 27; 11:12) and in both cases the appointment involves a solemn act in which tribal elders participate (Judg 11:5, 11; 1 Sam 9:22; 11:14-15). In both cases it is either stated or strongly suggested that this act followed successful military action. The spirit of Yahweh comes upon both (Judg 11:29; 1 Sam 11:6) and while Jephthah passes through the tribes himself to raise the levy Saul chooses a more original and impressive means to the same end (Judg 11:29; 1 Sam 11:7). Jephthah makes a vow which leads to the death of his daughter (Judg 11:30) while Saul issues a curse which seems to presuppose a vow and which almost leads to the death of his son (1 Sam 14:24).[40] Quite apart from these parallels the two episodes seem to belong to the same historical milieu. The adversary is the same, the tribes of Gilead and Benjamin are involved in both cases (Judg 10:9) and while the hostility of Ephraim is explicit in the Jephthah narrative it is to be inferred throughout the Saul traditions. The action of Nahash the Ammonite king, who lived on into the early years of David's reign and with whom David had a treaty (2 Sam 10:1), demonstrates the extreme weakness of the tribes after the crushing defeats recorded in 1 Samuel 4. As at the time of Jephthah, Ammonite hostility was directed not just against Gilead but against *kol yiśrā'ēl*, the tribal federation as a whole (11:2), though the term may of course refer only to some of the twelve tribes.[41] Thus the history of Jephthah, together with that of Abimelech,[42] provides the necessary historical context for understanding what was involved in Saul's ascent to power and in the transition from military overlordship to monarchy.

A special problem is posed by the mention of Saul's opponents after his successful campaign (11:12-13). This conclusion to the narrative does not seem to be in good order. The people ask Samuel for the death penalty for the opposition but then Saul not Samuel replies, magnanimously declining to punish them. Then Samuel, without further reference to the matter, invites the people to Gilgal to renew Saul's kingship. The phrase "let us renew the kingship" (vs. 14) is, as we have seen, an editorial adaptation to the account of the king-making at Mizpah in 10:17-27 in which also we hear of opponents of Saul, "sons of Belial" who refuse him allegiance (vs. 27). While there is more bias against the person of Saul in this instance ("how can this fellow save us?") the implication in both rhetorical questions is the same: only Yahweh can save Israel and therefore only he can be king. Faced with this theological objection to kingship Saul replies, in effect, that his acceptance of kingship does not imply rejection of the theocratic ideal of the federation (11:13). This situation will naturally bring to mind the offer of kingship to Gideon after the defeat of the Midianites. Though he appears to decline the offer (Judg 8:23) the subsequent narrative suggests rather that he was ruling out a dynastic, hereditary monarchy which would be inconsistent with the theocratic ideal.[43] In many respects the Saul episode is a piece of local history quite comparable with the Gideon-Abimelech and Jephthah episodes going on in different parts of the country and not too far removed in time. What set it apart was not only the scope of Saul's activity and jurisdiction — including the Joseph tribes to the north, Judah to the south and the Transjordanian tribes[44] — but also and especially the intent, whenever it was conceived, to establish a dynasty.[45]

In summary, then, Saul's first exploit which set him apart was against the

Ammonites not the Philistines and, as with Jephthah, it was this which led to his military overlordship and rule over a number of the tribes.[46] The anointing by Samuel must be considered historically doubtful, but if it took place it was after not before the Ammonite campaign.[47] There seems no need to doubt that Samuel did play a role alongside Saul — as other prophetic figures alongside charismatic leaders and kings — but what precisely it was is difficult to determine. He may have been instrumental in presenting this Benjaminite warrior to a wider circle of tribal elders or perhaps those of his own tribe of Ephraim. After the establishment of his overlordship by a solemn act at Gilgal the ancient Benjaminite sanctuary Saul went on to take up the Philistine challenge. To this, the last of the three sources alluded to, we now turn.

After the deuteronomist's regnal *incipit* at 13:1 there begins an account of a counterattack on the Philistines which, after an initial repulse, led to their defeat and expulsion from the territories of the tribes (13:2 - 14:46). Editorial expansions of this narrative are not difficult to detect, especially the first of two accounts of Saul's rejection by Samuel (13:7b-15a). There is also a long and entirely credible explanation of the success of the Philistine pacification program (13:19-21) which serves to place in higher relief the Israelite success. The account of Jonathan's ritual fault (14:24-46) may or may not have originated separately; at all events, it provides a fitting dramatic conclusion to the campaign.[48]

Even after the subtraction of these sections, however, the story-line is not free of difficulties. In the first place, the initial blow which triggered the uprising seems to be attributed to both Jonathan (13:3) and Saul (vs. 4).[49] What follows is difficult to read as a consecutive piece of narrative; it seems more likely that 13:2-4a and 14:1-23 are alternative versions of the uprising since in both cases the intention seems to be to describe an initial feat of Jonathan exploited by Saul at the head of the tribal levy. It is unlikely that this is meant to reflect unfavorably on Saul, for even though his oath was responsible for the failure to exploit the victory to the full, it was an outcome of his piety, as were also his reaction to the cultic sin of his troops, the building of an altar to Yahweh and the willingness to sacrifice his son. At the same time, his failure to consult the oracle before battle (vs. 18) and his failure in consulting it afterwards (vss. 36-37) may well have been seen as the first stages in his alienation from the divine source of validation on which he depended.

Moreover it is not easy to reconcile the dismissal of all but three thousand of his men (13:2) with the summoning of the tribal levy to Gilgal (vs. 4). Very likely this betrays the same "theological" intent as the reduction of Gideon's army to six hundred (Judg 7:2-8). After the initial reverse and the flight of many of the allied Transjordanian Hebrews the number was reduced yet further to six hundred and Saul's headquarters had moved from Michmash (and then Gilgal) to Geba (13:16) or perhaps Gibeah (14:2). Hence even in such an ostensibly straightforward and unpolemical narrative as this caution is needed. But at least the main lines are clear: Saul rose to power as a result of the Ammonite campaign and fought against the Philistines only after his appointment as overlord. The result was the liberation of much of the tribal territory and the retreat of the Philistines to their coastal cities where, of course, they were safe from further attack for the time being. While fighting continued sporadically during his reign (14:47, 52) it was several years before they were in a position to launch another all-out offensive against him (28:1; 29:1) which in the event resulted in his defeat and death.

On what happened between these early events connected with his rise to power and those which led to his defeat and death in battle we are very poorly informed indeed; but we can agree with the judgment of Eissfeldt that "there is no lack of indications that Saul exercised a strong and successful rule, and that his fall was not due to his sinful behavior but had all the elements of a personal tragedy."[50] In one quite sober notice we are told that he fought successfully against Moab, Ammon, Edom, the Aramean state of Zobah and the Amalekites in addition to the Philistines (1 Sam 14:47-48). It is of some interest to note that three of these occur as enemies of Israel in the final oracle of Balaam (Num 24:17, 18, 20), and in view especially of the earlier reference to a king greater than Agag (Num 24:7) it may be asked whether the events referred to in this chapter do not envisage the reign of Saul.[51] It is in every respect unfortunate that the official historians have allowed so little to survive from this heroic age of Israel's history. To take only one example, we have quotations from *The Book of the Upright* (*seper hayyāšār*) from the period of the settlement and the early years of David, and it would be strange if it did not contain material from the reign of Saul.[52]

One other important aspect of this period deserves attention. From one of the so-called appendices to the books of Samuel we learn that Saul violated the treaty made before his time with the Gibeonites by disenfranchising them from the position they had won within the federation and attempting to physically eliminate them (2 Sam 21:1). In the same notice the Gibeonites are described generically as "of the remnant of the Amorites," whereas in the account of the treaty we learn that they were a Hivite enclave comprising four cities of which the principal one was

Gibeon itself (Josh 9:7, 17). Indirect confirmation of Saul's action is at hand in the account of the assassination of Ishbaal by Baanah and Rechab from Beeroth (2 Sam 4:2) in the course of which we are informed that the inhabitants of Beeroth in Benjamin fled to Gittaim, though we are not told why. It would seem very likely that this flight from one of the member-cities of the Gibeonite tetrapolis was occasioned by Saul's hostile action and that therefore the assassination was an act of political revenge.[53] But why did Saul do it? The story of the immolation of his descendants by the Gibeonites during David's reign attributes it to his zeal for the people of Israel and Judah (2 Sam 21:2), and in view of other well attested examples of his religious zeal there is nothing improbable in this.[54] In other words, the action against these Hivites (thoroughly canaanized, no doubt, whatever their origin) would have been part of a policy of religious as well as political assimilation pursued with more zeal than wisdom. Also, there may well have been strategic considerations involved since the Gibeonite cities were uncomfortably close to the Philistine pentapolis and could have obstructed communications with Judah and the south. The possibility cannot, finally, be ruled out that at some point Saul attempted to make Gibeon, the great city like one of the royal cities (Josh 10:2) and the greatest high place (1 Kgs 3:4), his capital city, and that in so doing he antagonized its inhabitants. In this connection it is surely relevant to note that it was at Kiriath-jearim, another Gibeonite city, that the ark was deposited after it returned from its sojourn among the Philistines (1 Sam 6:21 - 7:1).[55]

3

The obscurity which surrounds so much of Saul's reign also encompasses his person. In 1 Sam 9:1-2 he is described as a Benjaminite, son of Kish, whose genealogy is traced back five generations to a certain Aphiah, and in 10:21 we learn that he belonged to the Matri clan of that tribe. The Philistines refer to him and his kinsmen as "Hebrews" (1 Sam 13:19; 14:11; cf. 4:6, 9; 29:3) and Saul himself calls the Hebrews to battle (13:3).[56] We also hear of Hebrews returning east of the Jordan after the initial reverse (13:7) and hiring themselves out to the Philistines (14:21) — in which respect at least David appears as a typical 'apiru condottiere of the kind we hear about in the Amarna letters three centuries earlier. As is well known, neither 'apiru nor 'ibrî is an ethnic term, and to describe Saul (or David, for that matter) as an Israelite is to say nothing about his background or provenance anymore than in the case of such earlier heroic figures as Shamgar ben-Anath, Jerubbaal or Samson. It must seem rather strange that in the notice referred to (1 Sam 9:1-2) his place of origin is not given. In 10:26 we learn that his home was in Gibeah and in 11:4-5 we find him ploughing at Gibeah of Saul (cf. 15:34). Yet he was buried not at Gibeah but at Zela where the tomb of Kish his father was located (2 Sam 21:13-14). This place occurs in the Benjaminite city-list within the Gibeon division (Josh 18:28) and it may be identified with Khirbet Ṣalah about a mile or so from Nebi Samwil, itself less than a mile from Gibeon (el-Jîb);[57] which makes it all the more interesting that the Chronicler associates Saul's family genealogically with the Gibeonites (1 Chr 8:29-40; 9:34-44).[58] It appears from the account of his secret designation as *nāgîd* that he was well known in the place where his journey ended, a place known as *haggibʿāh* (the hill) or *gibʿat haʾelohîm* (the hill of God).[59] While the relevant topographical and textual problems are probably insoluble, we may at least suggest that this hill was none other than "the great high place" (1 Kgs 4:3) or "the mountain of Yahweh" (2 Sam 21:6; cf. vs. 9) — namely, Gibeon itself or the nearby Nebi Samwil.[60] We have no means of knowing what this association implied, and we are certainly not justified in concluding that Saul was a Gibeonite, but it may at least help to explain how a situation arose between Saul and the Gibeonites in some respects analogous to that between Abimelech and the Shechemites with whom he (Abimelech) had matrilinear relations.

The question of Saul's origins is complicated by indications, admittedly for the most part obscure, of affinity with groups east of the Jordan. According to the Chronicler's genealogy both the Gibeonites and Saul's family are descended from Jeiel and Maacah (1 Chr 8:29; 9:35). In keeping with the character and purpose of these genealogical lists this would imply that both descend from a Jeielite group which settled at some time in the territory of Maacah in the northern Transjordanian region.[61] Elsewhere the name of Jeiel belongs to a Reubenite chieftain whose sphere of operation was the land of Gilead and beyond in the direction of the Euphrates (1 Chr 5:7), a region previously occupied by the men of Geshur and Maacah (Josh 13:11). The genealogy may then imply that the ancestors of the Gibeonites and of Saul came from that area. It should also be noted that the sixth in the list of Edomite kings in Gen 36:31-43 is also called Saul (Gen 36:37-38; 1 Chr 1:48-49) and his place of origin is given as Rehoboth on the Euphrates, which is in roughly the same area as that indicated by the Gibeonite genealogy.[62] Even if the Edomite king list represents local dynasts all more or less contemporary, this Edomite Saul could not have been far removed in time and space from his Israelite namesake, and it can hardly be a coincidence that the origins of both are traced back to the northern

Transjordanian region in the direction of the Syrian desert. Moreover, the suspicion that at this point the Chronicler has preserved genuine pre-Exilic tradition is strengthened by the observation that a significant number of the personal names in the Saulite genealogy also occur among the Edomite names in Genesis 36.[63] And we should note, finally, that one of the most highly placed and loyal of his officials was Doeg the Edomite or Syrian who slaughtered the priests at Nob.[64]

If these observations are given the weight they deserve it will be easier to understand the close associations of Saul and the tribe of Benjamin with elements settled east of the Jordan and how the center of gravity of his kingdom could shift so easily to the other side of the river after his death. It may also seem to strengthen the hypothesis of a Gilgal amphictyony or symmachy composed of Benjamin and related tribesmen in the Gileadite region, though substantial difficulties still remain in its way.[65] It would finally lead us to suggest that the historical model and analogy for his rule were not those of the great powers but of the mostly small Aramaean states to the north and the east.[66]

Just as mythical as the idea of ethnically distinct Israelites living as a group apart is that of religiously uncontaminated Yahwists living among idolatrous Canaanites. If other savior figures can carry non-Israelite theophoric names (e.g., Shamgar ben-Anath, Jerubbaal, Samson) we cannot simply assume that Saul was from beginning to end an "orthodox" Yahwist. It is, for example, significant that while his first son bears a good Yahwist name later children are named for Baal;[67] and we may add that no satisfactory Israelite derivation for the names of either Saul or Kish are known.[68] Having made this point, however, we must go on to note that in the earliest and most trustworthy traditions Saul is presented as ecstatic warrior and ecstatic prophet. In the account of the Ammonite campaign (1 Sam 11:6-7) he appears as a typical "war berserk" (Max Weber's term[69]) with which no doubt the practice of fasting (14:24), the taking of oaths and sexual abstinence (cf. 1 Sam 21:5; 2 Sam 11:11) were associated. The tradition of close affinity with the ecstatic prophetic conventicles ("plebeian technicians of orgiastics" as Max Weber called them) is more difficult to evaluate. The stories about him being seized with the ecstatic spirit at the hill of God and Naioth (1 Sam 10:6; 19:22) must clearly be understood in relation to the proverbial saying, "Is Saul also among the prophets?" (10:11; 19:24). We may agree that the stories have developed subsequently to the proverbial saying and that their function is to illustrate it, but we must also assume that there would be no proverbial saying without a genuine tradition about Saul as an ecstatic prophet;[70] especially since the question carries derogatory implications.

It seems to me that the most likely purpose of the *māšāl* in question form was to imply that Saul, far from being a prophet, was a sick and deranged person, afflicted with an evil spirit from Yahweh (1 Sam 16:14, etc.). In one of the versions dealing with his tendency to throw spears at people he did not like, he is described as "prophesying" (*vayyitnabbē'*, 18:10), in other words, raving out of control. This is not part of a wider polemic against orgiastic prophecy — which would have involved Samuel also (19:18) — but a quite specific polemic against Saul himself, a smear tactic not unlike those sometimes used by less reputable politicians today. But, to repeat, it would not have been necessary had there not been a tradition in existence attesting that he exercised prophetic gifts in some way. There is, of course, some affinity between the endowment of the charismatic *šopeṭ* and the *nābî'* but this seems insufficient in itself to explain the proverb.[71] We may come closer to an explanation if we can show that behind the account of Samuel's conception, birth and early life in 1 Samuel 1-2 there lies an older story about the consecration of Saul as nazirite. The main argument is, of course, the name etymology (*še'iltîw*, 1:20) which cannot be construed in any way (certainly not by assonance) to refer to Samuel but would very naturally refer to Saul. Moreover, the root *š'l* occurs nine times in all with reference to the child, including the passive participle *šā'ûl* identical with the name Saul.[72] The use of this verb is certainly to be understood with reference to the nazirite which is, in any case, clear enough from the vow of dedication, the mother's abstinence from strong drink and the commitment to let the child's hair grow (1:11, 15). The reading *nāzîr* in 4QSam[a] between vss. 11 and 12 does no more than make this explicit.

That the primary intent of 1 Samuel 1 is to describe the conception and birth of a charismatic *nāzîr* is confirmed by comparison with the story of the conception and birth of Samson in Judges 13. The *incipit* is stylistically identical, both mothers are barren and become fertile only with supernatural assistance, a sacrifice and meal take place in both cases, the mother eschews strong drink and no razor is to touch either child's head. The formulaic description of the birth and name-giving highlights the absence of an etymology in the case of Samson, an absence which, given derivation from *ŠMŠ* the sun-deity, is understandable. Both narratives, in addition, allude to the development of the child and the divine favor which he enjoyed.

However we care to formulate the relation between these two narratives, it is at least clear that both refer to the consecration of a nazirite and that such a characterization is inconsistent with Samuel as sanctuary attendant (1:22; 2:18-19; 3:1), *a fortiori* as a judgment-prophet. With Samson the charisma of the nazirite is in a function of the holy war against the Philistines (13:5) and manifests itself by possession of the spirit of Yahweh (13:25). This, again, suggests comparison with Saul not Samuel.[73] Samuel appears in many roles — sanctuary attendant, seer, judge, prophet — but not as nazirite.[74] It must of course be added that Saul does not appear explicitly as nazirite either. We find no mention in the Saul narratives of the nazirite vows and there is therefore no suggestion that his downfall, like that of Samson, was due to their violation.[75] Saul is, however, moved to deliver Israel by the spirit of Yahweh and we have noted some aspects of his conduct of war, such as the vow to fast in 14:2, which are consistent with the nazirite. Then there is the tradition of his prophesying which we have already discussed. In referring to his predecessors during the early years after the settlement Amos brackets *nebî'îm* with *nezîrîm*, the latter recruited from the *baḥûrîm*, the young men fit for warfare (Amos 2:11-12).[76] That there was a close link in the early period between ecstatic prophecy and war hardly needs demonstration; and although we know all too little about the nazirite we do know that it had close affinities with prophecy.

It will be clear from our survey — by no means exhaustive, needless to say — that if our sources allow us to know of him and his reign something more than *so gut wie nichts*[77] there is much that they do not tell us and that we shall never know. In particular, we know something about his early years and his downfall and death but of the period between, comprising most of his reign, very little indeed. This, I have argued, is due to the fact that the historiographical tradition which can be traced back to Judahite sources under David and which received definitive and official form in the hands of the deuteronomic historian allowed only certain traditions to survive most of which are made to testify against him. Perhaps more than with any other major biblical figure, therefore, the modern historian finds himself working, so to speak, against the grain of his sources. This is always a hazardous task, but the importance of the period in question, not to say the reputation of Saul himself, demands that it be undertaken.

1. A later tradition (Acts 13:21; Josephus, *Ant* 6.14,9) assigns to him a reign of forty years while some Greek minuscules have "thirty." Twelve or, better, twenty, would be more likely. See. O. Eissfeldt, "The Hebrew Kingdoms," *CAH* (vol. 2; 2nd facs. ed.; 1965) chs. 34, 39; J. Blenkinsopp, "Jonathan's Sacrilege," *CBQ* 26 (1964) 444-45.

2. See 1 Sam 14:40-42 where *yillākēd* is also used in a technical sense, and Josh 7:16-26, the fate of Achan ben-Carmi, where we have the same process of elimination from tribe to family or clan to individual, and where the technical term *hēqrîb* is used (vss. 14, 16, 17, 18).

3. *Ant* 6.4, 5-14, 9.

4. *Liber Antiquitatum Biblicarum* 58, 64. See M. R. James (ed.), *The Biblical Antiquities of Philo* (New York: Macmillan, 1971) 227-31, 239-42.

5. While Saul is praised for his zeal in disposing of the Gibeonites, his attachment to Torah and his modesty, and while the threat of Samuel's ghost (1 Sam 28:19) is turned into a promise of Paradise (Babylonian Talmud, *Berakoth*, 12b), his undoing is variously attributed to his not making his studies available to the public (Babylonian Talmud, *Erubin*, 53b), his failure to kill Agag from whom was descended the persecutor Haman (Babylonian Talmud, *Megillah*, 13a) and his arrogance (Babylonian Talmud, *Zebahim*, 102a).

6. E.g., Psalm 78 refers to the defeat of the Philistines and capture of the ark and then to the rejection of Joseph/Ephraim; 1 Mac 2:51-70, the last exhortation of Mattathias, goes from Caleb directly to David; 2 Esdr 3:4-36 directly from Sinai to David.

7. It will be seen that at this point I am following M. Noth, *Überlieferungs-geschichtliche Studien* (2nd ed.; Tübingen: Mohr, 1957) 18-27.

8. This implies that I do not believe the similarity is ruled out by the different order in Judges where the critical situation precedes the "raising up" of a military savior.

9. For details see J. Blenkinsopp, *Gibeon and Israel* (Cambridge: Cambridge University, 1972) 78 and notes.

10. The following phrases are deuteronomic: *wᵉlo' hālᵉkû bānāyw bidrākô; wayyiqhû šohad* (cf. Deut 16:19, *lo' tiqqah šohad*); *wayyattû mišpāt* (cf. Deut 16:19, *lo' tatteh mišpāt*). It is implied therefore that they did not live up to the (deuteronomic) standards for judges.

11. Cf. 1 Sam 8:11 with Deut 17:16 referring to horses. The attitude to monarchy is restrictive and deterrent in both. See H. Seebass, "Traditionsgeschichte von I Sam 8,10 17ff und 12," *ZAW* 77 (1965) 286-96.

12. See Noth, *Überlieferungsgeschichtliche Studien*, 5, 47, 54-55.

13. In both the extended and restricted usage of *šopet*. As Noth has shown (*Überlie-ferungsgeschichtliche Studien*, 48-49) Jephthah provides the key to the juxtaposition of major and minor judges by the D editor.

14. We may take as typical of the older school the work of C. H. Cornill and W. Nowack both of whom make much of E in 1 Samuel and assign the ark narrative to this source.

15. See also 1 Kgs 18:4, 13 referring to the hundred Yahwistic prophets hidden by

Obadiah, the survivors of Jezebel's persecution.

16. Amos 2:11-12; Hos 6:5; 9:7-8; 12:10.

17. Similarity with the vision of Isaiah in the temple (Isaiah 6) is striking. Both take place before the ark-God and issue in words of condemnation.

18. See esp. Num 11:16-30; Deut 18:15-18, with which cf. Deut 5:23-27 and Exod 20:18-21.

19. Hos 4:4 - 6:8; 5:1-2; 6:6, 9; 8:13; 9:4; 10:5; 12:10.

20. In 2:27-36 the intervention of the man of God who predicts doom and the fulfilment of whose prediction is noted is in line with the many similar prophetic interventions in the D history; and vs. 36 clearly refers to the dispossession of the $b\bar{a}m\hat{o}t$-priests as a result of the Josian reform (Deut 18:6-8; 2 Kgs 23:8-9). In 3:11 the phrase $t^e\dot{s}illeyn\bar{a}h$ $\dot{s}^et\bar{e}y$ $'ozn\bar{a}yw$ also appears to be deuteronomist (cf. 2 Kgs 21:12; Jer 19:3).

21. See L. Rost, *Die Überlieferung von der Thronnachfolge Davids* (BWANT 42; Stuttgart: W. Kohlhammer, 1926) 4-15.

22. Following N. Habel, "The Form and Significance of the Call Narratives," *ZAW* 77 (1965) 297-323, B. C. Birch ("The Development of the Tradition on the Anointing of Saul in I Sam 9:1 - 10:16," *JBL* 90 [1971] 55-68) argues that a modified prophetic call narrative has been superimposed on an early piece of folklore about Saul. While we may grant that any call to office or mission will have something in common with others, it seems that the call of the charismatic military overlords must be form-critically distinguished from that of the prophet.

23. There is no reason to doubt that Saul slaughtered the Nob priesthood (1 Sam 22:11-19). While he seems to have had close relations with the ecstatic conventicles the tradition about conflict with Samuel, however tendentious it may be, presupposes tension with some prophetic groups.

24. See 1 Kgs 18:20-40 which has to do essentially with the rebuilt altar (vss. 30-32) and represents a convenant-assembly.

25. The word of Yahweh came to Samuel (vs. 10) by night (vs. 16) and Saul is condemned for disobedience to the voice of Yahweh, that is, to his prophet (vs. 19; cf. vs. 23).

26. For substantiation see Blenkinsopp, *Gibeon and Israel*, 82 and "Kiriath-jearim and the Ark," *JBL* 88 (1969) 143-56.

27. E.g., Judg 19-20, the war of the federation against Benjamin which Judah was divinely appointed to lead (20:18) and which A. van den Born ("Etude sur quelques toponymes biblique," *OTS* 10 [1954] 201-19) has suggested may have had original reference to Saul; the transference of the grave-site of Rachel from Benjaminite to Judahite territory (1 Sam 10:2; Jer 31:15; cf. Gen 35:19; 48:7). It will be noted that much of the opposition to David came from Benjamin (e.g., 2 Sam 6:20-23; 16:5-14; 20:1-3) and that David progressively eliminated his Benjaminite rivals (2 Sam 3:22; 4:1-12; 21:1-14; 16:1-4).

28. It is not unusual to emend *mibbin yāmîn* (9:1) to *miggib'at bin yāmîn*, but this is

without support from the versions; anyway, we cannot assume that Gibeah was Kish's city since he and his family were buried at Zela in Benjamin (2 Sam 21:14).

29. It can be assumed to have been Ramah, Samuel's city, only if we ignore the editorial history of the narrative. Caution is suggested by the information supplied by the girls that the seer had just come to the city (vs. 12) and by the analogous account of David's anointing in which the seer visits Bethlehem but of course does not live there (16:1, 4).

30. Shalishah may or may not be identical with the Baal-Shalishah of 2 Kgs 4:42 (= Kefr Thilth SW of Hebron?); Shaalim may or may not be associated with the "land of Shual" (jackal) in 13:17; 'ereṣ yᵉmînî may refer simply to Benjamin though the more usual form is 'ereṣ binjāmîn and in this context it would naturally imply a destination outside of Benjamin.

31. M. Bič, "Saul sucht die Eselinnen, " VT 7 (1957) 92-97; B. C. Birch, "The Development," 55-68; F. Dornseiff, "Archilochos von Paros und Saul von Gibea," TLZ 80 (1955) 499. This last advances an interesting comparison with the Berufungsgeschichte of a certain Archilochos in a third century B.C. inscription from the island of Paros.

32. I would suggest that the journey was intended to be a symbolic circumambulation of Saul's future kingdom; cf. the equally providential journey of the ark from Ekron to Beth-shemesh and then to Kiriath-jearim, which follows the line of the boundary between Judah and Benjamin. See J. Blenkinsopp, "Kiriath-jearim and the Ark," JBL 88 (1969) 147-48. In a rather different way C. E. Hauer ("Does 1 Samuel 9:1 - 11:5 Reflect the Extension of Saul's Dominions?" JBL 86 [1967] 306-10) reads 9:1 - 10:16, 10:17-27 and 11:1-15 as progressive stages in the extension of Saul's jurisdiction.

33. Rather than just to the city elders as generally supposed. Whether the number thirty has any particular significance beyond the common stylistic use of three and multiples of three (e.g., 1 Sam 10:3; 13:2, 15; 14:2) is uncertain. H. Wildberger ("Samuel und die Entstehung der israelitischen Königtums," TZ 13 [1957] 442-69) sees them as official representatives of a restricted Yahweh-amphictyony to whom Samuel, the Gesetz-sprecher of the amphictyony, presented Saul. We may suggest comparison with the offering of the show-bread to David which perhaps even at this early time represented the tribes at the sanctuary (1 Sam 21:5-6; cf. Exod 25:23-30 and Lev 24:5-9); also, the symbolic tearing of Ahijah's cloak into twelve strips (1 Kgs 11:25-39). It may be significant in this respect that both Abiathar and Ahijah were descended from the Shiloh priesthood.

34. This was precisely the purpose of the anointing, 9:16; cf. 10:1.

35. See H. J. Stoebe, "Noch einmal die Eselinnen des Kîš (I Sam IX)," VT 7 (1957) 368.

36. The initiative for the revolt is in fact attributed to Jonathan at 13:3.

37. 2 Sam 2:4-7. See D. R. Hillers, "A Note on some Treaty Terminology in the Old Testament," BASOR 176 (1964) 46-47.

38. K. Möhlenbrink, ("Sauls Ammoniterfeldzug und Samuels Beitrag zum Königtum des Sauls," ZAW 58 [1940/41] 57-70) argued that Saul originally ruled over a Gilgal amphictyony or symmachy of three tribes: Benjamin, Reuben and Gad. The king-

making at Gilgal in which Samuel participated represented a union between the Shiloh and Gilgal amphictyonies which accounts for the tension and hostility which ensued.

39. The term "hero saga" (E. Sellin and G. Fohrer, *Introduction to the Old Testament* [Nashville: Abingdon, 1968] 219) may be considered appropriate.

40. It would be natural to assume that the ransoming of Jonathan (14:46) implied the ritual execution of a prisoner. Note the use of the verb 'kr in both episodes: w^e'$att\ h\bar{a}y\hat{\imath}t$ b^e'$okr\bar{a}y$, Judg 11:35; '$\bar{a}kar$ '$\bar{a}b\hat{\imath}$ 'et-$h\bar{a}$'$\bar{a}re\d{s}$, 1 Sam 14:29.

41. Similarly the phrase $b^ekol\ g^eb\hat{u}l\ yi\acute{s}r\bar{a}$'$\bar{e}l$ (11:3, 7), which also occurs in the account of the tribal war against Benjamin (Judg 19:28-29) and in the settlement of the Gibeonite question (2 Sam 21:5), and which Noth took to be a technical term for the sphere of the amphictyony (*Das System der Zwölf Stämme* [BWANT 4; (1930); reprint, Darmstadt: Wissenschaftliche Buchgesellschaft, 1966] 109-10), may have envisaged only some of the tribes.

42. For a comparison between Saul's relations with Gibeonites and Abimelech's with Shechemites see Blenkinsopp, "Did Saul make Gibeon his Capital?" *VT* 24 (1974) 6-7.

43. G. H. Davies, "Judges viii 22-23," *VT* 13 (1963) 151-57.

44. That Saul exercised jurisdiction over Judah is certain. Not only did the Philistines direct their attack against Judah (e.g., 1 Sam 23:1-5; cf. 2 Sam 23:13-17) during the reign of Saul; but Saul's own campaign against the Amalikites (1 Sam 14:48; 15) must have aimed primarily at defending this part of his kingdom. Judahites fought with him from an early period (1 Sam 15:4; 17:13) and he recruited men from Judah of whom the best known is of course David (1 Sam 16:14-23; 17:55-58). In his struggle against David he continued to find much support in the south (1 Sam 23:12, 19-24; 26:1), though the principal basis of his power resided in the coalition of Cisjordanian and Transjordanian Hebrews comprising the tribes of Benjamin, Reuben and Gad and the Josephite tribesmen on both sides of the river. See 1 Sam 13:3; 14:11, 21 and especially the list at 2 Sam 2:9.

45. This emerges most clearly from the relations between Jonathan and David; on which see especially 1 Sam 18:1-5; 20:8, 17, 20-21, 23; 23:17-18. There seems to have been no doubt that Ishbaal should succeed him, which he did.

46. There is no reason, then, to speak of "the rustic king" out ploughing in the fields when the bad news reached him (1 Sam 11:5).

47. In other recorded cases of anointing (David, 2 Sam 5:3; Jehu, 2 Kgs 9:1-7) the military charisma of the king-designate had already been established.

48. See J. Blenkinsopp, "Jonathan's Sacrilege," *CBQ* 26 (1964) 427-49.

49. It consisted, in all probability, in the assassination of a garrison commander or military governor, this being the time-honored way of starting a revolt (cf. Judg 3:15-30). The substantive $n^e\d{s}\hat{\imath}b$ is of doubtful connotation in all instances except 1 Kgs 4:19 (cf. 4:7) where it must refer to an individual.

50. *CAH* (vol. 2; 2nd fasc. ed.; 1965) 5.

51. While David also fought successfully against the same enemies (see especially 2 Sam

8:12) the very specific reference to Agag and to the security of the Kenites (Num 24:21; cf. 1 Sam 15:6), as well as the recurring use of "Jacob/Israel" in Num 23-24, would suggest that events prior to the reign of David cannot easily be excluded.

52. On this source and *The Book of the Wars of Yahweh* see O. Eissfeldt, *The Old Testament. An Introduction* (New York: Harper and Row, 1965) 132-33.

53. See J. Blenkinsopp, *Gibeon and Israel*, 8-9. In "Kiriath-jearim and the Ark," *JBL* 88 (1969) 143-56, I have argued that evidence for Judahite connections for the population around Kiriath-jearim may also be explained in this way.

54. E.g., his waiting the prescribed time for Samuel at great risk to himself and his men, 1 Sam 13:8-12; his oath after battle and willingness to sacrifice his son, 1 Sam 14:24-25; the expulsion of the mediums and wizards from his territories, 1 Sam 28:3.

55. See "Kiriath-jearim and the Ark," *JBL* 88 (1969) 143-56; "Did Saul make Gibeon his Capital?" *VT* 24 (1974) 1-7.

56. I am not persuaded that the text must be emended to "The Philistines said, 'the Hebrews have revolted'."

57. M. Noth, *Das Buch Josua* (2nd ed.; Tübingen: Mohr, 1957) 113; R. de Vaux, *Les Livres de Samuel* (Paris: Editions du Cerf, 1961) 234; K. D. Schunck, *Benjamin* (Berlin: Töpelmann, 1963) 89, 118-19.

58. On these and other relevant genealogies of the Chronicler see, in addition to the commentaries, M. Noth, "Siedlungsgeographischer Liste in I Chr 2 und 4," *ZDPV* 55 (1932) 97-124; A. Demsky, "The Genealogy of Gibeon (I Chronicles 9:35-44) Biblical Epigraphic Considerations," *BASOR* 202 (1971) 16-23.

59. We hear of the surprise of all who knew him, and his uncle is there to question him about the expedition.

60. Cf. also the reference to "the hill" where the ark was for a time located: 1 Sam 7:1; 2 Sam 6:3.

61. See B. Mazar, "Geshur and Maacah," *JBL* 80 (1961) 16-28.

62. Cf. the reference to the Syrians of Beth-rehob and Zobah in 2 Sam 10:6 and to Hadad-ezer son of Rehob king of Zobah who went to restore his power at the Euphrates in 2 Sam 8:3-8.

63. I.e., Matri (Matred), Yeush, Ishmael, Hanan, Aiah, Shimei (Shimeah); on which see my *Gibeon and Israel*, 59-60.

64. In view of the frequent confusion between *dalet* and *reš* the LXX *Syros* may well be the correct reading at 1 Sam 21:8 and 22:9, 18. Whatever their exact meaning, the phrases *niṣṣāb 'al 'abdē šā'ûl* (22:9) and *'abbîr hāro'îm 'ašer lešā'ûl* (21:8) certainly denote high status.

65. See Möhlenbrink, "Sauls Ammoniterfeldzug," 57-70. The hypothesis does not seem to explain adequately the important and very early references to the tribes in the Song of Deborah, Judges 5, nor does it give an adequate account of Ephraimite and Manassehite settlements east of the Jordan and the close ties between Benjamin and the Joseph tribes.

66. See the parallels to 1 Sam 8:10-17 from Ugarit and Alalakh adduced by I. Mendelsohn, "Samuel's Denunciation of Kingship in the Light of the Akkadian Documents from Ugarit," *BASOR* 143 (1956) 17-22.

67. Ishbaal (2 Sam 2:8, etc.); Meribbaal (1 Chr 8:34 cf. Mephibaal, 2 Sam 9:2, etc.); Malchishua (1 Sam 14:49). The last contains the same theophoric element as Elishua (2 Sam 5:15), Bathshua (Gen 38:2; 1 Chr 2:3) and Abishua (1 Chr 5:30).

68. See my *Gibeon and Israel*, 59-60.

69. Max Weber, *Ancient Judaism* (New York: Free Press, 1967) 90-95.

70. See J. Sturdy, "The Original Meaning of 'Is Saul among the Prophets?' " *VT* 20 (1960) 206-13, who ascribes it to Davidic propaganda, and B. C. Birch, "The Development," 66-67.

71. V. Eppstein, "Was Saul also among the Prophets?" *ZAW* 81 (1969) 287-303, thinks that the proverb arose out of the question whether Saul was to be considered the last of the Judges or the first of the Kings.

72. 1:17, 20, 27, 28; 2:20.

73. "the spirit of God came mightily upon him," Judg 14:6, 7-8; 14:19 and 15:14; "the spirit of God came mightily upon Saul," 1 Sam 11:6.

74. See J. L. McKenzie, "The Four Samuels," *BR* 7 (1962) 3-18.

75. As I argued in "Structure and Style in Judges 13-16," *JBL* 82 (1963) 65-76.

76. Cf. Jer 35:1-11 where Rechabites and prophets are likewise mentioned together.

77. R. Bultmann, *Jesus* (Tübingen: Mohr, 1951) 11.

JAMES W. FLANAGAN

Judah in All Israel

John L. McKenzie has dealt extensively with the problems surrounding the rise of the monarchy in Israel.[1] His recent writings rest upon presumptions that demand a dramatic reappraisal of the history of that time, for he presumes that Judah was not part of the kingdom of Saul and that the scribes of David were responsible for the books of Samuel.[2] He believes that understanding the meaning of the term "all Israel" (*kol yiśrā'ēl*) will support his assumptions.[3] He has called attention to my work in this area, and I am pleased to present him with this study on the occasion of his 65th birthday.

McKenzie is correct in noting that "all Israel" is a technical term in the Hebrew scriptures. With five exceptions, it is found exclusively in the deuteronomic history and in the writings of the Chronicler in the MT. We must determine whether the phrase was coined by these writers or whether it has a history of its own. If the latter, what did it mean at the various stages of usage, and how did Judah relate to this "all Israel" especially during the time of Saul?

The five exceptions reinforce the claim that the term is important for the deuteronomist because each of them has been influenced by his work. Exod 18:25[4] and Num 16:34[5] are both deuteronomic redactions; they contain the only references to "all Israel" in the Tetrateuch. Mal 3:22 (=LXX 4:4) falls within an appendix that is secondary and which attributes deuteronomic vocabulary to the prophet in an effort to sustain loyalty to the Mosaic law. Two references in Dan 9:7 and 11 are within a prayer that appears out of context and is written in a style that differs from the surrounding material which suggests that it is an editorial insertion, perhaps based on Deut 28:15-68 where "all Israel" is used.[6]

The complete absence of the term in the Tetrateuch contrasts sharply with its sudden and frequent appearance in the deuteronomic and in the Chronicler's writings. It appears nearly ninety times in the MT from Deuteronomy through 2 Kings and more than fifty times in 1 and 2 Chronicles, Ezra and Nehemiah. There are a few cases of textual uncertainty, but the frequency ranges from fourteen to twenty-two references per book except for Judges (2 times), 2 Kings (3 times), Ezra (5 times) and Nehemiah (3 times). Even this variation illustrates that the term may be associated with the monarchy.

The book of Deuteronomy uses *kol yiśrā'ēl* in a completely consistent manner. The term does not appear in material drawn from the traditions but is used repeatedly in units that stem from the compiler. The phrase appears most frequently in introductory and concluding formulae of Moses' speeches,[7] but it has also been inserted in deuteronomic revisions of the code (13:12; 18:16; 21:21),[8] in a command to appear for worship that was proclaimed to "all Israel" (31:11), and in a covenant form that has been conflated by the deuteronomist (11:6).[9] Thus, every use that has been credited to Moses or his time originated in the time of the deuteronomic historian.

In Joshua "all Israel" is linked with the book's hero by appearing only in passages that name him. "All Israel" was with Joshua at the crossing of the Jordan (3:7, 17; 4:14), in the Achan episode (8:15, 21, 24, 33) and during the so-called southern campaign where the term serves as a link between sites conquered (10:29, 31, 34, 36, 38). Finally, Joshua summoned "all Israel" to hear his last directives, a use that is similar to those in Deuteronomy (23:2). The entire section in which these are found is set completely within the territory of Benjamin, a setting which McKenzie recognizes as artificial.[10] The attempt to expand the setting to "all Israel" is the work of the deuteronomist.[11]

In the book of Judges, *kol yiśrā'ēl* is used only twice which makes it impossible to speak of a pattern. Still, both uses occur in sections that contain ancient material that has been reworked by the deuteronomist (8:27; 20:34), and both passages share a common concern for some type of strong central authority that would maintain order within the tribal community.[12] In the Gideon story, the reference follows the Israelites' call for Gideon to rule over them. He declined but then built an "ephod," and "all Israel" prostituted themselves before it (8:27). The monarchical and cultic context in which Yahweh was ignored makes it probable that the use is deuteronomic and that "all Israel"did not appear in earlier versions of the story.

The second use of this term is within the story of the Levites' concubine where a group fighting against the Benjaminites is called "all Israel" (20:34). The context speaks of all the tribes of Israel and refers to the boundaries of Dan and Beersheba (20:1), but the involvement of a Judahite and the separation of Benjamin from the rest of Israel in the story has led commentators to assign the usage to the final, so-called, deuteronomistic, i.e., Exilic, redactor.[13] Such an interpretation correctly distinguishes between the Josian, deuteronomic, and the Exilic, deuteronomistic, versions, but it fails to recognize what may be an ancient use of the term *kol yiśrā'ēl*.[14] It is not clear why the deuteronomistic redactor would have used the term here, since it appears nowhere else in his material. At the same time, a usage which stresses the division within the community contradicts the deuteronomic insistence upon unity that has been seen in Deuteronomy and Joshua. As will be seen in the Abner-Ishbaal episode in 2 Samuel 3, the term can be used to designate an early group that did not include the Benjaminites. A distinction between Benjamin and the rest of Israel in the time of the judges suggests an archaic usage that has escaped the deuteronomic redactor. We may recall that many of the traditions that have been "universalized" to tell the history of Israel during that period were originally Benjaminite traditions. The distinction between Benjamin and "all Israel" in the concubine story indicates that the universalizing process resulted from an alliance between the immigrant Benjaminites and an indigenous group known as "all Israel." For the present, however, we must state this as a possibility to be tested by comparison with other uses of the term.

A survey of the phrase leads us next to the books of Samuel. Since the classic study by Martin Noth, the books have been accepted as a predeuteronomic compilation that was incorporated into the deuteronomic history with only minor revisions.[15] If McKenzie is correct, we should credit the predeuteronomic compilation to David and should expect to find the narrative expressing the views of the Davidic court. The assumption deserves consideration in conjunction with our study of *kol yiśrā'ēl*, but since there are several meanings of the term in the books, it is not possible to assign them all to a single editor or to assume that their origin can be traced to one historical period.

The first period covered in the books is the time of Samuel. "All Israel" is associated with him at Shiloh (1 Sam 2:14, 22; 3:20; 4:1, 5), at Mizpah (7:5), in the introduction to his farewell address (12:1), and in the reports of his death (25:1; 28:3). The references appear in a variety of traditions about Samuel which have been reworked and submitted to several levels of theological interpretation so that not only Samuel's role, but also his historical context have become obscured.[16] At Shiloh, during the ministry of Eli and his sons, "all Israel" was the group that came to worship there. Two of the references associated with that site are found within a tradition that portrays Samuel as a priest, a role that must be considered as unhistorical (2:14, 22); a third is in a revised unit which speaks of him as a prophet, again unhistorical (3:20); and the last two are in the introduction to the ark narrative which has been edited to fit its present setting (4:1, 5). The Mizpah reference is within the tradition which casts Samuel as a judge and attempts to make him a judge of "all Israel" (7:5). A similar effort in 8:1-5 is recognized as a fiction.[17] Thus, every connection between Samuel and "all Israel" is found in material that either has been submitted to later reinterpretation or has been reworked in order to connect it with surrounding material. This makes it very difficult to determine which of these uses of the phrase are anachronistic.

A question may be raised about the political geography of the "all Israel" group that has been credited to Samuel. The only indication of the territory's expansiveness is found in 3:20 where Dan and Beersheba are mentioned as the limits for the worshipping community at Shiloh. This designation of boundaries appeared before in Judg 20:1 and is used again in 2 Sam 3:10; 17:11; 24:2, 15 and 1 Kgs 5:5. The Chronicler refers to the cities in inverted order and links them with "all Israel" in the census in 1 Chr 21:2 and during Hezekiah's attempted reform in 2 Chr 30:5. The pattern indicates that referring to the boundaries was a usual way of describing the territory during the united monarchy and that its use should be traced to that period and not before. An editor associated Samuel with Dan and Beersheba because the charismatic leader had provided continuity between the days of the tribal league and the period of monarchy that followed. The editor considered it appropriate and useful to expand Samuel's influence as far as the boundaries of the later kingdoms. Since there is no clear indication that all of these uses of "all Israel" have been placed in the Samuel accounts by the deuteronomist, we may assign them to an earlier editor but without deciding which of them, if any, date from Samuel's time. This leaves only three unexplained uses in the Samuel narratives. One is in the introductory formula to his speech in 12:1 and two are in the doublet reporting his death (25:1; 28:3). The first is commonly treated as deuteronomic,[18] and the last two are obviously the work of a later editor; they tell us little about the limits of "all Israel" at the time of Samuel.

The account of Saul's reign is so entwined with the story of David's rise that it is difficult to consider them separately.[19] The narrative portrays Saul as a shadowy and tragic figure who was faced with enormous problems that proved to be too much for him. The portrayal may accurately reflect the historical situation. The story of Samson in Judges reports that the Philistines had dominion over Israel (Judg 14:4) for an extended time (13:1) before they captured the ark which marked the end of the tribal league (1

Samuel 4-6). Faced with what must have seemed like extinction, Israel groped for a means of coping with such threats and chose to meet the Philistines on the Philistines' terms, that is, as a centralized military and political power. The decision met with strong resistance from factions within the community (1 Samuel 7-11) which meant that Saul was faced with the task of organizing an unwilling village population around his new central administration.[20] The history of Saul is, therefore, the story of his failure to cope both with the Philistines and with his own people. Although he may have judged David correctly when his family and his nation did not, his portrait is that of a small-time politician who was obsessed with his own security as much as he was concerned about the peace of his people. He fought frantically on many fronts to secure his kingdom, but apparently without the moral sensitivity that was characteristic of a Yahwist (14:47-48; 15:20-21).

"All Israel" is mentioned eight times within the stories of Saul. In episodes which do not involve David, it appears in the account of the battle with the Ammonites (11:2), in a summary of Saul's victories (13:4), in the remark that the Philistines controlled the iron crafts (13:20), and in the report of Jonathan's violation of the oath (14:40). In episodes which do involve David, Saul and "all Israel" feared Goliath (17:1), but "all Israel" and Judah loved David (18:16); Jonathan credited David with saving "all Israel" (19:5); Saul led "all Israel" in pursuit of David (24:2) and again in the battle against the Philistines which ended his life (28:4).

Since this material has come to us through Judahite compilers and editors, it is necessary to determine which of the uses may date from Saul's time and what part Saul actually played in the political affairs of the South. We are asking here whether his "all Israel" included Judah? In order to determine this, it is helpful to compare the uses of the two terms. In 1 Samuel, Judah is mentioned only twice in passages that do not include David. Both are glosses which report that Saul numbered his troops from Israel and Judah (11:18; 15:4).[21] The first statement is within the account of the Ammonite war that explains Saul's rise to power by portraying him as the last Israelite judge. The section has been extensively reworked by the deuteronomist, and so probably neither "all Israel" nor Judah were in the earlier tradition. The second reference is within the story of Saul's campaign against the Amalekites which reports that Saul led troops from Judah on a foray far from the frontiers of Israel. McKenzie has challenged the historicity of the Amalekite war on the grounds that we lack confirming archaeological and literary evidence and that it is unlikely for Saul to have been engaged so far from Israel.[22] I believe that McKenzie is correct, and further, that Judah is an insertion into the tradition. But even if the story and reference to Judah do have a basis in history, the episode would not confirm Saul's political jurisdiction over Judah or the Amalekites any more than his victories over the Philistines confirm his jurisdiction over them. In addition, the account is placed early in Saul's reign, a time when Israel was not strong, and it is used by the compiler as a theological explanation for Yahweh's displeasure with the first king.

We must pause before considering the rest of the references to Judah to point out the pattern that has already emerged. "All Israel" is used in passages that feature Saul without David and in passages which speak of them together. But Judah appears in no sections which feature Saul alone; it is used only in narratives that include David. It is hardly necessary to mention that in each case David is the hero, and Saul is cast in an unfavorable light. "All Israel" may have been Saul's, but Judah belonged to David.

The remaining references to Judah state the following: the Goliath battle took place at Socoh in Judah (17:1), David was from Bethlehem in Judah (17:12), the men of Judah took part in the battle against Goliath (17:52), "all Israel" and Judah loved David (18:16), Gad advised David to flee to the land of Judah (22:5), David's men were afraid to fight in Judah and feared even more fighting against the Philistines (23:3), and Saul sought David among the clans of Judah (23:23), Ziklag was reported to be the property of the kings of Judah (27:6), David fought in the Negeb of Judah (27:10; 20:14) and took booty from the land of Judah (30:16) which he sent to the elders of Judah (30:26). The list includes a number of anachronisms (17:52; 18:16; 27:6) and statements of fact that have no jurisdictional significance (17:1, 12; 23:3). Several references imply that Judah was outside the kingdom of Saul. These include Gad's advice to flee into Judah and away from Saul, and the subsequent remark that Saul pursued David with a contingent from "all Israel" (24:2). Although they are found within material taken from different traditions, the two statements imply that "all Israel" and Judah were not a single kingdom. The same conclusion can be drawn from David's vassalage to the Philistines at Ziklag and his gifts to the elders of Judah which show that there was an organization in Judah by the end of Saul's reign and that it did not join Saul's defense against the Philistines.

There are several more episodes that require investigation since they imply some sort of political bond between Judah and Israel during Saul's reign. In 1 Sam 27:1 David remarks that Saul had been searching for him within the boundaries of Israel. At the time, David was within the territory of Judah. However, the report is stated to be what David said "in his heart," and it stands at the junction connecting two scenes where it serves as a transition to the following episode, the story of David with Achish of Gath. The fact that the report is about what David was thinking and that it is used within a literary seam are both strong indications that the remarks stem from the compiler. A second episode which implies a political bond is the appeal which the men of Keilah and Ziph make to the king (*mlk*, Saul) for protection against David (23:19-20). But this request for support and protection is countered by an unprejudiced statement in David's speech to Saul after he had spared the king's life. David accused Saul of cutting him off from the inheritance of Yahweh and of commanding him to serve other gods (26:19). To a Yahwist who associated the land of Israel with its god, David's accusation would mean that he had been driven out of that land. Uttered in Judah, the statement affirms that the territory was not part of the "all Israel" that followed Saul.

The strongest evidence that "all Israel" at this time was confined to the North does not emerge until after Saul's death and David's accession to the throne of Judah. Under Abner's control, Saul's son, Ishbaal, succeeded his father as king of the North, including "all Israel" (2 Sam 2:9). By then David had moved from Ziklag to Hebron, with no noticeable objection from his Philistine suzerains, where the elders of Judah made him king over the house of Judah (2:4). A protracted war between the house of Saul and the house of David ensued, with David winning the upper hand (2:12-3:1). Behind the scenes, Abner had initiated the negotiations that would finally win David the kingship of the North.

The account of Abner's treason is important both because it appears to be ancient and because it contains explicit evidence regarding "all Israel." It contains a remark that is reminiscent of the fear which Saul had stated to Jonathan when he thought David had returned to Bethlehem (1 Samuel 20). Echoing Saul, Abner threatened Ishbaal that David would rule Israel and Judah from Dan to Beersheba (3:10). Next, he offered David "all Israel" (3:12) and returned home to speak separately with the elders of Israel and the men of Benjamin (3:17, 19) before returning to Hebron to report the agreement that had been made with Israel and the house of Benjamin (3:19). He departed from Hebron with a promise that he would rally "all Israel" for David (3:21). But Abner was murdered by David's men before he could complete his coup. When the news was heard "all the people" (*kol ha'am*) and "all Israel" knew that David had no part in it (3:37), and Ishbaal and "all Israel" were alarmed (4:1). Still later, in a summary of his reign, David is credited with ruling Judah from Hebron and afterwards with ruling "all Israel" and Judah from Jerusalem (5:5). Finally, "all Israel" is mentioned again in the first list of David's court officers (8:5).

In these references the meaning of "all Israel" is clear. It designates a completely northern group which was the union of two separate elements, namely, Israel and Benjamin. A distinction between them has been seen before in the concubine story, and will be seen again after the Schism, but in those cases, "all Israel" stands for Israel apart from Benjamin whereas here it includes the two groups. In neither case does "all Israel" include Judah, and we must conclude that the "all Israel" led by Saul did not either.

The hostility between the house of David and the house of Saul did not subside once the Jerusalem monarchy was established. The struggle for leadership of "all Israel" continued throughout the period narrated in the Court History (2 Samuel 9-20),[23] and was not finally resolved until the accession of Solomon. Before that "all Israel" was claimed by parties who supported unity and by those whose power depended upon disengaging the North from Judahite control.

David reigned over "all Israel," as has been noted (8:15), and he led "all Israel" against the Aramaeans (10:17). In the troubled times with Absalom, however, David's rebellious son sowed dissention at the city gates and "by behaving this way toward 'all Israel' " stole the hearts of the men of Israel (15:6). Ahithophel advised Absalom to take the royal harem so that "all Israel" would see the act (16:21, 22), and Hushai warned him that "all Israel" knew David's bravery (17:10) and counseled him to call up "all Israel" from Dan to Beersheba for battle (17:11). He predicted that they would destroy a city if David hid there (17:13). After Absalom was murdered by Joab, "all Israel" fled (18:17). Finally, when the news that "all Israel" was planning to escort him back Jerusalem reached David, he sent word to the elders of Judah to remind them of his special relationship to them (19:12). In the debate that followed, the Israelites protested that they had ten shares in the king, implying an earlier tribal league of ten rather than twelve members (19:44).

Because of the foolish advice and intentional deceit in the remarks of Ahithophel and Hushai, and because the Court History is written to explain how David overcame northern threats to his sovereignty, it is difficult to determine at times whether the speaker was using "all Israel" as a name for the united kingdoms or whether he was appealing to the old separatist sympathies by using it as it was used during Saul's reign or before. Since Absalom's revolt was supported only by the North, as was Sheba's (ch. 20), Ahithophel may be drawing upon political nostalgia in his advice.[24] The meaning of "all Israel" as the North does appear in 18:17, and David himself emphasized separation between North and South by appealing directly to the Judahites in 19:12. There can be no doubt, however, that "all Israel" from Dan to Beersheba was ruled by David and that the meaning applied during the time of the Court History (17:11). This meaning of "all Israel" under David is confirmed in the accession scene of Solomon. Although I do not believe that 1 Kings 1-2 were part of the earliest Court History, the historicity and antiquity of the material in the chapters cannot be questioned.[25] There, Bathsheba asserted that "all Israel" expected Solomon to be king (1 Kgs 1:20) while Adonijah made the same claim (2:15). The same use of the term to describe the united monarchy continues in the narratives which describe Solomon's reign after his accession. Solomon was recognized throughout "all Israel" for his wisdom (3:28), and he offered sacrifices with (8:62, 65), conscripted workers from (5:27) and ruled over "all Israel" (4:1; 11:42). A single reference to his administrators breaks this pattern by assigning them to "all Israel" and Judah, but the statement is found within a text that is corrupt and cannot be trusted (4:7).[26] Thus, the historical use of the term during the united monarchy was to signify the dual kingdoms, although the more archaic, northern meaning sometimes surfaced.

At the time of the Schism, the meaning of the term changed again. Benjamin remained in union with Judah and Jerusalem, as is clear from 1 Kgs 12:21; 2 Chr 10:1 and 11:3.[27] This means that the schismatic group was not exactly the "all Israel" of Saul, but was instead the northern group without Benjamin, the same group that was mentioned in the account of the Levite's concubine. This group took with it the label "all Israel" and retained it until the fall of Samaria. The usage of the title is consistent. Because of the treatment "all Israel" received from Rehoboam (1 Kgs 12:16), it elected Jeroboam (12:1, 18, 20). When Ahijah prophesied the death of Abijah, "all Israel" mourned (14:13, 16). Nadab, Baasha and Omri were kings of "all Israel" (15:27, 33; 16:16, 17), Elijah summoned "all Israel" (18:18), and Micaiah saw "all Israel" scattered (22:17). As noted, there is no change in the usage throughout the period, and there is no reason to doubt the historicity of the records since the meaning is not the deuteronomic meaning seen in Moses' and Joshua's accounts. The references to "all Israel" in 2 Kings fit this pattern even though they may be glosses:[28] Jehoram mustered "all Israel" and then sent word to the king of Judah (3:6); Jehoram is called king of "all Israel" (9:14); and Jehu sent messengers throughout "all Israel" (10:21).

Surprisingly, there is no further mention of "all Israel" in the deuteronomic history. Because the writer worked under Josiah and placed such emphasis upon the term in his reconstruction of the history of the wilderness and settlement periods, it is striking to find that he has not depicted Josiah as the king of "all Israel." His reasons can be understood, however, when we realize that Josiah did not rule "all Israel" like his model, David, had. The deuteronomic history was intended, not as a history of Josiah's reign, but as a legitimation of Josiah and as a basis for his policies and reforms. His hopes for an "all Israel" from Dan to Beersheba had not been completed, and subsequent events determined that they would never be fulfilled.

When we turn to the Chronicler's use of "all Israel" we find that it is predictable, but that it is not consistent. He uses the phrase in several ways. In passages which he adopted from the deuteronomic historian, he either copied the phrase or added it in a way that reflected the deuteronomic meaning. Since we are concerned with the development of the term, we need not be concerned about the originality of the additions because they parallel the earlier meaning.[29] Its appearance in the writings of the Chronicler would mean only that an older meaning had survived. The uses which are distinctive, however, are of concern for tracing the historical development of the term. In these, the Chronicler used "all Israel" to mean Judah and Jerusalem, which for him were the authentic Israel.[30] A review of the passages where the term occurs will demonstrate both the inconsistency and the peculiar meaning that has been imposed.

"All Israel" occurs first in an introduction which classifies groups as they are listed in the Books of the Kings of Israel and Judah (1 Chr 9:1). The phrase does not appear again until the Hebron monarchy of David because the writer ignores a separate Judahite reign in order to give the impression that David became king of "all Israel" immediately after Saul's death. "All Israel" gathered at Hebron (11:1) and escorted the king and the ark to Jerusalem (11:4, 10; 12:39; 13:5, 6, 8; 15:3, 28). The Philistines heard that David had been made king of "all Israel" (14:8), and (in a use of Nathan's oracle that may be archaic) David was reminded that Yahweh had not had a permanent dwelling when he wandered with "all Israel" (17:6). David ruled over "all Israel" (18:14; 29:26) and led the group against the Aramaeans (19:17). One episode does deserve special comment since it differs from its parallel in 2 Samuel 24 where "all Israel" is not mentioned. In the Chronicler's report of the census, Joab was told to go from Dan to Beersheba (1 Chr 21:2), and he traversed "all Israel" (21:4), but he reported regarding "all Israel" and Judah (21:5). This sequence indicates the persistency of archaic uses which has been mentioned above.[31]

The "all Israel" governed by Solomon is the same in the Chronicler as in 1 Kings. Midrashic materials found in Chronicles, however, are of interest because they reveal the later historians' interest in the legitimacy of David and Judah as Yahweh's choices to rule "all Israel" (28:4, 8). Casting Judah as "all Israel" served to legitimate David and Solomon (29:21, 23, 25; 2 Chr 2:1; 7:6, 8; 9:30). Although the Chronicler could accept the concept of the united kingdoms as "all Israel" during the time of David and Solomon at least partially, the Schism caused him to interpret the term differently from the deuteronomic historian.[32] Two things are clear from his references to the divided monarchy: first, that the term was used for Judah rather than for the North; and second, that he again was not able to suppress the earlier, northern meaning completely.

The older meaning of "all Israel" as the North is found in reports of the Schism (10:1, 3, 16), in the war between Abijah and Jeroboam (Abijam in Kings) (13:4, 15) and in the quotation of Micaiah's prophecy (18:16). "All Israel" meaning the united monarchy as it had been used by the deuteronomist is found in the passages that pertain to Hezekiah (29:24; 30:1, 5, 6; 35:3). But the "all Israel" which is distinctively that of the Chronicler is found in the reports of events surrounding the Schism that mention Judah and Benjamin explicitly (11:3, 13; 12:1), and in the report of Joash's collection for the temple which was carried out in Judah, "all Israel" (24:5). Ezra and Nehemiah continue the Chronicler's Jerusalemite interpretation by stressing the liturgical importance of the returning Exiles (Ezra 2:70; 6:17; 8:25, 35; 10:5; Neh 7:72) and the legitimacy of the Jerusalem kings (Neh 12:47; 13:26).

We have noted McKenzie's statements about the importance of "all Israel" for understanding the role of Judah in ancient Israel and his belief that the phrase was coined by the scribes of David. This study has shown that he is right about the importance, but that the Davidic court was not its place of origin.

To summarize: the term was used at least as early as the days of the Yahwistic tribal league when it meant a group that had bound together with the Benjaminites. We know little of the "all Israel" group, but the use of the term apart from the Benjaminites — whom McKenzie feels were the bearers of northern Yahwism[33] — may infer that the group and the term were pre-Yahwistic.[34] The "all Israel" ruled by Saul was the union of these two earlier groups, known to us as the premonarchic tribal league. His kingdom probably included the members listed in Judges 5, a group of ten members, the ten shares referred to in the Israel-Judah debate in 2 Sam 19:44. Saul's monarchy represented the beginning of a politicizing process which accelerated rapidly and brought about the paganization of the Israelite nation within a few decades. Under David the process hastened, and Judah was brought into union with Israel under a common monarch. The term "all Israel" was adopted by the Jerusalemite court and was used to describe the united kingdom. Even if Judah had been previously Yahwistic, as the Caleb tradition suggests, the change was drastic for the Israelite community. The enduring hostility toward David and, finally, the Schism are ample proof of the resistance toward such a union. David and Solomon were able to suppress opposition to themselves through the use of political force, and except for the period of David's exile, they were able to rule the territory from Dan to Beersheba in spite of strong resistance. The Schism, however, forced a redefining of "all Israel." The boundaries of the oldest group known by the title were re-established, leaving Benjamin and Judah bound to each other and to Jerusalem. From then until its fall to Assyria, the North was referred to as "all Israel." Hezekiah and Josiah each launched reforms aimed at restoring the Davidic ideal. The Josian reform included a return to the Mosaic covenant as a basis for Israelite life and a restoration of the Davidic kingdoms. Josiah invested great confidence in literature as part of his effort and demonstrated this by emphasizing the newly discovered law book and by commissioning the writing of a history that would explain Israel's failure while it coincidently legitimated his reforms, especially in the eyes of the northerners. Elsewhere, I have presented fuller evidence to support this and to demonstrate that Josiah imposed the Davidic ideal upon the times of Moses and Joshua.[35] These conclusions are completely compatible with the evidence McKenzie has presented regarding the deuteronomic use of the land theme in the prologue to Deuteronomy.[36] In a later period, the Chronicler imitated the deuteronomist, not only by copying much of his material, but also by laying claim to the phrase "all Israel" in order to legitimate the Jerusalemite leadership and cult of his day.

Although a final decision regarding Davidic authorship of the books of Samuel must await further study, the use of "all Israel" outlined here supports an assumption that they were written by the Davidic scribes. Other literary evidence corresponds with the information that we now have about "all Israel." I believe that the Solomonic sections of the Succession Document are secondary in the narrative of 2 Sam 9-20, 1 Kings.[37] Once the Bathsheba episode in 2 Sam 11-12 and the succession scene in 1 Kings 1-2 have been excised, what is left in the two books of Samuel is an explanation of David's rise and his survival. This means that the addition of the Solomonic material was made shortly after Solomon's accession and that the addition transformed the original thrust of the narrative in order to up-date it and to demonstrate that Solomon was his father's legitimate successor. My arguments for this development are based on literary evidence, but we must also note the importance of the books and of their principal figure, David, for subsequent kings, priests, and historians. The deuteronomist accepted both almost completely, and the Chronicler drew upon each, mediated by the deuteronomist, for his work. Each of their works, like the books of Samuel, were up-dated and revised shortly after its original compilation.[38] It may be a coincidence, but the parallels which emerge when comparing the three histories are striking: the books of Samuel, compiled to legitimate David and to cast him in a hero's role, later revised; the deuteronomic history, compiled to legitimate Josiah's reforms by enhancing the Davidic ideal, later revised; the Chronicler's history, compiled to legitimate the Jerusalem authorities by stressing Davidic legitimacy, later revised. Each work was directed against a claim made by the North; each work drew upon the same traditions.

The second factor which combines with this "coincidence" of literature is the history of the term "all Israel." We have traced its stages of development and have found that several of the detectable changes correspond with the times when histories were written. Shifts in the meaning of the term took place at times when the traditions were reinterpreted and the history of Israel was recast. Since Judah was not included in Saul's kingdom, its introduction under David constituted one of the most drastic changes in Israel's history. The pressures against David's leadership of "all Israel" were enormous, but he withstood them, changed the meaning of the term, and produced a history — the books of Samuel — that justified his monarchy in the light of Israel's past. Thus, the history of Judah, the use of "all Israel," and the formation and transmission of the books of Samuel are closely connected.

1. See *The World of the Judges* (Englewood Cliffs: Prentice-Hall, 1965); "The Dynastic Oracle: II Samuel 7," *TS* 8 (1947) 187-220; "Royal Messianism," *CBQ* 19 (1957) 25-53; "The Elders in the Old Testament," *Bib* 40 (1959) 522-40; "The Four Samuels," *BR* 7 (1962) 3-18.

2. J. L. McKenzie, *A Theology of the Old Testament* (Garden City: Doubleday, 1974) 236, 244. McKenzie is only one of a growing number who doubt that Judah was joined to Israel before the time of David. See A. Jepsen, "Zur Überlieferungsgeschichte der Vatergestalten," *Wissenschaftlich Zeitschrift der Karl-Marx-Universität Leipzig* 3 (1953/54) 265-81; R. E. Clements, *Abraham and David: Genesis XV and Its Meaning for Israelite Tradition* (SBT 2/5; London: SCM, 1967) 44; R. de Vaux, "The Settlement

of the Israelites in Southern Palestine and the Origins of the Tribe of Judah," *Translating and Understanding the Old Testament* (eds. H. T. Frank and W. L. Reed; Nashville: Abingdon, 1970) 108-35; R. P. Carroll, "Psalm LXVIII: Vestiges of a Tribal Polemic," *VT* 21 (1971) 133-50; A. D. H. Mayes, *Israel in the Period of the Judges* (SBT 2/29; London: SCM, 1974) 107. One of the best treatments of the problem has been done by S. Herman, "Autonome Entwicklungen in den Königreichen Israel und Juda," VTSup 17 (1969) 139-58.

3.   J. L. McKenzie, Review of Jakob H. Grøbaek, *Die Geschichte vom Aufstieg Davids (1. Sam. 15 — 2. Sam. 5): Tradition und Komposition, CBQ* 34 (1972) 221. The phrase has received mention in a number of studies but has received very little attention by itself. See J. N. Schofield, " 'All Israel' in the Deuteronomic Writers," *Essays and Studies Presented to Stanley Arthur Cook*, (ed. D. W. Thomas; London: Taylor's Foreign Press, 1950) 25-34. M. Noth, *Das System der zwölf Stämme Israels* (BWANT 4 [1930]; reprint, Darmstadt: Wissenschaftlich Buchgesellschaft, 1966) 109-10. T. Ishida ("The Leaders of the Tribal League 'Israel' in the Pre-Monarchic Period," *RB* 80 [1973] 529-30) has suggested a technical usage for the word "Israel" which at times included all of the league and at times did not. He has ignored the significance of "all Israel."

4.   =Deut 1:9 (16:18).

5.   =Deut 11:6.

6.   L. Hartmann, "Daniel," *JBC* 448, 457.

7.   Deut 1:1; 5:1; 27:9; 31:1, 7; 32:45; 34:12.

8.   " 'All Israel' shall hear and fear" has been added to Deut 13:12 and 21:21; its use in 18:16 presumes the demand for centralization. See G. von Rad, *Deuteronomy* (Philadelphia: Westminster, 1966) 122.

9.   von Rad, *Deuteronomy*, 84. ⁻

10. McKenzie, *Judges*, 5.

11. Schofield, "All Israel," 28; J. A. Soggin, *Joshua* (Philadelphia: Westminster, 1972) 52-55; 94-97; 130.

12. R. Boling, *Judges* (AB 6A; Garden City: Doubleday, 1975) 278-79. W. Richter, *Traditionsgeschichtliche Untersuchungen zum Richterbuch* (Bonn: Peter Hanstein Verlag, 1963) 194-95; 233-36.

13. Boling, *Judges*, 160.

14. For the dating of the deuteronomic and deuteronomistic editions and the assignment of passages to each I follow F. M. Cross, *Canaanite Myth and Hebrew Epic* (Cambridge: Harvard University, 1973) 274-75, 287. *Kol yiśrā'ēl* does not appear in the Exilic material.

15. M. Noth, *Überlieferungsgeschichtliche Studien* (3rd ed.; Tübingen: Max Niemeyer Verlag, 1967).

16. McKenzie, "Four Samuels," 16. Others have recognized the confusion within the traditions but have come to different conclusions regarding the historical Samuel. See M. Noth, "Samuel und Silo," *VT* 13 (1963) 391-92; W. F. Albright, "Samuel and the

Beginnings of the Prophetic Movement," *Interpreting the Prophetic Tradition* (ed. H. M. Orlinsky; New York: Ktav, 1969) 164-66.

17. McKenzie, "Four Samuels," 14.

18. D. J. McCarthy, "II Samuel 7 and the Structure of the Deuteronomic History," *JBL* 84 (1965) 131. See J. Muilenburg, "The Form and Structure of the Covenantal Formulation," *VT* 9 (1959) 360-64; H. Seebass, "Traditionsgeschichte von I Sam 8, 10:17ff. und 12," *ZAW* 77 (1965) 289.

19. A. Weiser, "Die Legitimation des Königs David. Zur Eigenart und Entstehung der sogen. Geschichte von Davids Aufstieg," *VT* 16 (1966) 325-54. See F. Schicklberger, "Die Davididen und das Nordreich. Beobachtungen zur sog. Geschichte vom Aufstieg Davids," *BZ* 18 (1974) 258-63.

20. G. E. Mendenhall, "The Monarchy," *Int* 29 (1975) 158-59. The complexity of the problems surrounding monarchy have been treated in greater detail in Mendenhall's earlier work. See his *The Tenth Generation* (Baltimore: Johns Hopkins, 1973) esp. ch. 7.

21. A. Weiser, *Samuel. Seine geschichtliche Aufgabe und religiöse Bedeutung* (Göttingen: Vandenhoeck & Ruprecht, 1962) 107-71. My own arguments for the deuteronomic character of 1 Samuel 11 may be found in "Faith in Crisis: A Lesson from Samuel," *That They May Live* (ed. G. Devine; Staten Island: Alba, 1972) 229.

22. McKenzie, "Four Samuels," 7. Against arguments such as C. E. Hauer, "Does 1 Samuel 9:1 - 11:5 Reflect the Extension of Saul's Dominions?" *JBL* 86 (1967) 306-10. His view fails to recognize the uneven historical quality of the traditions McKenzie has studied. Also, too little attention is paid to David's shifting allegiances during Saul's reign.

23. I have argued this at greater length elsewhere. See "Court History or Succession Document? A Study of 2 Samuel 9-20 and 1 Kings 1-2," *JBL* 91 (1972) 172-81. The tension is recognized by W. Brueggemann, "On Coping with Curse: A Study of 2 Sam 16:5-14," *CBQ* 36 (1974) 176.

24. A. Alt, "Die Staatenbildung der Israeliten in Palästina," *Kleine Schriften zur Geschichte des Volkes Israel* (3 vols.; München: C. H. Beck'sche, 1959) 2. 48.

25. Flanagan, "Court History," 181.

26. 11:16 is a gloss.

27. Although confused in 1 Kgs 12:1, 20.

28. Schofield, "All Israel," 33.

29. At least three levels of interpretation can be found in the writings of the Chronicler. I have not separated the material pertaining to "all Israel" according to these levels since the presence of the term in each serves to emphasize its importance for the historian and his redactors. See D. N. Freedman, "The Chronicler's Purpose," *CBQ* 22 (1961) 436-42; F. M. Cross, "A Reconstruction of the Judean Restoration," *JBL* 94 (1974) 4-18; J. D. Newsome, Jr., "Toward a New Understanding of the Chronicler and His Purposes," *JBL* 94 (1975) 201-17; D. N. Freedman, "Son of Man, Can These Bones Live?" *Int* 39 (1975) 182-83.

30. R. L. Braun, "Solomonic Apologetic in Chronicles," *JBL* 92 (1973) 503-16. J. M. Myers, *I Chronicles* (AB 12; Garden City: Doubleday, 1965) 85, 88.

31. Myers, *I Chronicles*, 147.

32. Schofield, "All Israel," 34.

33. McKenzie, *Judges*, 89.

34. Full discussion of this point falls outside the scope of the present study. However, the independent work of McKenzie, Mendenhall and Freedman is clarifying the nature of the settlement period, and Freedman's studies on the early Hebrew poetry are especially useful. The manner in which the term "all Israel" is used cannot be studied alone in order to determine the faith of the earliest league, but the pattern studied here clearly suggests a pre-Benjaminite, and therefore a pre-Yahwistic, usage.

35. Forthcoming in *Studies in Religion* (Montreal).

36. J. L. McKenzie, "The Historical Prologue of Deuteronomy," *Fourth World Congress of Jewish Studies* (Jerusalem: World Congress of Jewish Studies, 1967) 100.

37. Flanagan, "Court History," 176-77.

38. See notes 14, 20 and 29 above.

ROLAND E. MURPHY, O. CARM.

Wisdom and Yahwism

The long-standing division of the Tanak has left the $k^e t\hat{u}b\hat{i}m$ rather undefined with respect to the types of literature contained therein. Lamentations and the work of the Chronicler are cheek by jowl with books traditionally associated with wisdom: Proverbs, Job and Ecclesiastes. Already, therefore, we have an omen of the world-view which we wish to explore in this paper: Wisdom and Yahwism go together.

From one point of view, this might seem to be incontrovertible fact. Has not "wisdom" been found all across the Hebrew bible?[1] Nonetheless, the marriage between wisdom and Yahwism has been an uneasy one in the pages of scholarly writings. The dilemma faced by the late G. E. Wright some years ago has been taken up, but the solutions remain ambiguous. In *God Who Acts* Wright implied that he did not know what to do with wisdom literature in his view of biblical theology.[2] G. von Rad, who in virtue of his *heilsgeschichtlich* emphasis should have had even more difficulty with wisdom than Wright, gave a sweeping orientation to wisdom as Israel's "response." This insight is indeed attractive, but "response" loses its aptness when it is seen to be applicable as well to the Torah and the Prophets. The term is simply too broad to be effective, and it is significantly toned down in von Rad's final book on wisdom.[3] W. Zimmerli related wisdom to creation theology, especially as presented in the first chapters of Genesis.[4] While the writer agrees with Zimmerli, there is a lingering question: is this approach too apologetic, as though wisdom has to be justified because it is not salvation history? C. Westermann also seems to "justify" wisdom by subsuming it under the aegis of "blessing" in the OT (cf. Gen 1:28; 2:3).[5]

On the negative side some have seriously attacked wisdom as a genuine expression of Israelite faith. In 1970 H. D. Preuss concluded by denying a theological relationship of wisdom literature to the "real" OT. Indeed, he found it "dangerous" to take over wisdom literature into the texts for preaching.[6] In 1972 he returned to the topic and presented a portrayal of the God represented in the older wisdom of Israel. In this he seriously questioned if the Yahweh of the prophets or the Yahweh of divine law is also the Yahweh of wisdom, because what is said of him in the older wisdom (Proverbs 10 - 29) does not go beyond what ancient Near Eastern wisdom literature has said about "God."[7]

Although he has written more extensively concerning this thesis, Preuss is not alone in recognizing an antithesis between Yahwism and wisdom. G. Mendenhall has written, "With Solomon's charisma of wisdom, received at the old Gibeonite high place, almost certainly in connection with a pagan incubation ritual, the old pagan tradition of some god as the source of royal or other wisdom was reintroduced into Palestinian politics. And this had nothing to do with the Yahwistic tradition, while the gods as the donors of technical wisdom goes back at least to old Sumerian myth."[8] In a similar vein, but in a very broad generalization, E. Würthwein contrasts the picture of God in wisdom with that in the rest of the OT: the God of wisdom is without mystery, and his ways can be calculated by reason, whereas the God of the covenant is sovereign and free. Würthwein sees the work of Job and Qohelet as a corrective and purification of the wisdom concept of God which rests on "foreign" presuppositions.[9]

In this welter of controversy the present writer would make the following observations concerning wisdom and Yahwism, with the purpose of dissipating what should be considered a false problem. Ultimately the alleged incompatibility of wisdom and Yahwism is a logical creation (and Western logic, at that), and it is not real.

1. At the root of current discussion lies the assumption that Israel's understanding of Yahweh as working in the historical order is more orthodox, more "Yahwistic" than her understanding of him through nature or by human experience. In the conceptual order there is something to be said for the distinctiveness of Yahwism as an historical religion, despite the reserves of B. Albrektson.[10] One can select in the bible certain unique elements in Hebrew religion: the series of covenants (patriarchal, Mosaic and Davidic, however they are to be held together), the saving acts of the Exodus, the dominion of the Lord in history, the Torah, etc. One may even claim that these are the areas in which appears the exclusive quality of Israelite faith as "Yahwistic" faith. Here Israel stands in the particularity of her faith over against her neighbors.

But can this particularity carry the weight of "purity" with which many theologians (at least by implication) invest it? Everyone would grant that even in these essential aspects Israel was considerably influenced, at least in expression, by the surrounding culture (e.g., the concept of covenant and the Hittite treaties, etc.). The point to be made here is that, for all the uniqueness of Israel's view of the Lord and history, such a criterion is itself a mixed one. Emerging victorious from the conflict with Baal, Yahweh came to receive the epithets of Baal. There is nothing "pure," nor need there be, about Israelite religion. The logic of Hosea is helpful here. He tells Israel that it was the Lord who gave her "the grain, the wine, and the oil" (Hos 2:8). The claims of Baal are boldly usurped by Yahweh. Nature, as the area in which Yahweh's will and direction (cf. Isa 28:23-29) are also to be found, is not to be separated from history, nor is Yahweh's activity in nature viewed as secondary to his activity in history.

But the issue is deeper than outside influence upon Israel. Many theologians make the value judgment that the "essence" of Israelite religion lies in its historical framework. There is no question about these typical traditions constituting the heart of Israel's liturgy and "remembrance."[11] But life is larger than liturgy, and it is in life and its varied experiences that Israelite religion took shape.

Where was the centre of life? It was (and remains) in the daily experience of mankind: the human response to nature, the response of humans to each other, growth in self-understanding through experience and the acquired wisdom of the ages. It is true that large areas of this daily experience were covered by the stipulations of the covenant, especially by the decalogue. But there were other areas of life not really touched by the decalogue: personal diligence, self-control, attitudes (even if ambivalent) towards the poor, pride, trust in one's judgment, etc. In short, the formation of responsible character, over and beyond the goals of the decalogue, form the heart of wisdom teaching, and this was seen as responsible Yahwism. Within this sphere, between the limits of ethical and unethical conduct, lay the grey area which deserved to be put into perspective by the covenanted people of the Lord. They did so as worshipers of Yahweh, not merely as ancient Near Eastern tribes. The wisdom lessons and ideals were an essential expression of their understanding of the Lord and of life. It seems wrong-headed to separate all this out of their religion and faith.

In support of this view one may also adduce the thesis of E. Gerstenberger, which has been convincing to many.[12] The decalogue itself is largely the outgrowth of the community, the family or tribal ethos. Here lies the origin of much that came to be codified later in law, and presented also as wisdom. The expression of the people's faith, their living with the Lord, embraced both the sacral and the non-sacral, and the latter is not to be equated with the profane or the non-Yahwistic.

Hence, one may ask: By what right is Yahwism defined exclusively by the action of God in history: the patriarchal promises, the Exodus and Sinai events, etc.? This is a correct base, because it captures what is distinctive of Israel. But it may also be too narrow, when one considers the total religious experience of the Israelite, or at least, of the biblical record. Instead of inserting wisdom into Yahwism, with Yahwism as a kind of implicit determinant of orthodoxy, one might rather turn the question around: How is Yahwism to be inserted into wisdom, into what was the daily experience of the Israelite? The wisdom literature constitutes a significant index to this concrete experience of the worshipper of Yahweh, and it deserves to be heard, just as much as the liturgical kerygma.

2. The polarity of wisdom and Yahwism seems to be based upon a particular interpretation of wisdom as a search for a world order established and upheld by God. Particularly important within this order is the so-called act-consequence relationship: every good/evil deed produces its proper good/evil consequence. This view was first urged by K. Koch:[13] God does not intervene directly; he is outside of the mechanism of deed and result, but he is the guarantor of its working (Koch used the metaphor of *Hebammendienst*, or midwifery, for the divine role). At the present time the interpretation of OT wisdom is dominated by the concepts of order and the act-consequence relationship, as can be seen from the studies of H.-H. Schmid, H. Gese, and G. von Rad.[14]

The notion of a divinely established order in OT wisdom is influenced by the role of *ma'at* in the Egyptian world view. *Ma'at* is both goddess and the divine established order in the world. The term is variously translated as "justice," or "truth," etc. If man's life is to be a harmonious one, his actions must be geared to this order. The order is both ethical and cosmological; wise actions affirm and establish such an order in the world.

Is this reconstruction of the Egyptian view of *ma'at* really applicable to the Israelite understanding of wisdom and secondary causality? A distinction is necessary here. As C. Kayatz has shown, the description of personified wisdom in Proverbs 8 has been influenced by the Egyptian understanding of *ma'at*.[15] But it is another thing to say that wisdom is the order of creation, as *ma'at* was for the Egyptian, and the object of man's inquiry. I would prefer to say that wisdom attempts to establish or impose a kind of order upon the myriad human experiences that form the raw material of wisdom sayings and upon nature itself. The direction of Israelite wisdom is other than that of Egyptian *ma'at*. The sayings of the sages flow from experience and put order into the chaotic events that make up human life. How does experience help to categorize pride? It comes before a fall (Prov 11:2; 16:18). What judgment can be passed upon the appearance of things? Certain physical characteristics suggest mischief

(Prov 16:30), but on the other hand, it is the Lord who proves the spirit (Prov 16:12; 21:2).

Comparisons with nature are frequent in wisdom literature. Certain analogies are easy to make: pleasing words can be compared to a honeycomb (Prov 16:24), the lazy sleeper with a door turning on its hinges (Prov 26:14), etc. But this has nothing to do with the discovery of an order inherent in the world of conduct and nature. There is a coordination of experience and the created world; they illustrate each other. Human conduct is captured in observations and illumined by comparisons; specific ideals are formed, and then inculcated. Indeed, the didactic character of wisdom is not sufficiently adverted to by modern scholarship. It is easy to romanticize about the sages' openness to experience and their readiness to revise their insights. There are some observational sayings that betray this; but most of the time the sages were teaching, inculcating the lessons of tradition, and of (Yahwistic) experience.

It is true that several wisdom texts contemplate nature, as it were, for herself: the smallest but wisest creatures on the earth (Prov 30:24-28), the four things that never say "enough" (Prov 30:16-17). The influence of Egyptian onomastica, or name-lists, seems to underlie the listing of heavenly phenomena in such passages as Job 38. But one can hardly speak of discovering order. Where order does clearly appear, as in the stability of events in nature, it is a term of comparison rather than an object of discovery. The Davidic covenant is compared with the Lord's covenant with day and night (Jer 30:20-21). God and man are the really important parameters of Israel's understanding of nature: "the heavens declare the glory of God" (Ps 19:2); "when I behold your heavens, the work of your fingers, the moon and stars which you set in place — what is man that you should be mindful of him?" (Ps 8:5). Nature provides for man a language of, and about, God; it is an area in which God is at work, but it does not become a field for the investigation of order.

Although von Rad accepts an order in nature as the object of wisdom's search, he has also expressed his reservations about this: "In view of all this, one must therefore be cautious in one's use of the term 'order' which we, too, have felt unable to dispense with in our discussion. Can one really say that the teachers were searching for a world order? Our findings, especially the discussion of the Yahweh-proverbs, suggested, rather, that one can in no sense speak of a world order as really existing between God and man."[16]

Next, the order implicit in the theory of act-consequence needs to be considered. As indicated above, this view holds that the good or evil deed produces of itself a good or evil consequence; God stands outside of this "order," which he guarantees. One cannot easily deny that such an explanation is a fitting one for many so-called "retribution" texts (e.g., Prov 25:26-27). But the direct intervention of God, responding to good or evil human acts, is also clearly stated; indeed, the primary causality of God in all things is an OT cliché. Koch attempts to reconcile these points of view: God is portrayed as the guarantor of the working out of the mechanism of good and evil. This is a reconstruction, although there is no effort in the bible to correlate these views, just as there is no effort to correlate human responsibility or freedom with the omnipresent causality of God. Israel lives easily with both understandings. The casting of Yahweh as the guarantor or supervisor is a logical answer to the dilemma, but it remains on an abstract level. There may very well be a profound insight into good and evil present in the understanding of deed-consequence, but does this deserve to be elevated into an "order" of things? Even if many sayings in Proverbs and elsewhere suggest that the inner dynamism of an act produces certain consequences, was this insight more than simply an insight, according to which many sayings were phrased? Across the pages of the OT the Lord is represented as actively responding to man. The concept of the "fate-working" (*schicksalwirkend*) deed is overshadowed by the relationship in which man stands to the Lord who may "repent" of the evil/good which he intended to do (Jer 18:1-11).

Koch claims that the concept of the "fate-working" deed is overthrown by Job and Qohelet. But both of these works are concerned with God, not an abstract order, and not a "guarantor" God. It is the "work" (*ma'ăśěh*) of this God, his dealing with mankind, that Qohelet cannot figure out (8:17; 11:5). He has no doubt about the Lord's active role in life ("for to whatever man he sees fit he gives wisdom and knowledge and joy. . . ." 2:26; cf. 3:17; 7:26; 11:9). Job is not fighting with an order; he knows who is to be blamed, and he says this quite clearly (9:20-22). He will not be satisfied with an explanation of a breakdown in order; but he will be confronted in a theophany, and he will eventually yield (42:5). The relationship here is between God and man.

The above considerations concerning "order" and Israelite wisdom are important not only because they raise questions about a current view concerning wisdom. They also strike at the heart of the arguments (of Preuss and others) that would isolate wisdom thought from the rest of the OT. These arguments proceed as if the Lord were the "God of Order," as opposed to being the "God of Israel." Such a position sets up a straw man that is easy to knock down, but the position is itself irrelevant to the concrete experience of the Lord in the life of Israel.

3. Finally, we may give a brief consideration to some of the arguments put forward by H. D. Preuss against the legitimacy of wisdom, as opposed to Yahwism. Preuss' concern is to see if a distinctive or even transforming influence of Yahwistic faith can be detected in the sayings of Proverbs 10 - 29. This is the wrong question because it cannot be answered on the basis of the criteria which it is demanding. It is ultimately asking for the traditional, distinctive traits of Yahweh's intervention in Israel's history, and of course, this cannot be found. Hence it is easy game for Preuss to make his point: wisdom is dealing with the mechanical dynamism of deed and consequence; the divinity is not the savior of Israel, but the *Urheber* or creator-god; the expressions of human acts being approved by (*raṣôn*) or being an abomination (*tō'ēbāh*) to the Lord can be paralleled in Egypt; even expressions of "fear" and "trust" can also be found. In other words, the argument is so constructed that the "foreign" character of this block of wisdom (Proverbs 10 - 29) stands out irrefutably. It is not an answer, as von Rad long ago pointed out, to claim "Yahweh"-sayings as typically "Israelite." The use of the divine name is simply not sufficient, since it could be simply a question of substitution, as it were, of the divine name.

However, the real issue is whether or not the claim of illegitimacy for wisdom is in a sense game-playing. The question to be asked is: who is the god, and how are the factors of "fear," "trust," etc., understood in this block of material? It is incredible to suppose a simple game of substitution, or of mechanical derivation from Egyptian theology (not merely Egyptian wisdom).

My concern is not to deny influence from Egypt or any other quarter in the matter of Israel's understanding of the Lord. Zimmerli has pointed out that the God of the Fathers was only later identified with the Yahweh of the exodus experience, and we have already indicated that the Lord did inherit some of the prerogatives of Baal. If one were to view such realities or texts in the same way that Preuss interprets the wisdom literature, the patriarchal narratives, for instance, would be suspect, a *reductio ad absurdum*.

In this whole question it is important to distinguish between the historical situation in ancient times and the later settings — between the ancient Israelite who was gradually defining his belief, and the later Israelite who had the sacred traditions to call on for this belief. But surely it is decapitating even the early Israelite (Proverbs 10 - 29, by Preuss' theory), to imagine that he was not responding to the Lord of the covenant in the area of wisdom.

What is the real mistake behind Preuss' underestimation, if not denigration, of biblical wisdom literature? I think it is the principle of the canon within the canon. Obviously these books do not belong to *his* operating canon. He has made some configuration of (Christian) salvation-history as the principle of selection and interpretation. What does not fit here is to be excluded. However, if one accepts the total canon, and does not attempt to find an absolute *Sachmitte* from which all else is to be ever judged, a different possibility arises: how is one to hear the word of God that is not the result of salvation history, but the result of human experience suffused by God's presence? That is the interesting question which the wisdom literature proposes to us. Two significant answers can be only adumbrated here. First, there is the possibility that the style may well outweigh the content, i.e., the concrete "truth" of Proverbs or any other book may be far less important than the fact that a style of life is approved in the bible: a finding God in experience, a wrestling with what we would call the "secular" to find God. Secondly, does not wisdom serve as a corrective to a theology that is too exclusively defined in terms of sin and salvation? W. Brueggemann[17] has expressed this corrective aspect very well:

> Wisdom is a surprising resource for the continual re-examination of Israel's faith. The wise man in his method sought to be always in dialogue with the reality of his environment. He was always curious about the intricacies of his social order, the delicacy of human relationship, the marvel and mystery of his natural environment. He always wanted to know. He would not settle for yesterday's answers but asked how it looks today.
>
> Proverbs, of course, is an example of a style of life in which men really ask about the message given in their environment. In such a dialogue nothing is trivial or safely ignored. Each small turn of events speaks a word to us and discloses a freshness about the world in which we live. The word spoken is often a new word, unexpected, not in conformity with how we thought it should be and always was.

1. For a summary of views, and a judgment on the methodology involved, cf. J. L. Crenshaw, "Method in Determining Wisdom Influence upon 'Historical' Literature," *JBL* 88 (1969) 129-42. The scholar whom this Festschrift is honoring took a very broad view in his presidential address to the Society of Biblical Literature, "Reflections on Wisdom," *JBL* 86 (1967) 1-9. Here McKenzie makes an important distinction between wisdom as wisdom literature and wisdom as an approach to reality (2-3), although he seems to have overreached himself with his conclusion, "Evidently I have identified the wise men of Israel with the historians, and thus effectively designated the historical books as wisdom literature" (8). He applies the wisdom standard (the validity of experience) to the collective experience of the group, and hence to the salvation history; see the criticism by G. von Rad, *Wisdom in Israel* (Nashville: Abingdon, 1972) 291.

2. *God Who Acts* (SBT 8; London: SCM, 1952) 103-04.

3. Compare Israel's "answer" (under which von Rad grouped Psalms and wisdom literature in *Old Testament Theology* [New York: Harper & Row, 1962] 1, 359-455) with *Wisdom*, 307, where he writes: "the wisdom practised in Israel was a response made by a Yahwism confronted with specific experiences of the world." The present paper is an extended commentary on that basic insight.

4. "The Place and Limit of the Wisdom in the Framework of the Old Testament Theology," *SJT* 17 (1964) 146-58. Zimmerli returns to the problem in a 1973 article reproduced in *Studien zur alttestamentlichen Theologie und Prophetie: Gesammelte Aufsätze II* (Theologische Bücherei 51; München: Kaiser, 1974) 27-54. The article is entitled, "Considerations about the Form of an Old Testament Theology," and pp. 46-51 take up the question how wisdom is to be integrated into OT theology. Among other considerations (emphasis on the just/wicked contrast in Proverbs, significance of "fear of the Lord," and the name of Yahweh) he stresses the need of weighing the importance of Job and Ecclesiastes in the total view of wisdom (and why not Ben Sira and the Wisdom of Solomon?). He refuses to recognize wisdom as an "illegitimate" element in the OT and utilizes his previously expressed view about wisdom and creation. Then he writes: "By neglecting any reference to the historical memory of Israel's faith, wisdom puts a question to Old Testament theology: Must one always have an historical explanation, explicitly referred to and fully formed, as the center (of theology)? And another question: Did not Israel know the 'I am who I am,' whom she recognized only from the historical experience that explained the name of Yahweh, also as the One who is attached to his creation without being a captive of it?" (50).

5. *Der Segen in der Bibel und im Handeln der Kirche* (München: Kaiser, 1968) 40-42.

6. "Erwägungen zum theologischen Ort alttestamentlicher Weisheitsliteratur," *EvT* 30 (1970) 393-417; see 414, 416.

7. "Das Gottesbild der älteren Weisheit Israels," *Studies in the Religion of Ancient Israel,* VTSup 23 (1972) 117-45; see 144.

8. "The Shady Side of Wisdom," *A Light unto My Path: Old Testament Studies in Honor of Jacob M. Myers* (ed. H. N. Bream, et al.; Philadelphia: Temple University, 1974) 324.

9. E. Würthwein, *Die Weisheit Aegyptens und das Alte Testament* (Marburg: Elwert, 1960) esp. 10 and 13-17.

10. B. Albrektson, *History and the Gods* (Lund: Gleerup, 1967); see the criticism by von Rad, *Wisdom*, 290, and the review of W. Lambert, *Or* 39 (1970) 170-77.

11. Cf. H. Zirker, *Die kultische Vergegenwärtigung der Vergangenheit in den Psalmen* (BBB 20; Bonn: Hanstein, 1964). Even in the liturgy (Psalms) there is a striking absence of reference to typical sacral traditions. The psalmists in the main are appealing to human experience(s). They are buoyed up by the collective experience of the past in which they share (Ps 22:5, "in you our fathers trusted"), but the action is in the concrete present and the immediate past of the one who prays. How limited one's liturgical experience must be if liturgy and ultimately the essentials of religion are to be reduced to a center as a profession of faith.

12. E. Gerstenberger, *Wesen und Herkunft des "apodiktischen Rechts"* (WMANT 20; Neukirchen-Vluyn: Neukirchener Verlag, 1965); see the remarks of M. E. Andrew in J. J. Stamm - M. E. Andrew, *The Ten Commandments in Recent Research* (SBT 2/2; Naperville: Allenson, 1967) 44-75.

13. Koch's 1955 article is reproduced, along with other studies pertinent to the subject, in a volume edited by him: *Um das Prinzip der Vergeltung in Religion und Recht des Alten Testaments* (Wege der Forschung 125; Darmstadt: Wissenschaftliches Buchgesellschaft, 1972).

14. H. -H. Schmid, *Wesen und Geschichte der Weisheit* (BZAW 101; Berlin: Töpelmann, 1966); H. Gese, *Lehre und Wirklichkeit in der alten Weisheit* (Tübingen: Mohr, 1958).

15. *Studien zu Proverbien 1-9* (WMANT 22; Neukirchen: Neukirchener Verlag, 1966).

16. von Rad, *Wisdom*, 106-07.

17. Notably in "Scripture and an Ecumenical Life-Style. A Study in Wisdom Theology," *Int* 24 (1970) 3-19, and *In Man We Trust* (Richmond: John Knox, 1972), from which (115) the quotation is taken.

BRUCE VAWTER, C. M.

Prophecy and the Redactional Question

The problem which perennially faces the conscientious translator of the bible or its commentator is: which bible does he translate, on which bible does he comment? The problem looms largest for the Christian exegete of the OT; but it is no less a problem for the Jewish expositor of the OT and even, in some sense, for the Christian interpreter of the NT. The problem is common because it is constituted by the common historical fact of redaction, and the historical fact of redaction is that it dates almost from the first moment when the biblical word began to be committed to writing. The fact explains the phenomenon noted by Elias Auerbach:[1]

> the deeper one probes into the composition of the Hebrew Bible, the more he is confronted by a phenomenon unique in world literature: There are, in fact, two Bibles.

However unique the phenomenon may be, we are not prepared to say; but a phenomenon it undoubtedly is. Furthermore, on Auerbach's own principles, the number of bibles involved probably cannot be limited to two. He went on in his remarks:

> Even to the present day the reader's comprehension of the Bible as far as the important developments of Israel's external and spiritual history are concerned comes rather through the redaction than through the original traditions and the accounts of the older original sources.

Auerbach was concerned only with the "great" redaction of Israel's sacred literature, the rereading and recasting of its history that took place in the wake of the national disaster we call the Babylonian captivity, in the long generation that produced the deuteronomic history structured about a rigid (one might even say, deterministic) theology of covenant, and the Priestly theology and history with its somewhat different concerns and preoccupations. But just as it may be doubted that the redactional activity of this era may properly be reduced to one alone in inspiration and intent, it must also be observed that this particular "great" redaction was neither the first nor the last in the long process by which most of the OT writings have

127

come down to us who read them today.

The complexities of the redactional process present the biblical translator and expositor with his dilemmas and trilemmas.

What is to be said, for example, in reply to the apparently reasonable stance assumed by "conservative" translators, Jewish or Christian, who profess to render the OT texts as precisely as possible "as they stand" or "in their canonical form"? In this form, we are told, the OT is truly scripture, the finished product of a faith community. In this form, it is further alleged, the texts must be wrestled with in preference to all conjectural emendation however likely: as long as sense can be extracted from the texts in this form they are in presumptive possession against all the alternatives. We are confronted, we see, by two assumptions, one involving historical fact and the other deriving from it a methodological principle. But the fact, on the one hand, is not all that certain, while on the other hand the methodology begs the question in view of a history of transmission of the OT texts that is, indeed, certain.

Even in its finished form, it is doubtful that the entire Hebrew OT can be reduced to the status of a single canon. Rather, there are in it the residues of several canons, several redactions, which have not always been harmonized one with another. That harmonization which did take place, which justifies our speaking of *a* bible, is the working of a later tradition which most certainly sprang from the OT and continued its process, but just as certainly was subsequently imposed upon it. Therefore when we approach the OT not simply as a collection of ancient literary documents but as religious literature, it is necessary either that we select one canon of this literature at the expense of others or that we assume them all together, along with all of their internal tensions. In some instances, when redaction has not merely manipulated a received text but has actually altered it internally, we have only the option of choosing our canon.

An example of this necessary choice occurs in Amos 8:3, a line from the fourth of Amos' visions of the doom of Israel, which both RSV and NAB on "conservative" principles render: "The songs of the temple shall become wailings in that day." Contrast NEB and SBJ: "The singing women in the palace shall howl." RSV and NAB have chosen to translate the text as it was meant to be read by the Masoretic editors of the Hebrew OT, while NEB and SBJ have stripped it of its redaction and — admittedly by conjecture — have translated what the prophet Amos (or *his* editor) originally said.

There would seem to be no question about this.[2] The word *šîrôt* as "songs" would be an anomaly in this text. While it is true that there is a feminine singular form of *šîr* which turns up a number of times in the OT (never in Amos), it is likewise true that a feminine plural form never (otherwise) occurs. Always the plural is masculine: *šîrîm* (and so in Amos 5:23 and 8:10). The redaction on which the Masoretes depended produced the anomalous form by altering an earlier *šārôt* (cf. 2 Chr 25:35) in order to adjust to a post-Exilic Jerusalem scene a text that had at first applied to an eighth century Samaria situation. The same process forced an entirely new meaning upon the verb of the sentence.[3] There was no need to change the word *hêkāl* (ultimately derived from the Sumerian *ê-gal*, "great house"), since it already meant equally well palace or temple (in the latter acceptation, originally conceived as the palace of a god). Now that royal palaces were no more and *hêkāl* was replacing older expressions to designate the Jerusalem temple, it could not be allowed that there should be singing women there in defiance of the post-Exilic law which assigned the music of the temple firmly and exclusively to the male voices of the Levitical choirs. Thus this present redaction had a theological as well as a chronological motivation.

It might be objected at this point that the redaction in question has affected very little if at all the development of the human spirit, and that tracking it down is a matter chiefly of archival and philological interest. The objection has its measure of truth. However, there is some value in treating of an example of this kind, both to show how pervasive has been the influence of redaction, extending down to minutiae which at this remove may be thought trifling and of little practical consequence, and also to underscore the time-conditionedness of the redactional enterprise. The theological bias that first provoked the redaction and that may have addressed itself to what was then a significant issue, may no longer respond to any such issue at all. Instead, the theological issues of a later age may require quite different biases, including, perhaps, the one that was originally intended by the author of the redacted passage. We are cautioned, in other words, against assuming that the development of any given text within the life of a faith community has invariably reached some peak of relevance at the stage that has come to be designated "canonical." That peak, for a given age, might have been achieved earlier in the process, or it may be yet to come.

All of the prophetic works, Amos' included, have through redaction been made into books for the comfort and consolation of Israel, however inexorable may have been their original message of doom and condemnation. There can be no doubt about the necessary and vital function that these redactions served in nourishing the spiritual wants of a people during trying and perilous times, and of the hope that they offered in the face of every contrary human sign; but it would be obviously disastrous to interpret the whole of Israel's prophetic experience simply in the light of its postexilic redactional adaptation. To do this would be not only to cancel out an essential chapter in the history of Israel and of religion, it could also, in a time of other exigencies and imperatives, lead to an unintended triumphalism and unjustified self-righteousness, to a *Herrenvolk* conception of divine election from which the indispensable ingredients of judgment and service have been extracted. And if such a resultant caricature of prophecy has held perils for Judaism, how much more has it held them for Christianity! In their redacted form uncritically assimilated and with the accretion of an unbiblical and anti-biblical mythology of prophetical experience, the prophets for long in Christian history were oracular ciphers, at one with the Sibyls as providing chapter headings to a catalogue of putative predictions thought to have been fulfilled to the letter in NT times, with their historical individuality and reality almost totally obliterated in the process. Otto Eissfeldt has rightly claimed for modern critical biblical study the credit for having restored Israelite prophecy to its proper place not only in genuine history but also in the record of genuine religious experience,[4] a thing which it did and could do only by seeking the *ipsissima vox prophetae* behind the words of canonical redaction. Particularly in connection with the prophetical literature, indeed, has the biblical expositor found himself frequently in tension with the biblical translator; for if the latter felt it his duty to render the "canonical" text at every turn, the former knew that this could be universally done only at the expense of biblical misunderstanding. What is true of the prophetical literature, nevertheless, is true also in other measures of most of the rest of biblical literature.

We can add another twist of the screw of canonical complexity. Since canon was only begun in the bible and completed only after it, it could be fairly argued that the Christian has no business at all in translating as his bible the Hebrew OT. It could be fairly argued, that is, if we were willing to pursue down to its last logical conclusion the argument for translating a "canonical" text. When the Jewish translator takes for his basic biblical text the *masora*, to be rendered critically and discounting its occasional errors and lapses, he is acting consistently within a tradition — a Jewish, not a Christian tradition, of course — reflected and elucidated not in the *masora* alone but also in other Jewish sources that grew up together with it. Not so with the Christian translator of the MT. He approaches this text (as some Jewish commentators are careful to point out) as an alien, both factually and historically. Factually, because as it stands the *masora* testifies to a religious experience outside his own and usually outside his scholarly competence as well. It must be accounted passing strange, as Morton Smith has correctly observed,[5] that the so-called critical editions of the Hebrew OT most used today by scholars, which have been published under Christian auspices, are in reality reproductions of the *masora* down to its last synagogic detail, and that they make no attempt whatever, except by way of footnotes, to suggest the restoration of an original text — the conventional acceptation of the task of a critical edition of any document — even when the MT is clearly wrong and a suggested emendation is clearly right.[6] Historically, the Christian stands outside the MT tradition, because the OT of the early Christian church was not the Hebrew bible, let alone its *masora*, but rather the Greek LXX.

Obviously, we do not intend to argue, as some have argued,[7] that on the basis of its having formed the NT and the early Christian church the LXX is somehow a Christian or the Christian OT that ought to be preferred to the Hebrew. The LXX is a translation, sometimes accurate and sometimes inept, of another literature; and when it is inept a translation does not become right simply through the sanction of usage or because it has inspired Christian thoughts. Jerome's hardly won struggle for the *hebraica veritas* in the early fifth century,[8] which finally prevailed in the Reformation, was certainly no misdirection of energies. An historical religion like Christianity seeks contact with its literary origins, which are reflected only mediately through a translation. At the same time, the LXX is often deliberately "inept" in its translation: which is to say that it is also frequently a redaction — a Jewish redaction, as it happens, yet more proximate to Christianity than some of the redaction of the *masora* — representing the same kinds of adaptation and alteration that have occurred within the purely Hebrew transmission of the biblical text. Rigorous adherence to the principle that the text to be translated should be the redacted text of a faith community might seem to demand, therefore, that the LXX be heard in preference for its redactions, unless we are arbitrarily to set limits on the time, the geography, and the language of the redactional tradition.

Rigorous adherence to the principle we have never had, thank God. The Greek-speaking church, understandably, has retained the LXX for its OT, and Jerome never really succeeded in dislodging the LXX from the liturgical usage of Western Christianity. A conception of the "inspired," i.e., the canonical character of the LXX redaction/translation was certainly operative in both these instances, along with other considerations that doubtless add up to nothing more edifying than the inertia of custom. Jerome himself, despite his insistence on the *hebraica veritas* (which, to be sure, he understood in a rather naïve fashion), produced in the Vulgate a "Christian" OT which frequently owed to the LXX — or to the NT, indeed — as much as or more than it did to the Hebrew and Aramaic he had learnt through such toil and pain.[9] Martin Luther also professedly translated a "Christian" OT, sharing many of Jerome's presuppositions,[10] but he also thought it more important to get back to the language of the initial scriptural inspiration. Even modern biblical versions occasionally lapse into the habits of the past, as when, for example, the *'almâ* of Isa 7:14 is rendered "virgin" (NAB, RSV mg) in deference to the LXX and Matt 1:23 rather than to the evident sense of the Hebrew. Even when the LXX was widely accepted as possessing a normative tradition, the church was never of a single mind concerning the extent to which it determined or presupposed a canon of scripture. While the Council of Hippo in A.D. 393, for example, upheld in the West the longer, "Alexandrian" canon based on the LXX,[11] in the East the Council of Laodicea of about 360 had already restricted itself to what is essentially the "Palestinian" canon of the Hebrew OT and had explicitly rejected as noncanonical various of the books long contained in the LXX.[12] When during the Reformation and Counter-reformation the Roman church finally decided in favor of most — not all — of the additional books and parts of books that had been introduced into the canon through the LXX, while another course was followed by most of the Reformed churches, the basis of the choice in each case was a (disputed) Christian precedent.

We should hardly want the situation to be otherwise than it is. Obviously, no one would dream of translating the verbs in the second verse of the book of Amos into a past tense, as the LXX did, rather than into the present or future indicated by the Hebrew. This, despite the fact that the LXX choice was not done in ignorance but was doubtless deliberate, indicating the conviction of the translator concerning the relevance of the prophecy to his time. The LXX amounts here to a faith-inspired redaction, in other words, quite as respectable and as worthy of consideration as the post-Exilic Hebrew redaction of Amos 8:3 already noted. Our instincts rebel against the idea of reproducing what has been an obvious change of an original text. At least, they rebel in the case of the prophetic literature: in other areas of the bible acknowledged redactional alterations are accepted as a matter of course as constituting the ultimate text of the "final author." And, as we have shown, they do not rebel even in the case of the prophet's literature as long as it is a question of the received text of the *hebraica veritas.*

Proponents of our "conservative" translations of the OT, that is, those who for all practical purposes want to translate the *masora*, rightly point to the fact that it is only in this form that the substance of the Hebrew bible has been transmitted to the present-day translator. Unlike most of the other documents of antiquity — the Greek NT and the LXX pre-eminent within this other majority — the Hebrew OT was not allowed to descend through the normal process of a manuscript tradition, the process which results in the evidence of variants and recensions and which calls for proper critical editions, but instead was rigorously controlled and artificially standardized through the suppression of contrary witnesses so that only one form of the text survived: the *masora*. Essentially, of course, this contention is correct, or has been correct until quite recent times; and it alone can be the justification for perpetuating "critical editions" of the Hebrew OT which are in reality simply critical editions of the *masora*. The manuscripts, really only scraps and snippets of manuscripts, which had escaped the vigilance of the Masoretes and come down by other routes, were so insignificant as to deserve little or no attention. Indeed, the earliest of the Qumrân discoveries, which almost unbelievably revealed generous portions of the pre-Masoretic Hebrew bible, did so only to strengthen the case for the soundness of the *masora*. Both 1QIs*a* and 1QIs*b* differ from the MT very little, and only in a handful of cases does it appear intrinsically likely that they witness to a preferable reading. However, the evidence which has continued to flow from the same source during the past twenty-five years has also begun to unsettle the privileged place once enjoyed by MT in its splendid isolation. The evidence is, as it happens, largely corroborative of scholarly speculation that required only the positive proof that comes from manuscript testimony alone. For example, a fragment of the Hebrew of Samuel found among the earliest of the Qumrân documents has tended to confirm the hypothesis that the LXX of this work with its variants and "expansions" is in reality the rather faithful translation of *a* Hebrew recension of the text that must have coexisted with the one that was eventually adopted by the Masoretes. [13] It has become evident that the text of Samuel was in a rather fluid condition at the beginning of the Christian era, and that what has been handed down in the MT has no clearer title to being considered the "original" than to be recognized as an abbreviation of the "original." Conversely with the book of the prophet Jeremiah. [14] In this case the evidence of 4QJer*b* also appears to confirm what was long suspected, that this book existed in diverse redactional forms represented separately by the LXX and the MT. In this instance the MT chose to hand on the long form of the text; and while essentially both redactions must go back to the same school or circles (i.e., the deuteronomic redactors who are responsible for so much of the OT in its received form), the new textual evidence verifies the suspicion entertained by literary criticism, namely that most of the *plus* found in MT is secondary, created from and inspired by the "original" text of Jeremiah, but not properly part of it.[15]

All of the foregoing merely exposes the tip of an iceberg of available and weighable facts that enter into our present discussion. To expose the whole iceberg might seem to be self-defeating: we should end by demonstrating the practical impossibility of translating the OT at all. The Holy Bible invoked by fundamentalist piety with such confident and untroubled assurance simply does not exist. What bible there is must be reconstructed, always laboriously and often enough with ambiguous and indeterminate results.

Obviously, however, biblical translations are to continue, as they should. The bible will continue to be, in whatever a refracted form and in whatever a vernacular approximation, a source of inspiration and life to the many, who are the most who will ever read it, who have no firsthand acquaintance with the bundle of unsolved and insoluble questions which trail in the wake of every new translation, nor with the linguistic and other tools by which these questions are raised and got at. Responsible translation, on the other hand, will doubtless increasingly have to call attention by whatever means to those same questions, and will have to give an account of the degree to which it has resolved them. Measures of this kind ought to be taken not in any hope or desire of unsettling biblical fundamentalism, which they will not do, — in the worship of his nonhistorical bible the fundamentalist is the purest of the existentialists — but simply from the intention to deal candidly and honestly with the literary foundations of biblical religion.

There is a limit, nevertheless, to the cautions and controls that we can reasonably expect a translator to incorporate into his copy. A translation is not a commentary, even though a good translation ought to be the beginning of commentary and, indeed, in many instances eliminate the need of commentary. It cannot be expected to reflect line by line the many complexities of textual and literary criticism which the translator cannot ignore and of which he cannot permit his reader to remain entirely ignorant. There are obvious restrictions on footnotes and other critical apparatus which can be introduced into the translation of a biblical text to impede and annoy the progress of the ordinary reader. For a biblical translation, after all, is designed primarily for the ordinary reader, and a version whose idiosyncrasies must repel the general public would not only be self-defeating in terms of intention and effort, it would also deny the affirmation of biblical faith which holds that the bible mediates the word of God to men in the understood words of men.

The provisional resolution of this impasse has been to permit the translator and the expositor to go their separate ways, the one presenting at each juncture more or less arbitrarily that form of the text which seems right or convenient to him, the other supplying all the nuances in the lack of which even the best of translations must often be misleading. We should hope that there are better solutions than this one. For one thing, translations must undoubtedly become more forthright in acknowledging their presuppositions, and consequently require more sophisticated readers. Above all, however, we need studies of the biblical text, of the individual books of the bible, which will show how those messages which were once uttered orally came through the process of writing to be made into a living literature nourishing the spiritual aspirations of a people through continual adaptation, a process which is in turn the precedent for their subsequent adaptation in the preaching and hearing of the later communities of faith. Thereby we might hope to understand what is really entailed in the concept of biblical "inspiration," a rather different thing from the unreal and static irrelevancy that has so often been made into its caricature.[16]

The prophetical literature above all is suited to and requires such studies. True, it cannot be said that commentators on the prophets have failed their duty to point out the alterations that separate the putatively original words of the prophet in question from the received Hebrew text in which he has to be read. Only, they have generally undertaken this task with the intention of separating the "authentic" words of the prophets from the "deformations" introduced by the various editors of the prophetical books. And frequently enough the selfsame editors who are responsible for the "deformations" are precisely the ones to whom we are indebted for the preservation of the prophetical collections in the first place. Secondly, while the commentators have been adept at pointing out the editorial additions to the prophetic text that form one very important type of redactional change, they have not been equally sedulous in tracking down and interpreting internal alterations of the kind we have verified above in treating of Amos 8:3. And finally, in one or the other of these redactional situations, or that of the transfer of thought that occurred in a translation-redaction such as the LXX, the approach has been mainly lexicographical rather than from the standpoint of the sentence which is ultimately the true expression of theological thought.[17]

The book of Amos, it would seem, is one of the sections of the
prophetical literature best adapted to the kind of studies we have just
suggested.[18] It is this for several reasons. For one thing, this book
represents one of the oldest collections of poetry and prose to be found in
the OT. Certainly there are in the OT other segments of literature far older
than Amos, not only the smaller units found in isolated psalms, songs,
proverbs, and the like, but also such major efforts as the Yahwistic history
(itself a redaction of even older material) that has been incorporated into
the Pentateuch or Hexateuch. Amos, however, stands aloof in this
company as being the longest sustained unity of its kind that has been
largely retained for its own sake rather than for what it could contribute to
other purposes: through all its redactions, it has remained substantially a
document of the eighth century B.C. and has kept its identity in a way that
other ancient bits of the bible have not. Furthermore, for all its antiquity,
Amos is one of the best "preserved" of the books of the Hebrew OT. That is
to say, its text has suffered relatively little from the unintentional
alterations that have been introduced through human error and which, in
their most desperate state, have sometimes ended in a jumble of letters
which have preserved no thought at all. (The fact that Amos has been
affected by so little of this as over against the roughly contemporary work
of Hosea, which contains so much of it, has suggested to some authors that
greater care was exercised over the text of Amos which had attained an
earlier "canonical" fixation.) And lastly, as we already suggested, while
Amos like all books is a work of redaction, it is not a redactional work.
That is to say, by way of example, while some additions to the book of
Amos may be ascribed to the influence which we customarily call
deuteronomic,[19] there was never any attempt to bend either its content or
format into the well-known deuteronomic pattern; and the same may be
said of other recognizable redactional influences. (The only exception, as
already noted, would be the post-Exilic redaction which has converted
Amos into a salvation prophecy. But this purely mechanical and readily
detectable addition has scarcely affected the interpretation of the book
since the beginning of critical study.) It would appear, therefore, that this
straightforward text would be an ideal area in which to view the varied
redactional activity of the people of faith among which it was preserved in
the successive ages when it was found to have relevance.

The present writer hopes to be able to pursue these objectives in some
limited way at a future date or dates.

1. "Die grosse Überarbeitung der biblischen Bücher," VTSup 1 (1953) 1-10.

2. Cf. J. F. A. Sawyer, *Semantics in Biblical Research* (SBT 2/24; Naperville: Allenson, 1972) 5-6.

3. In every other instance of the use of *yll* hif in the Hebrew OT (all of them in the prophetical literature) the meaning is of a person or a personification actively engaged in weeping or wailing. See the lexica.

4. "Israelitisch-jüdische Religionsgeschichte und alttestamentliche Theologie," *ZAW* 44 (1926) 1-12 = *Kleine Schriften* (Tübingen: J. C. B. Mohr, 1962) 1, 105-14.

5. "The Present State of Old Testament Studies," *JBL* 88 (1969) 19-35. See pp. 22-23: with most of the rest of the article the present writer does not find himself in much agreement.

6. Preservation of the "literal" Hebrew text is taken to the limits of reproducing the suspended *nun* in Judg 18:30 where pious censorship transformed the name of Moses into that of Manasseh; in retaining what even the Masoretes noted as *tiqqûnê sōferîm*, scribal "corrections," i.e., intentional deformations of the text; the "bless" instead of the obviously original "curse" of Job 1:5, 2:9, and like passages; preservations of the *ketîb*, the erroneously written consonants which the Masoretes refused to change even though marginally and by punctuation they noted the *qerê* that they thought should be read, etc., etc. See D. M. C. Englert, "Bowdlerizing In the Old Testament," *A Light Unto My Path: Old Testament Studies in Honor of Jacob M. Myers* (ed. H. N. Bream; Philadelphia: Temple University, 1974) 141-43. It is interesting that the new BHS which is now replacing BH³ shows a tendency to shrink the truly critical apparatus appended to the text at the expense of expanding the Masoretic apparatus and includes with each fascicle a portable table of the 48 Masoretic accents which the vast majority of its users will find serviceable only as a bookmark. All such efforts are admirable when directed towards the preservation of postbiblical Jewish tradition, but they can only impede the reconstruction of a genuine edition of the Hebrew bible. Translators who work from these texts customarily ignore the evident excrescences, usually without indicating their departures.

7. In the most extreme form, perhaps, D. Barthélemy, "L'Ancien Testament a mûri à Alexandrie," *TZ* 21 (1965) 358-70, for whom the Hebrew OT stands in relation to the canonical OT of Christianity (i.e., the LXX) precisely as the J source of the Pentateuch stands in relation to, say, the book of Genesis, namely as a *propaedeuticon*. There is a considerable literature on the subject, mainly the work of some esteemed French colleagues, which the present writer must regretfully assess as an excursion into futility and a defence of the indefensible.

8. For an engaging appreciation of the impact of Jerome's effort over against the LXX establishment represented by Augustine, Bishop of Hippo, see the opening pages of the article by J. A. Fitzmyer, "A Recent Roman Scriptural Controversy," *TS* (1961) 426-44.

9. For what was Jerome's idea of a "literal" translation, see my *Biblical Inspiration* (Philadelphia: Westminster, 1972) 29.

10. Cf. H. Bornkamm, *Luther and the Old Testament* (Philadelphia: Fortress, 1969) 219-46.

11. *EB* §§ 16-17.

12. *EB* §§ 14-15. Actually, it is probably incorrect to think of separate canons as far as these councils were concerned, except to the extent they had come to embody Christian rather than Jewish tradition. Though the two questions are often confused, it is by no means evident that acceptance of the LXX as inspired scripture carried with it acceptance of the LXX's "canon." Indeed, as we have just indicated, where the LXX was most firmly established at the time, in the East, the tendency was to adopt a narrower canon of the OT, whereas in the West the longer canon became the rule. As is known, Jerome in opting for the canon of the Hebrew OT was an exception to the western rule.

13. See F. M. Cross, "A New Qumran Biblical Fragment Related to the Original Hebrew Underlying the Septuagint," *BASOR* 132 (1953) 15-26.

14. Cf. E. Tov, "L'incidence de la critique textuelle sur la critique littéraire dans le livre de Jérémie," *RB* 79 (1972) 189-99.

15. An easy instance from literary criticism: Jer 33:14-26 is the longest continuous passage of this book in MT that is lacking in LXX. The style is anthological: vss. 14-16 are a pastiche of 29:10 and 23:5-6; vs. 17 comes from 35:16; 31:35-37 have served as the model for vss. 19-22 and vss. 25-26; and there are other reminiscences. Jeremiah's words have been used partly in a sense different from that of the authentic passages: the *Yhwh ṣidqēnû* and *ṣemaḥ ṣaddîq* of 23:5-6 turn up in vss. 14-15 (the received MT actually has *ṣemaḥ ṣᵉdāqâ* in vs. 15, but at least four MSS testify to *ṣaddîq* instead, and this was read by Theodotion); but the former now means Jerusalem rather than the king thereof, and the latter in turn refers to the kingship itself rather than to a scion of David. This passage is discussed at the beginning of my "Levitical Messianism and the New Testament," *The Bible in Current Catholic Thought* (ed. J. L. McKenzie; New York: Herder & Herder, 1962) 83-99.

16. For the ongoing character of inspiration, see again my *Biblical Inspiration*, esp. 95-131.

17. Here we recall the position of J. Barr, *The Semantics of Biblical Language* (Oxford: Oxford University, 1961), who devoted the conclusion of his book to this thesis after having propounded it several times previously in passing. He later returned to the same topic in "Hebraic and Greek Thought-forms in the New Testament," *Current Issues in New Testament Interpretation* (ed. W. Klassen and G. F. Snyder; New York: Harper and Row, 1962) 1-22. As he sometimes does, Barr somewhat overstated his case (which was formulated against such works as the Kittel-Friedrich *TDNT*): what the semanticists call "full words," which account for the great majority of the entries in the theological dictionaries, can have significance in themselves even apart from context; cf. S. Ullman, *Semantics. An Introduction to the Science of Meaning* (New York: Barnes & Noble, 1962) 44-49. It is "form-words" which cannot be regarded of themselves as having theological significance and take on meaning only when they are part of a phrase or sentence. Both types of word are obviously involved in our discussion, but the commentators do not always advert to the distinction and its implications.

18. J. A. Arieti's article, "The Vocabulary of Septuagint Amos," *JBL* 93 (1974) 338-47, even though exclusively lexicographical, offers many suggestive observations on the

LXX adaptation of Amos which point to the new nuances which it introduced into the prophetic text.

19. As *certain* additions of this kind, we would doubtless have to instance 2:4-5 and 3:7 among others. See T. R. Hobbs, "Amos 3, 1b and 2, 10," *ZAW* 81 (1969) 384-87, criticizing W. H. Schmidt, "Die deuteronomische Redaktion des Amosbuches," *ZAW* 77 (1965) 168-92, regarding the delicacy of the application of "deuteronomic" to these and other redactions.

KATHLEEN O'BRIEN WICKER

First Century Marriage Ethics: A Comparative Study of the Household Codes and Plutarch's Conjugal Precepts

1

John L. McKenzie initiated a small band of devotees into the mysteries of Hellenistic religions scholarship at Chicago's Loyola University in 1961. He was affectionately known among us then as "Two-Edged Sword," not with reference to his famed rapier wit but to the title of his then most recent volume, *The Two Edged Sword.* Professor McKenzie's goal in this course was to present a survey of the philosophical and religious thought and practice of the Hellenistic-Roman world as a context for understanding both the historical influences upon the development of Christianity and the radical distinctiveness of Christianity in relation to its historical milieu. The material under consideration in the course also afforded McKenzie the opportunity to raise an issue which has been of long standing concern to him, the problem of whether or not there can be a Christian ethic. Both the question of the relationship of Christianity to the philosophical-religious thought of the Hellenistic period and the problem of a Christian ethic are relevant to the study I am contributing to this Festschrift on the marriage ethics of the Christian Household Codes and Plutarch's *Conjugal Precepts.* Though this topic has not been a primary focus of Father McKenzie's research, it is an issue he has discussed with his usual clarity and insight in several volumes.[1]

In this paper,[2] the marriage ethics of the Household Codes[3] will be compared with those found in the *Conjugal Precepts,*[4] a treatise of Plutarch, a Greek philosopher and man of letters of the first century. These two sets of texts lend themselves well to a comparative study since they are relatively contemporary, they share a similar ethical vocabulary, they have a common paraenetic purpose, and they are directed to adherents of a specific philosophical or religious group. There is little likelihood, however, that the Christian texts were known to Plutarch or Plutarch's

141

treatise to the Christian community.

Secondly, the ethics advocated in both the Household Codes and the *Conjugal Precepts* will be examined in the context of the ethos or social practice of marriage in the first century.[5] An attempt will be made to assess the degree to which these texts contain an affirmation, a modification, or a negation of the marriage practices current in that period.

Finally, the results of this research will be related to the ideas McKenzie has expressed on the nature and extent of the philosophical and religious syncretism of the first century and on the problem of a Christian ethic.

2

Plutarch's *Conjugal Precepts* was an oration delivered at the wedding of his two young friends, Pollianus and Eurydice. Its stated purpose was to recommend to them the practice of philosophy which "weaves a spell over those who are entering together into a lifelong partnership and renders them gentle and amiable toward each other" (138C). This treatise provides practical illustrations of the demands of a virtuous life in forty-eight graphic examples and comparisons which constitute the body of the speech.

Plutarch's ethical ideal of marriage in the *Conjugal Precepts* is clearly influenced by Aristotle's notion of *sōphrosynē* or control of the passions, which is the basis, according to Aristotle, for all training in virtue. The practice of *sōphrosynē* by the husband was reflected in his exercise of authority. Its practice by the wife was reflected in her submissiveness and silence.[6] Plutarch expresses the same view. His paradigm of the ideal marriage is that of Odysseus and Penelope, the sensible (*phronimos*) man and the virtuous (*sōphrōn*) woman. Its opposite is the marriage of Helen and Paris, one a lover of wealth (*philoploutos*) and the other a lover of pleasure (*philēdonos*) (140F). Plutarch describes the ideal marriage as a *symbiōsis*. He says:

> It is a lovely thing for the wife to sympathize with her husband's concerns and the husband with the wife's, so that, as ropes, by being intertwined, get strength from each other, thus . . . the copartnership may be preserved through the joint action of both (140E).

Plutarch also characterizes marriage as a relationship informed by mutual love, but the authority in the relationship clearly rests with the husband.

> Control ought to be exercised by the man over the woman, not as the owner has control of a piece of property, but, as the soul controls the body, by entering

into her feelings and being knit to her through goodwill. As, therefore, it is possible to exercise care over the body without being a slave to its pleasures and desires, so it is possible to govern a wife, and at the same time to delight and gratify her (142E).

In Plutarch's ideal marriage the husband also has the responsibility of serving as a model of virtue for his wife and of training her in the practice of philosophy, lest she, "left to [herself] conceive many untoward ideas and low designs and emotions" (145DE).

The wife, in turn, is to be subordinate to her husband. She should regard him as "guide, philosopher, and teacher in all that is most lovely and divine" (145A). Her aim should be to "have no feelings of her own, but she should join with her husband in seriousness and sportiveness and in soberness and laughter" (140A). She should "do her talking either to her husband or through her husband, and she should not feel aggrieved if, like the flute-player, she makes a more impressive sound through a tongue not her own" (142D). Modesty and moderation should characterize her behavior at all times. She should appear in public only in her husband's company and be carefully guarded in her speech. She should dress simply and avoid excessive adornment, since her true adornments are dignity, good behavior and modesty. Plutarch tells the bride, Eurydice:

> You cannot acquire and put upon you this rich woman's pearls or that foreign woman's silks without buying them at a high price, but the ornaments of Theano, Cleobulina, Gorgo, the wife of Leonidas, Timocleia, the sister of Theagenes, Claudia of old, Cornelia, daughter of Scipio, and of all other women who have been admired and renowned, you may wear about you without price, and adorning yourself with these, you may live a life of distinction and happiness (145EF).

Plutarch also holds that the wife should share her husband's gods, just as she does his friends. She is "to shut the front door tight upon all queer rituals and outlandish superstitions. For with no god do stealthy and secret rites performed by a woman find any favor" (140D).

Marriage for the procreation of children is inferior to marriage for love, according to Plutarch. However, he describes "the marital sowing and ploughing for the procreation of children" as more sacred than all the sacred ploughings which were part of religious rituals. He directs the husband and wife to indulge in this with reverent awe,

> keeping themselves pure from all unholy and unlawful intercourse with others, and not sowing seed from which they are unwilling to have offspring, and from which if any issue does result, they are ashamed of it, and try to conceal it (144B).

Turning now to the Household Codes, the ideals of marriage which they express have been shaped by OT conceptions, by the Christian experience and faith, and by contact with the Hellenistic milieu.

1 Timothy uses the example of Adam and Eve to justify the subordination of the wife to her husband. Adam's superiority is established by his priority in the order of creation and by his wisdom in not being seduced by the serpent. The same rationale is used to forbid women to teach or have authority over men in the churches. Women are "to learn in silence and all submissiveness" (2:11), undoubtedly from their husbands. They are also to dress modestly and be attired in "good deeds as befits women who profess religion" (2:10).

Sarah's obedience to Abraham is lauded in 1 Peter as a model for Christian wives. Those who have pagan husbands are particularly exhorted to be submissive in the hope of converting their husbands by their good example. Women are also encouraged to be modest in dress, following the example of holy women on the OT. 1 Peter advises:

> Let not yours be the outward adorning with braiding of hair, decoration of gold, and wearing of fine clothing, but let it be the hidden person of the heart with the imperishable jewel of a gentle and quiet spirit, which in God's sight is very precious (3:3-5).

Ephesians[7] grounds the ideal of marriage initially in the law of love in Lev 19:18, in the marriage command of Gen 2:24, and in the image of Israel as the bride of God.

1 Clement justifies the subordination of wives to their husbands as part of the order which God imposed on his creation to secure peace and harmony in the universe. Though 1 Clement used a Stoic source in this passage, he undoubtedly intended to appeal primarily to the OT tradition of God as creator.[8]

Several concepts which appeared in the Pauline literature and may have been common in the Christian tradition are also appropriated by the authors of the Household Codes. One is the notion of the Christian's incorporation in the mystical body of Christ. It occurs in 1 Cor 6:12-20 and 12:12-31 and also in the baptismal formulae of Gal 3:28 and Col 3:11: "all are one in Christ Jesus . . . Christ is all in all." The analogy of the role of Christ as head of the church with that of the husband as head of his wife, which occurs in 1 Cor 11:2-16, and the image of the church as bride found in 2 Cor 11:1-6 are also utilized in the Household Codes.

The earliest and simplest of the Household Codes is in Colossians. It states: "Wives, be subject to your husbands, as it is fitting in the Lord. Husbands, love your wives, and do not be harsh with them" (3:18-19). The phrase "in the Lord" puts the marriage relationship in the context of incorporation in Christ. The love command, applied here to the husband, is also characteristic of Christ's attitude toward the church in 1 Corinthians 11. The subjection of the wife to the authority of her husband is implicit in the analogy of husband as head of the wife. The phrase "as it is fitting" reflects the influence of the Stoic notion of duty in discussing the mutual relations of husband and wife.[9]

The author of Ephesians works out a complex analogy between the relationship of husband and wife, and that of Christ and the church. He begins with the general statement, "Be subject to one another out of reverence for Christ" (5:21). Then he proceeds to specify what this entails for the Christian husband and wife. The husband is to love his wife as his own flesh just as Christ loved his bride, the church. The wife is to be subject to her husband, the head, as to the Lord, just as the church is subject to Christ. This injunction is summarized in the conclusion: "Let each one of you love his wife as himself and let the wife see that she respects her husband" (5:33). Ignatius to Polycarp refers to this passage from Ephesians in his directives given to husbands (5:1).

The influence of Hellenistic ethical vocabulary on the Household Codes is reflected in the lists of virtues and vices found in Titus and 1 Clement.[10] In Titus, women are "to be reverent in behavior, not . . . slanderers or slaves to drink . . . to be sensible, chaste, domestic, kind and submissive to their husbands, that the word of God may not be discredited." Husbands are to be "temperate, serious, sensible, sound in faith, in love and in steadfastness" (2:2-5). Titus regards these ethical directives as based on the revelation of Christ. 1 Clement exhorts wives "to do all things with a blameless and seemly and pure conscience, to manage their households with all seemliness, in all circumspection . . . to show forth the innocent will of meekness, to make the gentleness of their tongue manifest by their silence" (1:3; 21:7).

Special emphasis is placed on the role of the wife as mother in 1 Timothy, Titus, and Polycarp to the Philippians. 1 Timothy states: "woman will be saved through bearing children, if she continues in faith and love and holiness with modesty" (2:15). This concept of salvation through motherhood is also found in the OT and in Judaism.

In summary, the virtuous behavior expected of husband and wife in the *Conjugal Precepts* and in the Household Codes is similar in many ways. Both expect the husband to be the thoughtful, loving, sensible and considerate leader, teacher and exemplar of virtue for his wife. She, in turn, is expected to defer to his authority and profit from his teaching and example. She is to remain in the home, silent, kind, faithful to her domestic duties, avoiding superstition and error in the practice of religion.

The *Conjugal Precepts* also differs from the Household Codes in several ways. It considers procreation as only a secondary purpose of marriage. However, Plutarch does discuss sexual union for the procreation of children in distinctly religious terms. The Household Codes view procreation as a means both of transmitting the faith and of winning the salvation of the mother. The Household Codes also emphasize purity and marital fidelity for both husband and wife. In addition, the wife is urged to love not only her husband and children but also all other members of the Christian community "equally in all chastity" (Pol Phil 4:2). In the *Conjugal Precepts*, the sexual freedom of the husband is regulated by the wife's sensitivities. The obligation of love is defined only within the circle of the family.

The most significant, indeed, the essential, difference between the *Conjugal Precepts* and the Household Codes, however, lies in the fundamental principles upon which the ethical ideals of each is based. Aristotle's notion of virtue as the mean state between the extremes of virtue and vice is the major philosophical principle upon which Plutarch bases the ethics of the *Conjugal Precepts*. Those who control their passions through reason and live in moderation attain the perfection which is the goal of human life. Plutarch also recognized, however, the important role the emotions have in affecting human behavior. Thus he modifies the Aristotelian scheme of the superiority of the husband and the subordination of the wife by affirming in addition the need of the spouses for mutual respect, consideration and love. His image of the nature of the marital relationship is the intimate unity of soul and body in a single living person. The reward Plutarch promises to those who live the life of virtue is personal happiness and the admiration of fellow human beings.

Christianity has a different view of human nature from that found in Aristotle and Plutarch. In the Christian conception, human beings are fallen, sinful, weak creatures. But they are also capable of being redeemed and enjoying an eternal life of happiness. Salvation is not found in reason, however, but in the redemptive death of Christ. Through baptism, Christians become members of the body of Christ. Their relationships with other persons also affect their relationship with Christ. The marital relationship is the most intimate of all human relationships and most closely resembles the relationship between Christ and the church. Therefore, the husband must imitate the love of Christ for the church and the wife must reflect the respect and submission of the church toward

Christ in her relationship with her husband. The reward of a virtuous Christian life is eternal happiness with Christ in heaven. Hell is the punishment of those who fail to meet those expectations.

3

Having examined the ethical ideals of marriage in the *Conjugal Precepts* and in the Household Codes and the principles underlying these ideals, let us turn now to a brief resume of what is known about the social practice of marriage in the ancient world.[11]

Classical Greek literature often expressed a lofty ideal of woman. However, in practice, the wife had an inferior status in the home and her public activity was severely restricted. Sparta appears to have been an exception to this general practice. Monogamy was the rule, though men enjoyed freedom for extra-marital affairs. The Socratic notion, which Plato also adopted, that the virtues of women and men are the same, was in direct contrast to the prevailing view and practice. Plato's recommendation in the *Republic* that women should be freed from some of the restraints of home and family to contribute more fully to the state was realized probably only in the Hellenistic period.

The Romans traditionally held the wife's position in the household relatively high. In the period of the Empire she had equality in the home and could move about freely. She could choose either to come under the *manus* or legal power of her husband and become the *mater familias* or remain in the power of her father and marry as *uxor*. Later she was able to assume her own legal identity. Roman marriage was also monogamous, though extramarital relationships were tolerated.

In the Roman period, there was a trend toward the emancipation of women from the home and from the absolute control of the husband. The Stoics in particular contributed significantly to the improvement of the lot of women. They affirmed the Socratic principle that men and women have the same *aretē*. They insisted on a single strict standard of morality for both men and women, motivated by the vision of marriage as a living spiritual community or *symbiōsis*. They encouraged women to study philosophy so that they might be better able to realize the ideal of the philosophic marriage.

There are also indications, however, that the traditional structure of the family was being weakened in this period. In both Greece and Rome, divorce was not uncommon and could occur by mutual consent or by the unilateral action of either party. Childless marriages became more usual.

The liberation of women advocated by the philosophers contributed, in one sense, to the dissolution of the traditional family structure. Their recognition of the dignity and equality of women with men as fellow human beings led inevitably to a change in the attitudes of both sexes toward themselves and each other and, correspondingly, to a change in social behavior. But given the strict standards of morality which the philosophers advocated, they should not be blamed for the negative aspects of the breakdown of the family structure observable in this period. Rather they should be credited with attempting to establish a higher standard of morality in marriage and the family.

Plutarch, a Greek who had spent considerable time in Rome before writing the *Conjugal Precepts*, was doubtless influenced in composing this work by these philosophical discussions of marriage and by what he had observed of human behavior over a lifetime. He, too, was concerned about the breakdown of the marital relationship, judging from his examples of the deplorable behavior of spouses in the *Conjugal Precepts*. His views on marriage ran counter to the common social practice of the period. But he did not accept the Stoic view that the *aretē* of men and women is always the same. He held the Aristotelian notion that in some circumstances the *aretē* of men and women takes different forms. Though he advocated a superior-subordinate relationship of husband and wife, he modified this hierarchical status by insisting that respect and consideration be shown by each spouse to the other in the symbiotic relationship of marriage.

The social practice of marriage in the OT and Judaism must be considered along with that of the Graeco-Roman world for an understanding of the background against which the ethics of the Household Codes was developed. In the OT, women were legally regarded as the property of their husbands. Polygamy was allowed. The most important role of the wife was to bear children, particularly male children. Despite her legal inferiority, however, the wife was ordinarily regarded as the invaluable helpmate of her husband. She also enjoyed a great of social freedom.

Jewish literature, with a few notable exceptions in the wisdom materials, reflects a decidedly negative attitude toward women. The wife was regarded as the moral, social and religious inferior of her husband. She was considered to be greedy, inquisitive, lazy, vain and frivolous by nature. To curb her basic sensuality, the wife was to submit to the authority and rationality of her husband and to live in servitude to him. Her participation in religious activities was severely curtailed. She was subject to divorce if she had not borne children after ten years, or for even more trivial causes.

Her position in the family was always threatened by the possibility of a polygamous marriage. Even Philo and Josephus shared these views, despite their contacts with Stoic ethics which influenced their views strongly in other areas.

Christianity did not initially adopt the model of Judaism in its attitude to marriage and the family. Jesus himself demonstrated a considerate attitude toward women. Many of his disciples appear to have been women. The early Christian community may even have considered kinship ties to have been transcended among believers. The communal life of the early church described in Acts 2:43-47 is not based on the kinship model. Jesus' relatives became for a time symbols of unbelief: "Who is my mother and who are my brothers?" (Mark 3:33//Matt 12:48). Belief in the unity and equality of all in Christ through baptism and an imminent eschatological expectation were the basic principles governing human relationships in early Christianity.

Paul's writings reflect the influence of both Jewish and Hellenistic attitudes toward women and marriage. In 2 Cor 11:3 he discusses the seduction of Eve. In 1 Cor 11:3 and 7, he observes that woman is second to man in the order of creation. He follows Jewish tradition in 1 Cor 14:33b-36 in advocating the silence of women in the churches. But in 1 Corinthians 7 he assumes the equality of husbands and wives and discusses their mutual rights and responsibilities from that perspective.

The Household Codes appear in the Christian literature only late in the first century. Initially they were intended to counteract the radical social practices affecting the household which developed in heretical groups within Christianity. Later they were directed against the disintegration of the traditional family structure and thus ran counter to the general social practice of marriage during this period. They appropriated the OT view of the sanctity of the marital relationship, the Jewish emphasis on the subordination of the wife, the Stoic notion of duty, and some of the traditional virtues associated with male and female roles in Graeco-Roman culture. However, by viewing marriage in the perspective of incorporation in Christ and the love command, the Household Codes both radically transformed the ideal of marriage and supported a conservative social practice of marriage within Christianity.

4

McKenzie emphasized in our Hellenistic Religions course and in the introductory chapter of his major volume on the interpretation of the NT,

The Power and the Wisdom,[12] the importance of historical influences in shaping the events and tests of early Christianity. He placed equal stress, however, on the radically distinctive characteristics of Christian thought which clearly distinguished it from the other philosophical and religious movements of the Hellenistic-Roman period. Our study of the marriage ethics of the Household Codes and Plutarch's *Conjugal Precepts* also illustrates the importance of distinguishing between the historical factors affecting the practical behavior advocated by Christians and non-Christians, which in this case led to the adoption of quite similar life styles, and the fundamental principles upon which such behavior was predicated, which in this case as elsewhere were quite different.

McKenzie discusses the uniqueness of the Christian moral revolution at considerable length in *The Power and the Wisdom*.[13] He views Paul as the principal formulator of the theological truths of Christianity, impelled by the crisis he faced of establishing the proper relationship of Christianity to its Jewish heritage. Paul's gospel proclaimed salvation through faith and baptism. Neither the natural law of Stoicism nor the revealed Law of Judaism, in his view, were sufficient for salvation. McKenzie interprets Paul's teaching as follows:

> The Christian is left with only one saving act which he can perform; this is the saving act of love. The Christian would be incapable of this spontaneous movement were the spontaneity not given him by the indwelling Spirit . . . . Freedom then is the exercise of a power communicated in baptism, the power to do that which is impossible for unregenerate man.[14]

Paul further emphasized that all Christians are united in the body of Christ, the church. This unity demands that differences among Christians "become totally irrelevant as determinants of how one man shall deal with another . . . . One cannot have several bodies of Christ and several lives of Christ and several spirits."[15]

Given this understanding of the Christian moral revolution and the absoluteness of the love command, McKenzie questions the possibility that a Christian ethics can exist. He defines ethics as "a theory of moral obligation in general and a system of moral obligation in particular based on a rational consideration of nature."[16] He argues that the historical development of Christian ethical systems "shows that they are ethical but not that they are Christian."[17] He denies that "a Christian ethical system is needed to solve the moral problems which are not solved in the New Testament,"[18] because "the ethical solution of these problems will often prove to be a rational evasion of the full weight of the Christian duty of love."[19]

How, then, should the marriage ethics in the Household Codes be regarded in the light of McKenzie's views on the impossibility of a Christian ethics? He himself suggests a solution to the dilemma.

> Admitted that the gospel is a moral revolution, the revolution must be worked out by the personal decision of each Christian. . . . The gospel does not give specific directions for each situation either; and the Christian can make his moral decisions only by the intelligent use of Christian moral principles applied to particulars — which is a morality of reason.[20]

The marriage ethics of the Household Codes may, then, be regarded as the attempt by Christians in particular historical circumstances to implement the love command of Christian morality in a specific sphere of their lives. Such an ethical code should not be regarded as absolutely normative, however. It can be a valid Christian morality only when and to the extent that the observance of the prescribed behavior by specific individuals is a legitimate means of fulfilling the love command.

Unfortunately, the marriage ethics of the Household Codes have become absolutized in the Christian tradition rather than being regarded simply as one way in which husbands and wives might fulfill their Christian commitment. One reason for this development may be that the Church adopted the Household Codes as the basis for rules of Church order, thereby, as we have observed above, providing an example and reinforcement of the orthodox social relationships in marriage. Today, however, when many Christians are reexamining and questioning the ideal of the dominance of the male and the submissiveness of the female in marriage and society, which the Household Codes advocate, it is helpful to remember McKenzie's *caveat* that an ethics which does not have the unity of Christians in love as its primary motivation cannot make the claim of being a Christian ethics. McKenzie concludes his essay "Neither Slave Nor Freeman, Male Nor Female" with the observation that Christians have the theological "framework for a kind of male-female relationship which is really quite new in the world."[21] But, he adds, "the culture frightens me."[22] Will Christians meet the challenge of shaping their human sexual relationships, both within and outside of marriage, in accordance with their theological traditions? This is one of the serious challenges confronting Christianity and society in the twentieth century.

1. See "Natural Law in the New Testament," *BR* 9 (1964) 1-11; "Marriage" and "Woman," *Dictionary of the Bible* (New York: Macmillan, 1965) 548-51, 935-37; *The Power and The Wisdom* (Milwaukee: Bruce, 1965) 194-232; "Sex Is in the Bible,"

Mastering the Meaning of the Bible (Wilkes-Barre: Dimension Books, 1966) 77-95; "And the Two . . . Remain Two" and "Neither Slave Nor Freeman, Male Nor Female," *Did I Say That?* (Chicago: Thomas More, 1973) 39-44, 207-10.

2. The second and third sections of this paper were originally presented as a Presidential Address to the Society of Biblical Literature — Pacific Coast Section in San Jose, California, on April 19, 1975, under the title "The Virtues of Women: A Comparative Study of Plutarch and the NT."

3. I include Gal 3:18-19; Eph 5:21-32; 1 Tim 2:8-15; Tit 2:2-6; 1 Pet 3:1-7; 1 Clem 1:3; 21:6-9; Ign Pol 5:1-2; Pol Phil 4:2. Texts and translations of the Apostolic Fathers are based on *The Apostolic Fathers* (tr. Kirsopp Lake, LCL 1; Cambridge: Harvard University, 1970).

4. Plutarch, "Advice to Bride and Groom," *Moralia* (tr. Frank Cole Babbitt, LCL 2; Cambridge: Harvard University, 1962) 297-343. This text and translation will be cited throughout the paper.

5. The importance of studying the social context of early Christianity and its literature is discussed by L. E. Keck, "On the Ethos of Early Christians," *JAAR* 42 (1974) 435-52. See also E. A. Judge, *The Social Pattern of Christian Groups in the First Century* (London: Tyndale, 1960) and H. Preisker, *Das Ethos des Urchristentums* (Gütersloh: Bertelsmann, 1949).

6. Aristotle, *Politics* 1260a 20-24; 1277b 21-25.

7. A helpful analysis of the traditions found in Eph 5:21-33 is found in J. P. Sampley, *'And The Two Shall Become One Flesh'* (Cambridge: University Press, 1971).

8. See W. Jaeger, "Echo eines unerkannten Tragikerfragments in Clemens' Brief an die Korinther," *RhM* 102 (1959), 330-40.

9. See J. E. Crouch, *The Origin and Intention of the Colossian Haustafel* (Göttingen: Vandenhoeck & Ruprecht, 1972) and E. Lohse, *Colossians and Philemon* (Hermeneia; Philadelphia: Fortress, 1971) 154-58.

10. See M. Dibelius and H. Conzelmann, *The Pastoral Epistles* (Hermeneia; Philadelphia: Fortress, 1972) 139-43 and W. Jaeger, *Early Christianity and Greek Paideia* (Cambridge: Belknap, 1961) 12-26.

11. See J. Leipoldt, *Die Frau in der der antiken Welt und im Urchristentum* (Gütersloh: Gerd Mohn, 1953); McKenzie, *Dictionary*, 548-51; A. Oepke, "*gynē*," *TDNT* 1(1972) 776-89.

12. *The Power and the Wisdom*, 1-26.

13. Ibid., 213-32.

14. Ibid., 207.

15. Ibid., 211.

16. "Natural Law in the New Testament," 10.

17. Ibid., 11.

18. Ibid., 10.

19. Ibid., 11.

20. *The Power and the Wisdom*, 224.

21. "Neither Slave Nor Freeman, Male Nor Female," 210.

22. Ibid.

JOSEPH A. FITZMYER, S.J.

Reconciliation in Pauline Theology

In Christian theology reconcilation has always played an important role.[1]
The doctrine of reconciliation is rooted in biblical teaching, but it has also
been developed in various ways through the course of the centuries, as
theologians wrestled with the concept in their explanations of the ways of
God with man. The Christian doctrine of the reconciliation of sinful man is
rooted in the OT as well as in the NT, and an adequate discussion of the
biblical treatment of the topic would demand a monograph. But one of the
main proponents of reconciliation in the bible is the Apostle Paul, and since
the role of reconciliation in his theology has recently been called in
question,[2] there is reason to reconsider it. My purpose, then, is to discuss
the notion of reconciliation in Pauline theology.

Before we examine the idea of reconcilation itself, however, it might be
wise to situate it in a general way in Pauline theology as a whole. As the first
Christian theologian, Paul left us in his letters many teachings, and among
them are the various ways in which he interpreted the Christ-event. In
reflecting on what Christ Jesus accomplished for mankind and what his
effect was on the history of mankind, different writers of the early Christian
community summed up his words, his deeds, and his personal impact in
various ways. Paul showed little interest in the earthly life of Jesus or in
what he actually did and said — in what is for so many Christians of today
a thing of no little importance. Paul did learn indeed of some of the sayings
of Jesus and of his teachings, as a number of passages in his letters reveal.[3]
But because most of his letters were composed prior to the composition of
the earliest gospel, it is understandable that he did not echo much of what
we know of today as the gospel-tradition.[4] Paul's dominant interest was in
what Jesus accomplished for man in his passion, death, burial,
resurrection, and exaltation. This complex of the last phases of Christ's
earthly career can be referred to as "the Christ-event," even though Paul
himself never so expressed it; it is a convenient way of labelling that about
which he preached and wrote. Some writers call it the "whole work of
Christ."[5] It has also been termed the "objective redemption," i.e., that

155

aspect of man's redemption wrought in Jesus which is wholly independent of man's cooperation and which consequently underlines its gratuitous character. In this view, it stands in contrast to man's attempt to appropriate the effects of the Christ-event to himself (through faith and baptism), which is often then regarded as the "subjective redemption." This terminology, actually born of a later problem, is not biblical or Pauline; but it does help at least to sharpen the aspects of the Christ-event about which we are talking.

Looked at in this way, it is not difficult to single out the various ways in which Paul objectively viewed the Christ-event, because in many instances he himself employed abstractions which enable us to grasp what he had in mind. As labels for the effects of the Christ-event, Paul used a series of abstract nouns, and we can cull at least nine of them from his letters; or in some instances there are verbal forms. Thus, as Paul looked back at the Christ-event, he interpreted its effects as (1) "salvation" (*sōtēria*), a restoration of man to safety, health, or wholeness from a state of danger or sickness (2 Cor 7:10; Rom 1:16; 10:10; 13:11);[6] (2) "expiation" (*hilastērion*),[7] a wiping away of man's sins by the crucified Christ who is now the new "mercy seat," superseding the *kappōret* of old (Rom 3:25);[8] (3) "ransom/redemption" (*apolytrōsis*), an emancipation or manumission of man bringing about his liberation through a ransom, so that God thereby acquires a people in a new sense (Rom 3:24; Eph 1:14);[9] (4) "sanctification" (*hagiasmos*), a dedication of man to God's service, thus removing him from the profane (1 Cor 1:30; 6:11);[10] (5) "freedom" (*eleutheria*), a liberation of man that gives him new rights and an outlook that frees him from the anxiety of Self, Sin, Death, and Law (Gal 5:1, 13; Rom 8:1-2);[11] (6) "justification" (*dikaiōsis*), an acquitting of man, whereby he finds himself, as he stands before God's tribunal, innocent, upright, or righteous (Gal 2:16; Rom 3:26-28; 4:25; 5:18);[12] (7) "transformation" (*metamorphōsis*), a gradual reshaping of man by the glory of God reflected in the face of Christ; it is the effect of the Creator God, who through Christ shines light anew into man's life (2 Cor 3:18; Rom 12:2; Eph 4:22-24);[13] (8) "new creation" (*kainē ktisis*), a creating of a new life, a new humanity, of which Christ is the head as the Adam of the *eschaton* through his life-giving Spirit (Gal 6:15; 2 Cor 5:17; Rom 6:14; 1 Cor 15:45);[14] and (9) "reconciliation" (*katallagē*), a restoring of man (and the world) to a status of friendship with God and his fellowmen (2 Cor 5:18-20; Rom 5:10-11; 11:25; Col 1:20-22; Eph 2:16).[15] These, then, are the main ways in which Paul looked back at the Christ-event and characterized it.[16]

It is important to note that when Paul refers to the Christ-event in these ways, he is applying to it various images or figures derived from his background, Jewish or Hellenistic. For instance, his view of the Christ-event as justification can only be explained from his Jewish or OT background; or his view of it as redemption cannot be adequately accounted for without some reference to modes of emancipation in the Hellenistic world of his time. For in his interpretation of the whole work of Christ he applies to it figures which have definite connotations, and these have to be respected. In certain developments of later Christian theology these figures were eventually erected into propositions, with all sorts of baneful results. But the effort to depict Paul's understanding of any one of the figures must treat them for what they are.

Reconciliation is one of these figures, and my concern here is to comment (1) on the figure and its background or origin; (2) on Paul's use of it; (3) on problems in the modern interpretation of it; and (4) on the pertinence of it to modern life.

1. The Figure of Reconciliation and Its Background

The basic idea that is conveyed by the figure of reconciliation is the restoration of men and women to a status of friendship and intimacy. The Greek words, *katallagē, apokatallassō, diallassō, katallassō*, are all compound forms of a root meaning "other" (*all-*), and denote a "making otherwise."[17] The words are abundantly used in the literature of the Greeks, both in a secular sense and a religious sense.[18] In the secular sense, they denote a change or alteration of relations between individual persons or groups of persons (e.g., nations); it is a change from anger, enmity, or hostility to love, friendship, or intimacy. The words do not express primarily a change of feelings or a psychological reaction. This may be present, but the essential change is rather in the relationship or situation vis-à-vis another. It is a change of relationship in the social or political realm. This secular use of the word is even found in the bible. In Judg 19:2-3 we read of a Levite who took to himself a concubine, who eventually became angry with him and went home; the Levite went to talk to her "to reconcile her to himself,"[19] i.e., to restore a relationship with her. Similarly, in the Sermon on the Mount Jesus teaches: "If you are offering your gift at the altar, and there remember that your brother has something against you, leave your gift there before the altar and go; first be reconciled to your brother, and then come and offer your gift" (Matt 5:23-24; cf. 1 Cor 7:11).

In the religious sense, the words are used of the reconciliation of gods and man (e.g., Sophocles, *Ajax*, 744).[20] This use is likewise found in the Greek OT. In 2 Mac 1:5 the Jews of Jerusalem and Judea write to their brethren in Egypt and pray, "May he [God] hear your prayers and be reconciledto you" *(katallageiē hymin)*. See further 7:33; 8:29. Similarly, the Jewish historian Josephus tells of Samuel the prophet who learned that God had repented of having made Saul the king: "Samuel was quite disturbed and all night long undertook to entreat God to be reconciled to Saul and not to be angry with him" *(Ant* 6.7,4 n. 143). What is noteworthy here in these two instances of Jewish authors who wrote in Greek is the use of the very *katallassein* in the passive of God; God is expected to be reconciled with men. What should also be noted is that in Greek writings the verb plays no essential role in the expiatory rites of the Greek and Hellenistic religion, for in these rites "the relation between divinity and humanity does not have this personal nearness."[21] Such examples suggest that Paul derived this figure for the Christ-event from the Greco-Roman world,[22] even though he makes his own use of it. Before we try to describe his use of the figure, there is one further remark that must be made about the figure itself, and that concerns the relation of reconciliation to atonement.

Fundamentally, reconciliation as we have described it above is the same as atonement. But the history of the use of the latter term has loaded it with connotations that are not part of the Pauline figure. "Atonement" is, in fact, a peculiarly English word, lacking any real counterpart in other modern European languages. It really means at-one-ment and denotes the setting of two or more persons at one with each other, implying the restoration of them to a mutually shared relationship after a period of estrangement. The word was so used in English in a secular sense. But it also developed a theological sense, and the *Oxford English Dictionary* says of it: "As applied to the redemptive work of Christ, *atonement* is variously used by theologians in the senses of *reconciliation, propitiation, expiation*, according to the view taken of its nature."[23] Now it is precisely the confusion of reconciliation with "expiation" (the wiping away of man's sins by the crucified Christ who is now the new "mercy seat," superseding the *kappōret* of old)[24] and with "propitiation" (the appeasing of an angry God by rites and sacrifices) that creates the difficulty in interpreting Paul's use of the figure of reconciliation. As we examine the texts in which he speaks of reconciliation, we shall see that reconciliation can be understood as atonement (= at-one-ment), but that it is not the same as expiation, and has, practically speaking, nothing to do with propitiation. So much for the idea of reconciliation and its background.

2. The Pauline Use of the Figure of Reconciliation

Paul describes the status of man without Christ as one of hostility with God. "If, while we were enemies, we were reconciled to God by the death of his Son, much more, now that we are reconciled, shall we be saved by his life. Not only so, but we also rejoice in God through our Lord Jesus Christ, through whom we have now received our reconciliation" (Rom 5:10). This is said by Paul in a passage in Romans in which he has just finished setting forth his thesis on the justification of man by faith in Christ Jesus and apart from what he calls "the works of the Law" (1:16 - 4:25). He sees man's situation vis-à-vis God as having been basically changed by what Christ did; if man is now justified in the sight of God because of the Christ-event, then his relationship has been radically altered, and not merely in a legalistic, juridical sense that the figure of justification connotes, but in the fundamental way of reconciliation. Similarly, in writing to the Colossians,[25] to a congregation that was made up largely of Gentile Christians, Paul says of their former relation to God: "You . . . once were estranged (*apēllotriōmenous*) and hostile in mind . . . " (Col 1:21). This is, then, the situation of mankind without Christ according to Paul, a situation of hostility or estrangement. This is but another way of describing the human condition that Paul spoke about in Rom 1:18 - 3:20, mankind without the gospel.

Wherein lies the cause of this hostility or estrangement, as Paul sees it? In 2 Cor 5:19 he cites man's "trespasses" as the root of the difficulty. In Rom 8:5-7 he probes more deeply and shows that it is man's preoccupation with "flesh" (*sarx*): "Those who live according to the flesh set their minds on the things of the flesh. . . . To set the mind on the flesh is death, but to set the mind on the Spirit is life and peace. For the mind that is set on the flesh is hostile to God; it does not submit to God's law." One must understand what Paul means by "flesh" in such a passage, especially in its contrast to the Spirit. On the one hand, it has the OT connotation of *bāśār*, meaning "flesh" as opposed to blood, or, in a collective sense, "man," "mankind," "humanity."[26] On the other hand, it often has for Paul a pejorative connotation, meaning the humdrum, non-elevating condition of human existence in its down-trodden, earth-oriented propensities. It represents all in man that makes him close in on himself and refuse openness to the Spirit, to God, and to his fellowman. In this sense, Paul says, "To set the mind on flesh is death." By contrast, the spirit in man is that aspect of human nature that makes him open to God's Spirit. Hence, the mind that is set on flesh does not submit to the law of God and is actually hostile to God. As Paul sees it, man left to himself cannot help but set his mind on flesh and cannot help but be alienated and estranged from God. This is why Paul lists "enmity" among the "works of the flesh" in Gal 5:20.

Paul also finds another cause for the hostility, when he addresses Gentile Christians and refers to their former condition as pagans as a separation from Israel; in this he finds another source of alienation from God. "You were at that time separated from Christ, alienated from the commonwealth of Israel and strangers to the covenants of promise" (Eph 2:12). This estrangement implied the very futility of their existence: "They are darkened in their understanding, alienated from the life of God because of the ignorance that is in them, due to their hardness of heart" (Eph 4:18). Thus Paul writes, as he exhorts the Gentile Christian recipients of his letter to realize that they must "no longer live as the Gentiles do, in the futility of their minds" (4:17). These may sound like harsh words, but Paul's view of the condition of pagans in his day is otherwise well known to us (Rom 1:18-32). These then are the two main causes of the hostility between mankind and God, "trespasses," coming from minds set on flesh, and the estrangement of pagans.

But how has God remedied this situation, or brought about the reconciliation of hostile, alienated man? Paul never says that God is reconciled (in the passive) to man, as did the author of 2 Maccabees or Josephus.[27] He rather sees God actively taking the initiative and bringing about the reconciliation of mankind through his Son, Jesus of Nazareth. True, Paul invites men to be reconciled to God (2 Cor 5:20), but that is an invitation to appropriate the effect of the Christ-event to themselves (the aspect of subjective redemption). What Christ-Jesus did is actually the restoration of the relationship of friendship, love, and intimacy. Once man reacts to the invitation and accepts it through faith in Christ Jesus, he is introduced into the realm of reconciliation; he is no longer *echthros*, "hostile," *asebēs*, "impious," *asthenēs*, "weak," or *hamartōlos*, "a sinner." These are the adjectives that Paul uses of man in his enmity in Rom 5:6-8. Moreover, the change of status is not just a legal fiction; it is a genuine renewal of man's way of life, a radical altering of his relation with God.

Paul attributes this reconciliation of mankind with God especially to the death of Jesus. "We were reconciled to God by the death of his Son — now that we are reconciled, we shall be much more saved by his life" (Rom 5:10). Here the figure of reconciliation is associated closely with the death of Christ, whereas that of salvation is associated with the risen life of Christ (i.e., with the influence of the risen Lord on Christian life and conduct). Sometimes instead of speaking of the "death" of Christ, Paul will refer reconciliation to the "blood" of Christ, i.e., the blood shed in his passion and death. Thus, "You [Gentiles] who were once far off have been brought near in the blood of Christ"; this is said in the context of reconciliation in Eph 2:13. Or again, "he has now reconciled [you] in his body of flesh by his death, in order to present you holy and blameless and irreproachable before him [God]" (Col 1:21). "For in him [Christ] all the fulness of God was pleased to dwell, and through him to reconcile to himself all things, whether on earth or in heaven, making peace by the blood of the cross" (Col 1:19-20).

There are two other aspects of Paul's reflection on the Christ-event as reconciliation which call for comments. The first is his calling Christ "our peace," ascribing to him in an abstract way the very effect of reconciliation that he has brought into the lives of men. Paul sees this as a breaking down of barriers, between Jew and Greek, and between man and God — or, if I might so put it, as a horizontal and a vertical reconciliation.

> 11 Therefore remember that at one time you Gentiles in the flesh, called the uncircumcision by what is called the circumcision, which is made in the flesh by hands — 12 remember that you were at that time separated from Christ, alienated from the commonwealth of Israel, and strangers to the covenants of promise, having no hope and without God in the world. 13 But now in Christ Jesus you who once were far off have been brought near in the blood of Christ. 14 For he is our peace, who has made us both one and has broken down the dividing wall of hostility, 15 by abolishing in his flesh the law of commandments and ordinances, that he might create in himself one new man in place of the two, so making peace, 16 and might reconcile us both to God in one body through the cross, thereby bringing the hostility to an end. 17 And he came and preached peace to you who were far off and peace to those who were near; 18 for through him we both have access in one Spirit to the Father (Eph 2:11-18).

Thus Paul sees the Christ-event as having achieved reconciliation, peace, at-one-ment for Jews and Greeks alike and for both with God through faith in Christ Jesus. In a similar way he writes in Rom 5:1, "We have peace with God through our Lord Jesus Christ."[28]

The other aspect of Paul's reflection is the cosmic dimension of Christ's reconciliation. In the earliest passage in which he discusses reconciliation (2 Cor 5:18-21) he introduces it thus: "All this is from God, who through Christ reconciled us to himself and gave us the ministry of reconciliation; that is, God was in Christ reconciling the world to himself. . . . " Now "the world" (kosmos) may seem to mean the world of men at first,[29] but it is probably to be understood in the sense of the universe of creation, since that is what is implied in Col 1:20, where Paul speaks of God reconciling to himself through Christ "all things, whether on earth or in heaven." In this view of things, Paul sees reconciliation as having not merely an anthropological dimension, but also a cosmic dimension; it affects not only man's relation to God, but also that of the created universe. It thus recasts in terms of reconciliation what Paul wrote about in Rom 8:19-23, where he saw material creation, subjected to futility because of man's sinfulness, now sharing in the hope that is born of the Christ-event: "creation itself will be set free from its bondage to decay and obtain the glorious liberty of the children of God" (8:22). In Romans the figure used was freedom, in 2 Corinthians and Colossians it is rather reconciliation.

This, then, is a brief description of the main elements of Paul's use of the figure of reconciliation to describe an effect of the Christ-event. What is striking is the absence of any allusions to expiation, propitiation, or even sacrifice in any of the passages which deal with the notion of reconciliation.[30] Paul clearly says that the reconciliation was effected by the death of Christ, by his blood, or the blood of the cross; yet he does it without importing these nuances. And with that we may now pass to another phase of our discussion.

3. Problems in the Modern Interpretation of Reconciliation

From the foregoing survey of Pauline passages dealing with reconciliation we can see that the figure being used is derived from the sociological or political spheres of life. The notions of enmity, hostility, estrangement, and alienation, as well as their counterparts, reconciliation, atonement, friendship, and intimacy are derived from social intercourse of human persons or from the relations of ethnic and national groups, such as Jews and Greeks, Palestinians and Romans. There is nothing in the Pauline passages that suggests a cultic or liturgical background to the figure, and even less a sacrificial origin. By contrast, expiation (used by Paul only in Rom 3:25) does have a cultic or liturgical background, since it is derived from the *Yôm Kippûr* ceremony of Leviticus 16. In saying that Christ himself has been proposed as the *hilastērion*, "the means of expiation" or the "mercy seat," Paul sees the blood of Christ achieving what the ritual sprinkling of the mercy seat in the Holy of Holies on the feast of *Yôm Kippûr* was supposed to achieve. That was a yearly rite, a cultic act; and Paul's figurative use of expiation reflects that background. But it is a distinct figure, having nothing to do with reconciliation.[31]

A few years ago E. Käsemann, contributing an article to Bultmann's third Festschrift, *Zeit und Geschichte*, penned some "Erwägungen zum Stichwort 'Versöhnungslehre im Neuen Testament.' "[32] His purpose was to show that "the whole soteriology of the New Testament" could not be summed up as a doctrine of atonement, as he sees it done "in the Anglo-Saxon theological world in particular." Though he names no Anglo-Saxon authors and refers only to "a large number of theological textbooks," his critical finger is not entirely misdirected. Though he speaks of the "Versöhnungslehre im Neuen Testament," he finds that "the motif [of reconciliation] appears only in the general realm of Paulinism, though without having any significant meaning for Pauline theology as a whole."[33] And he concludes that "there is no such thing as a doctrine of reconciliation which is regulative for the whole New Testament. It does not exist even in Paul, who only occasionally makes use of the motif, however important it becomes in the context of 2 Cor 5.18ff."[34] The bulk of Käsemann's subsequent discussion is devoted to the Pauline passages.

Though he may be right in castigating the Anglo-Saxon theological world for thinking of atonement as the summation of NT soteriology, I am not sure that he rightly understands the role of reconciliation in the Pauline writings or that one can write it off as having no significant meaning for Pauline theology. Part of the difficulty is Käsemann's understanding of Pauline theology. It is not until the next-to-last page of the article that one learns that "to Paul the doctrine of justification is the heart of the Christian message; it establishes the legitimacy and sets the limits of all varieties and even interpretations of NT teaching."[35] Let us grant for a moment — *dato, non concesso* — that for Paul the doctrine of justification is the heart of the Christian message, does that mean that since reconciliation is not the same as justification, it plays no significant role in Pauline theology as a whole?

Käsemann arrives at this understanding of reconciliation in Pauline writings by deciding initially that reconciliation "acquires terminological significance in Rom. 5.10f.; 11.15; and — here only with theological emphasis! — II Cor. 5.18ff.," whereas "it appears as a catchword in the hymnic fragments in Col. 1.20, 22 and Eph. 2.16."[36] Now this is a subtle way of writing off unwanted evidence, since we are never told just what the acquiring of terminological significance in the two passages in Romans and the one in 2 Corinthians really means, or what having "theological emphasis" in 2 Corinthians implies. How can a motif acquire terminological significance or theological emphasis "without having any significant meaning for Pauline theology as a whole?" And who decides that?

Käsemann further confuses the issue by associating *katallassein* and *hilaskesthai*; he writes, "The exegete can, strictly speaking, find the New Testament speaking of 'reconciliation' only in those passages in which *katallassein* and *hilaskesthai* and their derivatives occur."[37] Then he asks "to what extent the translation 'reconciliation' ought to take the place of (the surely more appropriate) 'expiate'."[38] By this association and this query, he falls into the same trap that has bedevilled Anglo-Saxon theology for the last four hundred years. In associating *katallassein* and *hilaskesthai*, he does what Paul has never done, and this enables him to attribute to the figure of reconciliation a cultic nuance and a liturgical background which it does not have. Again, when he says that "eschatological reconciliation does not exist apart from the 'means of expiation' mentioned in [Rom] 3.25, which is the dying Christ himself, or apart from his vicarious mediation,"[39] he implies the same confusion. For though it is true that no effect of the Christ-event (described under any of the nine figures mentioned earlier) can exist apart from the event itself, it does not mean that reconciliation is expiation or that *hilastērion* and *katallagē* are the same figure, having the same connotation or origin.

When we look at Käsemann's treatment of the Pauline passages in which reconciliation is mentioned, there are further problems in his discussion. He finds the phrase "the reconciliation of the world" in Rom 11:15 to be used without any preparation and to be obviously a formula that "can only be explained on the grounds of a fixed tradition."[40] Since this is the passage in which Paul discusses the so-called rejection of Israel and finds that in God's providence the reaction of the Jews to the Christian gospel has opened it up to the Gentiles *de facto*, he reflects on how wonderful it will be when they too accept it: "For if their rejection means the reconciliation of the world, what will their acceptance mean but life from the dead?"[41] "Reconciliation of the world" is here used as a tag, without any preparation indeed; that it is part of a "fixed tradition" is quite plausible. But does that mean that it is not Paul's own? Why could it not be echoing Rom 5:1-11 or, better still, 2 Cor 5:19, "God was in Christ reconciling the world to himself." Again, the problem is how to decide that a formulaic expression is echoing something other than Pauline teaching, and not an important element in his theology.

When Käsemann turns to Rom 5:9-10, he finds that reconciliation is used "in a non-cultic sense and means bringing hostility to an end."[42] This is accurate enough; but when he continues that reconciliation takes place "by his blood" (Rom 5:9) or "by the death of his Son" (Rom 5:10) and "for us" (*hyper hēmōn*, 5:8), he immediately decides that these phrases "have a liturgical colouring."[43] But is this clearly so? The "cultic associations" in these phrases are not *per se* evident, and they could just as easily express social or political associations of interpersonal, intergroup relationships quite independently of cult.

The real question in Romans 5 is whether Paul has introduced the motif of reconciliation to heighten the concept of *justificatio impiorum*, viz., by the assertion of *justificatio inimicorum*.[44] There is no doubt that justification and reconciliation are related in Romans 5; but the real question is, what is the nature of that relation? Is reconciliation subordinated to justification? In Rom 5:1 Paul says, "Having been justified . . . , we have peace with God." As I read that verse, it suggests that justification takes place in view of something, viz., reconciliation, so that reconciliation does not "sharpen and point up the doctrine of justification" in Pauline thought. It is rather the other way round. Further involved in this issue is the subtle question of the relation of Romans chs. 1-4 to Romans chs. 5-8, and indeed the place of Romans 5 in the whole of chs. 1-8.[45] No matter how one decides this question, it seems to me to be clear that the climax of chs. 1-8 is not in ch. 4, and as Paul begins ch. 5 he moves from justification to the manifestation of God's love in Christ and through the Spirit (ch. 8), so that the latter is the climax of it all. If so, justification is only a part of the process and a stage in the development of his thesis in Romans chs. 1-8 — and then justification finds a more adequate expression in reconciliation; indeed, "reconciliation" becomes the better way of expressing that process.

When Käsemann takes up 2 Cor 5:18-21, he finds that it is most likely a piece of tradition which was handed down to Paul and that Paul is there echoing a Jewish-Christian tradition, with vss. 19-21 being "a pre-Pauline hymnic fragment."[46] But if Paul has indeed "taken up and used motifs from earlier forms of the Christian proclamation," does that mean that they do not become part of Pauline theology? And the same question has to be asked about the "hymnic fragments in Col. 1.20, 22 and Eph. 2.16."[47] Once we ascertain that there is pre-Pauline material in Paul's writings, does that mean that it is not really part of his thinking or that it cannot be considered a part of his theology?

The extreme to which this sort of analysis of Pauline writings is carried is found in Käsemann's discussion of the relation between what he calls anthropological and cosmological reconciliation. It is the question that we mentioned earlier in terms of cosmic reconciliation over against the reconciliation of man to God. For Käsemann the anthropological reconciliation presupposes cosmological reconciliation; the latter is especially prominent in the "two deutero-Pauline texts" of Col 1:20 and Eph 2:16.[48] Käsemann argues thus:

We have already seen in Rom. 5.10f. the goal and result of the reconciling act to
be peace; similarly these texts [Colossians and Ephesians] are clearly
concerned with cosmic peace, the revelation of which is dreamed of as early as
Vergil's Fourth Eclogue. This peace is thought of as the eschatological state of
salvation, not as a psycholgoical attitude, something in which the NT is very
rarely interested. In this situation of peace what was formerly separated
becomes solidly united, i.e., the heavenly is united with the earthly, just as
warring earthly camps are united with one another. Even religious antipathies
now become irrelevant, as may be seen in a radical way in the antithesis
between Israel and the Gentile world. The world is made peaceful, as under the
pax romana, in that it is everywhere subjected to its new Lord, Christ, as
Cosmocrator.[49]

Now in this paragraph Käsemann has caught up beautifully some of the
Pauline or Deuteropauline nuances of reconciliation, and his paraphrase of
them leaves little to be desired. And again,

Though the world may not yet know of the transformation that has taken
place, the Christian community does. Its message is characterized by the open
proclamation of the seizure of power by God and his appointed Savior and by
the verification of that proclamation in the union of both Jews and Gentiles in
the Christian church.[50]

But the difficulty is that Käsemann sees the affirmation of cosmic
reconciliation as something that precedes anthropological reconciliation
and understands both Col 1:20-22 and 2 Cor 5:19-20 implying a "transition
from a cosmological to an anthropological message of reconciliation."[51] He
seems to mean that Paul or the author of the Deuteropaulines only came to
the idea of the reconciliation of mankind from the notion of the
reconciliation of the world (or the All), and that this was a notion current in
the Hellenistic world of the time, as is dreamed of in Vergil's Fourth
Eclogue.[52] But there are several comments that are in order in this regard.
First, one may concede that there is a vague idea of reconciliation in the
Fourth Eclogue. In it Vergil sings of the *ultima aetas*, when "a new
generation descends from heaven on high" and "a golden race springs up
throughout the world," putting an end to "the iron brood." As it begins in
Pollio's consulship, "lingering traces of our guilt shall become void and
release the earth from its continual dread." And the child to be born "shall
have the gift of divine life, shall see heroes mingled with gods, and shall
himself be seen of them, and shall sway a world to which his father's virtues
have brought peace." And the untilled earth shall pour forth its bounty of
flowers and plants and vegetables, while "the herds shall fear not huge
lions" (*Eclogues* 4.4-22). I regard the idea of reconciliation that may be

contained in this Eclogue as vague because it is really dealing with another matter, the birth of the Golden Age, when all will be blissful and bountiful. To compare such a view of cosmic progression with the cosmic reconciliation of Pauline or Deuteropauline writings is somewhat farfetched. What they have in common is only a rosy, utopian view of a future age; but all the details are remarkably different.

Second, it seems to me that the prime analogate in the Pauline writings that deal with reconciliation is anthropological reconciliation, and that the transition is from mankind to the world, or to the All, not the other way round. Cf. Rom 8:21-23 for the progress of his thought (under another image, to be sure).

Thirdly, it is difficult to understand how a notion that Käsemann generally relegates to Deuteropauline writings, cosmic reconciliation in Colossians and Ephesians, can be considered the source of something that is found in the Pauline writings themselves, anthropological reconciliation.

These are, then, some of the difficulties that I have with the Käsemann interpretation of the role of reconciliation in Pauline theology. Despite them I have recognized that there are some excellent paragraphs in the article on the consequences of this notion for Christian life and conduct. And this brings me to the last point of my discussion.

4. The Pertinence of Pauline Reconciliation to Modern Life

Having reflected on the figure of reconciliation that Paul uses to describe one of the effects of the Christ-event and that emphasizes the gratuitous initiative taken by God to bring mankind closely into a sphere of friendship and intimacy with himself, we can see that this idea has to be proclaimed anew by Christians of today. Ours is a world in which we have struggled to put an end to war, not merely because we fear the consequences of a Third World War of atomic- or hydrogen-bomb dimensions, but because men of varying religious backgrounds, Judeo-Christian or other, have come to a stage of cosmic or worldwide awareness that simply as men we can no longer act that way with one another. "Jamais plus la guerre," said Paul VI, addressing the United Nations. For Christians in particular the motivation for this is found in Paul's idea of reconciliation, in the breaking down of the barriers between men (and by implication, between nations).

But on another level of dealings between groups and individuals within a given national or ethnic society there is still further need for reflection on the Pauline message of reconciliation. There is a feeling abroad that our human society is sick — for all sorts of reasons. One aspect of it is precisely the alienation of men and women from those things or those persons with which they have been intimately identified in the past. To such as are estranged and alienated the Pauline message of reconciliation addresses itself ever anew: "For all of you who were baptized into Christ have put on Christ; there is neither Jew nor Greek, there is neither slave nor free, there is neither male nor female; for you are all one in Christ Jesus." This Paul wrote in another context (Gal 3:27-28), but it supplies the background to his thinking on reconciliation. The Christian, regardless of his or her ethnic origin, social status, or sexual identity is expected to meet the challenge of putting on Christ, of donning his outlook on life. If he is "our peace" and has made us both one (Eph 2:14), then in him the Christian finds the remedy to the alienation that besets him or her in the society in which he or she lives.

In the earliest passage in which Paul deals with reconciliation, he speaks of himself as having been given "the ministry of reconciliation" (2 Cor 5:18) and of being an "ambassador for Christ" (5:20). In this, as in some other passages (cf. Col 1:24), Paul did not hesitate to depict himself as having the task of extending, in a sense, one of the effects of the Christ-event. Paul never would have substituted himself for Christ, implying that anything that he would do would replace or substitute for the Christ-event itself. But he could speak of himself as a "minister of reconciliation," proclaiming to the world the message of reconciliation, announcing the effect of the Christ-event, and striving to get more and more of mankind to appropriate to itself the benefits thereof. So, as ambassador for Christ, he extends the ministry of reconciliation.

Paul's teaching about reconciliation obviously has something of the idyllic about it. We look at other Christians who surround us, and we see all the forms of estrangement and alienation among them as among many others who are not Christian. We wonder why it is that such an effect of the Christ-event has not taken root and manifested itself in the lives of such persons, if faith in Christ Jesus and baptism into his life really mean all that they are supposed to mean. This is a real problem, and it has often been called the problem of the integration of Christian life. How does a Christian become aware that his outlook and life are to be dominated by the person of Christ and all that he stood for and taught? Paul was not unaware of this himself. Writing in a context that did not deal with reconciliation as such, he said, "I have been crucified with Christ; it is no longer I who live, but Christ who lives in me; and the life I now live in the flesh (*kata sarka*) I live by faith in the Son of God," or that the ontological reality of Christ-in-me has somehow or other to be brought to the level of psychological awareness. This is the problem of Christian life: "Be what you are." You are in Christ; you have entered a state of reconciliation with God and with your fellowmen through your faith and baptism into Christ Jesus. The challenge is thus given to men and women of all ages and generations to be what they are.

By extension of the last two points that have been made, it would not be false to say that the Christian of today shares in a sense in that "ministry of reconciliation" of which Paul spoke. The role of the Christian in the twentieth-century would be to manifest that reconciliation to others, to other Christians, to his/her Jewish brother or sister, to other members of the human race not part of the Judeo-Christian heritage.

There is obviously a greater problem here today than that envisaged by Paul. His horizons were limited to the Christian message that he was explaining to the Christians to whom he wrote, whether they came from a Jewish or a Gentile background. He found the reconciliation of them in Christ Jesus, who is "our peace." Today the role of the Christian is to be faithful to his/her own Christian heritage, yet so manifest his/her love and friendship as to include even those who are not of his/her own immediate Christian circle. If the Roman poet Terentius could write, "Homo sum; humani nihil a me alienum puto" (*Heaut.* 1.1, 25), the Christian could also boast, "Christianus sum; christiani nihil a me alienum puto." That Christian challenge would be at once a loyalty to one's own heritage and an openness to and love of what is not of it.

In Paul's ken the reconciliation of Jew and Greek that he spoke of was envisaged as an at-one-ment brought about between them through faith and baptism in Christ Jesus — through the conversion of both Jews and Greeks to Christianity. This is Paul's sole perspective. Today we have all witnessed in one way or another the alienation of Christian and Jew. It is an age-old problem of a barrier that exists between us, born of what Paul calls "their rejection." This stern word, used of his former co-religionists, was likewise associated with his sorrow about that barrier (see Rom 9:2-3). But as we ponder the implications of his teaching about the reconciliation of all men in Christ, we cannot be blind to the problems that that teaching has created and can still create. For Christian theologians have never been able to explain why it is that the God that they worship has in his providence continued to favor a people which nourishes itself on a great deal of the same scriptures that feed our Christian lives and yet have not accepted the reconciliation that is at hand in Christ Jesus. Christian theologians have no adequate theology of Israel. This is the enigma that the Pauline theology of reconciliation proposes.

If I was somewhat critical of Käsemann earlier in this paper, I should like to end by making my own some of his comments on an aspect of reconciliation. Without buying all the connections which he establishes between the NT hymns and "the unbridled enthusiasm . . . of the earliest Hellenistic community and the beginnings of its world mission," I can agree that the Pauline teaching on reconciliation could be viewed too enthusiastically and with too rosy a hue, so that an "individual Christian will understand the salvation he experiences as devoid of temptation and consequently cease looking toward the future and giving himself to the service of others. So it is no accident that the anthropological statements about reconciliation occur in a parenetic context, portraying existence as still hanging in the balance. The message of reconciliation is not an eschatological myth, as in Vergil's Fourth Eclogue. It is actualized between the indicative of the gift of salvation and the imperative of the duties of salvation, i.e., in the historical realm, the realm of concrete daily life and corporal community. Cosmic peace does not settle over the world, as in a fairy tale. It takes root only so far as men in the service of reconciliation confirm that they have themselves found peace with God."[53]

* * *

In concluding this discussion of the theological notion of reconciliation, I should like to stress that I have sought merely to situate it in Pauline theology as a whole and to restore it to its merited relation to justification. I have not tried to say that it is in Pauline theology more important than justification or that the essence of Pauline theology can be summed up by it. It expresses an aspect of the Christ-event that justification does not, and it is really impossible to say which is more important. In certain discussions of Paul (e.g., Romans 5) one may debate, as I have above, whether justification is not subordinated to reconciliation, but that still leaves the question open about the place of reconciliation in Pauline theology as a whole.

1. See F. Büchsel, "Allassō, . . . ," TDNT 1 (1964) 251-59; R. Bultmann, Theology of the New Testament (London: SCM, 1956) 1. 285-87; T. R. Clark, Saved by His Life: A Study of the New Testament Doctrine of Reconciliation and Salvation (New York: Macmillan, 1959) 179-83; J. Dupont, La réconciliation dans la théologie de Saint Paul (ALBO 3/32; Bruges: Desclée de Brouwer, 1953); L. Goppelt, "Versöhnung durch Christus," Christologie und Ethik: Aufsätze zum Neuen Testament (Göttingen: Vandenhoeck & Ruprecht, 1968) 147-64; E. Käsemann, An die Römer (HNT 8a; Tübingen: Mohr, 1973) 129; "Erwägungen zum Stichwort 'Versöhnungslehre im Neuen

Testament'," *Zeit und Geschichte: Dankesgabe an Rudolf Bultmann zum 80. Geburtstag* (ed. E. Dinkler; Tübingen: Mohr, 1964) 47-59; "Some Thoughts on the Theme 'The Doctrine of Reconciliation in the New Testament'," *The Future of Our Religious Past: Essays in Honour of Rudolf Bultmann* (ed. J. M. Robinson; New York: Harper & Row, 1971) 49-64; A. F. N. Lekkerkerker, "Dialectisch spreken over de verzoening," *Nederlands theologische Stemmen* 1 (1946-47) 212-32; W. Michaelis, *Versöhnung des Alls: Die frohe Botschaft von der Gnade Gottes* (Gümligen/Bern: Siloah, 1950) 23-30, 122-51; J. Michl, "Die 'Versöhnung' (Kol 1, 20)," *TQ* 128 (1948) 442-62; A. Nygren, *Die Versöhnung als Gottestat* (Studien der Luther-Akademie, 5; Gütersloh: Bertelsmann, 1932); E. Percy, *Die Probleme der Kolosser- und Epheserbriefe* (Acta regiae societatis humaniorum litterarum Lundensis, 39; Lund: Gleerup, 1946) 85-92, 271-73; A. Ritschl, *Die christliche Lehre von der Rechtfertigung und Versöhnung* (3 vols.; 3d ed.; Bonn: Adolf Marcus, 1888-89); V. Taylor, *Forgiveness and Reconciliation: A Study in New Testament Theology* (2d ed.; London: Macmillan, 1948) 70-108; B. N. Wambacq, "Per eum reconciliare . . . quae in caelis sunt," *RB* 55 (1948) 35-42; D. E. H. Whiteley, "St. Paul's Thought on the Atonement," *JTS* ns 8 (1957) 240-55; *The Theology of St. Paul* (Oxford: Blackwell, 1964) 130-54. G. Wiencke, *Paulus über Jesu Tod: Die Deutung des Todes Jesu bei Paulus und ihre Herkunft* (Beiträge zur Förderung christlicher Theologie, 2/42; Gütersloh: Bertelsmann, 1939) 69-78; G. W. H. Lampe, *Reconciliation in Christ* (Maurice Lectures 1955; London: Longmans, Green, 1956); J. Denney, *The Christian Doctrine of Reconciliation* (London: J. Clarke, 1959).

2. By Käsemann, "Some Thoughts."

3. E.g., 1 Thes 4:2, 15; 1 Cor 7:10 [cf. 7:25]; 9:14; 13:2; Rom 12:14; 13:9; 16:19. See further W. D. Davies, *Paul and Rabbinic Judaism: Some Rabbinic Elements in Pauline Theology* (London: S.P.C.K., 1948) 136-41; B. Gerhardson, *Memory and Manuscript: Oral Tradition and Written Transmission in Rabbinic Judaism and Early Christianity* (ASNU 22; Lund: Gleerup, 1961) 302-06; D. M. Stanley, "Pauline Allusions to the Sayings of Jesus," *CBQ* 23 (1961) 26-39; D. L. Dungan, *The Sayings of Jesus in the Churches of Paul: The Use of the Synoptic Tradition in the Regulation of Early Church Life* (Philadelphia: Fortress, 1971); F. F. Bruce, "Paul and the Historical Jesus," *BJRL* 56 (1974) 317-35.

I do not mean that Paul did not know the words or the teaching of Jesus or that his interpretation of the Christ-event was wholly derived from his conversion-experience or something similar. His mention of his visit to Jerusalem (*historēsai Kēphan*, Gal 1:18) was almost certainly intended to suggest that he had obtained some information about Jesus from Cephas. One can also debate the meaning of 2 Cor 5:16, his knowing Christ according to the flesh. But whatever one wants to say about his knowledge of the earthly Jesus, the fact still remains that he is interested much more in the interpretation of the Christ-event for Christians who had never witnessed the earthly ministry of Jesus of Nazareth.

4. Most of the letters of the Pauline corpus were composed prior to the composition of the earliest gospel (Mark, ca. A.D. 65).

5. E.g., Whiteley, *The Theology of St. Paul*, 130.

6. See F. Amiot, *The Key Concepts of St. Paul* (New York: Herder and Herder, 1962);

S. Lyonnet, "The Terminology of 'Salvation,' " *Sin, Redemption, and Sacrifice: A Biblical and Patristic Study* (eds. S. Lyonnet and L. Sabourin; AnBib 48; Rome: Biblical Institute, 1970) 63-78; W. Foerster and G. Fohrer, "*Sōzō, sōtēria, . . .*," *TDNT* 7 (1971) 965-1024.

7. In this instance one can ask whether Paul is using the word *hilastērion* as an adjective or as a noun; in the interpretation which I prefer it would be a concrete noun, best translated as "a means of expiation," with an allusion to the *kappōret* of Exod 25:17-20, which is translated in the LXX as *hilastērion*.

8. See my "Pauline Theology," *JBC*, 2. 815-16 (§83-89); S. Lyonnet, "The Terminology of 'Expiation' in the Old Testament," "The Terminology of 'Expiation' in the New Testament," *Sin, Redemption, and Sacrifice*, 120-66; Whiteley, *The Theology of St. Paul*, 145-47. Contrast L. Morris, "The Biblical Use of the Term 'Blood,' " *JTS* ns 3 (1952) 216-27. See further L. Moraldi, *Espiazione sacrificale e riti espiatori nell'ambiente biblico e nell'Antico Testamento* (AnBib 5; Rome: Biblical Institute, 1956).

9. See my "Pauline Theology," §90-93 (Redemptive Liberation); S. Lyonnet, "The Terminology of 'Liberation,' " *Sin, Redemption, and Sacrifice*, 79-119; Whiteley, *The Theology of St. Paul*, 137-45.

10. See O. Procksch and K. G. Kuhn, "*Hagios, hagiazō, . . .*," *TDNT* 1 (1964) 88-115; L. Cerfaux, *Christ in the Theology of St. Paul* (New York: Herder and Herder, 1959), 296-315.

11. See H. Schlier, "*Eleutheros, eleutheroō, . . .*," *TDNT* 2 (1964) 487-502; H. D. Betz, "Spirit, Freedom, and Law: Paul's Message to the Galatian Churches," *Svensk Exegetisk Årsbok* 39 (1974) 145-60; R. Schnackenburg, "Freedom in the Thought of the Apostle Paul," *Present and Future: Modern Aspects of New Testament Theology* (Notre Dame: University of Notre Dame, 1966) 64-80; D. Nestle, *Eleutheria: Studien zum Wesen der Freiheit bei den Griechen und im Neuen Testament* (Hermeneutische Untersuchungen zur Theologie, 16; Tübingen: Mohr, 1967).

12. See P. Stuhlmacher, *Gerechtigkeit Gottes bei Paulus* (FRLANT 87; Göttingen: Vandenhoeck & Ruprecht, 1965); K. Kertelge, *"Rechtfertigung" bei Paulus: Studien zur Struktur und zum Bedeutungsgehalt des paulinischen Rechtfertigungsbegriffs* (NTAbh ns 3; Münster in W.: Aschendorff, 1967); J. A. Fitzmyer, "Pauline Theology," §94-97; E. Käsemann, "Justification and Salvation History in the Epistle to the Romans," *Perspectives on Paul* (Philadelphia: Fortress, 1971) 60-78; J. A. Ziesler, *The Meaning of Righteousness in Paul: A Linguistic and Theological Enquiry* (SNTSMS 20; Cambridge: Cambridge University, 1972); D. Lührmann, "Rechtfertigung und Versöhnung: Zur Geschichte der paulinischen Tradition," *ZTK* 67 (1970) 436-52.

13. In this instance the abstract noun is not found in Paul's writings, but he does use the verb *metamorphoun*. See further J. Dupont, "Le chrétien, miroir de la gloire divine, d'après II Cor. 3,18," *RB* 56 (1949) 392-411; W. C. van Unnik, " 'With Unveiled Face,' an Exegesis of 2 Corinthians iii 12-18," *NovT* 6 (1963) 153-69; I. E. Friesen, *The Glory of the Ministry of Jesus Christ: Illustrated by a Study of 2 Cor. 2:14-3:18* (Theologische Dissertationen, 7; Basel: F. Reinhardt, 1971); D. M. Stanley, *Christ's Resurrection in*

Pauline Soteriology (AnBib 13; Rome: Biblical Institute, 1961) 131-34; S. Schulz, "Die Decke des Moses," *ZNW* 49 (1958) 1-30.

14. See W. Foerster, "*Ktizō, ktisis*, . . . ," *TDNT* 3 (1965) 1000-35, esp. 1033-35. Cf. E. Sjöberg, "Neuschöpfung in den Toten-Meer-Rollen," *ST* 9 (1955) 131-36.

15. On this figure, see the literature cited in n. 1 above.

16. One further figure might be added, viz. "forgiveness" (*aphesis*), a remitting of the debt implied in the sins of mankind. However, since this figure is found only in the Captivity Letters of the Pauline corpus, some might prefer to consider it a Deuteropauline figure, which is closer to the Lucan way of viewing the Christ-event. In any case, one would have to discuss here the very problematic word *paresis* in Rom 3:25, which may be nothing more than a synonym for *aphesis*.

17. See Büchsel, "*Allassō*, . . . ," 251.

18. There is no need to rehearse this evidence here, since it has been adequately presented by Dupont, *La réconciliation*, 7-15. — An interesting additional example of the secular use of the Greek expression comes from a papyrus contract of remarriage found in one of the Murabba'at caves in Palestine. It is dated to the year A.D. 124 (the seventh year of Hadrian, in the consulate of Manius Acilius Glabrio and Bellicius Torquatus) and bears witness to the remarriage of Eleaios, son of Simon, of the village of Galoda, to Salome, daughter of John Galgoula. The crucial part of the text reads: "Since it happened some time ago to Eleaios (son of) Simon to disagree with and divorce *(apallagēnai kai apolyein)* Salome (daughter of) John Galgoula [. . .] for the sake of living together (?), now the same Eleaios agrees anew (*ex ananeōseōs*) to reconcile and to take to himself (*katallaxai k*[*ai*] *proslabesthai*) the same Salome (daughter of) John Galgoula as wedded wi[fe] with dowry of 200 denarii, which make 50 Tyrian (shekels)" (Mur 115:3-5). Here one finds not only the use of *apolyein* in the sense of "divorce" (as in Matt 1:19; 5:31-32; 19:3-9; Mark 10:2-12; Luke 16:18; contrast 1 Cor 7:10-11), but also *katallassein* in a secular sense. What is interesting is the active use of the verb with an object (to reconcile the same Salome). P. Benoit, who published the Greek text, translates it, however, differently: "est d'accord pour se réconcilier à nouveau et reprendre la même Salomé." See *Les grottes de Murabba'at* (DJD 2; Oxford: Clarendon, 1961) 250.

19. So at least reads the LXX MS A (the purpose infinitive *diallaxai* in MS A has as its counterpart in MS B the infinitive *epistrepsai*); the MT has an infinitive, *lhšybw*, which is vocalized as *lahªšîbāw*. Since the latter makes no sense in the context, emendations have been suggested. As far as our discussion is concerned, it seems rather obvious that the exact nuance in *diallassein*/*katallassein* is not rooted in the Hebrew scriptural tradition and that Greek translators have introduced the idea of "reconciliation" which is otherwise well attested in Hellenistic writers. I am aware that compounds of *allassein* are used in the LXX to translate various Hebrew words; but the question is whether the Hebrew words so translated actually denoted what the Greek words did or whether the Greek words have introduced a further Hellenistic (if not Hellenic) nuance.

20. It should be noted, however, in this instance that we are not told how Ajax was reconciling himself with the gods. J. Dupont (*La réconciliation*, p. 13) speaks of his

doing this "au moyen de purifications rituelles." This may be involved, but Sophocles does not even hint at them; and it seems more likely in view of the fundamental thrust of the play that what is meant is that Ajax has gone to reconcile himself to the gods by his own death. The extent to which anyone can read a cultic or ritual sense into Sophocles' expression in *Ajax* 744 is highly questionable. — See further 163-65 below.

21. Büchsel, "*Alassō*, . . . ," 254.

22. This is also the conclusion of Dupont, *La réconciliation*, 28. He also rightly admits that Paul invests the figure with certain nuances derived from his Jewish background. But I am not sure that the figure of reconciliation has "le caractère essentiellement juridique" which he associates with it.

23. See *The Compact Edition of the Oxford English Dictionary* (New York: Oxford University, 1971), 1. 135. — The first instance of the verb "atone" is cited from Shakespeare (*Richard the Second*, 1.i 202). One will find its use there is in the secular sense. The *OED* continues: "*Atone* was not admitted into the Bible in 1611, though *atonement* had been in since Tindale."

24. See note 8 above.

25. In this discussion of Pauline passages dealing with reconciliation, I am treating ten letters of the corpus as authentic (1-2 Thes, Gal, Phil, 1-2 Cor, Rom, Phlm, Col, Eph). If one prefers to regard 2 Thes, Col, and Eph as Deuteropauline, even though not in the same sense as the Pastorals, it would require but a slight adjustment to speak of the author of these letters rather than of Paul. In any case, they belong to a Pauline circle and reflect a view of the Christ-event that it represented in the early Christian church. The interpretation of the Christ-event as reconciliation that one encounters in Col and Eph is so similar to that in 2 Cor and Rom that it is almost impossible to distinguish a Pauline and a Deuteropauline view of this matter. See further my remarks on Käsemann's treatment of the Pauline material below, 165-67.

26. See further Bultmann, *Theology of the New Testament*, 1. 232-38; Fitzmyer, "Pauline Theology," §119.

27. See 158 above; cf. Dupont, *La réconciliation*, 10-18.

28. Here one could add further Pauline passages that deal with the peace of Christ. He is "the peace of God" that surpasses all understanding and that will keep your hearts and your minds in Christ Jesus" (Phil 4:7). Or "let the peace of Christ rule in your hearts, to which indeed you were called in one body" (Col 3:15). Cf. 2 Thes 3:16. Moreover, "peace" is not to be understood in this connection merely as the absence of war or enmity, for it carries with it further the OT nuances of *šālôm*, the wholeness or perfection of bounty that can come only from God himself.

29. As in Rom 3:6; 5:12. But Paul also used *kosmos* in the sense of the created universe; see Rom 1:20; 1 Cor 3:22; cf. Eph 1:4. See Bultmann, *Theology of the New Testament*, 1. 254-59.

30. Dupont (*La réconciliation*, 39-42) associates reconciliation with both sacrifice and propitiation. But in this I have to disagree. It is not that Paul did not consider the death of Christ a sacrifice (cf. Eph 5:2), but rather whether in the passages in which he deals

with reconciliation he uses the expressions, "his death," "the blood of the cross," or "the blood of Christ" with the sacrificial connotation. No one will deny that the saying of Lev 17:11 ("for the life of the flesh is in the blood; and I have given it for you upon the altar to make expiation for yourselves; for it is the blood that makes expiation") underlies Paul's use of "blood" in Rom 3:25, where it is closely associated with *hilastērion*. That meaning of blood is thus clearly related to expiation. But in Romans 3 Paul does not introduce the figure of reconciliation.

I cannot help but think that Whiteley ("St. Paul's Thought on the Atonement," 240-55, exp. 247-49) comes closer to Paul's sense when he relates the mention of blood in the reconciliation passages to "covenant blood" (cf. Exod 24:3-8): "The Apostle means that through his death Christ constituted a relationship with all things analogous to that established in the Old Testament by means of the blood of the covenant" (249). Cf. his *Theology of St. Paul*, 140. Lührmann ("Rechtfertigung und Versöhnung," 438-40) speaks of the use of blood in Rom 3:24-26 as also related to "Bundestheologie." In a footnote he recognizes the connection with Leviticus 16 and the similar use of material in Qumran literature. To my way of thinking the primary reference in Romans 3 is to Leviticus 16 — and only thereafter possibly a reference to "Bundestheologie. The reason is that it is only in Romans 3 that "blood" and *hilastērion* are associated, whereas elsewhere the "blood" or "death" of Christ (e.g., when related to reconciliation) could have the covenant reference more directly.

31. What is curious is to recall that English-speaking Jews translate *Yôm hak-Kippûrîm* as the "Day of Atonement." See *The Torah: The Five Books of Moses* (Philadelphia: Jewish Publication Society, 1962) 226 (Lev 23:27). This name is undoubtedly influenced by the translation of Christian English bibles. In French the Hebrew expression is more accurately translated as "Jour de l'Expiation." The JPS *Torah* uses, however, the noun "expiation" in Lev 16:6, 10, 11, 17; 17:11 (where the *RSV* has "atonement"; but cf. Lev 16:34 in the JPS *Torah*). — Apparently, English-speaking Jews have never used any other translation for the Hebrew name of this feast-day; at least so I have been informed by Prof. Harry M. Orlinsky and Dr. Philip Goodman, the compiler of *The Yom Kippur Anthology* (Philadelphia: Jewish Publication Society of America, 1971). To both of these gentlemen I owe my thanks.

32. See note 1 above for details. The article was translated under the title "Some Thoughts on the Theme 'The Doctrine of Reconciliation in the New Testament,'" but in view of the article's starting-point it would have been better to render "Versöhnungslehre" as "the doctrine of Atonement," for this is the term more properly used in the Anglo-Saxon theological world, which Käsemann criticizes.

33. "Some Thoughts," 51. Käsemann considers Colossians and Ephesians to be Deuteropauline, but in reality this distinction means little in his discussion.

34. Ibid., — Käsemann continues: "In the deutero-Paulines [presumably Colossians and Ephesians] it also characterizes only very limited contexts, specifically the liturgical tradition contained in two passages" [presumably Col 1:20, 22; Eph 2:26]. But the fact that the image is used in a text of "liturgical tradition" does not mean that the image itself is of a liturgical background; liturgy does use figures and language drawn from other contexts and relationships.

35. "Some Thoughts," 63 — I can understand how one might say that the doctrine of justification establishes the legitimacy and sets the limits of *Pauline* teaching, but "of [presumably, all] NT teaching"? How does Paul become a norm for John, or Pauline theology a criterion of, say, Lucan theology?

D. Lührmann ("Rechtfertigung und Versöhnung," 446) likewise asserts that reconciliation has "keine eigenständige Bedeutung" in Paul's theology, but is subordinated to the "Hauptthema seiner Theologie, das in der Antithese von Glaube und Gesetz zu beschrieben ist." Though Lührmann tries to refine Käsemann's position somewhat, he is still operating with the basic presupposition of the latter. He breaks with Käsemann, when the latter describes "Versöhnung" as only one soteriological variant among others that were taken up in early Christianity, especially in those circles in which Christ was hailed as the cosmic victor. But he still derives the whole idea of anthropological reconciliation from cosmic reconciliation, as does Käsemann.

36. "Some Thoughts," 50.

37. Ibid.

38. Ibid. — This is not merely a problem of the English translation of Käsemann's article, to which I referred above in note 32, but it is even true of the German original: "Blickt man von da aus auf die um *hilaskesthai* kreisende Wortgruppe, muss sofort gefragt werden, ob und wie weit die Übersetzung 'versöhnen' überhaupt an die Stelle des sicher angemesseneren 'sühnen' treten darf" ("Erwägungen," 48). The problem is by what right one can say that the *katallassein*-words belong to the orbit of *hilaskesthai* in Pauline thinking. *Sühnen*/expiate has cultic, liturgical, and even sacrificial overtones; but does *versöhnen*/reconcile imply any of that? Moreover, Paul never uses the two together in the same passage. That atonement, reconciliation, expiation, and even propitiation, came to imply all that is part of the history of the doctrine of the atonement. But is it so in Pauline theology?

39. "Some Thoughts," 52. — To show that *hilaskesthai* and words related to it designate "an event in the cultic realm," Käsemann cites Rom 3:25; Heb 2:17; 8:12; 9:5; I John 2:2; 4:10. Then he adds, confusing the issue still more, "to which may be added the ransom-sayings in Mark 10.45 and 1 Tim 2.6" (50). But the image in *lytron* (or *antilytron*) is distinct. The mere fact that Paul links both *apolytrōsis* and *hilastērion* in Rom 3:24-25 does not necessarily mean that they have the *same* background or, for that matter, share a cultic background, let alone the *same cultic* background. That *hilastērion* has a Palestinian Jewish cultic background can be readily admitted; but if one were to insist rather on its Hellenistic background (e.g., on its derivation from expiatory rites in the Greco-Roman world), it could also be of cultic origin. But it is not at all clear that the figure involved in *apolytrōsis* is necessarily cultic. Here one would have to discuss the extent to which the (fictive) emancipation of a slave or a prisoner at the shrine of a god in the ancient eastern Mediterranean world was really considered to be an act of worship or cult. And if it were, would that imply the same cultic background that the Hellenistic origin of *hilaskesthai* might?

40. "Some Thoughts," 51.

41. The phrase, "life from the dead," is very difficult to interpret and has been

understood in many ways; for my preferred understanding of it, see the commentary on Romans in *JBC*, 2.§112 (p. 323).

42. "Some Thoughts," 51.

43. Ibid., 52.

44. Ibid. — Käsemann's starting-point was a criticism of Anglo-Saxon theology and its use of the doctrine of atonement as a summation of NT soteriology. Given all the overloading of the term "reconciliation" or "atonement" with the nuances of expiation, propitiation, satisfaction, penal substitution, etc., that ensued in that "theological world," Käsemann was rightly critical. But when he employs the tag *justificatio impiorum* in the context of a discussion of Pauline theology and fashions another in imitation of it, *justificatio inimicorum* (thereby subordinating reconciliation to justification), he runs the risk of importing into Pauline theology nuances born of a later problematic. For that Latin abstract phrase, though based on Rom 4:5 (*dikaiounta ton asebē*), is not found precisely in Paul's writings — and I do not mean simply that Paul did not write in Latin. The abstraction with the genitive plural is not his way of putting it; in using it, Käsemann betrays a later theological stance.

45. For a brief summary of the discussion about the relation of ch. 5 to the whole of Romans, see my commentary in *JBC*, 2.§49 (305) and the literature cited there. Cf. U. Luz, "Zum Aufbau von Röm. 1-8," *TZ* 25 (1969) 161-81. — As for the relation of reconciliation and justification, it might be well to recall the treatment of J. Weiss, *The History of Primitive Christianity* (ed. F. C. Grant; New York: Wilson-Erickson, 1937), 2. 496-504, esp. 497: "The most common and comprehensive expression for the event which Paul had experienced, and which all Christians must experience, is undoubtedly 'reconciliation' . . . ."

46. "Some Thoughts," 53.

47. Ibid., 50. — Obviously, it would not be part of it if one insists on the Deuteropauline character of these hymnic fragments in Colossians and Ephesians.

48. Actually cosmic reconciliation is not found in Eph 2:11-22. Since it is found in Col 1:20-22, it may be called Deuteropauline. But it should be remembered that it is explicitly mentioned in 2 Cor 5:18-19 and is echoed in Rom 11:15. Hence it cannot be simply written off as a Deuteropauline motif, as Käsemann implies in his discussion of the idea in *An die Römer* (HNT 8a; Tübingen: Mohr, 1973) 129.

49. "Some Thoughts," 54.

50. Ibid., 55.

51. Ibid., 55.

52. Ibid.

53. Ibid., 55-56.

RAYMOND E. BROWN, S.S.

Luke's Method in the Annunciation Narrative of Chapter One

For Roman Catholicism the narratives of Jesus' birth and infancy found in Matthew and Luke may well constitute the last frontier to be crossed by biblical criticism. The Roman Church has taken a somewhat liberal position regarding the composition of the gospel accounts of the ministry of Jesus: they are *not* literal, chronological reports of his words and deeds.[1] But even with such an official directive it has been difficult to move Catholics from a literalistic view. The church has taken no official position on the birth narratives in the gospels; and so *a fortiori* it is and will be more difficult to correct the general impression that Matthew and Luke preserve literal family histories of Jesus' origins. True, some Catholic writers, particularly in Europe, have stressed the OT atmosphere and midrashic character of the infancy narratives; but most often even informed clergy and laity treat the birth stories as if they had the same historical value as the passion stories. Sentimentality, emotion, and doctrinal fears have discouraged forays across the last frontier.

While Protestant biblical criticism breached this frontier a long time ago, it never really settled the territory and made the desert bloom. Early in this century most Protestant scholars recognized that the two infancy stories were different in kind from the rest of the gospel material and sometimes in conflict with it — indeed, sometimes in conflict with each other. But the popular character of such narratives, featuring magi, a birth star, the wicked king, angelic messengers and choruses, led to debunking and almost to a contempt whereby such material was deemed unworthy to be a vehicle of the pure gospel message. Thus, the frontier territory of Jesus' birth, once it had been "scouted" by critics, was judged capable of only marginal scholarly cultivation, and likely to be settled only by primitives and romantics.[2]

Through a commentary on the infancy narratives of Matthew and Luke,[3] I hope eventually to argue the case that, although of different origin and

179

historical character from the rest of the gospel, these stories are truly gospel, integrated into the purposes of the respective evangelists, and proclaiming vividly the good news of salvation. This essay treating the two annunciation scenes in Luke 1 is a small gesture in that direction. Let me begin with a few background reminders.

If we assume that Mark was written before Matthew and Luke, it is clear that the gospel narrative once began with the public ministry of Jesus, inaugurated by the baptism. No matter how early they circulated in a popular setting, it was only late in the century that the birth stories came to be included as part of the gospel account (and even then perhaps not in all churches). A late dating for the birth stories in their present form is harmonious with the modern approach to christology, for they reflect a "higher" and more developed christology. While formulas found in the Pauline letters and in the sermons in Acts associate Jesus' divine sonship with the resurrection, and while the body of the gospels associates divine sonship with the beginning of the ministry (the baptism), the infancy narratives associate divine sonship with conception in the womb of Mary. Jesus is clearly God's Son from the first moment of his earthly existence. Granting all of this, we are still faced with particular problems about the Lucan infancy narrative. There is no real doubt that the author we call Luke,[4] who wrote the body of the gospel and the book of Acts, wrote the two chapters of infancy narrative.[5] But did he write the infancy narrative before or after he wrote the rest of his two-volume work? The very solemn passage that is now Luke 3:1 may once have served as the opening of the Lucan narrative of Jesus; there are good parallels in Josephus and Thucydides for such an opening, as H. J. Cadbury has pointed out. Acts 1:1 and 1:22 may be interpreted to mean that the Lucan Gospel once began with the baptism of Jesus, so that it was the story of what Jesus did and taught as attested by those who were with him from that baptism. But whether Luke began his work with 3:1 and only at the end of his labors added chs. 1-2 (as I incline to think)[6] or he began with the infancy narrative so that the present order represents the order of composition, it is important for this discussion that the material in the body of the gospel was preached and known before the infancy narrative was made a part of the consecutive message about Jesus.

Did Luke himself compose the material in the infancy narrative, or for the most part did he take over and touch up material already shaped (in whole or in part)? The latter possibility, which implies a source or sources, has been defended on the grounds of theology, language, and content.

First, theology. In his famous analysis of Lucan thought and plan, H.

Conzelmann virtually ignored chs. 1-2 wherein he found a theology different from and even contrary to that of the rest of the gospel. For instance, Conzelmann maintained that in proper Lucan theology John the Baptist (henceforth JBap) belongs to the period of the law and the prophets, not to the period of the preaching of the kingdom of God (Luke 16:16). But in the infancy narrative the birth of JBap is clearly part of the good news of salvation, fulfilling the prophets (1:20, 70, 77). Other writers on Lucan theology, like H. Oliver, W. Tatum, and G. Voss, while accepting Conzelmann's general analysis, have sought to work the infancy narrative into that analysis. Still others, like J. -P. Audet, P. Minear, and H. Songer, have used the infancy narrative to challenge the validity of the Conzelmann analysis. They have insisted that the infancy narrative is a true introduction to the main themes of the gospel and is thus harmonious with Luke's theology.

Second, language. The Greek of the infancy narrative is more Semitized than that of much of the gospel; it is similar to the more Semitized sections of Acts. Accordingly, some have suggested that Luke drew upon and translated written or oral sources in Aramaic (M. Dibelius, W. Michaelis, A. Plummer, F. Spitta, B. Weiss), or in Hebrew (G. A. Box, G. Dalman, P. DeLagarde, H. Gunkel, R. Laurentin, B. Streeter, C. Torrey), or in both languages (P. Winter). On the other hand, many scholars have denied the necessity of positing extended Semitic sources for the main infancy narrative and have explained the Semitized Greek by Luke's deliberate use of a Septuagintal style when he was composing a narrative imitative of the OT (P. Benoit, H. Cadbury, M. Goulder and M. Sanderson, A. von Harnack, N. Turner, J. Wellhausen).[7]

Third, content. There have been complicated theories about pre-Lucan material, with as many as seven or more sources posited (K. L. Schmidt; H. Schürmann); but, as regards ch. 1,[8] the debate often centers around whether or not there was a "Baptist source" and a "Marian source." Let me stress that I am talking about a *source*, meaning an oral or written consecutive narrative, rather than scattered bits of information. Many scholars who deny the existence of sources admit that Luke picked up items of tradition, historical or non-historical, from which he shaped the present narrative; but they insist that it was Luke who composed the consecutive story.

The Baptist source is sometimes thought to have had Christian origins but more often to have been composed by followers of JBap.[9] Indeed, it is posited that the Baptist source once contained not only the material in Luke 1 that now refers to JBap but other material that has been shifted in application to Jesus. For instance, some have proposed that originally there was an annunciation to Elizabeth (as well as to Zechariah) but this has been reshaped into or replaced by an annunciation to Mary. A more popular suggestion (with some minor textual backing) is that the *Magnificat* was originally the song of Elizabeth, corresponding to the *Benedictus*, the song of Zechariah, but has been shifted to Mary. A prominent reason for positing a Baptist source is the contention that the view of JBap in Luke 1 is different from Luke's own view of him as represented in the gospel proper (see the reference to Conzelmann's theory above) and that, with the deletion of certain small Lucan touches, the portrait of JBap that emerges from Luke 1 is not subordinate, so that in the source he may have been the principal salvific figure, the prophet, etc.

The Marian source has its advocates today almost entirely in Roman Catholic circles; usually it posits an oral communication of Mary's experiences to Luke, either directly or indirectly (through family).[10] The basic argument is that, since Mary is pictured alone on the occasion of the annunciation, only she could be the source of the dialogue found therein. Leaving aside the simplistic aspects of such an argument,[11] including presuppositions about historicity, I would point out that there is something to be said in favor of the priority of the annunciation to Mary when that annunciation is compared to the annunciation to Zechariah. The two annunciations share so many common features[12] that in their present form they cannot have arisen independently of each other in two different sources. Luke has shaped the parallelism by making one match the other or by composing both of them. The scholars who favor the Baptist source maintain that Luke found therein an annunciation of the birth of JBap and that he composed an annunciation of the birth of Jesus to match it. A contrary suggestion has been made by Benoit that Luke had a tradition of an annunciation of the birth of Jesus and that he freely composed an annunciation of the birth of JBap to match that. This theory is not easily dismissable as Marian piety once we bring Matthew's gospel into consideration. In an account that betrays no dependence on Luke, Matthew tells of an annunciation (to Joseph) of the birth of Jesus. This is explicable if, anterior to both Matthew and Luke, popular interest in Jesus' origins had produced a tradition of an annunciation of the birth of Jesus by an angel,[13] a tradition that Matthew and Luke each used in his own way. Matthew fitted it into a narrative that patterned Joseph the father of Jesus on the Genesis model of the patriarch Joseph, using the two prominent aspects of that story, namely, that revelation came to Joseph in dreams and that Joseph went down to Egypt.[14] Luke filled out the annunciation tradition in a manner to be discussed below and fitted it into a narrative set up on a parallelism between JBap and Jesus.[15] For Luke, Mary was a more important figure than Joseph, even as she is more important than Joseph in the body of the gospel story of Jesus' ministry. Each evangelist in his own way succeeded in making the story of the annunciation (and birth) a miniature gospel and thus brought popular traditions into the service of the good news of salvation.

Working with this hypothesis that an annunciation pattern (of the birth of Jesus) was pre-Lucan, *first* I shall seek to show that Luke filled out this pattern with christological statements from Christian preaching and with a portrait of Mary known to him from the body of the gospel (the account of Jesus' ministry). Thus, I maintain that there is no need to posit a Marian source in the sense of a narrative stemming from Mary concerning her conversation with the angel and her feelings on that occasion. *Second*, I shall propose that in imitation of the annunciation of Jesus' birth Luke shaped an annunciation of the birth of JBap. While he may have had some items of historical information (the names of JBap's parents; the fact that they were of priestly stock),[16] I see no need to posit a JBap source in the sense of an already composed annunciation narrative. I shall briefly sketch how the angelic statements about the future of JBap in 1:13-17 could have been composed by Luke out of what is found in the body of the Lucan gospel about JBap, especially from Luke 3:1-20 and 7:18-35.

I. The Annunciation of the Birth of Jesus

It is well known that the OT supplies us with a virtually stereotyped pattern for the annunciations of the forthcoming births of famous figures in salvation history,[17] narratives obviously written in retrospect after the figure had become famous. Regularly there are five features in the pattern:

— Appearance of an angel or of God, sometimes greeting by title the subject of the vision.

— Fear or prostration on the part of the subject confronted with this supernatural presence.

— The annunciation message, sometimes prefaced by the injunction not to fear and the mention of the visionary's name. The basic message contains the follows(ing items:

  (a) the woman is or is about to be with child;

  (b) she will give birth to the child;

  (c) the name by which the child is to be called;

  (d) an etymology interpreting the name;

(e) the future accomplishments of the child.

— An objection on the part of the visionary as to how this is to come about.

— The giving of a sign to reassure the visionary.

In comparing Matthew and Luke's accounts of the annunciation of the birth of Jesus (to Joseph and to Mary, respectively), we find that Matthew preserves three of the features while Luke preserves all five. Thus, many items in Luke's account the annunciation are simply the stereotyped features of the OT pattern for which he needed no special source, Marian or otherwise: the angelic appearance in 1:26; the angelic greeting in 1:28 (cf. Judg 6:12); Mary's being startled in 1:29; the "Do not be afraid" in 1:30; the message of conception in 1:31; Mary's "How can this be?" in 1:34; a sign given by the angel in 1:36-37. But there remain three major aspects of the Lucan scene which cannot de explained simply from the OT annunciation pattern: (1) the content of the description of the child and his future; (2) the idea of a virginal conception; (3) Mary's reaction. Let us discuss these one by one.

(1) *The content of the description of the child and his future.* This is embodied in two angelic pronouncements (1:32-33 and 1:35), semi-poetic in their structure.

First Pronouncement:

    32a: He will be great and will be called Son of the Most High.

    32b: And the Lord God will give him the throne of his father David;

    33a: and he will be king over the house of Jacob forever,

    33b: and there will be no end to his kingdom.

Second Pronouncement:

    35b: A Holy Spirit will come upon you,

    35c: and power from the Most High will overshadow you.

    35d: Therefore the child to be born will be called holy — Son of God.

The first angelic pronouncement in Luke clearly echoes the promise of Nathan to David (2 Sam 7:8-16), the promise that came to serve as the foundation of messianic expectation:

    9: I shall make for you a *great* name . . .

    13: I shall establish *the throne of his kingdom forever.*

    14: I shall be his father and he will be *my son* . . .

    16: And your *house* and your *kingdom* will be made sure *forever.*

The second angelic pronouncement in Luke echoes in its wording (and in its sequence to the first) a creedal formula of the type that Paul quotes in Rom 1:3-4, where he describes Jesus Christ, God's Son:

    3: Descended from David according to the flesh;

    4: and *designated Son of God* in *power* according to a *Holy Spirit* [Spirit of Holiness] by resurrection from [of] the dead.

(In citing both 2 Samuel and Romans I have italicized verbal parallels to the first and second Lucan pronouncements.) Just as the pre-Pauline formula in Romans speaks first of the son of David and then of the Son of God, the Lucan annunciation pronouncements deal first with Jesus as the fulfillment of the Davidic promise and then with Jesus conceived as the Son of God. In Paul the two are contrasted: through human origin Jesus is the son of David, while through resurrection, Holy Spirit, and power, Jesus is designated as God's Son in a special way. For Luke there is no contrast: the Son of the Most High in whom the Davidic promise is fulfilled is the child to be called the Son of God, conceived through the Holy Spirit and power.

This difference is understandable if we reflect on the development in christology separating the pre-Pauline creedal formula (pre-58 A.D.) and the Lucan infancy narrative (final form in the 80s?). The pre-Pauline formula, like other echoes of early preaching, makes the resurrection the christological moment[18] when God begot Jesus as His Son, exalted him at His right hand, and bestowed on him the name Lord (Acts 2:36; 5:31; 13:33; Phil 2:9). The ministry before the resurrection was accordingly considered a ministry of lowliness (Phil 2:7). Intermediary between this early christology and that of the infancy narratives was the christology evident in the body of the gospels (Mark written in the late 60s?) where the christological moment has moved back to the baptism of Jesus where God's voice declares Jesus to be His Son[19] and the *Holy Spirit* descends on him so that he can begin his ministry with *power* (Luke 4:14 — note the same terminology formerly attached to the resurrection). Consequently, the ministry becomes less and less a ministry of lowliness as we progress through Matthew, Luke, and John: and the fact that Jesus is God's Son, not simply His servant, becomes more apparent in the pages of the gospel story.

But for many Christians the moving of the christological moment from the resurrection to the baptism still did not solve the mystery of who Jesus was, and in the prefaces of the later gospels we see two parallel further movements of the christological moment. In John it is moved back to pre-existence before creation;[20] in Matthew and Luke it is moved to conception.[21] And particularly in Luke 1:35 terminology drawn from the early creedal formulas is also moved back to the conception. By giving two angelic pronouncements, one phrased in the language of Nathan's prophecy to David, the other in the language of Christian christological proclamation and creed, Luke is showing that the fulfillment matches the promise: God told David that David's offspring would be His son, and through the power of the Holy Spirit the son of David comes into the world as the Son of God.

(2) *The idea of a virginal conception.* If Luke needed no special Marian source for the content of the angelic proclamation about the child and his future, did he need personal information stemming from Mary for the idea of a virginal conception? Elsewhere at length[22] I have discussed this subject and found nothing in the OT, in pagan sources, in Jewish Hellenistic mysticism, or in early Christian preaching that would explain convincingly why both Matthew and Luke maintain that Jesus was conceived of a virgin without the intervention of a human father. Others who have come to similar results from their investigations have concluded that therefore the virginal conception is either a pure theologoumenon in the sense of a dramatization and historicizing of a theological statement (e.g., Jesus is the Son of God, therefore not the son of a man) or else a historical reminiscence passed down through family tradition stemming from Mary. The theologoumenon approach suffers from the difficulty that there is no real evidence that the theology of Jesus as God's Son would lead *Jews* to conclude that he had no human father — and the pre-Matthean story especially, with its Joseph/Moses pattern, suggests Jewish Christian not Gentile Christian origin.[23] The family-tradition approach faces a formidable difficulty in explaining why such a memory left no traces in *any* of the early NT writing and preaching outside the infancy narratives[24] and indeed seems to have been totally unknown to Mark writing in the 60s (Mark 6:2-3; see also footnote 28 below).

Perhaps it is possible to explain the origin of the idea of a virginal conception by combining the suggestions of theological conclusion and historical fact (without resorting to intimate family tradition for the latter). The marriage situation envisaged in Matthew and (seemingly) in Luke where Mary has conceived or will conceive before living with Joseph implies that Jesus was born at a *noticeably* early period after his parents came to live together. This could have been a historical fact known to Jesus' followers and opponents. (I cannot believe a Christian freely invented the awkward marriage situation posited in Matthew, or that a Christian would not have denied it if opponents had invented it.) The Jewish opponents of Christianity eventually accused Jesus of being illegitimate[25] — their interpretation of the fact of his noticeably early birth — but Christians rejected any implication of sin in Jesus' origins as part of their theology that Jesus was totally free of sin (2 Cor 5:21; 1 Pet 2:22; Heb 4:15; 1 John 3:5) and that his parents were holy and righteous (Matt 1:19; Luke 1:42). And so interpreting the historical fact in the light of a theology of sinlessness and divine sonship Christians concluded that the child was conceived of the

Holy Spirit before Mary lived with Joseph.[26] I mention this very tentative hypothesis to demonstrate that positing a historical basis for the virginal conception does not necessarily imply a Marian source.

(3) *Mary's reaction to the annunciation.* A key argument for a Marian source has been the understanding that we have Mary's *ipsissima verba* in 1:38: "Behold the handmaid of the Lord; let it be done to me according to your word." Rather, I propose, we have here a Lucan echo of the one scene in which Mary appears in the common synoptic tradition of the ministry.[27] As this scene is narrated in Mark 3, it has two parts. First, in 3:20-21 "his own"[28] go out to seize him because the frenzied pace of his ministry is provoking charges of madness; second, in 3:31-35 his mother and his brothers arrive and stand outside the place where he is, asking for him; but Jesus responds that the listeners seated around him who do the will of God are his mother and his brothers. The first part of the Marcan scene reveals the attitude of Jesus' relatives toward him and it is scarcely one of belief. Luke and Matthew do not report this first part of the Marcan scene, so that the closest parallel is John 7:5, "Even his brothers did not believe him." The second part of the Marcan scene reveals Jesus' attitude toward family relationship. His real family is established through a relationship to God, not by human origin. (The Johannine parallel is in 2:4 where Jesus resists his mother's interference, seemingly because she has no role in the coming of his "hour.") When the two parts of the Marcan scene are read together, the impact of 3:33-34 is very strong: "And Jesus replied, 'Who are my mother and my brothers?' And looking around on those who sat about him, he said, 'Here are my mother and my brothers!'" — it is a replacement of his natural mother and brothers and can even be read as a rejection of his family altogether.

Be that as it may, Luke's parallel scene is quite different.[29] Luke omits not only the first part of the Marcan scene (Mark 3:20-21) but also the lines just quoted from the second part. The scene in Luke 8:19-21 reads as follows:

> Then his mother and his brothers came to him, but they could not reach him because of the crowd. He was told, "Your mother and your brothers are standing outside, desiring to see you." But he said to them, "My mother and my brothers are those who hear the word [*logos*] of God and do it."

This is not to be read as if the hearers of the word of God replace Jesus' mother and his brothers as his real family (so Mark), but as a statement that his mother and his brothers are among his disciples: the physical family of Jesus is truly his family because they hear the word of God. Luke preserves Jesus' insistence that hearing the word of God and doing it is what is constitutive of his family, but Luke thinks that Jesus' mother and brothers meet that criterion. Luke is quite logical, then, in reporting that among the 120 "bretheren" who constituted the believing community after the resurrection-ascension were "Mary the mother of Jesus and his brothers" (Acts 1:14).

It is this Lucan tradition that Jesus' mother was one of "those who hear the word of God and do it" that supplied the response placed on Mary's lips at the end of the annunciation scene: "Behold the handmaid of the Lord; let it be done to me according to your word [*rēma*]" (1:38). Luke needed no special source nor Mary's reminiscence for this response; he needed only to make the picture of Mary in the infancy narrative consistent with the picture he had of her from her sole appearance in the common Synoptic tradition of the public ministry.

This conclusion is reinforced if we press beyond the annunciation to the visitation which is the last long description of Mary in the infancy narrative.[30] It is noteworthy that the Lucan account of the public ministry has not just one saying about Jesus' mother (the parallel to Mark 3:31-35) but a second saying for which there is no parallel in the other gospels, namely Luke 11:27-28:[31]

> As Jesus said this, a woman in the crowd raised her voice and said to him,
> "Fortunate is the womb that bore you and the breasts you sucked." But he said,
> "Fortunate rather are those who hear the word [*logos*] of God and keep it."

This may be a doublet of the first saying since it has the same contrast between family relationship and hearing the word of God. (Curiously, although found only in Luke, it is more negative in thrust than the Lucan adaptation of Mark 3:31-35.) This second Lucan saying provided the background for Elizabeth's reaction to Mary in the visitation (1:42, 45):

> Blessed are you among women,
> and blessed is the fruit of your womb . . . .
> Fortunate is she who believed that the Lord's word to her would
>   be fulfilled.

Like the woman in the crowd, Elizabeth praises Mary's physical motherhood; but since Elizabeth is the vehicle of the prophetic spirit, she continues by praising Mary's real value as the one who hears the word of God with persevering belief — the value Jesus praised in 11:28 in response to the woman. Once again Luke seems to have found his material (and this time even the form of the material, a macarism) in what he knew from the public ministry.

II. The Annunciation of the Birth of John the Baptist

Space limitations imposed for contributions to this volume do not permit me to show in detail that Luke used this same technique of borrowing from the public ministry (especially from Luke 3:1-20 and 7:18-35) for his description of the future of JBap in the annunciation of Gabriel to Zechariah in 1:13-17. But lest I tantalize unduly, let me at least list my key suggestions in this area with the hope that I shall be able to develop them elsewhere.

1:13 — In constructing an annunciation of birth for JBap (in imitation of a pre-Lucan tradition of an annunciation of Jesus' birth), Luke follows the standard pattern discussed above.

1:14 — Joy and gladness greet the salvific event of the resurrection-ascension-gift of the spirit in Luke 24:41 and Acts 2:28. In the infancy narrative the salvific event has been moved forward to the conception and birth of Jesus, and the same reactions appear (see also Luke 2:10).

1:15 — "Great before the Lord" = 7:28.

— "Drink no wine or strong drink" = theme of JBap's asceticism in 7:33, adapted to an infancy format in free imitation of the infancy narratives of Samson and Samuel (Judg 13:14; 1 Sam 1:15).

— "Filled with a Holy Spirit" hints at the prophetic role of JBap.[32] In the OT the *spirit* of the Lord and the *word* of the Lord are equivalent descriptions of the divine source of prophecy. Here Luke uses the former of the two for JBap; in 3:2 he uses the latter for JBap.[33]

1:16 — "Turn many of the sons of Israel to the Lord their God" = standard OT terminology for the repentance of a people, sometimes in relation to the word of a prophet moved by the spirit of God (2 Chr 15:1, 4). Thus the ending of 1:15 and 1:16 simply spell out in OT language that JBap is a prophet, nay more than a prophet (7:26).

1:17 — "In the spirit and power of Elijah." Despite the oft-stated claim that Luke reserves the Elijah role for Jesus not JBap, in 7:27 Luke applies to JBap the classical Elijah passage from Malachi.[34]

> "To turn the hearts of the *fathers* to the *children*,
> and the *disobedient* to the wisdom of the *just*."

This is more Elijah language from Mal 3:24 (4:6) and Sir 48:10. However, there is a peculiar twist in the second line of Luke's adaptation of the Elijah motif. Malachi speaks reciprocally of "the hearts of the fathers to their children *and the hearts of the children to their fathers"*; Sirach speaks of "the heart of the father to the son *and to restore the tribes of Israel.*" But Luke, if taken in strict synonymous parallelism, identifies the fathers with the disobedient whereas the children seem to be the just whose wisdom is noted.[35] Is it coincidental that most of this language echoes Lucan passages concerning JBap in chs. 3 and 7? In 3:8 JBap warns those who claim that Abraham is their *father* that they can be replaced by new *children* to Abraham (3:8). In 7:33-35 Jesus says that, in contrast with those who criticize JBap, *wisdom is justified by her children.* A possible interpretation of 1:17 is to see the children who have the wisdom of the just as those who accept the challenge of the kingdom which the disobedient fathers will refuse, so that JBap's task is to break down this refusal on the part of those who claim to be descended from father Abraham.

* * *

To conclude, I think that in composing ch. 1 Luke had some items that came to him from tradition, e.g., the names of JBap's parents and that they were of priestly origin; the songs of an early Jewish Christian community (at Jerusalem?) now adapted as the *Benedictus* and the *Magnificat*; the tendency to compare the conception of Jesus to the conception of OT salvific figures by the use of an annunciation pattern; the idea of a virginal conception. He combined and fleshed out these traditions with a Christian creedal formula about Jesus as Son of God and with portraits of JBap and Mary gleaned from the gospel account of the public ministry. The two chapters of the infancy narrative were meant by Luke to provide a bridge from the OT to the gospel story of Jesus (even as the first two chapters of Acts were meant to provide a bridge from the gospel story of Jesus to the story of the church). Those dramatis personae in the infancy narrative who appear in the gospel (JBap, Mary) were shaped from the gospel portraits; those who do not (Zechariah, Elizabeth) were shaped from OT portraits (Abraham, Sarah, Hannah). The infancy narrative, then, is a key to the Lucan conception of salvation history.

1. For information on the 1964 statement of the Roman Pontifical Biblical Commission, see *JBC*, article 72, §§8, 35.

2. Proportionately, the infancy narratives often receive little attention in introductions to the NT or in seminary courses.

3. To be published by Doubleday, probably in 1977. Because that commentary will carry complete bibliography, I shall not take up space here with long bibliographical footnotes. For those unfamiliar with the literature on the Lucan infancy narrative, the writings of the authors to whom I refer can be tracked down in B. Metzger, *Index to Periodical Literature on Christ and the Gospels* (Leiden: Brill, 1966), covering articles up to 1961, and in the cumulative index to *NTA* (1956-71).

4. I use the common designation without deciding the question whether the author had been a companion of Paul, specifically Luke the physician. The theory that he was such a companion has often been accompanied by the thesis that, while in Palestine during Paul's imprisonment at Caesarea (*ca.* A.D. 58-60), Luke uncovered the sources from which he composed the infancy stories, e.g., the "Baptist source" and the "Marian source" to be mentioned below.

5. Marcion's form of the Gospel of Luke did not include the infancy narrative, but this omission scarcely reflects manuscript tradition; it probably resulted from Marcion's excision of material which had such strong OT background.

6. Additional arguments include: (a) The placing of the genealogy in ch. 3 rather than in ch. 1. Seemingly the genealogy was already part of the gospel before the infancy narrative was prefixed but had to be adapted to the thesis of virginal conception after the addition of 1:26-38, whence the parenthetical insertion of "as was supposed" in the description of Jesus as the son of Joseph. (b) The many similarities between the Lucan infancy narrative and the opening two chapters of Acts, especially as regards prophecy and the Spirit. Both were probably composed after the gospel proper (in which the influence of Mark had been a guiding factor).

7. Notice that I have spoken of sources for the main infancy narrative. Many who deny the existence of such sources allow a source for the three hymns: the *Magnificat*, the *Benedictus*, and the *Nunc Dimittis*. Personally I think that substantially these hymns came to Luke from early Jewish Christianity, perhaps from the Jerusalem community. Luke edited them, made additions, and inserted them into his narrative, almost as appendages in the respective scenes.

8. I omit from this discussion ch. 2 which may have had very different origins from ch. 1. See note 30 below.

9. Followers who were anti-Christian and maintained that JBap, not Jesus, was the Messiah; or followers who simply did not become Christian; or even followers who did become Christian. The last suggestion is similar to the thesis that the Baptist source had its origins in early Jewish Christianity.

10. See note 4 above.

11. The whole account could be the product of Luke's creative imagination. The theory grows more simplistic when it is claimed that the *Magnificat* was composed by Mary on the occasion described, so that she is the source of the hymn as well.

12. Note the following: (a) both annunciations have an introduction that mentions the husband, the wife, and the tribal origin; (b) in both the angel is identified as Gabriel; (c) in both Gabriel addresses the visionary by name and urges "Do not be afraid"; (d) the

phrasing of the messages in 1:13 and 1:31 about the birth and naming of the son is very similar; (e) each message is followed by a poetic passage predicting the future greatness of the child; (f) in turn, this prediction is greeted by a "How?" question posed by Zechariah and by Mary respectively; (g) the "How?" question is answered by a sign from the angel showing the power of God.

13. We shall see below that the OT supplied very close antecedents for angelic annunciations of the births of salvific children.

14. The narrative continued by comparing the baby Jesus to the baby Moses (since it was Moses who led Israel back from Egypt), with Herod playing a role patterned on that of the wicked Pharaoh who, in Jewish tradition, sought to kill Moses and so ordered the killing of all the Hebrew male children.

15. The logic seems to have worked thus: for Luke the conception and birth of Jesus had become a proclamation of the good news of salvation (2:10-11); historically, JBap had a ministry before Jesus began his ministry of proclaiming this good news; and so if now the good news was to be attached to Jesus' birth, his birth should be preceded by the birth of JBap. JBap came first, before God's voice at the baptism proclaimed Jesus to be His Son; an annunciation of the birth of JBap should come first, before an angel announces the birth of Jesus as God's Son. We can trace through the gospels a development in the church's thought about JBap, increasingly subordinating him and his ministry to Jesus. In the infancy narrative Luke goes farther than elsewhere in the gospels in the process of Christianizing JBap: he makes JBap a relative of Jesus, something difficult to reconcile with the baptismal story (cf. John 1:31).

16. This seems less demanding on the imagination than the theory mentioned by Goulder and Sanderson wherein the identification of JBap as the Elijah-figure of Malachi brought in an association with the priesthood (since Malachi directs his words to priests) and the name Zechariah (the prophet who precedes Malachi in the canon); and the fact that Jesus' mother was named after Moses' sister Miriam gave Luke the idea of naming JBap's mother after Aaron's wife Elizabeth.

17. Good comparisons for the study of Luke 1 can be found in the annunciations of the birth of Isaac (Gen 17:1, 3, 15-16, 17, 19) and of Samson (Judg 13:3a, 22, 3b-5, 20). The pattern has been studied minutely by X. Léon-Dufour among others.

18. A still earlier christology, leaving only faint traces in the NT, may have made the parousia the christological moment: Jesus would be the Messiah, the Son of Man, when he would return again — but that is not of importance for our purposes here. What does it mean to an orthodox Christian that there were different christologies in the NT, some of them, especially the earlier ones, clearly inadequate in the light of later faith? It means that the full appreciation of Jesus' divinity took time. Each of the christologies had positive value in emphasizing the importance of a particular moment (the parousia, the resurrection, the baptism, the conception) but did not express the full truth about Jesus.

19. In the Western text of Luke 3:22 God *begets* Jesus as His Son at the baptism. In all the gospels I am assuming that the heavenly voice is the evangelist's way of communicating to the Christian reader God's revelation about who Jesus was; it is not a historical revelation to Jesus or to bystanders at the baptism who heard God speaking.

20. Christological development is not strictly chronological, for pre-existence christology antecedes John's Prologue and is found in Paul. But John's Prologue is the first clear example of a theory of pre-existence before creation, since Phil 2:6 can refer to a pre-existence of an Adam-like figure (Adam was in the image of God but grasped at being equal to God), and Col 1:15 has Jesus pre-existing as the first-born of all creation. (See also 1 Cor 8:6).

21. Although the subsequent church quickly combined pre-existence christology and conception christology by having the pre-existent Word take flesh (John) in the womb of the virgin Mary (Matthew, Luke), originally these were two different answers to the same problem. In particular, I interpret Luke 1:35 to mean that Jesus *became* God's Son by being conceived through the action of God's Holy Spirit. His being "called" God's Son means his being recognized for what he is. I find no suggestion of pre-existence in the Matthean or Lucan infancy narratives.

22. R. E. Brown, *The Virginal Conception and Bodily Resurrection of Jesus* (New York: Paulist, 1973). Also "Luke's Description of the Virginal Conception," *TS* 35 (1974) 360-62.

23. Many who speak of the Hellenistic origins (or even Gentile Christian) origins of the infancy material base themselves on the christological language found therein and do not distinguish the possibility that the christological interpretation of the virginal conception may be one of the latest factors in the infancy narrative, indeed the factor that caused the story of Jesus' conception to be seen as gospel. Often too there is insufficient allowance for the fact that the idea of a virginal conception arose long enough before Matthew and before Luke to be able to be fitted into two very different annunciation stories.

24. The case against a secret family tradition has been argued strongly by the Catholic scholar A. Vögtle, *BLeb* 11 (1970) 51-67.

25. For hints of this accusation in the gospels, see Brown, *The Virginal Conception*, 66.

26. The veracity of this conclusion cannot be scientifically proved. This is an area where one's acceptance of divine inspiration and of the authority of traditional church teaching will play a deciding role.

27. Mary is mentioned but does not appear in Mark 6:3 where Jesus returns to Nazareth. There is a parallel in Matt 13:55 and John 6:42, but not in Luke 4:22 which mentions Joseph but not Mary.

28. *Hoi par' autou*, literally "those from him," which theoretically could mean emissaries. But we must consider the sequence in Mark where "they set out to seize him" in 3:21 is followed shortly by "his mother and his brothers came and, standing outside, sent to him" in 3:31. It seems likely that Mark understood the *hoi par' autou* to be his mother and his brothers. However, the absence of an equivalent for Mark 3:21 in Matthew and Luke, plus the fact that the Johannine parallels are widely separated (John 7:4; 2:4), raises the possibility that Mark has joined two once independent traditions. The Johannine parallel confines disbelief to the Jesus' brothers; in the NT his mother is never mentioned by name as a disbeliever.

29. Matt 12:46-50 follows Mark 3:31-35 closely, so that Luke's differences are probably to be attributed to his editing.

30. Mary's role in 2:1-40 is very brief; nothing there presupposes a virginal conception or an annunciation. The story in 2:41-51 is almost certainly a tradition independent in origin of ch. 1, and is perhaps an early reflection of the tendency to shape stories about Jesus' precocious boyhood that we find in the apocryphal gospels. The Mary of 2:48-49 does not seem to be the Mary who was told about Jesus by an angel or even the Mary who heard from the shepherds reports of an angelic proclamation about Jesus. I would be more inclined to posit a narrative source behind some of the material in Luke 2.

31. In what follows I translate *makarios* by "fortunate" and a word related to *eulogētos* by "blessed" to signal the distinction between the macarism and the benediction. See R. E. Brown, *The Gospel According to John* (AB 29; Garden City: Doubleday, 1970) 553.

32. Scholars often trace to a non-Christian Baptist source the association of the Holy Spirit with JBap in 1:15, precisely because the Christian tradition distinguishes between JBap's baptism with water and Christian baptism with the Holy Spirit (Luke 3:16; Acts 1:5; 19:2). The Holy Spirit attached to Christian baptism is the Spirit of Jesus communicated by him after the resurrection; obviously that cannot be associated with JBap. But in the infancy narrative we are dealing with the prophetic spirit that Christians knew of from the OT, and that is quite appropriate for JBap.

33. Compare Luke 3:1-2 with the opening description of the career of the prophet Zechariah, remembering that Zechariah is the name of JBap's father. Luke's stress in 1:15 that JBap was filled with a Holy Spirit "even from his mother's womb" is reminiscent of the opening of Jeremiah's prophetic career which also began in the womb (Jer 1:5). A parallelism with Samson is also echoed here (Judg 16:17).

34. Unfortunately Conzelmann has persuaded many that Luke was a highly systematic theologian shaping all things toward a master goal. Luke has an overall plan but has not leveled out all the inconsistencies in what he reports. In many passages he casts Jesus in an Elijah or prophet role (perhaps an older christology); but even in the body of the gospel he leaves traces of the thesis that JBap had an Elijah role. In the infancy narrative, composed after the body of the gospel and with an even higher christology, there is a contrast between Jesus who is conceived as the Son of God and JBap who is conceived as an Elijah-like prophet.

35. This identification is so startling that many interpreters want to see a chiastic relation of the terms: fathers = just; children = disobedient.

JOHN DOMINIC CROSSAN

Jesus and Pacifism

The writer is not defined by the use of specialized tools which parade literature ... but by the power of surprising, by some formal device, a particular collusion of man and nature, i.e., a meaning: and in this 'surprise,' it is form which guides, form which keeps watch, which instructs, which knows, which thinks, which 'commits'; this is why form has no other judge than what it reveals.

Roland Barthes, *Critical Essays.*

This article wishes to debate an interpretation of Matt 5:39 which Professor McKenzie has offered at various places throughout his writings across the years. Since the article was prepared precisely in his honor, it presumes that contradiction is the sincerest form of flattery.

One citation will suffice to state his position, from *The Power and the Wisdom* (107): "[Jesus'] own death illustrates better than anything else his principle of not resisting evil (Matt 5:39)." The point at issue is actually quite narrow, but it has two separate elements. First, does Matt 5:39 constitute a manifesto for pacifism and announce a "principle of not resisting evil"? Second, does this come from the historical Jesus, the ecclesial tradition, or the editorial activity of the evangelist?

This article will not discuss certain wider and probably far more important issues in this context. It will not debate whether Jesus' life and death presents, either in his own deliberate intention or in the tradition's deliberate interpretation, a normative example of pacifism unto death, even unto death upon the cross. And neither will it discuss the much larger question of the value of pacifism as a spiritual challenge to faith, a political tactic for hope, or a human imperative of love. Only one small point is under consideration and this concerns the aphorism attributed to Jesus in Matt 5:39b, "if any one strikes you on the right cheek, turn to him the other also," and its parallel version in Luke 6:29a, "to him who strikes you on the cheek, offer the other also." What exactly does this mean, and who said it?

195

I. The Meaning of the Aphorism

The saying in Matt 5:39b and Luke 6:29a will be discussed under three separate but connected rubrics: historical, literary, and philosophical analysis.

A. Historical Analysis

Lest quotational familiarity may have bred hermeneutical contempt the logion needs to be read most carefully once again in its present two locations within the synoptic tradition. My procedure will be to consider the unit from the viewpoint of source, form, and redaction and to do this in four circles of diminishing textual scope. This will serve to delimit what can be done through historical criticism before literary and philosophical concerns must take over the investigation.

1. Matt 5:1 - 7:27 and Luke 6:17-49.

The aphorism is presently contained in a section which, in the more usual Two-Source hypothesis, comes from Q. Matthew included it in his great inaugural Sermon on the Mount (5:1 - 7:27) and Luke has it in what those who like to be pedantic term the Sermon on the Plain (6:17-49). Before redaction criticism gave scholars a better sense of humor, this could all have been harmonized in terms of a small plain on top of a large mount.

2. Matt 5:38-48 and Luke 6:27-36.

The more proximate context is the units in Matt 5:38-48 and Luke 6:27-36. In Luke this unity is underlined by the opening admonition to "love your enemies" in 6:27b and its closing repetition, "love your enemies," in 6:35a. Matthew has modified his source much more radically in order to fit it into his set of six antitheses in 5:21-26 (murder), 27-30 (adultery), 31-32 (divorce), 33-37 (oaths), 38-42 (revenge), and 43-48 (hate). In all six cases Matthew has Jesus oppose his own interpretation of the Mosaic tradition to other and different interpretations: "You have heard that it was said (to the men of old) . . . . But I say to you" (5:21, 27, 31, 33, 38, 43). In doing this he made two major changes over the source whose original sequence is presumably still evident in Luke 6:27-36. He divided the material over his fifth and sixth antitheses, and he rearranged its order so that Matt 5:38-42 (fifth) = Luke 6:29-30, and Matt 5:43-48 (sixth) = Luke 6:27-28, 32-36.

The cheek saying, therefore, now appears in the fifth of Matthew's six antitheses, but within the more general frames of "love your enemies" in Luke. Or, in other words, the aphorism is *within* the "love your enemies" command in Luke 6:27b=35a but comes *before* the sixth antithesis on hating/loving your enemies in Matt 5:43-48.

3. Matt 5:38-42 and Luke 6:29-31.

The immediate context of the logion can be compared more easily in tabular format, as in Table 1.

Table 1:

Main Elements in the Context	Matthew	Luke
You have heard: Eye, eye; tooth, tooth	5:38	—
But I say to you: Do not resist evil one	5:39a	—
To one who strikes you, turn other cheek	5:39b	6:29a
To one who takes coat, give cloak	5:40	6:29b
To one who forces you one mile, go two	5:41	—
Give to asker, do not refuse borrower	5:42	6:30
Do unto others as you would they do to you	7:12a	6:31

There are two quite significant differences between Matthew and Luke in this table, and both bear on the precise interpretation of the cheek saying. First, Matthew but not Luke has the opening interpretive comment, "Do not resist one who is evil," in Matt 5:39a. Second, Luke but not Matthew has the closing and equally interpretive statement, "And as you wish that men would do to you, do so to them," in Luke 6:31 (see Matt 7:12a).

And since the Golden Rule has just been noted, one other facet of this entire synoptic section must be faced. It is characterized by a disturbing range of motivational dicta. Motivation moves from the rather banal if supremely practical invocation of the Golden Rule just quoted to admonitions motivated by hope of heavenly reward in Luke 6:35a (see also Matt 6:4, 6, 18) and on to far more profound levels of motivation such as becoming sons of the impartial God who "makes his sun rise on the evil and the good, and sends rain on the just and the unjust," in Matt 5:45 = Luke 6:35b, or becoming perfect as God is perfect in Matt 5:48 = Luke 6:36.

One general conclusion arises from all this. The proximate frames of "love your enemies" (Luke 6:27b=35a) and the immediate interpretive comments of Matt 5:38-39a and/or Luke 6:31 pertain to the redactional handling of the cheek logion by the evangelists and do not therefore form its original interpretive context. It is perfectly correct to say that Matthew, for instance, interprets the cheek aphorism as an admonition not to resist

evil because that is exactly how he prefaced it in 5:39a. But this
understanding belongs to Matthew and not to any original meaning of the
saying.[1] As usual in any comparative synoptic study the interpretive frames
of present position are traditional and redactional rather than original.

4. Matt 5:39b-42 and Luke 6:29-30.

Leaving aside, then, these interpretive comments in both Matt 5:38-39a and
Luke 6:31, we have isolated the series of sayings in Matt 5:39b-42 and Luke
6:29-30. The next step is to study very closely the form of these aphorisms to
see if any further separation is required.

(a) Matt 5:39b-42. This is actually a series of five logia with striking
formal similarities, as summarized in Table 2.

Table 2:

	5:39b	5:40	5:41	5:42a	5:42b
1	if any one	if any one	if any one	to him who	him who would
2	you	you	you	you	you
3	strikes	sue, take	forces go	begs	borrow from
4	rt. cheek	coat	one mile	---	---
5	turn	let have	go with	give	do not refuse
6	him	him	him	---	---
7	other	cloak	two miles	---	---

When the five sayings are displayed schematically the resemblances and
also the differences become immediately apparent. The three dicta in 5:39b-
41 are separated from the two concluding ones in 5:42 by three factors.
First, there is a basic sequence of seven elements followed quite clearly in
the former three, but only three or four of these elements reappear in the
latter sayings. Second, the former three are specific, concrete, and separate
from each other. In effect, they are capsule stories. The last two are general,
abstract, and may well be but positive (give) and negative (do not refuse)
formulations of the same admonition. Third, the imperatives of the first
three sayings are all positive while the last two balance a positive and
negative imperative. This raises the strong possibility that the three logia of
Matt 5:39b-41 must be further isolated from the generalizing summaries in
5:42.

(b) Luke 6:29-30. The case is remarkably similar with the set of sayings in
Luke, as shown schematically in Table 3.

Table 3:

	6:29a	6:29b	6:30a	6:30b
1	to him who	from him who	to every one who	of (=from) him who
2	you	your	you	your
3	strikes	takes away	begs from	takes away
4	cheek	cloak	---	(goods)
5	turn	do not withhold	give	do not ask return
6	other cheek	coat	---	---

As with the Matthean series there is a break between the former and the latter two aphorisms and on the same points: full set of formal elements as against broken format: specific, concrete, and different as against general, abstract, and redundant. But the divergences between the Matthean and Lukan sets are also clear. First, Luke has no equivalent to Matt 5:41 on conscript travel. Second, there is more of a balance created between the former pair in 6:29 and the latter pair in 6:30 in that each set has a balanced positive and negative imperative and also in that the opening of 6:29b is repeated verbatim in the Greek of 6:30b. Third, the Greek version of the former two aphorisms in 6:29 is more compact and terse than the parallel versions in Matthew.

5. Historical Conclusions

Some general conclusions can now be suggested. The series of sayings in Matt 5:39b-41 (three) and Luke 6:29 (two), which includes the cheek logion, must be isolated from their present redactional and interpretive contexts both in Matt 5:38b-39 (do not resist evil) and Luke 6:31 (Golden Rule). They must also be separated from the appended generalizing logia attached to them by both Matt 5:42 and Luke 6:30 which were already present, of course, in (by?) Q.

B. Literary Analysis

At this point we must turn to literary analysis to understand these sayings against the functional possibilities of language. Very important work has already been done in this area by both Robert C. Tannehill and William A. Beardslee, and my own discussion will be in very conscious dependence upon and debate with their conclusions.

1. Form of the Aphorisms

Despite the somewhat more condensed form of the sayings in Luke as compared with Matthew, a basic form is quite recognizable behind both sets. With due allowance for the vagaries of translation and adaptation, the form can be outlined schematically as follows:

(a) Casuistic Opening

(b) Double Object: You/Yours   (b′) Double Object: Him/Yours
(c) Indicative Verb: Take   (c′) Imperative Verb: Give

The casuistic opening appears as an "if any one" clause in Matt 5:39b, 41 but as a "to one who" clause in Matt 5:50; Luke 6:29a, 29b. In the protasis, the double object is always implicit and is explicit in most cases. It is "you" and/or "your" specific possession. The verb of the protasis always involves some form of violence against this double object. In the apodosis the double object is again always implicit, is left so by Luke but rendered explicit by Matthew. It is "him" and "your" other and corresponding specific possession. Finally, the verb of the apodosis is always imperative, always in first place in the clause and always positive save for Luke 6:29b (to parallel with 6:30b?), and is always a verb of giving.

From this point on we shall concentrate on the Matthean set and leave aside the Lukan parallel. The main reason is that it seems much more likely that Luke omitted one of the three sayings than that Matthew added it in as his own 5:41. The threesome would have been present in Q and reduced to two by Luke because he did not find the conscriptive travel saying either understandable or relevant and also because he wanted a better formal balance between his own 6:29 and 6:30. The original Q trilogy follows Olrik's Law of Three,[2] and it also has a progressive logical expansion in the object of the protasis from one's body (5:39b), to one's possessions (5:40), to one's time and labor (5:41).

2. Characteristics of the Aphorisms

Professor Tannehill[3] has noted two major characteristics of these sayings, their "specificness" and their "extremeness."

This specificness was seen above and was one of the characteristics which distinguished Matt 5:39b-41 from 5:42. Each of the three aphorisms points to a very specific and individual case and not to an everyday happening. Any one might well happen only once, if at all, in any given hearer's lifetime.

The extremeness of the cases is also clear. In Matt 5:39b the attack is an insulting *backhanded* blow because it is to one's *right* cheek (not in Luke

6:29a). In 5:40 both tunic and cloak are given up which both leaves one more or less naked and even goes beyond and against Exod 22:26-27 and Deut 24:12-13 where a poor man's cloak, given in pawn or pledge, must be restored by that same nightfall "that he may sleep in his cloak and bless you." And 5:41 presumably refers to the conscripted service demanded (as of Simon of Cyrene in Matt 27:32) by imperial invaders.

Using these twin characteristics Professor Tannehill has postulated a mode of language in these three sayings which he calls *focal instance* because, "It is the focus or point of clarity within a larger field of reference of which the instance is a part, a field which appears because of the tension in this extreme instance" (380). The aphorism thus opens up the closed limits of the possible and focuses an entire range of new options in one terse and shocking admonition. "It is an extreme instance and therefore is able to call in question our established patterns of thinking and acting" (384). The article then exemplifies all this by contrasting *focal instance* with *legal rule* under three rubrics. This latter speech mode has (1) literal applicability, (2) general reference to wide areas of human behavior, and (3) clear expansive possibilities by deduction or analogy to other cases. But, he argues, the focal instance lacks these three features and therefore "leaves room for the uniqueness of complex situations" (382).

3. Function of the Aphorisms

It is on this final point that I would wish to qualify Professor Tannehill's conclusion although I think his contrast of focal instance with legal rule is a very important insight. The three differences which he argued between them are less persuasive the longer one thinks about them. Turning the other cheek, for example, *is* literally possible, and the very presence of *three* sayings referring respectively to one's body, one's clothes or possessions, and one's time and labor indicates clear deductive and analogous possibilities for other situations. I would argue that, besides their specificness and extremeness, these logia are also characteristically ridiculous. We experience a certain immediate disharmony and discontinuity or, less politely, a certain sensation of nonsense. Somebody, somewhere, is laughing at us. Both legal rules (cases) *and* focal instances are literally applicable and analogously expansible but, while the former are sensible and logical, the latter strike us as weird and illogical. In fact, these three logia are a satiric parody of case law's careful statement of rights between litigants and should be termed, I would argue, *case parody* rather than focal instance. This latter term can be left as a synonym for legal rules and case laws since these function precisely as focal instances. Two arguments can be offered for this interpretation of the aphoristic trilogy in Matt 5:39b-41 as a mode of speech called *case parody*, one intrinsic and the other extrinsic.

Intrinsically, one can ask how else might these sayings have been formulated if they were to have done different things, if they had different speech functions from case parody.[4] The element of ridicule or nonsense is established in the discontinuity between protasis and apodosis. The protasis always opens like good, solid, helpful case law concerning acts of personal attack and aggression: if somebody does . . . against you. We await legal or ethical advice or decision in the apodosis. We imagine in an instant such conclusions as, in a biblical seven ranging from extreme negative to extreme positive: kill him, maim him, strike him, run away from him, forget him, forgive him, love him. This spectrum of apodictic possibilities, extending from the negative ethics of Lamech in Gen 4:23 to the positive ideals of Luke 6:35, has this in common that it is in continuity with the protasis and, easy or difficult, bad or good, lethal or loving, it would not be termed ridiculous or nonsense. All these options have apodictic harmony with the protasis even if, at the end, they challenge us to our limits and already ask of us more than many or any can readily furnish. But instead of such possible if terribly difficult apodoses we get the ridiculous admonition to join in our own dispoiling. The alternatives were there in language and they were not used. Unless one wishes to invoke authorial incompetence, the conclusion must be that they were not used because they were functionally inapplicable. We are expecting *case law*, that is, a problem and its solution. We get instead, *case parody*, that is, a problem and its dissolution.

This disjunction shows up syntactically in the very form of these aphorisms. First, the aggressive verb of the protasis is countered with an apodictic command to join in one's aggression. Second, the double object of the protasis (you‖your possession) results in a double object which is not the expected one (him‖his possessions) but rather: him‖more of your possessions.

The exact speech function of such case parody can be illustrated, extrinsically, by a comparison with William A. Beardslee's[5] studies on the *proverb* in the synoptic tradition and in the coptic Gospel of Thomas. Two of his main conclusions are of present interest. In comparing different versions of individual proverbs and different layers of the synoptic and Thomas gospels he noted a steady escalation from banal truism to hyperbolic and paradoxical challenge. Even more significantly, he argues that this gradual intensification operates in reverse to the history of the tradition so that the historical sequence was *from* intensified paradox *to* generalized truism. "The intensification of the Synoptic proverbs is, by its closeness to the function of the parable, to be regarded as a trait of the tradition at a very early stage (indeed, of Jesus himself)."[6] The function of such hyperbolic and paradoxical proverbs, which Beardslee derives from the origins of the tradition in Jesus, is summed up as follows: "The paradox of intensified antithesis is putting pressure on the very presupposition on which the clusters of wisdom insights had been gathered together. This presupposition is the project of making a continuous whole out of one's existence."[7] Clearly, then, these proverbs were not *in*tensified. They started as intense paradox with Jesus and were muted and *dein*tensified by the tradition.

In parallel with all this I would suggest that case parody challenges the presuppositions on which case laws are based, and it shakes and shocks the project of making a continuous whole of one's existence by law. Or, again, case parody and paradoxical proverb challenge this project's successful completion by either law or wisdom. What is wrong with such a project is, of course, that God is either inside one's projected whole and in that case is idolatrous or is outside the whole and experienced therefore only in that whole's being challenged and broken.

The comparison between paradoxical proverb and case parody is very instructive. In both cases, the tendency of the tradition's development has been to mute, to soften, to generalize, to smooth out the satiric and sardonic thrust of such aphorisms. We saw earlier that Q had already muffled the force of these three case parodies with the added generalizing conclusion in Matt 5:42 = Luke 6:30 which makes it all sound rather like an injunction to fervent almsgiving. But at the tradition's earlier level the paradoxical proverb challenges proverbial wisdom to a deeper and more difficult wisdom and the case parody undermines case law in the name of a profounder and more pervasive law. Or, in that address which Rilke[8] wrote as "The Words of the Lord to John on Patmos,"

> Sometimes, when they howl that I'm in ire,
> lovingly I fling my trial of fire
> over those possessive sons of earth.
> And I taste some thing of theirs to see
> whether it is fit for me: —
> if it blazes it has worth.
> ....
> I am not concerned with form,

> for I am the fiery story,
> and like jagged lightning is my gaze.

The search for other examples of case parody will have to be left, of course, for other times and other places.

C. Philosophical Analysis

Questions of speech function and language mode point ineluctably towards what the poet Henry Rago called "the ontology that is hidden in words." A few words, then, and only a few, to note the ontological dimensions of this mode of language here termed case parody.[9]

In his *Letter on Humanism*[10] of 1947 Martin Heidegger was responding to three questions posed by the French philosopher, Jean Beaufret. The second query was how one might make clear and precise the relationship between ontology and ethics. Heidegger answers with Aristotle's story about the visitors who came to see the philosopher Heraclitus. They were surprised and probably disappointed to find the great thinker in so mundane an occupation as warming himself at the stove. He invited them in with the reassurance that, "Here too there are gods present." As Heidegger interprets this it indicates that the thinker must warm himself at the divine fire before and if he is to have anything to say. So he concludes that the most original and fundamental ethics is, as the word *ēthos* (dwelling) shows, man's abiding with Being. In Heidegger's words: "More essential than any establishment of rule is the abode in the truth of Being." And this, I would suggest, is the ontological function of case parody. It stops and arrests the forward development and expansion of case law by satirical laughter. This is not done, however, in order to furnish law with new insights or directions contained within these sardonic aphorisms. Rather does its parody turn case and law and rule backwards towards their source and, by blocking any literal interpretation of its own dictum as ridiculous, remind us over and over again that to abide with God is more fundamental than any case law and is itself original ethics and fundamental morality.

When we are confronted with any form of language or mode of speech thus parodied and so turned backward towards its source we can see what Robert Frost learned from that "West-Running Brook."[11] He noticed how "that white wave runs counter to itself" and concluded:

> It is this backward motion toward the source
> Against the stream, that most we see ourselves in,

> The tribute of the current to the source.
> It is from this in nature we are from.
> It is most us.

So much, then, for the meaning of the aphorism. We can turn now to the second half of the initial question and discuss its origin.

II. The Origin of the Aphorism

It has already been established that the case parody logia in Matt 5:39b-41 or Luke 6:29 were not created at the redactional level by either of these two authors. They came to them from Q. Neither were they created by Q since it already contained (or created?) with them a softening generalization in Matt 5:42 = Luke 6:30 which turned them from instances of case parody into admonitions to exuberant almsgiving. If the case parody set is earlier than Q, the next question is whether it goes back to the historical Jesus himself. And that raises the question of one's criteria for determining whether a given unit goes back to Jesus or stems from the primitive church at some early date in its tradition.

Any criteria for historical authenticity of sayings or stories from Jesus must face four narrowing circles of preliminary problematic. There is, first, the ambiguity, uncertainty, and insecurity of any and all historical research. Second, there is the difficulty that all this happened long ago and in another country, and besides they all are dead. Third, there is the nature of our sources which are, quite openly and honestly, confessional witness rather than uncommitted chronicle. Fourth, there is the problem of constant adaptation, application, and interpretation which offers us multiple versions of the same unit within successive layers of the tradition.

It is, in fact, this last problem that brings with it the best avenue of solution. If, and only if, one agrees that creative reinterpretation for renewed relevance is the constant in our data and if one can chart the trajectory of such readaptation and reapplication, one could see what was there originally in need of all this reinterpretation. This is why the "criterion of dissimilarity" must be the basic criterion for authenticity in historical Jesus research. This criterion or principle proposes that the most likely authentic material coming from Jesus will appear where there is divergence from or dissimilarity to the emphases of the primitive community which both transmitted and transformed such materials. The principle is logically persuasive *only* if one has decided that creative change is what strikes one most forcibly in any careful reading of the texts. Indeed, in many cases, one discovers that the material is being changed back into greater harmony with certain emphases in contemporary Judaism by the early church. Any other criteria, such as multiple attestation or content similarity, must be secondary to and dependent on this criterion of dissimilarity. It should also be stressed that dissimilarity does not of itself claim either superiority let alone uniqueness for Jesus. Any such claims will have to be vindicated by what one finds by this criterion but they were not the presupposition which created it.[12]

I accept the criterion of dissimilarity as a necessary and negative discipline imposed by the nature of the materials themselves. But, and this is a very important qualification, I would apply it, first and foremost, to *form* rather than to *content*. What forms of language and modes of speech did Jesus use which were dissimilar to those of the primitive church and which this tradition tried valiantly to change into greater harmony with its contemporary Judaism? Even *a priori* one would feel more hopeful that forms might perdure even if multiple changes of content took place.

It might be useful at this point to recall the classic division of *basic forms* given by the Dutch scholar André Jolles in 1929.[13] His nine basic or simple forms were: Legend, Saga, Myth, Riddle, Proverb, Case, Memoir, Tale, Joke. It will be seen that the dissimilarity in Jesus' language concerns (at least) three of these basic forms: Case, Proverb, and Tale.

In the present article the form of *case parody* was found in opposition to case law, and the attempt to smooth it back into harmony with case law was also noted. So also, in recent work on the proverb, the form of *paradoxical proverb* was found to be set against proverbial wisdom, and again the tradition was attempting to domesticate the former by changing it back into its opposite. In my own work on parables[14] I have argued that *parable* is a form of story which undermines example-story and myth, and yet the tradition tried, rather unsuccessfully, to change such parables back into example-stories. In all three situations (in Jolles' basic forms of Case, Proverb, and Tale) the principle or criterion of dissimilarity indicates that this is the historical Jesus at work. Indeed, it is becoming steadily clearer that the main *content* of Jesus' message was an attack on *form*. The kingdom of God comes as the forms of our language are shattered and the world we have created in and by them is shocked into awareness of its relativity. It is Jesus who created the anti-forms of satiric parody on case law, on proverbial wisdom, and on example-story. It is Jesus who attacked case with parody, proverb with paradox, and example-story with parable. And it is the thrust of the tradition to mute this formal attack by turning the attackers back into the attacked. But with Jesus we hear again the voice of

Israel's ancient aniconic imagination. This time it does not warn against a God caught in forms of wood and stone, of silver and gold, but of a God trapped in the forms of language itself, in the forms, for example, of case law, proverbial wisdom, and example-story.

Matt 5:39b comes from Jesus, but it is not a case law and it does not enjoin pacifism upon us. It does something far more fundamental and more radical. It takes away from us all our case absolutes, even the beautiful absolute of pacifism itself.

1. The break between Matt 5:39a and 39b-42 is underlined in the Greek text by the plural "you" in 5:39a followed by a reiterated singular "you" in 5:39b-42. And the suture is further evident in the negative imperative in 5:39a ("do not resist") followed by the positive imperative in 5:39b ("turn the other").

2. From 1909, translated as "Epic Laws of Folk Narrative," *The Study of Folklore* (ed. A. Dundes; Englewood Cliffs: Prentice-Hall, 1965) 129-41.

3. "The 'Focal Instance' as a Form of New Testament Speech: A Study of Matthew 5:39b-42," *JR* 50 (1970) 372-85.

4. In the words of F. Bovon ("Le structuralisme français et l'exégèse biblique," *Analyse structurale et exégèse biblique* [Neuchâtel: Delachaux et Niestlé, 1971] 20) "On imagine ainsi — ce qui conduit à des découvertes surprenantes — un contre-texte." Or, in those of M. A. K. Halliday ("The Linguistic Study of Literary Texts," *Proceedings of the Ninth International Congress of Linguists* [ed. H. G. Lunt; Janua Linguarum: Series Maior 12; The Hague: Mouton, 1964] 302-3) "a text is meaningful not only in virtue of what it is but also in virtue of what it might have been. The most relevant 'might have been' of a work of literature is another work of literature."

5. "The Wisdom Tradition and the Synoptic Gospels," *JAAR* 35 (1967) 231-40; *Literary Criticism of the New Testament* (Philadelphia: Fortress, 1970) 30-41; "Uses of the Proverb in the Synoptic Gospels," *Int* 24 (1970) 61-76; "Proverbs in the Gospel of Thomas," *Studies in New Testament and Early Christian Literature* (Essays in Honor of A. P. Wikgren; ed. D. E. Aune) NovTSup 33 (1972) 92-103.

6. W. A. Beardslee, "Gospel of Thomas," 103.

7. W. A. Beardslee, "Uses of the Proverb," 67.

8. Rainer Maria Rilke, *Poems 1906 to 1926* (New York: New Directions, 1957) 222.

9. For general background see R. E. Palmer, *Hermeneutics* (Northwestern University Studies in Phenomenology and Existential Philosophy; Evanston: Northwestern University, 1969).

10. *Philosophy in the Twentieth Century* (eds. W. Barrett and H. Aiken; New York: Random House, 1962) 270-302 gives a translation by Edgar Lohner.

11. R. Frost, *Complete Poems of Robert Frost* (New York: Holt, Rinehart and Winston, 1967) 329.

12. For a full discussion see N. Perrin, *Rediscovering the Teaching of Jesus* (NT Library; New York: Harper & Row, 1967) 15-53; W. O. Walker, "The Quest for the Historical Jesus: A Discussion of Methodology," *ATR* 51 (1969) 38-56; M. D. Hooker, "Christology and Methodology," *NTS* 17 (1970-71) 480-87; H. K. McArthur, "The Burden of Proof in Historical Jesus Research," *ExpT* 82 (1971) 116-19; D. G. A. Calvert, "An Examination of the Criteria for Distinguishing the Authentic Words of Jesus," *NTS* 18 (1971-72) 209-19; N. J. McEleney, "Authenticating Criteria and Mk 7:1-23," *CBQ* 34 (1972) 431-60; J. G. Gager, "The Gospels and Jesus: Some Doubts about Method," *JR* 54 (174) 244-72. See also J. Eckert, "Wesen und Funktion der Radikalismen in der Botschaft Jesu," *MTZ* 24 (1973) 301-25.

13. *Einfache Formen (Legende, Sage, Mythe, Rätsel, Spruch, Kasus, Memorabile, Märchen, Witz)* (2nd ed.; Tübingen: Niemeyer, 1958) = *Formes simples* (Paris: Seuil, 1972). See the discussion in K. Ranke, "Einfache Formen," *Journal of the Folklore Institute* 4 (1967) 17-31 [English translation of 1959 original], and also in R. Scholes, *Structuralism in Literature* (New Haven: Yale University, 1974) 42-50.

14. *In Parables. The Challenge of the Historical Jesus* (New York: Harper & Row, 1973); and the debates in *Semeia: An Experimental Journal for Biblical Criticism* 1 (1974) and 2 (1974). N. Perrin ("Wisdom and Apocalyptic in the Message of Jesus," *SBL 1972 Proceedings* [2 vols.] 2.543-72; and also *The New Testament: An Introduction* [New York: Harcourt Brace Jovanovich, 1974] 277-303) has already drawn attention to the similarity of these conclusions concerning the forms of proverb and parable in the teaching of the historical Jesus.

Robert W. Funk

The Significance of Discourse Structure for the Study of the New Testament

Introduction

A random agglomeration of words does not constitute a phrase, and an arbitrary juxtaposition of phrases does not produce meaningful clauses or sentences. Analogously, a random collection of sentences would not be recognized as a coherent discourse, say, as a gospel, letter, or miracle story. On the contrary, just as phrases, clauses, and sentences are governed by a grammar that gives them meaningful coherence, so the longer text must also have a grammar by which it is ordered. Supersentential grammar — grammar having to do with units larger than the sentence — is currently being pursued under the rubric *discourse structure*.

Among various types of discourse, the structure of narrative discourse has thus far received the greatest amount of attention. The thread of narrative discourse is a chain of events to which participants and props are related by various rôles, such as agent, recipient, affected. These rôles may be compared to corresponding rôles in sentence grammar: subject, direct object, indirect object. However, the two sets of rôles must also be distinguished since particular rôles in the sentence are not always realized as the same rôles in discourse.

The event line is segmented into various actions, which are given a spatial and temporal setting and hooked together into a chain by a variety of other devices. And a narrative will be constructed in such a way as to focus on certain participants, events, or themes; focus thus provides still another form of cohesiveness.

This brief sketch indicates that the grammar of the linguistic unit larger than the clause will have a grammar strikingly similar to that of the sentence, although it will also differ in important respects. It also suggests that the study of segmentation, participant patterns and rôles, temporal and spatial connectives, and focus will be elements of such a grammar.

The aim of this essay is to elucidate the report of the miracle at Cana in John 2:1-11 by an analysis of the structure of the narrative. The result of the analysis will be relatively simple, and could perhaps be established by other means. Nevertheless, the exercise will hopefully demonstrate the significance of discourse structure for the study of the NT.

It is generally agreed that the miracle story functions very differently in the Fourth Gospel than it does in the Synoptic Gospels and Acts. Various observations are adduced in support of this claim, including matters of form and style. Nevertheless, supporting evidence tends to be impressionistic; an analysis of the structure of the narrative will introduce a crispness into the demonstration which has hitherto been lacking.

The study of John 2:1-11 will be reserved until the last. It will follow upon a sketch of a narrative grammar based on other miracle stories in the NT. The elements of the narrative grammar which shall be sketched are tentative at best. Yet they may offer sufficient footing for the purpose at hand. The uncommon structure of the story of the miracle at Cana becomes most evident in comparison with the structure of other miracle stories. The analysis will thus be both comparative and contrastive.[1]

1. Participants

In the typical healing miracle story in the gospels and Acts there are three participants. They are: the healer, who may be designated A, the person healed (B), and the observers (C). A brief example is found in the healing of Aeneas reported in Acts 9:32-35:

	Now as *Peter* went here and there among them all, he came down also to the saints that lived at Lydda. There he found a man named *Aeneas*, who had
AB	been bedridden for eight years and was paralyzed. And Peter said to him,
B	"Aeneas, Jesus Christ heals you; rise and make your bed." And immediately
C(B)	he rose. And all *the residents of Lydda and Sharon* saw him, and they turned to the Lord.

The skeleton of this story may be said to consist of three parts: A heals B, B confirms the results (often but not always a demonstration), C witnesses to the miracle. This yields the pattern: AB / B / C, where the first letter in a cluster indicates the initiator of an action, and the succession of clusters represent the narrative sequence. This basic structure of the healing narrative is well known from form criticism.

Another abbreviated example is the healing of Peter's mother-in-law (Mark 1:29-31 pars):

AB
B/C(B)

[29]And immediately *he* left the synagogue, and entered the house of Simon and Andrew, with James and John. [30]Now *Simon's mother-in-law* lay sick with a fever, and immediately they told him of her. [31]And he came and took her by the hand and lifted her up, and the fever left her; and she served *them*.

In this story Jesus takes the woman by the hand and lifts her up; the fever leaves her and she ministers to them. The pattern here is AB followed by B. The witness of the observers, C, is apparently omitted; C therefore appears to be an optional item in the structure of the healing miracle (AB / B / [C]). C may be said to belong to the deep structure of the healing story, if by deep structure one means constituent items which do not always come to expression.

In this story, however, there is a third participant, viz. the four disciples just called by Jesus (cf. Mark 1:29 with 1:16-20). They are made to witness indirectly to the healing in 1:31: "she served *them*."

The witness of observers, C, may nevertheless be omitted in longer, more complicated tales. It does not appear, for example, in the healing of a leper (Mark 1:40-45 pars; note Matt 8:1-4 especially) and the healing of the blind man at Bethsaida (Mark 8:22-26).

It should be emphasized that in simple, one-scene miracle stories there are never more than three animate participants. Extended narratives may, of course, have four or more participants, but only three of them normally appear on the stage in any one segment. The appearance of four participants in a tale immediately suggests that the narrative consists of more than one segment. These restrictions hold for folk literature generally.

2. Segmentation

Many of the healing miracle stories preserved in the NT are of the one scene, single segment variety, with two or three animate participants. Occasionally, however, there appear stories with more than one segment and four or more participants. What is the nature of these stories, and how are their segments to be identified?

Healing miracles reported in the Fourth Gospel and Acts sometimes serve as the basis of a much longer narrative. The healing of the lame man at the pool of Bethzatha in John 5:1-9 is expanded into a narrative of six scenes occupying the whole of the chapter (47 verses). This pattern is repeated in John 9 with the healing of the man born blind. In Acts, Luke develops the healing of the lame man at the Gate Beautiful into a narrative of five scenes, some with subscenes, extending from 3:1 to 4:31. In all three cases, the longer complex narratives begin with a typical miracle story.

In the gospel of John these longer narrative complexes with a healing miracle as nucleus appear to serve a rather different purpose than do the simple healing stories in the other gospels. To this point we shall return later in connection with the miracle at Cana.

An intermediate stage of the tendency to expand the healing story into a complex narrative may be observed in the story of the healing of the infirm woman on the sabbath (Luke 13:10-17). In this case we have another simple narrative unit, a pronouncement story, joined to a miracle story, but the two parts of the story constitute separate scenes. The text runs:

(i)   [10]Now he was teaching in one of the synagogues on the sabbath. [11]And there was a woman who had a spirit of infirmity for eighteen years; she was bent
AB   over and could not fully straighten herself. [12]And when Jesus saw her, he called her and said to her, "Woman, you are freed from your infirmity." [13]And
B   he laid his hands upon her, and immediately she was made straight, and she praised God.

DC (ii) [14]But the ruler of the synagogue, indignant because Jesus had healed on the sabbath, said to the people, "There are six days on which work ought to be done; come on those days and be healed, and not on the sabbath day." [15]Then
AD   the Lord answered him, "You hypocrites! Does not each of you on the sabbath untie his ox or his ass from the manger, and lead it away to water it? [16]And ought not this woman, a daughter of Abraham whom Satan bound for
D   eighteen years, be loosed from this bond on the Sabbath day?" [17]As he said
C   this, all his adversaries were put to shame; and all the people rejoiced at all the glorious things that were done by him.

Several close observations on this story will yield the sketch of an elementary narrative grammar on segmentation.

The first observation follows from the previous discussion of participants. The narrative has two sets of participants, Jesus and the infirm woman in the first scene, the ruler of the synagogue, the people, and Jesus in the second scene. The number of different participants is four. The axiom of folk literature that only three animate participants may be permitted on the stage at any one time suggests the first rule of segmentation: where more than three participants appear in a narrative, segmentation will occur at a shift in the set of participants.

In this story, since the set of participants shifts from Jesus and the woman to a scene with the ruler, Jesus, and the people, it is certain that the narrative is segmented at this shift (vs. 14).

This mark of segmentation is reinforced by a second related mark.

A new set of participants may or may not involve the introduction of a new participant into the narrative. However, when a new participant is formally introduced into the narrative in connection with a shift in the set, it is doubly certain that the narrative has been segmented. The ruler in the synagogue is introduced as a new participant, i.e., with full identification, at vs. 14 in the narrative of the infirm woman, in conjunction with a change in the set, thus underscoring the break.

A third sign of segmentation is closely related to the first two.

In the parable of the Laborers in the Vineyard (Matt 20: 1-16), the leading character is called "a householder" at the outset of the story. At the beginning of the second scene ("When evening came. . . "), he is referred to as "the master of the vineyard." A third rule therefore is: it is a mark of segmentation that a participant is given a new name or title.

In the first scene of the account of the infirm woman, Jesus is referred to by his common name, as frequently in the gospel narratives. In the second scene, at the point where he becomes initiator of the action (vs. 15), he is called "lord." This change in nomenclature marks the second scene off from the first.

A variation of this rule concerns the full identification of a continuing participant who might, in a non-segmented narrative, be referred to by pronoun or some other reduced form of identification. This rule will be illustrated by reference to the miracle at Cana subsequently.

As might be expected, an explicit shift in time also indicates a change in scene or a new segment of the narrative. In the parable of the Laborers in the Vineyard, to which reference has already been made, the story opens "early in the morning." The householder repeats his visits to the marketplace to hire workers until the eleventh hour. Then, "when evening comes . . . " he calls his steward to pay wages. The shift in time to evening clearly marks a new segment in the story.

Correspondingly, when a subsequent segment of the narrative looks back on previous events *as past*, the reader also knows that a new narrative segment has been created. In the same parable, agreements made and work done earlier in the day are referred to in the second scene as though they were past. This temporal distancing by means of the pluperfect (past from the standpoint of a narrative told in past time) also marks temporal segmentation.

An explicit time shift is not provided in the story of the infirm woman. However, the reader is told that the ruler of the synagogue was indignant "because Jesus *had healed* on the sabbath." In the second segment, the activity of the first scene is cast into the past, indicating obliquely that the second scene is set in a new and subsequent time.

Thus far the following marks of segmentation in the story of the infirm woman have been noted:

    (1)   the introduction of a new set of three participants

    (2)   the formal introduction of a new participant

    (3)   a change in nomenclature for a participant

    (4)   reference to events in the same narrative as past

To these should be added two other possibilities not illustrated by the story of the infirm woman:

    (5)   the full identification of a continuing participant

    (6)   an explicit temporal shift

There are, of course, still other marks of segmentation. In order to round off this portion of this rudimentary narrative grammar, note should be taken of three other symptoms of segmentation. There will be occasion to make use of two of them in connection with the analysis of the miracle at Cana.

It will come as no surprise that a shift in locale is often employed as a sign of segmentation. Both scenes of the healing of the infirm woman take place in the synagogue; there is thus no change of locale to mark the second segment. The healing of the lame man in Acts 3, on the other hand, takes place at the gate of the temple. In the next scene, Peter addresses the multitude in Solomon's portico: the change in locale sets off the new narrative segment.

A shift in locale is often preceded by a departure at the conclusion of the previous segment. Occasionally a departure is the only clue to a change in place. A departure and a new spatial setting tend, of course, to reinforce each other, although one or the other may stand alone as a signal.

In the account of the healing of the ten lepers (Luke 17:11-19), which is also made up of two segments, the ten lepers depart at the end of scene one. The grateful leper returns to open the second scene. We do not know whether the locale in the two scenes is identical. For the purposes of the narrative that knowledge is unnecessary. For purposes of segmentation, departure and arrival are clear enough indicators.

Finally, narrative segments, particularly initial narrative segments, are formally opened with what may be called a "focalizer." In a general way, it may be said that a narrative is opened with some indication of the time and place events were supposed to have transpired, as well as some minimal identification of the participants. But for the narrative to become narrative, preliminary descriptions of time, place, and participants must be succeeded by at least one specific action (just as each sentence must have a verb). How is the transition from the more general descriptive statements to the particulars of action managed in narrative discourse? The transition is managed by a "focalizer."

An example will be more lucid than further generalizations.

In the story of the lame man in Acts 3, the reader is told first that Peter and John were on their way to the temple (locale), at the hour of prayer (time). Further, a lame man was customarily placed at the gate of the temple (closer specification of place: temple > gate of temple) to ask alms. There is thus a more general and more specific indication of the place, and a precise indication of the time. There is thus the general picture: the lame man is lying at the gate prepared to beg; simultaneously, Peter and John are on their way. The narrator next focuses attention in such a way that the first action of the story gets underway: the lame man "sees," i.e. focuses on Peter and John (and the reader along with him) and asks for alms. With this the story proper gets underway.

Having a participant "see" something is a formal device by means of which the attention of the reader (hearer) is focused on the first action of the narrative. The illustration given provides the first of a wide variety of such devices. It will be possible here only to list a few of the most common of these devices, without amplification.

(1) Someone "sees" something

(2) Someone "hears" something (a report or the like) (cf. the story of Peter's mother-in-law)

(3) Someone "finds" something (cf. the story of Aeneas)

(4) An object or person is "brought"

(5) Someone "arrives"

(6) Persons "meet" (mutual arrival)

(7) A sound signal (cry, rush of wind, earthquake, etc.) focuses attention

(8) A visual signal (vision, flash of light, etc.) focuses attention

All of these are commonly found in the narratives of the NT and related hellenistic literature.

To recapitulate: the rudimentary narrative grammar being sketched here contains the following marks of segmentation, now arranged schematically:

With reference to participants:

(1) the introduction of a new set of participants

(2) the formal introduction of a new participant

(3) a change in nomenclature for a participant

(4) the full identification of a continuing participant

With reference to time:

(5) an explicit temporal shift

(6) reference to events in the same narrative as past

With reference to place:

(7) an explicit shift in place

(8) departure (segment end)

Focalizer:

(9) formal means to focus attention on the specific action

3. Formal Structure of the Narrative

The treatment of participants and segmentation has been in sufficient detail to afford a glimpse of what a full narrative would be like. It will not be possible to treat other components of such a grammar in this context. Rather, it will be necessary to move on briefly to two larger considerations in preparation for the analysis of the miracle at Cana in John 2.

A narrative may be said to consist of three parts: an introduction, a nucleus, and a conclusion.

In the story of Aeneas, the introduction consists of the introduction of Peter (vs. 32) and the introduction of Aeneas, with some indication of the gravity of his malady (vs. 33). The focalizer, 'Peter finds Aeneas,' occurs in vs. 33, in anticipation of the first action in vs. 34: Peter's pronouncement over Aeneas. Peter's healing words and Aeneas' response constitute the nucleus of the narrative. In terms of the participant analysis given earlier, the nucleus comprises the AB / B sequences. The conclusion of this mini-narrative is equivalent to C, the witness of the residents of Lydda and Sharon.

One may describe this tripartite division in a formal way in relation to the healing narrative: the introduction serves to introduce the major participants (together with temporal and spatial notices); the nucleus consists of the AB / B sequences; and the conclusion is provided by C, the witness of onlookers.

This same structure is found in rather full form in the narrative in Acts 3:1-10. Peter and John (A) and the lame man (B) are introduced in vss. 1 and 2; place and time are also given. The focalizer, 'the lame man sees Peter and John about to go into the temple,' opens the nucleus in vs. 3. The nucleus in this case consists of the sequences BA / AB / BA / AB / B, which is merely an elaboration of the simpler sequence AB / B. The conclusion of this narrative is provided by vss. 9, 10, which is set off as a subscene with its own focalizer ("all the people saw him . . . "). The conclusion is once again the witness to the miracle.

These structures may be represented schematically as follows:

[1]Now Peter and John were going up to the temple at the hour of prayer, the ninth hour. [2]And a man lame from birth was being carried, whom they laid daily at that gate of the temple which is called Beautiful to ask alms of those who entered the temple.

BA   [3]Seeing Peter and John about to go into the temple, he asked for alms. [4]And

AB   Peter directed his gaze at him, with John, and said, "Look at us." [5]And he

BA   fixed his attention upon them, expecting to receive something from them.

AB   [6]But Peter said, "I have no silver and gold, but I give you what I have; in the name of Jesus Christ of Nazareth, walk." [7]And he took him by the right hand and raised him up;

B   and immediately his feet and ankles were made strong. [8]And leaping up he stood and walked and entered the temple with them, walking and leaping and praising God.

C   [9]And all the people saw him walking and praising God, [10]and recognized him as the one who sat for alms at the Beautiful Gate of the temple; and they were filled with wonder and amazement at what had happened to him.

Even a two scene narrative like that found in the story of the infirm woman follows this same general pattern. Jesus' teaching in the synagogue is the setting for both scenes (vs. 10). This is followed by the introduction of the infirm woman (vs. 11), which serves as the introduction to scene one. The nucleus of scene one consists of an AB / B sequence.

Scene two opens with the introduction of the ruler of the synagogue. The nucleus of the second scene is the exchange between the ruler and the people, followed by an exchange between Jesus and the people.

Verse 17a ("his adversaries were put to shame") serves as the conclusion to scene two, and 17b ("the people rejoiced . . .") as the conclusion to the whole narrative. The element C, the witness of the people, is reserved for the conclusion to the whole narrative; this conclusion indicates that the healing miracle still dominates this complex narrative.

We thus have a introduction, nucleus, and conclusion to each of the segments, as well as to the narrative as a whole.

4. Plot Structure

Vladimir Propp, in his now famous *Morphology of the Folktale*,[2] defines a fairy tale as any development proceeding from villainy (A, in his code) or a lack (a), through intermediary functions, to marriage (W*), reward, the liquidation of misfortune or lack, or other terminal function. Such a development Propp terms a move.

Each new act of villainy or situation of lack creates a new move, i.e. the villainy or lack are finally overcome.

The healing miracle story follows this general pattern, as do many other types of stories.

The healing miracle is developed out of a lack or misfortune: a sufferer is introduced, usually with some indication of the gravity of the malady (the woman had been infirm for 18 years). This misfortune is overcome in the act of healing. Sometimes, as in Acts 3, the healing segment is rather more developed than in the simpler forms of the healing narrative. The witness of observers then serves as the conclusion, and this type of conclusion connects the narrative to its larger context, the witness to Jesus of Nazareth as the wonder worker.

In anticipation of the Cana story, notice should be taken of just how the conclusion to the miracle story is handled.

In the account of the infirm woman, the woman herself praises God at the end of scene one, presumably in gratitude for his goodness to her. But the conclusion to the narrative as a whole indicates that all the people rejoiced at the glorious things done by Jesus.

Similarly, in the story of the lame man at the gate of the temple (Acts 3), the lame man praises God, in addition to jumping up and down in the temple. But the people recognize this man as the one who used to lie at the gate and so are filled with wonder and amazement.

This motif is extremely common in the healing stories, but it is not lacking in the nature wonders. At the conclusion of the story of the stilling of the storm (Mark 4:35-41 pars), for example, the disciples are filled with awe, viz. they are impressed with the powers of Jesus. When Jesus comes walking to them on the water (Mark 6:45-52 pars), they are terrified, and when the wind ceases, they are astounded.

It is thus characteristic of the miracle stories we have examined that either the ones affected by the miracle or those observing testify to the impression made on them. In some cases, both forms of testimony appear. The purpose of this motif is to call attention to the marvelous powers of the miracle worker.

5. The Miracle at Cana (John 2:1-11)

An effort has been made to present those elements of a rudimentary narrative grammar which might be helpful in an analysis of the miracle at Cana. The discourse analysis should be developed in relation to a problem of interpretation, in order to demonstrate the potential applicability of this type of study.

The question in the Fourth Gospel is whether the miracle stories serve the same function that they do in the Synoptic Gospels and Acts. We have noted that the miracles in the latter are told to underscore the wonder working powers of Jesus. In John, on the other hand, it has been argued that the miracles are told for the sake of the symbolic possibilities latent in them. The miracle itself is unimportant; it is the symbolic meaning that counts with John.[3] Can discourse analysis assist in resolving this question?

It is necessary, first, to establish the segments and formal structure of the narrative. These may be presented schematically and then commented upon.

[1]On the third day there was a marriage at Cana in Galilee, and the mother of Jesus was there; [2]Jesus also was invited to the marriage, with his disciples.

AB (i)   [3]When the wine failed, the mother of Jesus said to him, "They have no
BA   wine." [4]And Jesus said to her, "O woman, what have you to do with me? My
AC   hour has not yet come." [5]His mother said to the servants, "Do whatever he
           tells you." [6]Now six stone jars were standing there, for the Jewish rites of
BC   purification, each holding two or three measures. [7]Jesus said to them, "Fill the
           jars with water." And they filled them up to the brim. [8]He said to them, "Now
           draw some out, and take it to the steward of the feast." So they took it [to
           him.]

    (ii)   [9]When the steward of the feast tasted the water now become wine, and did
           not know where it came from (though the servants who had drawn the water
DE   knew), the steward of the feast called the bridegroom [10]and said to him,
           "Every man serves the good wine first; and when men have drunk freely, then
           the poor wine; but you have kept the good wine until now."
           [11]This, the first of his signs, Jesus did at Cana in Galilee, and manifested his
           glory; and his disciples believed in him.

The first two verses comprise the introduction. Jesus' mother, Jesus, and his disciples are introduced. The occasion is specified (a marriage), the time (on the third day) and place (Cana) are indicated.

The participants in scene one are Jesus' mother, Jesus, and some servants. It is curious that the disciples, who were introduced earlier, do not appear.

In scene one a lack is established (no wine) and the lack is overcome (six jars are filled with water). The scene closes with the departure of the servants bearing water, now presumably turned wine, to the steward of the feast.

We have assumed that segmentation recurs with vs. 9. What are the reasons for this assumption?

First of all, the servants depart at the end of vs. 8 (departure ends a segment). A new set of participants appears in the next stretch of narrative (the steward, the bridegroom and the servants, rather than Jesus, his mother, and the servants), and the steward, who is proleptically introduced in vs. 8 is reintroduced in vs. 9 with full identification. (Were there no segmentation at this point, we would expect vs. 9 to read: "When *he* tasted the water . . . ," i.e. pronominal reference.) Further, in vs. 9 there is pluperfect reference back to events in scene one. And finally, there is a new focalizer in vs. 9: the steward "tastes" something (cf. seeing and hearing).

It is thus clear that vss. 9-10 constitute a second scene in this brief narrative. This fact is not often noted. The participants are the steward, the bridegroom, and the servants. The disciples again do not appear.

Verse 11 functions as the conclusion to the whole. The disciples now reappear. They appear at both the beginning and end of the narrative and thus mark its limits, but they do not participate in the narrative except as silent witnesses. Nevertheless, they are important to the author's larger purpose: the disciples are those who witness the event and believe; it is to the disciples' point of view that the author invites the reader. But to what do the disciples witness that leads to faith?

The plot structure of the conventional miracle is misfortune or lack/overcoming of that misfortune or lack/and the witness to the powers of the miracle worker (§4).

In John 2:1-11 the lack (failure of the supply of wine) is established and presumably overcome in scene one, although testimony to that fact does not occur until scene two, and when it does, it is oblique testimony. On the conventional pattern, one would expect the testimony of witnesses in scene two (Acts 3) or at least a controversy dialogue related to the miracle (infirm woman). But the steward strangely ignores the miracle and reprimands the bridegroom for holding back the good wine until the inferior has been consumed. The steward's pronouncement is in fact unrelated to the miracle as such; it has to do rather with the significance of the new and better wine.

The discussion in scene two is thus patently a non-literal treatment of the changing of the water into wine. The structure of the narrative bears this out: testimony to the powers of the miracle worker is suppressed in favor of a dark saying about the order of wine service. And the disciples believe in him; they do not marvel, are neither astounded nor thunderstruck. The comparative structure of the miracle narrative in John accordingly demonstrates that in John it is the symbolic meaning that counts.

6. Conclusion

This elementary treatment of discourse structure in relation to the New Testament has hopefully demonstrated two things. First, discourse structure will enable the form critic to analyze narrative structures with greater precision. It will be possible, as a consequence, to develop a more vigorously controlled typology of narrative forms. This aspect of the significance of discourse structure is reflected only obliquely in the section on narrative grammar.

Secondly, discourse structure will make possible the resolution of interpretative problems by making available new comparative and contrastive data with respect to the structure and form of larger units of discourse. The treatment of the marriage feast at Cana is a minor though not insignificant example.

The task before the biblical scholar is to develop a full narrative grammar for a variety of discourse forms. The process of developing such a grammar will itself undoubtedly suggest a myriad of applications of the emerging data.

1. This essay is dedicated to the pioneering spirit and achievements of John L. McKenzie. He has an established interest in the form and function of biblical narratives, as illustrated most recently by a seminar paper presented to the Society of Biblical Literature at its annual meeting in 1974 ("Primitive History: Form Criticism," *Society of Biblical Literature, 1974 Seminar Papers* [vol. 1; Missoula, Mont.: Scholars Press, 1974] 87-99).

2. *Morphology of the Folktale* (2nd ed., rev. and ed. with a preface by L. A. Wagner; Austin: University of Texas, 1968).

3. B. Olsson, *Structure and Meaning in the Fourth Gospel. A Text-Linguistic Analysis of John 2:1-11 and 4:1-41* (Lund, Sweden: CWK Gleerup, 1974).

GERARD S. SLOYAN

Postbiblical Development of the Petrine Ministry

In an essay which attempts to be fully faithful to the NT data John L. McKenzie, a priest of the Roman Church of now thirty-six years, observes that "all the Christian churches have evolved their ministerial structures and offices with almost serene indifference to the NT."[1] Neither pope, bishop, priest, nor stated clerk in the modern form of those offices, he observes, can be found in the canonical books. "This [viz., the pluriform ministerial structure actually attested to in the NT] does not imply that development beyond the NT is impossible or undesirable; it does imply that such a development, when it occurred, was based on other than biblical reasons."[2] McKenzie concludes from this mode of development that, to the degree to which these reasons were historical, other structures can be suggested by other historical reasons.

The scholar in whose honor the present essays are collected is not an anti-papalist or an opponent of the offices of bishopric or presbyterate, the latter two whether understood as priestly or not. He has rather spent an adult career being in favor of things, for example, ministry understood as service and, more broadly, the interpretation of the bible in terms of what it says rather than what any reader or ecclesial body would like it to say.

An interesting NT question is that the authorship of 1 Peter, a document redolent of Pauline thought, was attributed to Peter.[3] If the Symeon whom Jesus called Rock wrote it, a supposition which should not be dismissed out of hand, that would account for the fact best. Only on the hypothesis that he did not must the problem of the pseudonymous claim of authorship be faced; at 2 Peter there is no doubt of its pseudonymous composition, well into the second century. The question of attributed authorship is, in turn, part of the larger one of the measure in which Peter serves as touchstone of right faith throughout the books of the NT.[4] This is not the much later question of the primacy of the Roman See but touches on the indubitable fact of Peter's firstness in the apostolic community — the latter understood as either the Twelve or the larger group which saw the risen Christ and was commissioned by him to preach the gospel. If Peter did not write the first epistle attributed to him (and he certainly did not write the second; cf. 2 Pet 1:14, 15; 3:15, 16 which show familiarity with Peter's martyrdom and the canonical status of Paul's letters), the question is, how did this apostle to diaspora Jews (cf. Gal 2:7-9) become a natural candidate for authorship of a letter to Gentile converts (cf. 1 Pet 1:14; 2:10; 4:3) in areas associated with the labors of Paul ("Pontus, Galatia, Cappadocia, Asia, and Bithynia," 1:1)? It is true, Peter might also have gone there on mission, but the whole tenor of 1 Peter is not Jewish Christian (but cf. 1:15-16; 2:5, 9; 3:20; 5:8). Assuming 1 Peter to be fairly early in composition (before A.D. 64 if Peter wrote it, before 1 Clement — ca. 96 — if he did not), it can be asked what his eminence consisted in, as the churches recorded it, that would best account for the literary attribution.

The author of 1 Peter places him *en Babylōni* (5:13). Most commentators think that this testifies cryptically to the tradition of Peter's presence in Rome,[5] but the language used throughout the letter testifies to spiritual and cultural exile (cf. 2:9, 11; 4:7, 12; 5:1b, 6, 9-10) and hence the mention of Babylon may be entirely figurative. Peter's authorship of an epistle while in Rome would, however, fit in with the tradition of his ending there, again assuming that we have a case of attribution. (His actual writing from Rome is an obvious alternative.) It is a time when scattered Christians (1:1) are being maligned by pagans as criminals (2:12). The letter calls Peter a *martys* of the sufferings of Christ and *koinōnos* of the glory that is soon to be revealed (5:1). This vocabulary is taken by some as the technical speech for martyrdom and its crown, hence an indication of the writer's awareness of such a tradition about Peter.[6] But Peter's martyrdom alone, even if it be further attested to by ch. 21 of the Fourth Gospel and/or the Revelation of John,[7] does not seem sufficient cause to make him that leading apostolic figure to whom writings as disparate as 1 Peter (an elegant Hellenistic Jewish catechesis) and 2 Peter (a warning in a parousian context against corrupters of the faith, employing the donor-recipient formula of Roman decretals) are assigned. There must have been a sufficient association between Peter and the city of Rome in the popular Christian mind, and Peter as the apostolic teacher, *kat'exokēn*, that a pastoral summary of faith and conduct, concluding with an exhortation to tend the flock of God (cf. 1 Pet 5:2), should fittingly have been thought to come from him in that city. Peter is likewise conceived of as the natural opponent of false teachers who multiply destructive heresies (cf. 2 Pet 2:1), in what seems to be the expanded version of a letter attributed to Jude. The writer of 2 Peter is claiming for his adaptation an even higher authority than Jude's, namely, that of Peter. (Interestingly, despite its lateness 2 Peter does not mention Rome, even though when it was written the tradition of Peter's having ended there was already taking hold.)

It has been demonstrated by Cullmann and others that Peter's unquestionable spokesmanship and rôle as representative among the disciples in the gospel tradition cannot be fully correlated with the choice Jesus made of him as Rock.[8] In other words, there is no satisfactory answer to the question: did his character and psychological makeup bring on the designation or was he named by Jesus to a function that he subsequently "grew up to"? His constant being to the fore is never described as a leadership of the others or a superior position to theirs during Jesus' earthly days. It is probable that the singling out of Simeon as Cephas was pre-paschal (cf. Mark 3:16; Matt 10:2; 16:18; Luke 6:14; John 1:42), like the designation "Boanerges, that is, sons of thunder" (Mark 3:17). Against this, Pesch points out that in the synoptic tradition (the evidently redacted Luke 22:34 is an exception) Jesus always calls him Simon, which makes Pesch and others think the name $Kēpha$ came from the community.[9]

There is no way to be sure whether the naming of a special rôle for Peter in the future is an occurrence of the earthly or the risen life (cf. Matt 16:18-19; Luke 5:10; 22:31-32; John 21:15-17) but the affinity of Luke 5:10 with John 21:10-11, and the absence of any charge to Peter in Mark's Caesarea Philippi account (8:27-30), suggest the latter, or better still the life of the community.[10] Peter's being the first among the intimate disciples to see the risen Lord (cf. the developed "$Kēphas$" of 1 Cor 15:5 from "$Simon$" of Luke 24:34, and Mark 16:7, following 10:2; in John, the entering of the tomb first, 20:6, and acting on the beloved disciple's recognition of Jesus, 21:7) complements of the leadership rôle he is assigned in the Jerusalem church (cf. Acts 1:15; 2:14, 37-41; 3; 4; 5:29; 8:20; 10; 12; 15) and probably accounts for it. The reported designation of him by Jesus as Rock, wielder of the keys and binder and looser, and the charges to catch men, feed Christ's sheep, and strengthen his brothers may be summed up as the tradition of Galilee, from which the synoptics came, on his leadership function.

It would be a mistake to view the NT traditions on Peter as all of a piece. They came from different places in the early Christian world and arose in different decades and circumstances. Those in the synoptics represent the earliest layer, deriving from the sayings of Jesus, but they reach us as part of a redactional unity which incorporates materials from as much as sixty years later. Thus, Luke has some of the earliest Peter traditions but works out of a Gentile Christian framework. Matthew is interested in putting those he possesses in the service of a claim for Peter's doctrinal authority (16:18-19) in his Syrian church[11] and applying the tradition of "the interpretative application of the Petrine saying [of 18:18] to the community [of Matthew] as a whole . . . [which] legitimately claims for itself the authority imparted to Peter."[12] By the time the gospels are written the churches from which they come have already institutionalized certain offices and practices.

If the Syrian, even Antiochene, provenance of Matthew is sustained (a hypothesis contributed to strongly by the use made of this gospel by Ignatius a generation later), the departure of Paul reported as final from that Hellenist Jewish community (cf. Acts 15:35-36) would be explained by the increasingly Jewish Christian presence testified to in the gospel of Matthew. The tensions of Jewish and Gentile Christians in proximity stalk the pages of Matthew, with its promulgation of fulfillment of the law in a particular Jesus-spirit which is demonstrably not that of the James community of Jerusalem. Peter's coming to Antioch and his ambivalence about taking his meals with Gentiles, coupled with Paul's unhappiness over his reversion to Jewish custom (cf. Gal 2:11-14), is a further indication of the uneasy balance.

The book of Acts with its Jerusalem and Antioch traditions sees in Peter a witness to Jesus as the Christ in Jerusalem (chs. 1-5, 12, *passim*) and leader of the community there (4:9; 5:3; 12:3; 15:7) who defers to James (12:17; 15:13; cf. Gal 1:18-19); as a missionary to Samaritans (cf. 8:14-17) and to Gentiles (ch. 10; 11:15-18; 15:7). His visits to Joppa, Lydda, and Caesarea, which some critics place after ch. 12,[13] prepare him for the missionary career that Paul hints at in 9:5 (less surely attested to in 1:12). Peter's stay at Antioch is not to be found in Acts except by the doubtful procedure of identifying it as the "other place" of 12:17 from Gal 2:11.[14] The silences of Acts and Romans on any connection of Peter with that city are well known but nothing positive can be concluded from them.[15]

Cephas is reputed to be one of three pillars of the Jerusalem church and its foundations in the diaspora, along with James and John (cf. Gal 2:6, 9). His calling as an apostle is enshrined in the legend of Mark 1:16-17. The tradition-history of two basic narratives about him found in Mark, his confession of Jesus as the Christ (8:27-33) and his denial of Jesus (14:54, 66-72) is not available to us.[16] We can only observe the twofold tradition in Mark of Peter's strength and weakness. In the first instance it is Peter who answers after Jesus tries to evoke a faith response from all (8:29) and Jesus gazes on all while calling Peter a Satan (vs. 33); in vss. 29 and 33 Peter is so termed without mention of the giving of the name (cf. the earlier 3:16,

"Simon whom he surnamed Peter"). Despite the Semitic phrases found in Matt 16:17-19 (the addendum to Mark 8:29), the sayings of the three verses are probably not *verba Jesu* but of the Jerusalem church tradition introduced into Hellenist Christianity for a Matthean purpose.[17] Clearly a risen Jesus is being claimed as the speaker. He "will build" (vs. 18) a christologically oriented community ("my *ekklesia*" as opposed to the emerging *synagōgē*) which will survive the eschatological powers of death, and "will give" keys that admit to God's realm. "In terms of content it is Matt 21:33-46; 22:1-14, and above all Matt 28:18-20 which conform most closely to this meaning,"[18] namely of a worldwide community in which Peter's authority over the Jerusalem church is extended indefinitely. Matt 16:13-20 must be read as chiefly a Christ-confession of the Matthean church in the total setting of Matt 7:24-27; 11:25-27; 18:18; 23:13.[19]

Cullmann is of the opinion that Peter in his Rock rôle is the archetype of all apostolic faith. The leadership of the primitive church, in fact the church of Jerusalem (which he yielded to James as he became a missionary) is a never-to-be-repeated laying of the foundation.[20] Cullmann has Jesus thinking of the lifetime of Peter when he promises him the power of the keys, the power to bind and loose. That exercise of authority (a better word than Cullmann's "power," which a particular theory of church governance has long sanctioned) will die when he does. The whole construct is a little too neat and also redolent of later historical categories. The hypothetical succession of James to the headship of the Jerusalem church relies heavily on the pseudo-Clementines and Hegesippus[21] and can scarcely be read from the two texts in Acts and one in Galatians. The fullblown "missionary apostolate" sounds suspiciously like a modern career-change or reassignment. Weakest of all is the supposition that we have here authentic *logia* of Jesus reworked, when a church-theory of the Matthean community, which placed them on Jesus' lips, would account for the data far better. In sum, the historicizing tendency is very clearly at work on materials which are obviously symbolic.

A careful review of the literature on Peter's place in the NT and especially of the sayings of Jesus that single him out reveals the all but universal assumption of exegetes that the method of critical history holds the key to his religious significance. If we could know the words of Jesus that underlay the Peter tradition, or Peter's career in Jerusalem, or his subsequent moving about in the Mediterranean world we should then know why he was so highly regarded during the last quarter of the first century when the post-Pauline literature was written.

Since, however, we are operating in the realm of myth and symbol or "type," it is highly unlikely that even relatively sharp tools like composition criticism will be satisfactory if they are used to gain historical information as the key to all. Robert A. Spivey has brought to notice lately a quotation which may be unfair to two great traditions, the one religious and the other scholarly, but it is not without merit in reminding exegetes of the nature of their work:

> The return to symbolism (structuralism) would be the end of the Protestant era, the end of Protestand literalism.
>
> Protestant literalism: the crux is the reduction of meaning to a single meaning — univocation.
>
> Protestant literalism is modern scholarship.
>
> Modern humanistic, literary, and historical scholarship . . . is the Renaissance counterpart of Reformation literalism.[22]

Brown is clearly not describing fundamentalist literalism here but the quest for historicity to which the present essay has referred so liberally. The exegete and hermeneutist have long described "historicism" as the enemy of their craft. There is pride in the more than century-old search for literary *genres*, including poetry and myth. When, however, the poet of long standing or the language structuralist of briefer tenure reminds biblicists that they are literary critics *nolens volens* and that the primary setting of the "historical" in the NT is religious myth, there is resistance. The battle was hard-won which established that history was the locus of salvation for Jew and Christian. The apologetic necessities imposed by the last century, moreover, have left their mark. The scholar of religion even when most determinedly a person of faith has not fully recovered from the conviction that fighting postivists with their own weapons will down them soonest. Although faith has no need of history, the argument runs (an extreme position but the one in a measure held by all), *this* much can be said as to what really happened.

What really happened was that a religious myth grew on the basis of resurrection faith and historical reminiscences. The reminiscences were real but their mythical elaboration was just as real. The biblical critic may not forget that. Any neat distinction between myth and reality establishes a basic ignorance of religion: not religion as a debased counterpart of faith, but religion as an important guise that faith has always worn. The warning that God is not confined to history in communicating with the human race is a familiar one. Equally important is the reminder that the language of symbol is his oldest tongue.[23]

Recalling this, we have said, causes anxiety in exegetical circles. The reason is not so much fear of linguistic or anthropological attempts to co-opt religion as an awareness on the biblicist's part of the uncharted depths of those disciplines. Who wishes to be told in mid-course that myths the world over follow certain laws of which one has not heard, that binarism is intrinsic to the process of human thought, that the essence of a myth is not so much what it *means* as how it *works*? The initial temptation is to dismiss all reports that reach one's ears as faddism: Jung one season, Lévi-Strauss the next, but durable historical criticism the constant that will not fade.

This may be true of historical method. It may, on the other hand, prove increasingly unsatisfactory as a way to deal with biblical material. Thus, to read the balanced views of Professor Cullmann and others on Peter is to suspect that in their conclusions they may not have a clue as to what is going on here. History adds two and two and gets four. Myth gets twenty-two. The man who was once called Rock — by Jesus, by the community, by a long-forgotten child is of no consequence — is he whose faith in Jesus is such that he is the archetypal believer. How did this faith of his and that name come together? We shall never know. At least, or so it is thought, the Rock figure as foundation-stone is so solid that it cannot be thought of as moving, as being transmitted to another. Uneasily one thinks of 1 Cor 10:4. But is not this part of a Pauline polemic against the Petrine party and its claims (cf. 1 Cor 1:12; 3:10-11, 21-23; 9:5)? It may be. It may just as readily be what it seems *prima facie*, the figure of the God of Israel as foundation-stone put to another use. The laws of myth-making are such that one does not say, like King Canute to the waves, "Thus far and no farther." What is to keep a group from thinking thughts of a "succession" in spiritual authority, however abhorrent it may be to the modern mind without documentation, with indeed a gap of a century and a half?

The hazards of canonicity and of declaring a primordial age (like the apostolic one) unique should be clear to all. In the one case some writings are called inspired and others not. In the other a community puts itself under the judgment of the settlements that fall within a certain period, however diverse they may be. Well and good. The sacred literature and the unique epoch both have normative force. Peter becomes the type of man of faith and trustworthy teacher. Simon Magus serves the same function as type of the charlatan, the false teacher.[24] Who can govern the way in which either type will function? The dynamic that was at work to create the symbol may continue in the same direction, it may change course, or it may spend itself and die. It is always there to be appealed to, to function quite as it did in the earliest epoch. But if this does not suit the needs of a living community the primitive symbol may be disregarded, or asked to function quite differently. Tradition is both inflexible and manipulable. Humanity may serve it briefly, but in the long run it serves humanity. A community brought Simon into existence as Rock and wielder of the keys (though there was a real Jesus and a real Simon). The Christ of glory, the *mou hē ekklēsia*, the martyred bishop of Rome (a simple *sympresbyteros* before the monoepiscopate existed in that city) are just as real. In their symbolic existence they are more powerful than history. They are inauthentic only for those who have the historical as their sole norm of authenticity, a group much smaller than the body of believers.

These reflections on the workings of religious symbol are not to be taken as a repudiation of critical historical method, least of all as an apologia for the Roman development. They are a plea for critical attention to the symbolic and the narrower semiotic. An application of linguistic structuralism to the Petrine myth such as Leach has done with the three creation stories in Genesis[25] or Chabrol with three gospel accounts of the passion[26] would be quite in order, but the present appeal is broader. It asks for a hard look at NT data on their own terms, which are historical only secondarily. The tradition history of a given pericope is historical by definition. The main concern of its content is typological and functional. This fact erases the difference between canonical and extracanonical in the category of history. It is sensitive to the distinction in the realm of faith but not to the the extent that the biblical is declared of consequence and the extrabiblical inconsequential. The consequences are different but the differences are more in degree than in kind.

Expositors and leaders of living religions have always known this fact, which is why their use of noncanonical traditions is instinctively sound, even if in practice it may be distressing. They cannot be faulted for a use of symbols and types which is true to the nature of these phenomena, nor with using symbols "historically," for that is the way they have always been used. Religious officials can be charged with desertion of the primary symbolism but not with ignorance of the language or power of symbol. This means that the biblical critic must know the language of symbol well and press its claims if it is to serve its function and be fruitful in a living tradition.

Thus, Josef Blank in the essay cited above concludes that while the Petrine office is not to be found in its developed form of Roman primacy in the NT, it is there "in the much wider sense of the symbolic point of departure perhaps of ecclesiastical office as a whole, for the purpose of witnessing to the authentic tradition, safeguarding it and making continuous renewal in teaching and practice possible."[27] Blank has provided the necessary corrective to this one-sided Petrine symbolism with the reminder that ancient tradition is free of any glorification of Peter apart from mention of his role as adversary (Mark 8:31-33), his weakness in faith (Matt 14:28-31), and his denial of Jesus (Mark 14:29-31, 53-54; 66-72). This ambivalence is not erased by the reality of Easter, as Paul's reference to his vacillating conduct indicates (Gal 2:11-16).[28] The symbol of Peter has worth if it is transmitted whole, not if it is so manipulated as to distort it. The NT Peter is a type of the believer as much as of the teacher, of the strengthener at peer level ("your brothers") as much as of the shepherd or fisherman. To present him as leader and not as learner is to deface his image in the NT, where but one is to be called Rabbi.

Hans Küng has written that the ministry of Peter should constitute the preserving and strengthening of church unity and not a "gigantic, apparently immovable, insuperable and impassable block of granite barring the way to any mutual understanding on the part of the Christian Churches."[29] He asks for deep pondering on this absurd situation by all convinced of the usefulness of a Petrine ministry. An important start would be repeated calls to the rock-like apostolic faith of all Christians by the incumbent of the Roman See. If he sees himself, like any Christian, as a wavering believer, a faithful adversary, and a compromising inheritor of the apostolic teaching, he will inspire confidence that he comprehends the NT teaching on this symbolic figure whom he embodies in a unique way.

1.   "Ministerial Structures in the New Testament" in *The Plurality of Ministries* (eds. H. Küng and W. Kasper; Concilium 74; New York: Herder and Herder, 1972) 13.

2.   Ibid., 21.

3.   "Entire passages are little more than an expansion or restatement of Pauline texts, and whole verses are a kind of mosaic of Pauline words and forms of expression." F. W. Beare, *The First Epistle of Peter* (2d ed.; Oxford: Basil Blackwell, 1958) 25. J. N. D. Kelly does not hold as strongly for direct dependence but (and in this he adds the Pastorals and Hebrews) for "the influence of accepted patterns of teaching and preaching, traditional ideas and ways of looking at things, and a common vocabulary," *A Commentary on the Epistles of Peter and Jude* (New York: Harper and Row, 1969) 13. E. G. Selwyn in a long, appended essay in *The First Epistle of St. Peter* (London: Macmillan, 1947) 363-466, laboriously traces the Pauline paraenetic tradition verbally, attributing many common elements to Silvanus (cf. 1 Pet 5:12; 1 Thes 1:1; 2 Thes 1:1). Neither Beare (189-90) nor W. L. Knox (review in *Theology*, 49 [1946], 342-44) is much impressed with this hypothetical amanuensis. They find the Thessalonian letters far short of 1 Peter in polished style and having very little material in common with it. J. H. Elliott in *The Elect and the Holy* (Leiden: Brill, 1966) examines 1 Pet 2:4-10 and the phrase *basileion hierateuma*, finding the letter a paraenesis probably related to baptism;

cf. 207-18. For a summary of arguments in favor of Peter's authorship, cf. C. Spicq, *Les Epîtres de Saint Pierre* (Paris: J. Gabalda, 1966) 17-26.

4.   B. Rigaux provides an ample bibliography on this question, although unfortunately not an exegetical essay of the same quality, in "St. Peter in Contemporary Exegesis" in *Progress and Decline in the History of Church Renewal* (ed. R. Aubert; Concilium 27; New York: Paulist, 1967) 147-79. See also the discussion and citations found in R. E. Brown, K. P. Donfried, and J. Reumann, eds., *Peter in the New Testament* (New York and Minneapolis: Paulist and Augsburg, 1973); O. Cullmann, *Petrus: Jünger, Apostel, Märtyrer. Das historische und das theologische Petrusproblem* (2d ed., Stuttgart: Evangelisches Verlagswerk, 1960; ET, London: SCM, 1962); R. Pesch, "The Position and Significance of Peter in the Church of the New Testament" in *Papal Ministry in the Church* (ed. H. Küng; Concilium 64; New York: Paulist, 1971) 21-35.

5.   Cf. Rev 14:8; 16:19; 17:5-7; 18:2-24; also the discussion of the symbolic usage of this city for Rome in K. G. Kuhn, *"Babylon," TDNT*, I, 516-17.

6.   Thus Cullmann, *Peter*, 87, n. 83, who cites R. Knopf, Windisch-Preisker, Heussi, and Lietzmann as concluding the same as he from this verse, and Hauck, Bigg, and Strathmann (in Kittel) as supposing that the office of apostle or a literal share in Christ's sufferings are in question but not the martyrdom of Peter already known to the author.

7.   Bultmann thinks John 21:18 merely a proverb about the fate of the elderly, while granting that vs. 19 specifies martyrdom (*Das Evangelium des Johannes* [15th ed.; Göttingen: Vandenhoeck and Rupprecht, 1966] 552; ET, 713). It may be that the verb *ekteinein*, "stretch out," points to crucifixion while not making it certain. Vs. 19 about glorifying God through Peter's death all but assures it, while John 13:36-38 and Luke 22:33 are supportive of the hypothesis of Peter's martyrdom if not his crucifixion. On the two witnesses of Rev 11:3-12, see J. Munck, *Petrus und Paulus in der Offenbarung Johannis: Ein Beitrag zur Auslegung der Apokalypse.* (København: Rosenkilde og Bagger, 1950.)

8.   For Peter's unique position, cf. Mark 1:16, 29, 36; 3:37; 8:29-30; 9:2-8; 11:21; 14:29, 37; 16:7; Matt 10:2; 14:28; 15:15; 16:17-20; 18:21; 21:21; Luke 5:1-11; 8:45; 9:32; 12:41; 22:31. John has the complication of the firstness of the disciple whom Jesus loved, yet he never leaves Peter out of account; cf. 1:37-42; 13:24; 18:15; 20:2-8; 21:2-23.

9.   Pesch, "Significance of Peter," 26.

10.   Thus G. Bornkamm, "Die Binde- und Lösegewalt in der Kirche des Matthäus," *Die Zeit Jesu: Festschrift für Heinrich Schlier* (Freiburg-i-B.: Herder, 1970) 105; ET, "The Authority to 'Bind' and 'Loose' in the Church in Matthew's Gospel," *Jesus and Man's Hope* (vol. 1; Pittsburgh: Pittsburgh Theological Seminary, 1970) 47. The scene is located in Caesarea Philippi precisely because it is "far from Jerusalem" (107; ET, 49).

11.   Cf. H. Strathmann, "Die Stellung des Petrus in der Urkirche. Zur Frühgeschichte des Wortes an Petrus Mt. 16, 17-19," *ZST* 20 (1943) 259-62.

12.   W. Trilling, "Ist die katholische Primatslehre schriftgemäss? Exegetische Gedanken zu einer wichtige Frage," *Zum Thema: Petrusamt und Papstum* (Stuttgart: Katholisches Bibelwerk, 1970) 57. Cf. Bornkamm, "Die Binde- und Lösegewalt," 106; ET, 48. This essay on the sources of Matthew's gospel examines ch. 18 in detail, "The

Discourse Concerning the Congregation," finding in it a Hellenist Christian source but not one in which Peter has lost the position he had in the Jerusalem church — as Bultmann holds — with a group of leaders in the congregation now taking his place (ch. 16).

13. E.g., W. Grundmann, "Die Apostel zwischen Jerusalem und Antiochia," *ZNW*, 39 (1940), 129.

14. For the claims that the bishops of Antioch derive from Peter, which begin in the 3d century, see D. W. O'Connor, *Peter in Rome. The Literary, Liturgical, and Archaeological Evidence* (New York: Columbia University, 1969) 31, 33, 34, 36n.

15. Ibid., 8-11; cf. Cullmann, *Peter*, 80-83.

16. See the attempted reconstructions of E. Dinkler, "Peter's Confession and the 'Satan' Saying," in J. M. Robinson, *The Future of Our Religious Past* (New York: Harper and Row, 1971) 169-202; G. Schneider, *Die Passion Jesu nach den drei alteren Evangelien* (München: Kösel, 1973) 27-31, 43-50, 55-63, 73-79, 83-87, 94-98, 104-08, 111-14, 117, 123-28, 133, 136-45, 143-49, 155-59.

17. Cf. Bornkamm, "Die Binde- und Losegewalt," 104.

18. Ibid.

19. Cf. J. Blank, "The Person and Office of Peter in the New Testament" in *Truth and Certainty* (ed. E. Schillebeeckx; Concilium, n.s. 3, 9; New York: Paulist, 1973) 50.

20. Cullmann, *Peter*, 228-29.

21. Cf. Hegesippus as quoted by Eusebius in *History of the Church*, II, 23, 1 and 4.

22. N. O. Brown, *Love's Body* (New York: Vantage, 1968) 212. Spivey writes, "Structuralism and Biblical Studies: The Uninvited Guest," *Int* 28 (1974) 143, and credits James A. Boon, *From Symbolism to Structuralism* (New York: Harper and Row, 1972) with putting him onto this quotation and another from Claude Lévi-Strauss.

23. E. Voegelin provides such a reminder in "The Gospel and Culture," *Jesus and Man's Hope*, II, 83-84, while R. M. Frye in the same volume ("A Literary Perspective for the Criticism of the Gospels," 194-95) laments the "radically nonliterary enterprise" which he finds in much NT criticism.

24. Cf. K. Beyschlag, *Simon Magus und die christliche Gnosis* (Tübingen: J. C. B. Mohr [Paul Siebeck], 1974).

25. E. Leach, *Genesis as Myth and Other Essays* (London: Jonathan Cape, 1969) 7-23.

26. C. Chabrol, "Analyse du 'texte' de la Passion," *Languages* 22 (1971) 75-96.

27. Blank, "Person and Office," 55.

28. Ibid., 45.

29. *The Church* (New York: Sheed and Ward, 1967) 464.

BERNARD COOKE

The "War-Myth" in 2nd Century Christian Teaching

Support for the peace movement, scholarly effort to clarify the function of religious symbolism — two involvements of John McKenzie that appear quite unrelated, though perhaps by their co-existence helping to destroy the stereotype of the scholar as a detached, half disinterested observer of the human condition and its problems.

Concerned attention to world peace should not be seen, of course, as some additional activity of a scholar (particularly of a theologian). If there is to be a genuine establishment of peace, we must come to understand much better than we now do the underlying dynamics of human behavior that lead to war. Points of view, prejudices, fears, aggressive drives, motivations all play their part, and we cannot profitably work to remove the causes of war until we know what part these forces play and how. Are we, for example, to take for granted that humans are by nature aggressive toward one another, or is aggression a learned attitude?[1] And this is where myth and symbol enter the picture.

Whatever posture a given group of people has toward war or peace is rooted in that group's basic world view, its "cosmic myth." If all of life and nature is seen as involved in battle, if enduring creation-wide war is the story that best explains the progression of events and of human experience; people expect war to continue, they prepare for it as inevitable, they include it in their plans for the future. It is a matter of vital importance, then, whether such a battle-myth is an authentic symbol for the historical process in which we find ourselves, whether the long-standing religious story of a holy war in which God's followers are carrying out the divine will by exterminating God's enemies (and theirs!) is revelation from God or human rationalizing.[2] Vietnam is but the last in a long list of wars that have been glorified as crusade; and it seems that as long as crusades remain a cherished religious ideal, the moral support of religion will be invoked in defense of mankind's wars.[3]

Genuine myth is an imaginative expression of an insight into the causative structures of existence, an insight that is deeply philosophical though not formulated in philosophical language. If the philosophical insight be faulty, the myth cannot but be misleading. In the case of the battle-myth as a view of the universe, there does seem to be a faulty understanding of the pervasive phenomenon of conflict: this conflict is seen as contradictory opposition of good and evil, i.e., of opposites that are irreconcilable; but the actual situation may be one of a dialectical tension between contrary positive principles, an interplay of forces in creative interaction. Thus, there is struggle, but it is the struggle indicative of emergent life and organic development; and the over-riding imagery appropriate to such a situation is that of life rather than of death, as with war. In human society, there is competition and lack of easy agreement; there is pluralism of views and ideologies and values; there is inevitable tension increased by ignorance and prejudice and fear. However, the resolution need not come through the outbreak of hostility; a solution can come through the emergence of human community grounded in love.

This latter is, of course, the thrust of the thirteenth chapter of 1 Corinthians; but despite the idealistic picture of charity's role provided by Paul, much of Christian tradition — and much of Jewish tradition before it — assumes the battle-myth.[4] Gregory VII may have been the first to launch the Christian Church on a formal course of crusade;[5] but by his day the Christian community, the *societas christiana*, had long seen itself as the Church militant. The ideal of the Christian as *miles Christi* goes back at least as far as Basil,[6] perhaps even to the first Clementine epistle, or further back to Paul himself.[7] But is such a battle image really consonant with Christianity; or is it one of the alien elements that it inherited from its cultural origins or that entered it later from the cultural influences it encountered?[8] It is the purpose of this present essay to examine one small portion of that question: the existence or non-existence of an underlying battle-myth in the explanatory (catechetical, apologetic, homiletic) non-biblical writings of mainstream Christianity prior to Irenaeus.

Late first and early second century Christian writers inherited a mixed Christian tradition regarding the use of battle as a description of life's conflicts. In the sayings of Jesus, the statement that he came "to bring not peace but the sword" (Matt 10:34; Luke 12:51), frequent reference to "the enemy" (Satan, the devil), and the presupposition in several of the parables that there is some person or force that is working in hostile opposition to God, all seem to point towards some underlying warfare between godly and evil hosts. This was, at least to some extent, reinforced by the Pauline use of military imagery to describe the Christian struggle against the forces opposed to the gospel (e.g., 2 Cor 6:7; 10:4).

On the other hand, the basic gospel — Jesus having overcome the powers of evil by non-resistance to their attempt to destroy him, by enduring suffering and death and thus passing into newness of life — reverses the previous battle-myth interpretations of human history. Salvation is attained for mankind by love absorbing the attacks of evil; the one who appears defeated is actually the victor. Thus, the risen Lord calls no one to battle in the ordinary understanding of the term, but rather to patient and loving endurance; he is the triumphant Suffering Servant. The earliest traces we have of baptismal instruction suggest that Christians were exhorted to shape their behavior according to this paradoxical wisdom.

The basic story remains the same throughout the later writings of the NT: there is a conflict between God and His Christ on the one side and the Evil One on the other; the world is enslaved by evil, but the divine action is one of liberating creation — and particularly humans — from this slavery. Patient endurance of injustice (1 Pet 2:18-24), countering hurt with blessing (1 Pet 3:19), escaping from a vice-ridden world (2 Pet 1:4) — these, rather than a militant attack upon evil, are the appropriate Christian response. The Evil One is working against God, working to deceive and enslave Christians; the Christian should fight the good fight against such a foe (1 Tim 6:12), and endure suffering like a good soldier of Christ Jesus (2 Tim 2:3). The first Johannine letter agrees that Christians are called to overcome the Evil One, but precisely by keeping free from his blandishments and by loving their fellow humans and God.

In trying to assess such evidence and more specifically the evidence from the late first and early second century, an important distinction must be kept in mind. Use of imagery similar to that employed in a basic battle-myth explanation of the world can mean either of two things: it can mean that the "Jesus event" is absorbed into the already existing myth, reinterpreted so to fit, and stripped of his historical uniqueness in the process; or it can mean that the basic "story" is changed, that the "Jesus event" is considered the actuality to which other explanations must conform, and that the old battle-myths are radically demythologized. The emergence of the gospel as literary type and the role of the collected gospels as focus for the formation of canonical scriptures point to the second of these two alternatives. If this be true, then one must be careful not to conclude that use of military language and imagery in second century writings necessarily indicates an underlying battle-myth.

1 Clement

The first Clementine epistle is a case in point. Its well-remarked comparison between military and Christian orderliness (1 Clem 37) would appear at first reading to be a clear reflection of the underlying view that life is a battle.[9] In this battle, Christians would be well advised to manifest the virtues of good soldiers. "In all earnestness, brothers, should we march under his [Christ's] orders. Consider the soldiers who serve under our generals, how they carry out their assigned tasks with discipline, alacrity, and obedience" (37:2). The passage would seem to draw from Roman military usage, from Stoic imagery, and from the background of Judaism. In her study of the passage, A. Jaubert makes a strong case for emphasizing the Jewish background of the text; and this could tempt one to link it, therefore, with OT and late Jewish notions of "holy war."[10]

Yet, a closer look at the letter as a whole and at the precise argumentation that leads up to the passage in question does not seem to indicate that Clement's basic view of life is that of a war. Immediately preceding this military comparison, the letter is describing the manner in which salvation is achieved, entirely in terms of *knowledge*, of Christ as illuminator and as reflection of God. Speaking of Christ in this context leads to citation of a sequence of OT texts similar to that used in the opening chapter of Hebrews to underline Jesus' pre-eminence. The last of these, Psalm 110, speaks of "enemies" (I will make your enemies your footstool), and Clement remarks that the enemies in question are the wicked who resist Christ's will. It is this line of thought, tangential to the immediately preceding reasoning but very germane to the main thrust of the letter, that seems to trigger the imagery of orderly military behavior.

No other passage of the letter suggests that Christian life and action are involvement in fighting a war. Indeed, Christians are told to ally themselves to those who are religiously devoted to peace (15:1), to seek peace as their goal and to cling to the marvelous gift of peace that God has bestowed on them (19:2-3). This peace, Clement prays, will be extended to all men (60:4). God works to establish harmony in creation; the heavens, the earth, and the underworld all obey him peacefully; and Christians, too, are to remain in their proper place in this harmonious dispensation (20) — here, entirely in terms of a non-conflict image of creation, the same basic point is made as in 37:2. Given the situation of the early church, it is particularly significant that Clement sees great peace and continuity between the two covenants (e.g., 42-43).

Clement is, of course, aware that life involves conflict; in more than one place the letter reflects the opposition encountered by the early Christians. Typical of early Christian writing, the letter attributes such opposition and hatred to more than just human forces; it sees both this opposition and the dissension within Christian churches (as at Corinth) as coming from "the adversary" (51:1). However, the proper Christian response in this conflict situation is not one of aggression: rather, it is one of obedience to God and of patient endurance of misunderstanding and suffering (9-10). Both Peter and Paul are presented as models of such patience (5); but more importantly the letter draws from the Suffering Servant ideal as realized in Jesus (16). It is in terms of this ideal that the closing exhortation of the epistle encourages the Corinthian community to "please almighty God by uprightness, veracity, and patience. Live in harmony, bearing no grudges, in love, peace, and genuine considerateness. . . . " There is no hint that they are involved in a crusade against evil.

Christians' basic response to the conflicts of life is epitomized, not in the image of the soldier, but rather in the image of the athlete (5:1). Obviously drawn from Paul's letters (perhaps purposely so in a letter addressed to Corinth), this metaphor concretizes the *persevering endurance* that Clement adovcates. That such endurance is the precise focus of the metaphor is abundantly clear from the context: Peter and Paul are not proposed as ideal "athletes" because they overcame their rivals (which is the ordinary way that athletes become heroes). Instead, the entire passage in which the metaphor is found is an attack upon rivalries within the Christian community; and it is explicitly stated of both Peter and Paul that they won the prize ("were taken up to the holy place") for their patient endurance (5:4-7).

The Didache

Turning from 1 Clement to another late first century document, the Didache, one finds neither direct reference to life as warfare nor implicit reflection of such an underlying myth.[11] There is clear recognition of conflict: the opening chapters' presentation of the "two ways" places one immediately in the context of opposing wisdoms; but the imagery in question is that of a journey — one follows the path of truth to life, or one follows the path of error to death. The "enemy" is seen in terms of this imagery: he is "the deceiver of this world" (16:4); and the task of Christians is to cling to the truth with patient endurance (16), to take care lest anyone lead them from the way of truth (6:1). Christians are not to oppose anyone aggressively: at the very beginning of "the way of life" the sayings about loving enemies, praying for those who persecute you, etc., are invoked — and the Didache adds "In fact, have no enemies" (1:3).[12]

Perhaps one could challenge this judgment about absence of a battle-myth in the Didache because of the closing section's clear reference to a final apocalyptic struggle (16:3-8). Explicitly, the passage describes the opposition that the good will encounter in the final days as a *testing* and as an attempt to *mislead* them; and it describes the salvation and triumph of the faithful by saying that "the signs of truth will appear" (16:6). There is no suggestion that faithful Christians, during the time of this final struggle, are expected to be an army opposing "the deceiver." On the contrary, though the word "endurance" does not occur, it seems quite clear that the Didache advocates the same kind of persevering endurance that 1 Clement proposes as the Christian ideal.[13]

Epistle of Barnabas

Another early Christian writing that is strongly influenced by the "two ways" is the Epistle of Barnabas which, like 1 Clement and Didache, comes from Jewish Christian circles.[14] By way of some contrast, however, the Epistle of Barnabas does seem to reflect more of the battle mentality. Exactly how much and what kind of battle-myth underlies the letter's outlook is not easy to ascertain.

Like 1 Clement and Didache, Barnabas views the "enemy" as basically a deceiver, one who attacks Christians by trying to lure them from the path of truth (2:10). The basic story is again that of a journey, or rather of two possible journeys ("the two ways"): God is leading men to the land of milk and honey, the Evil One is leading to perdition (6). Yet, there are overtones of overt struggle. The epistle mentions early that the times are evil, and adds that "the Agent" (quite clearly the Evil One) is gaining power (2:1); it then speaks of Christian resources to withstand this attack by employing terms that have rather clear military resonance: the *auxiliaries* of our faith . . . our *allies* (2:2). Again, the notions of *power* and *force* are attached to the Evil One when the petition is made that "the wicked Ruler never gain power over us and force us away from the kingdom . . ." (4:13).

Perhaps the passage that is most suggestive of a "battle" view of life is the one that relates good and bad angels to the two ways: "There is a great difference between the two ways: the one is controlled by God's light-bringing angels, the other by angels of Satan. And as the latter is the ruler of the present lawless epoch, the former is lord eternally" (18:1-2). There is no mention of a battle between these two angelic groups, yet the myth of such an angelic struggle was such a widespread element of religious belief among those to whom the letter would have been addressed, that it is difficult to see how it would not have been recalled to their minds.[15]

Still, when one has gone as far as possible to discover some trace of battle imagery or connotation, the fact remains that the Epistle of Barnabas does not in any way view Christians as soldiers involved in battle. Patient endurance rather than aggressive resistance is the true Christian course of action; on the other hand, it is those who follow the way of death who "are total strangers to gentleness and patient endurance" (20:2). Christ's own task of salvation consisted in enduring death (5:1), for he is the servant who submits to suffering in order that men might have life (5:14; 7:2). Indeed, there is a remarkable stress in Barnabas on a soteriology of the cross: almost half of the letter is devoted to clarification of the saving role played by the cross of Jesus.

Ignatius of Antioch

The letters of Ignatius of Antioch, despite their quite precise purpose and the limitations of the epistolary form, provide a considerable amount of evidence about our topic. There is, though, one particular problem in assessing Ignatius' use of military imagery: the circumstance of his being escorted to Rome by a contingent of soldiers could largely explain the use of such imagery and weaken any argument that the imagery reflects an underlying battle-myth.[16]

Evidence in favor of such an underlying myth centers around the title applied to "the evil one": for Ignatius the name generally given Satan is "the prince of this world." While this name is not new with Ignatius, it does seem to reflect the image of a kingdom (the kingdom of evil and death, Ign Eph 19) existing in opposition to the kingdom of God; and the ruler of this opposing realm has destructive power (Ign Eph 13) that is directed against life and truth (Ign Eph 16-17). Ignatius seems clearly to feel that "the prince of this world" is hostile to him and to other Christians (Ign Magn 1:2), and to this hostility is linked the world's hatred for Christians (Ign Rom 3:3). If possible, the "prince of this world" would capture Ignatius and keep him from witness to Christ and from reaching God (Ign Rom 7:1).

The one passage in which there is clear application of the military metaphor to Christians and to their life is Ign Pol 6:2; but the very detailed manner in which the metaphor is utilized indicates its rhetorical rather than mythical character. Apparently occasioned by the idea of receiving reward from God, and following immediately after use of the athletic metaphor to describe the persevering effort needed to receive this reward, the passage in question exhorts Christians to give satisfaction to the God in whose ranks they serve and to remain faithful in their service. Paralleling the Pauline language of Eph 6:11-17, Ignatius speaks of baptism as one's weapons, faith as one's helmet, love one's spear, and endurance one's armor. Then, returning to the principal point of the comparison, and referring to the practice of placing a portion of soldiers' wages on deposit until they finished military service,[17] Ignatius says, "Let your deeds be your deposit, so that finally you will receive your savings in abundance." Significantly, the passage ends with an exhortation, not to "fight the good fight," but to be gentle and patient.

However, a genuine use of metaphor always supposes some underlying relation of real similarity; if Christian life can be compared to battle, there must be something about it that is similar to battle. The similarity here would seem to be the element of *struggle*, of having to withstand an enemy; but the manner of withstanding the enemy in question is what makes it clear that for Ignatius the role of the Christian "soldier" is not one of aggressive resistance. Ign Magn 1 and Ign Rom 7 speak of *escaping*, not resisting, the hostility of "the prince of this world"; Ign Smyrn 3 exhorts Christians to overcome death by *despising* it; Ign Eph 13 points out that Satan's power is overcome by *faith*, and the same letter adds a bit later (17) that the prince of this world's attempt to rob them of truth can be foiled by accepting Jesus Christ who is God's knowledge.

Christians will be hated by the world (Ign Rom 3), but they should accept and endure this ill treatment (Ign Rom 5); for the prince of this world is overthrown by gentleness (Ign Trall 4). It is this patience, endurance, and compassion that the letter to Polycarp advocates in its use of the athlete metaphor that is found side by side with the military metaphor examined above. Christians are positively exhorted to avoid contention and to love one another (Ign Smyrn 7); and Ign Eph 13 states that war itself is the enemy, an enemy to be overcome by peace.

If there is a deeper level to the "real story" as Ignatius sees it, this lies in his statements that evil is destroyed by God revealing himself as man and so bringing newness of life (Ign Eph 19), that the power of new life comes in the passion of Christ that must be appropriated by faith (Ign Magn 5; Ign Trall 2:2), that the cross is the source of immortality (Ign Trall 11:2). Moreover, the nature of the enemy that works in opposition to God and to Christians in their journey to God is described most often in Ignatius' letters by metaphors of "evil seed" (Ign Trall 11, Ign Eph 3:3), "poison" (Ign

Trall 6), "corruption" (Ign Eph 16-17), "disease" (Ign Eph 7) — all of which pertain to the basic image of life.

2 Clement

The early second century homily that goes by the misleading name of the second letter of Clement offers an interesting and significant change of viewpoint.[18] With the exception of one quick reference to the "devil's lures" (18), there is no allusion to an outside enemy who is in conflict with God's saving action. Consistent with this, there is no trace in the homily of a battle-myth as an underlying story about human life. At least part of the significance of this piece of evidence lies in the fact that the second Clementine is exhortation to appropriate Christian behavior: it is in such a context that one would expect to find some counsel to "fight the good fight" or to "resist the enemy of your souls," if Christian life was viewed as a battle. One cannot, of course, generalize from this one instance of early second century preaching, but the fact that this document enjoyed such widespread acceptance and circulation indicates that its point of view is reflective of "mainstream" Christianity in the second century.

There is mention in 2 Clement that Christian life involves struggle, but the struggle is *within* the Christian — against the unbelief and dishonesty and undisciplined desires that would keep one from the kingdom of God (19). True, "this world" with its false values and seductions appeals to a person's unspiritual tendencies (6); the devil does work to deceive one (18); and the Christian must constantly work to renounce whatever has led him away from God and to avoid the false pleasures that would lead him astray in the future (16). But it is against one's own sins and lusts and weakness that the Christian — with the help of God and his fellow Christians — must struggle (17:2).

This struggle is metaphorically described by the athletic imagery that is so prevalent in early Christian writings. Christians are engaged in a contest, and they must run the straight race perseveringly if they are to win the crown (7:1-3). Having once entered upon the race in baptism, they must continue sincerely without cheating; if those involved in earthly contests are disqualified and punished for not following the rules, what just punishment must come to those who cheat in the race for an incorruptible prize (7:4-5)? The present life is a time of training, and there can be no relenting from such discipline of life, because God does not grant the laurels of victory until the life to come (20:2-4).

Two other metaphors are employed in the homily to characterize the Christian life. Probably the more basic is that of a *pilgrimage*: Christians (and for that matter, all humans) are in the situation of passage during their earthly life. Christians are urged not to tarry in this life, nor to be reluctant to leave it for better things (5:1). Man's stay in this world is short, and the reward of future life and rest is unending; so Christians should be wise, regard this present world as alien and its promised pleasures as misleading (5:5-7), flee vice and impiety (10:1), and with single-mindedness seek to do the will of God (11:5-7).

The other metaphor, which along with "athlete" was destined to have a long history in Christian ascetical writings, is "freedom from defilement." Christians are exhorted to serve God with "a pure heart" (11:1), but more often the notion of *free from defilement* is applied to "the flesh" (8:4, 14:4-5) which should be guarded as the temple of God (9:3), or to the baptismal "seal" (7:6, 8:6). The defilement in question is broader than sexual immorality, but "adultery" consistently begins the list of sins to be avoided (e.g., 4:3, 6:4), and the writer, towards the end of the homily, speaks of "the advice I have given about continence" (15:1).

Justin Martyr

Turning to the apologetic writings of the second century, the works of Justin Martyr are a logical place to search for some evidence of a battle-myth mentality, since he was both creative and influential in shaping the early Christian "theology of history."[19] Actually, there is very little in Justin's Apologies to support such an underlying myth of human life (or beyond that, of the created cosmos) as a battle. What there is pertains to Justin's explanation of the functions of the good and bad angels; but even here Justin does not have a developed angelology, but rather a taken-for-granted mention of these supra-human spirits.[20]

Two passages represent a bit of an exception; for in them Justin gives a brief explanation of the hostility and persecution that Christians face, opposition that Justin sees as coming ultimately from unfriendly spirits. Chapter 5 of 2 Apol describes the origin of these evil spirits, their infidelity to the task of caring for the orderly functioning of creation which divine providence had entrusted to them, and their ensuing hostility to God and to those allied with God. In 1 Apol 5-6 Justin delineates the corrupting and terrifying activity of the evil demons and states that men mistakenly called these demons "gods." Thus, the evil demons were able through such idolatry to work all kinds of mischief; for example, they could see that

Socrates who was trying to draw men from such impiety was put to death on charges of atheism. So, too, Christians are being accused of impiety and atheism, because they will not give worship to these evil demons but instead worship the Father of all righteousness and the Son, with whom the good angels are associated, and the prophetic Spirit.

In his view of history, then, Justin does see a continuing conflict: the evil demons working to deceive and corrupt humans, in opposition to the illumining and saving activity of the Father who sends his Son as mankind's teacher. So, behind the evil actions of men and the hostility that Christians encounter lies the activity of these bad spirits. The evil demons work — through fornication, dreams, and magic — to deceive mankind, and so render men and women their slaves and the instruments of their destructive designs (1 Apol 14). It is these evil demons, Justin points out, that Christians have renounced in their baptismal promises; and so their way of life is drastically different from that of the men who denounce and persecute them. Yet, Justin persistently thinks of Christians as *persecuted*; they do not form an "army of God" fighting these evil demons and their human minions.

One other element of the conflict needs mentioning, though Justin gives it nothing more than passing attention. At one point, when he is discussing the manner in which the Divine Word, in his work of teaching mankind, is opposed by the falsehoods spread by the evil demons, Justin says that these demons operate in conjunction with "the evil desire" that is in every man (1 Apol 10). Whether or not Justin derives this notion from the Jewish *yṣr hr'*, it seems quite clear that he believed that opposing tendencies toward good and evil are part of each human's psychological makeup. But there is no indication that his understanding of this "evil desire" is colored by some underlying view of human life as warfare.

Justin's Dialogue with Trypho has essentially the same view, with the evil deeds of men (and angels) explained by their own abuse of freedom rather than by some story of a cosmic battle (e.g., 141). However, there is somewhat more emphasis on the non-resistance of Christians who are faced by persecution; the new law given by Christ lays on his followers the precept to "bear patiently all the evils imposed by vicious men and demons and, even in the midst of torture and death, to pray for mercy for our persecutors" (96). This is linked in the logic of the Dialogue with Justin's clarification of the servant role of Jesus himself, a role forecast in Isaiah 52-53 and in Psalm 22. It is in his suffering and death that the saving power of God was revealed, the power that overcomes all evil, human and demonic (49). Expanding this point, Justin has a rather lengthy "theology of the saving cross" (89-97) in which he argues from OT types such as the brazen serpent; but there is no hint that Jesus in his death was a triumphant warrior.

Athenagoras

Writing not long after Justin, the Athenian apologete Athenagoras has basically the same outlook, but argues in a more philosophical manner.[21] With him, as with Justin, there is no suggestion that Christians form an army that is engaged against the forces of evil. Instead, in his basic defense of Christians' moral behavior, Athenagoras directs almost all his attention to the fact that Christians actually live out the command to love their enemies (11-12). He does emphasize Christian idealism in sexual behavior along with aversion to violence at the end of his apology (32-35), but that is because he is directly responding to the charges of cannibalism and incest.

Study of Athenagoras' worldview, a view that depends concomitantly upon Greek philosophical cosmology and the Genesis creation accounts, is aided greatly by the succinct presentation he gives of that view about midway through his apology (24-25). Most attention in this section is paid to a fairly lengthy demonology, for it is Athenagoras' purpose to show (as had Justin before him) that most of the supposed "gods" of the pagan religions are really demons. The passage opens and closes with the assertion that the triune God of Christian faith is the only true God, that this God alone exercises final over-all providence, and that within this providence partial tasks of "overseeing" have been entrusted to various angelic beings. To this trust some angels have been faithful, others unfaithful; and so there are some demons who now work in opposition to the orderly divine plan for creation. Above all, there is "the prince of matter" who governs in opposition to the goodness of God, and who is assisted in his chaotic work by his "demonic cohorts." Yet, the basic pattern of the universe's existence is not one of conflict and disorder, for creation under God's ruling providence is ultimately orderly.

Athenagoras never states explicitly that a war is going on in the universe; and there is never any question about the indisputable providential power of God. But it does seem that the basic story about "reality" is that orderly guidance of nature (including man) by God and the cooperative angels is being constantly challenged and opposed by the demonic forces allied with "the prince of matter"; and men and women, though their fundamental human nature functions in orderly fashion under divine providence, are driven in opposing directions by the good and evil spirits. In Athenagoras there is more of the battle-myth than in any of the other authors we have studied; but even in his view humans, including Christians, are cast in the role of potential or actual victims of the evil hosts rather than themselves serving as soldiers.

Epistle to Diognetus

One other piece of early Christian apologetic writing should be handled in our present study, despite the uncertainty of its dating. More probably the first ten chapters of the Epistle to Diognetus come from a source in Asia Minor quite early in the second century, though the final two chapters may well be later, perhaps from Hippolytus; and these earlier chapters in particular deserve to be classified as "apology."[22]

In Diognetus there is recognition of conflict in the life of Christians, but there is no hint of battle imagery nor of an underlying battle-myth. Instead, the picture given of creation and of its providential guidance by God is that of harmonious process in which the proper place and function of each thing is determined by a kind of patient God. It is his grand design for the universe that this God has revealed in his only Son (8:7-9). Men have deviated from this plan, so that they need the ransom provided by Jesus; but this sin of men came from their own abuse of freedom, their own free abandonment to their undisciplined impulses (9:1).

Thus, there is some tension within man and in the creation of which he is a part. The author of Diognetus accepts a rather radical dichotomy between body and soul in man and maintains that the soul is imprisoned in the body. Parallel to this, Christians are in the world, but are not part of it; in the midst of what is corruptible, they await their heavenly incorruptibility. There is antagonism between body and soul, between the world and Christians; but the antagonism is one-sided: while the flesh hates the soul, the soul loves the flesh, and Christians love those who hate them for condemning worldly abandonment to pleasure (6:3-8). Rather than advocating a crusade against evil-doers, the author is praising Christians because they teach and practice love of one's enemies.

The picture given of the Christian community by Diognetus is not, then, that of an army marshalled under the banner of Christ; rather it is that of a band of pilgrims, living out their temporary earthly experience in the midst of hostility and misunderstanding. Though not yet possessing the full transformation which has been won for them by Christ, they have begun to live on this earth the kind of loving and peaceful existence that they hope for in the life to come (5).

Conclusions

This study has necessarily stopped short of the major theological achievements that close the second century and inaugurate the third: Irenaeus, Hippolytus, Tertullian and Clement of Alexandria; and the expository kind of writings, which we have studied, in no way reflects adequately the underlying attitudes of second century Christianity. Still, some pattern seems to emerge from this limited evidence:

1. There is an unquestioned awareness of conflict in life, a conflict that comes to focus for Christians of this period in their persecution. Quite generally, though not universally, the observable opposition of men and women to Christians is attributed more ultimately to evil spirits.

2. This conflict is one-sided: the evil spirits, and their human associates, attempt to mislead, corrupt, or destroy Christians; they inflict suffering and even death. Christians, however, are not to resist in kind.

3. Instead, Christians are patiently to endure such attacks during this earthly pilgrimage. This kind of behavior is epitomized by Jesus' death on the cross and exemplified in the Apostles. The common metaphor for this situation is that of the athlete; but the underlying "story" is a journey.

4. It is clear that the Suffering Servant ideal is still quite operative; this militates basically against any aggressive Christian retaliation.

5. Somewhat unexpectedly, there is little or no carry-over from Judaism of a notion of "holy war," despite the presence of this notion in the OT traditions, in the spirituality associated with the Maccabean developments, and in sect literature, such as 3Q 15.

6. On the contrary, the documents that are most influenced by Greek philosophy, i.e., by Middle Platonism, are most battle-minded, though even in them Christians are not viewed as soldiers. These are Justin and Athenagoras.

7. There is minimal use of military imagery, but there is no passage that indicates that the underlying myth is that of a war.

These conclusions must, of course, be placed in context and either confirmed or corrected by examination of the myth that is implicit in second century liturgy, of the mythic underpinnings of early Christian apocalyptic, and of the mythology contained in Christian Gnostic writings as well as that contained in contemporary Jewish and Hellenistic culture. However, there is still some significance in the fact that the instructional writings of second century Christianity give no support to the ideal of a church militant.

1. The most recent addition to the literature on this question is E. Fromm, *The Anatomy of Human Destructiveness* (New York: Holt, Rinehart & Winston, 1973).

2. Cf. P. Berger, *Sacred Canopy* (Anchor ed.; Garden City: Doubleday, 1969) 29-51, where he describes religion's function of providing legitimation for human institutions and practices, such as war. An associated process, that of projecting guilt and failure onto a scapegoat, often effected by "religion" in times of war, is described in H. Duncan's classic on social symbolism, *Symbols in Society* (New York: Oxford University, 1968) 135-50.

3. The NT Theology of *mission* (applied both to Jesus and to Christians) as a principal source for ecclesiology demands distinction between mission and crusade.

4. On religious support for war, cf. D. Wells, *The War Myth* (New York: Pegasus, 1967) 127-69.

5. Urban II was actually the first to implement the idea of a great Christian war to recover the holy places in 1095; but Gregory VII had already framed the policy and was prevented from carrying it through only by unfavorable circumstances.

6. *Praevia institutio ascetica*, 1.

7. Paul's use of military imagery and the early circulation of collected Pauline letters were influential in the widespread use of this imagery in the second century; but the question remains whether such usage reflects an underlying battle-myth. For one thing, Paul's own use of such imagery (e.g., 2 Cor 6:7) does not seem to suggest that life is a war as strongly as do the relevant passages in the Pastorals (2 Tim 2:3).

8. Historical evidence is ambiguous; cf. D. Wells, *War Myth*, 83-126.

9. For a review of the opinions on the sources and interpretation of this passage, cf. A. Jaubert, "Les sources de la conception militaire de l'Eglise en 1 Clement 37," *VC* 18 (1964) 74-84.

10. Ibid., 84: "En ce qui concerne la discipline communautaire, si facile à exprimer en termes militaires, nous croirions volontiers que Clément est en dépendance d'une tradition juive, déjà acclimatée en milieu hellénistique, et vécue dans la communauté chrétienne de Rome."

11. See the discussion of J. -P. Audet, *La Didaché* (Paris: J. Gabalda, 1958) 252-350 on "the two ways," particularly 348-49, where he points out the stress placed by the Didache on individual moral responsibility.

12. This sentence is found neither in the gospel texts (Matt 5:44; Luke 6:27) nor in the parallel use of the two ways teaching in the Epistle of Barnabas.

13. Cf. J. -P. Audet, *Didaché*, 469.

14. On the Jewish Christian character of the Epistle of Barnabas, cf. J. Daniélou, *The Theology of Jewish Christianity* (Chicago: Regnery, 1964) 33-36. P. Prigent, *L'Epitre de Barnqbé I-XVI et ses sources* (Paris: J. Gabalda, 1961) 219, rejects the common assignment of the document to an Egyptian source and argues instead for a Syrian

origin; but he, too, notes the close link of Barnabas to Jewish Christian writings like the Odes of Solomon and the Gospel of Peter.

15. On the demonology of Jewish Christian circles, cf. Daniélou, *Jewish Christianity*, 187-92.

16. Cf. C. Richardson, "The Letter to Polycarp," in *Early Christian Fathers* (vol. 1; Library of Christian Classics; Philadelphia: Westminster, 1953) 119, n. 36.

17. Ibid.

18. On the character and dating of 2 Clement, cf. J. Quasten, *Patrology* (vol. 1; Westminster, Md.: Newman, 1950) 53-54.

19. Cf. E. Osborn, *Justin Martyr* (Tübingen: Mohr, 1973) particularly 154-70. Osborn does not dispute the role of Justin in helping to create a Christian view of history; but he maintains that to fit Justin's contribution into a theology of history is to limit excessively his vision. See also L. Barnard, "Justin Martyr's Eschatology," *VC* 19 (1965) 86-98.

20. On Justin's demonology, cf. E. Osborn, *Justin Martyr*, 55-65; for the role of the evil spirits in temptation (and their conquest by Christ) see M. Steiner, *La tentation de Jesus* (Paris: J. Gabalda, 1962) 11-22.

21. On the dating and nature of Athenagoras' apology, cf. L. Barnard, "The Embassy of Athenagoras," *VC* 21 (1967) 88-92. Regarding the philosophical tone of Athenagoras' writing, cf. A. Malherbe, "The Structure of Athenagoras, 'Supplicatio pro Christianis'," *VC* 23 (1969) 1-20. He characterizes Athenagoras as "a Christian Platonist" (20).

22. For the most recent review of the divergent theories regarding the literary unity of the Letter to Diognetus, cf. J. Lienhard, "The Christology of the Epistle to Diognetus," *VC* 24 (1970) 280. One of the most balanced views of the question seems to be that of E. Fairweather, in his introduction to the Letter in vol. 1 of *Early Christian Fathers*, 209-10; he agrees with Andriessen in attributing the first ten chapters to Quadratus and thinks Connolly's arguments for connecting chs. 11 and 12 with Hippolytus are quite convincing. Our own use of Diognetus will be confined to the earlier chapters, which seem quite clearly to come from a pre-Irenaean source.

JOHN E. BURKHART

Authority, Candor, and Ecumenism

Ecclesiastical authority is in trouble. No matter how it is defined or defended, there are few theologians alive who would readily volunteer the judgment that such authority as the churches have known in the past is now alive and well and living in — perhaps Canterbury, Geneva, or Rome. Of course many have offered explanations or excuses for the shadow which now seems to hover over churchly authority, and some have sought to conceal its darkness from others and even from themselves; but it is now obvious that the traditional exercise of authority in the churches no longer seems plausible to countless numbers of faithful Christians. For some, especially those who think of themselves as occupying positions of authority, this has become a cause for alarm; while for others, more given to the wise candor which characterizes the sound scholarship of John L. McKenzie, it seems to afford good grounds for owlish glee. Nevertheless, it is quite possible that intelligent openness about the breakdown of the customary forms of authority in the churches may prove to be an ecumenical blessing in disguise, for if many Christians — too long separated behind the high battlements of authoritarian customs and inflated rhetoric — were to share the white truth of candidness about their common plights and their own modest prospects, all might find themselves drawn closer to each other. Indeed, they might discover the real focus of their faith. Such, surely, is worthy of hope. In any event, the problems of church authority deserve further scrutiny.

In his discerning study, *Authority in the Church*, McKenzie writes, "If Church authority has been losing prestige, in the last analysis it is because authority has here and there failed to be truly ecclesiastical."[1] Its failures, he argues, are basically from defects of purpose and style. In a word, many ecclesiastical functionaries are overbearing, self-serving, and given to pontificating on matters where they have no genuine competence.[2] Whatever ends they serve, and from whatever mixed motives, the consequences of what they do and say are often other than the flourishing

251

of the gospel and the well-being of the faithful given to their care. All too frequently, their manner belies their calling to ministry. Too many of the servants of God parade and posture as if they were his masters. Such is McKenzie's diagnosis. It is cogent and — given his lapidary sentences — quite telling. It may yet do much to recall Christians, Catholic and Protestant, to a renewed understanding of the appropriate place, manner, and function of authority within the churches. What is needed is more genuinely Christian leadership. McKenzie is right. Such leadership cannot simply be traditional. It must be charismatic, given and living by the Spirit of God. Its shape is to be determined by the needs of the church, realized as an authentically new society, a new kind of reality in the world, creating fresh forms and structures and novel patterns of behavior. The church is a unique society, requiring its own types and modes of authority.

Precisely because of this vital uniqueness, McKenzie deliberately avoids setting his comprehension of ecclesiastical authority within the wider context of theological, philosophical, or sociopolitical forms and definitions — although his distinction between traditional and charismatic is surely reminiscent of Max Weber. Throughout his study in *Authority in the Church*, McKenzie rarely deviates from the NT; and, for his purposes, this is both judicious and compelling. Nevertheless, it leaves room for additional studies to introduce other materials, in order to illuminate more clearly some of the topics upon which he has touched so persuasively and helpfully. This paper, therefore, is a brief attempt simply to rehearse something of the logic inherent in the more traditional notions of ecclesiastical authority, to indicate a few of the historical realities which have made that logic appear questionable to many of our contemporaries, and then to suggest that McKenzie's own thoughtful descriptions of the Roman Catholic Church may need to be evaluated in the light of a broader understanding of the crisis of authority in our time.

1

From the earliest times of the Christian churches, there has been evident the need not only to proclaim but also to declare and defend the truth of the gospel. Whatever the merit of Harnack's argument that Christian dogma developed as a consequence of the strange intrusion of Greek speculative ways of thinking upon Jewish ethical soil, it is clear from many sources that concern for correct thinking was an early and widespread phenomenon. And whether or not Walter Bauer was right in his thesis that orthodoxy was in many places the child of heresy, there is clearly, even within the pages of the NT itself, vigorous interest in sure proclamation, thoughtful pondering, and watchful protection of "the faith which was once for all delivered to the saints" (Jude 3). Rightly or wrongly, but nonetheless quite early in its history, the church tended to earn the description of it as an "essentially doctrinal society" (*societate essentialiter doctrinali*). Hence when the exercise of authority among the faithful came to be located in special positions of leadership, some form of authoritative teaching office was almost bound to emerge.

Among the church fathers, Irenaeus has often been cited as the patristic warrant for many aspects of the developing Roman Catholic doctrine of the teaching office. It is tempting to recount his thought at some length. However, without going into the vexed questions of whether he espoused the notion of Roman primacy, or in what form, the following passage does offer profound illumination of some of the basic doctrinal assumptions articulated in the growth and development of an authoritative teaching office.

> Therefore we ought to obey only those presbyters who are in the Church, who have their succession from the Apostles, as we have shown; who with their succession in the episcopate have received the sure gift of the truth according to the pleasure of the Father. The rest, who stand aloof from the primitive succession, and assemble in any place whatever, we must regard with suspicion, either as heretics and evil-minded; or as schismatics, puffed up and complacent; or again as hypocrites, acting thus for the sake of gain and vainglory. All these have fallen from the truth.[3]

Irenaeus clearly senses some vital need for doctrinal certainty, and his theological endeavors may be interpreted as efforts to calm and settle the uneasy minds of the faithful. For him the wandering thoughts of the heretics offer no stability, while believers require some solid rock of assurance. So he speaks of "the sure gift of the truth" (*charisma veritatis certum*). *Certus* means fixed, settled, established, reliable, unerring, sure. Irenaeus uses the Greek word *asphales* (as in asphalt!), which means unfailing, reliable, firm, sure, certain, safe, secure. Thus, because of God's pleasure, and in the midst of the quite fleeting but yet dangerous winds of doctrine, the truth remains available and sure. Apostolic succession is its surety and guardian.

Obviously, Irenaeus here shares something of the classical Greek notion of the nature of truth.[4] He equates truth with immutability. Since truth is changeless, error is a passing deviation from truth. Error is letting the mind wander astray, roaming from the sure terrain of the established into the uncharted lands of the new and fanciful. The new is to be feared, since what is new is not immutable and hence cannot be true. Thus Irenaeus speaks of the "primitive" (*archaias*) succession. For him, as for the ancient Greeks and Romans, "archaic" is a compliment. There is here an inveterate veneration of the ancient, since its very survival testifies to its immutability, and hence to its truth. Therefore, to strive for novelty, or even to be forgetful of the past, is to die to the truth. Heresies change, that is their fashion, while truth remains constant. Consequently, the surest way to know the truth is to go back to the original sources. Perhaps for this reason, Augustine was to call memory the seat of the mind, and in so doing to undercut expectation by replacing charism with tradition!

Irenaeus' emphasis upon the "presbyters" (read elders, senators, or old men — they amount to the same thing!), upon "succession," and upon the "archaic" resonates remarkably well with what we know of ancient Roman politics, especially from Hannah Arendt's instructive description in her seminal essay "What Is Authority?"[5] At Rome's heart, she observes, was a firm belief in the "sacredness of foundation," so that what had been established remained binding upon all successive generations. In such a context, the basic aim of all politics was to preserve the sacred founding of the city of Rome, and to be religious meant to be tied to the past. Since the founding of the city provided a permanent home for the gods, religious and political activity were almost identical.

> It is in this context that word and concept of authority originally appeared. The word *auctoritas* derives from the verb *augere*, "augment," and what authority or those in authority constantly augment is the foundation. Those endowed with authority were the elders, the Senate or the *patres*, who had obtained it by descent and by transmission (tradition) from those who had laid the foundations for all things to come, the ancestors, whom the Romans therefore called the *maiores*. The authority of the living was always derivative, depending upon . . . the authority of the founders, who no longer were among the living. Authority, in contradistinction to power (*potestas*), had its roots in the past, but this past was no less present in the actual life of the city than the power and strength of the living.[6]

All true authority derives from the foundation, "binding every act back to the sacred beginning," so that every present moment carries the whole weight of the past. In this understanding, partially expressed by Cicero, *religio* comes from *re-ligare*; and, quite contrary to our concept of growth, where growth is into the future, the Romans believed that growth was properly directed toward the past. Hence leadership was in the hands of the elders, since time had given them time enough to grow close to their ancestors and the past. "Tradition preserved the past by handing down from one generation to the next the testimony of the ancestors, who first had witnessed and created the sacred founding and then augmented it by their authority throughout the centuries." It was precisely this amalgam of religion, tradition, and authority which Christianity assimilated from Rome in order to become institutionalized as the Church of Rome.

Therefore, the basic theological foundations for traditional readings of ecclesiastical authority were already laid in the patristic period — since the religious quest for certainty, the Greek notion of truth as archaic and immutable, and the Roman conviction of succession from the founders are the very groundwork for later elaborations of the power and jurisdiction of traditional ecclesiastical authority. These needed only to be developed and rationalized to their plausible, if not so strictly logical, conclusions in order to create the climate in which formal definitions of an infallible teaching office could flourish and abound. In this sense, it is obvious that Vatican I was a truly Roman development, for it simply gave institutional expression of a mentality in which uniformity replaced pluralism, tradition replaced progress, and truth was fixed somewhere outside the vagaries of the ongoing historical process. It is little wonder that many who exercise such traditional authority can do it with the bold assurance of being veritable oracles of God and with that studied indifference to human sensibilities born of caring primarily for the sanctity of the past.

2

Traditional ecclesiastical authority is in crisis in our time. There are many reasons for this, but important among them may well be that while traditional authority has customarily derived its dignity and strength from a cultural hallowing of the past, much of humankind is no longer persuaded that the past is normative. Too many historical realities have intervened, giving humankind an historical consciousness and a sense of emergence from the past.

When people still patterned their lives by the seasons, perceived themselves as mirrors of the cosmos, and equated their nature with the inherited past, they were prehistorical in consciousness, if not in fact. When only one style of life and culture was known or honored as truly human, historical consciousness was dormant or unborn; and so long as European society remained somewhat isolated, unified, and stable, antiquity and continuance were the foundations of legitimacy. There was little sense of history when sons followed fathers and grandfathers in trades they did not choose and dared not forsake without loss of identity and livelihood, bearing as they did such names as smith, miller, shepherd, or cartwright. There was little sense of history when heroes were examples of virtue, saints were guides to heaven, and Christ was simply to be imitated. Typically, the past served as pattern for the present and as prediction of the future, because there was no fundamental or admitted discrepancy between them.

However, events have changed the human prospect. Humanity's static self-understanding has been thrown into question. With the excited reports from explorers among the Aztecs, Incas, Asians, and others, the horizons of time and space were suddenly broadened and alternative possibilities were revealed for humanity. Secular delight in other cultures was matched by commercial interest in distant places, while the invention of printing spread the new to the newly literate. Human ingenuity, evidenced in the invention of the mariner's compass, literally found new worlds to conquer, and was able to overturn and rearrange the social, cultural, and religious orders through the ideas spread by newly printed pamphlets. The new middle classes were less and less impressed by transcendent goals and explanations and were more and more interested in the obvious results of the this-worldly virtues of shrewdness and practicality. Those who had reverenced, indeed even imitated, the cosmos, began to discover and transform it. Nationalism found eager exponents, theological controversy blossomed and its seeds spread, while scholarship bravely dared to scrutinize the past and sift its wisdom. Humankind began to remake itself and its environments with revolutions in politics, education, skills, and imagination. New worlds were born and new orders of things.

In these new worlds, humanity defines itself by those human events which have formed its destiny and are the matrices for its decisions. Human identity is a consequence of those changes which have brought people into the present. People may think of themselves as the products of their own initiative, as the inheritors of political liberty, as the acculturated children of immigrants, as successful transplants from farm to factory, or even as the result of several historic occasions which influence and nuance the character of human life. In any event, they understand themselves in those moments when someone somehow turned from the past, thereby rejecting the stability of repetition for the sake of some new good. In a word, no matter how much people may speculate about the supposed constancy of something called human nature, history is the distinguishing mark of humanity, and historical consciousness is a sure measure of human sophistication.

More than three centuries ago, Joseph Glanvill already glimpsed the power of the present, and testified that the inventor of the mariner's compass deserves more thanks than is due to

> a thousand Alexanders and Caesars, or to ten times the number of Aristotles. And he really did more for the increase of knowledge and the advantage of the world by this one experiment than the numerous subtile disputers that have lived ever since the erection of the school of talking.[7]

More recently, perhaps no one has been more conscious of the traumas of change, or written more sensitively of its demands, than did Henry Adams. He was a man born out of time, cherishing the medieval more than the modern, the Virgin more than the dynamo; but he felt the need to adapt himself to a world he had not made or chosen and did not always like. *The Education of Henry Adams: An Autobiography* is a monument to momentous changes and to the sheer accelerating potency of forces unleashed by social revolutions and modern technology. More than others, he found "his historical neck broken by the sudden irruption of forces totally new," and opined that

> the new forces would educate. History saw few lessons in the past that would be useful in the future; but one, at least, it did see. The attempt of the American of 1800 to educate the American of 1900 had not often been surpassed for folly; and since 1800 the forces and their complications had increased a thousand times or more.[8]

Such was the judgment of a patient scholar who had devoted years to writing nine exhaustive volumes on the administrations of Jefferson and Madison but saw the need for a "new social mind" which would not only react but could "jump." For him and numerous others in our time, history has become the realm of change, and its temples are filled with chants in praise of the new.

Despite the exaggerations of the gospel of historical progress, and the exuberance of its evangelists who would proclaim any relevance at the price of all authenticity, some of its fundamental tenets have worked their way into our bones, putting much of the past and not a few of its traditional apologists on the defensive. The present *is* quite different from the past in many crucial ways, and we all know it. For one thing, the political revolutions of recent centuries have actually undermined or overthrown most of the secular analogs to ecclesiastical absolutism. Few human figures still claim divine rights to anything, and rulers whose will is unquestionable law are now rather scarce. Effective rule has always been by consent, since rule by force is not rule but force; and consent is now given more sparingly. It has, in a way, to be earned. Function, not office, has become the operative clue to authority. Genuine leadership is exercised by those who manifest charisms of competence.

Furthermore, competence has now been dispersed among the experts. No one can successfully claim more than a limited and specialized knowledge. In McKenzie's gentle statement, "The Roman Church is not competent by its teaching office to write an exegetical commentary on the Bible."[9] The requisite critical, historical, and philological skills simply do not appear to be transmitted by apostolic succession. Indeed, given the rapid progress of the various intellectual disciplines, both secular and sacred, it is no longer patently obvious precisely what the specific competence of traditional ecclesiastical authority now is. When church bureaucrats find themselves pushing someone else's papers, their own specific competence is open to some question. It may be that a plausible and functional definition of what their actual competence now is remains *the* unfinished business on the bureaucratic agenda.

Such a definition, when it is got round to, must now take rather more seriously the adulthood of the faithful. Insofar as we are all now children of the Enlightenment, it behooves bishops and others who would be in authority to grant and respect the maturity of those to whom they would minister. Immanuel Kant's classic definition of the Enlightenment as the courage of maturity continues to indict those who treat adults as if they were children, as much as those who let themselves be treated as children. The unhappy state of traditional ecclesiastical authority was surely this. Given the models of authority in relations of masters and slaves, teachers and students, parents and children, it could not make up its mind between them; and so it chose perpetual docility as the cardinal virtue of consent, little realizing that people who understand themselves to have reached the age of consent no longer think of themselves as children. Hence, in its fear of "scandalizing the faithful," it has created a greater scandal by denying them their rights to know, to think, and to decide freely. Humane authority requires that candor in which those who would lead open themselves as mature persons to those whose mature responses they would elicit. Genuine authority under the gospel, then, is manifest as a charism in specific realms of competence among those with whom it is candid. Discriminate response is each person's task, uncertain of result but honest in endeavor, as he or she reflects upon experience — though, as always, common experiences may engender various clusters of consent and delight in the gospel.

3

In his provocative study in *Authority in the Church*, McKenzie observes that the Church

> is open to the temptation which threatens any organization of attributing to
> structure a sacredness which structure does not have. Structure is a means to an
> end, and with the passage of time and the change of conditions the means can
> become inept. The forms of Church authority, we have noticed, have been
> frozen at an absolute level reached by a combination of Renaissance tradition
> and a defensive posture against modern attacks on Church authority.[10]

He is right. Structure *is* properly understood as a means to an end.
Nonetheless, perhaps it is not unfair to ask why this basic insight did not
shape his own ordering of material in his thoughtful studies of the Roman
Catholic Church. His volume on *The Roman Catholic Church* commences
with lengthy descriptions of ecclesiastical structure, almost as if it mattered
most, and his *Encyclopaedia Britannica* exposition of "Roman
Catholicism" discusses structure before beliefs, worship, and practices.[11]
Surely something is wrong here. If McKenzie is correct in his theological
judgment that structure is a means to an end, then one is left wondering why
this crucial judgment did not inform the ordering of materials in his surveys
of Roman Catholicism. Since he is not usually given to thoughtlessness but
is prone to objectivity, it may just be because he is here describing the
actual, if tragic, state of affairs of an institution in crisis. If he is right in his
opinion that "the structure of the Roman Church is one of its most evident
features," so that "no other factor can be much more important," is this also
a theological diagnosis of its plight? Of course, it should be noticed that
many other churches easily merit the same assessment and diagnosis, for
they too are often top heavy.

In any event, there is now surely a widespread crisis of authority among
both Catholics and Protestants; and such candor as honors the humanity of
those from whom we are separated and with whom we disagree requires
that our ecumenical conversations should speak the truth as it is now given
us to see it in our varied situations. Nothing less than such perceptions of
the truth spoken in love will suffice to serve the gospel.

John L. McKenzie is a devout Roman Catholic. Few things are much
clearer to this Presbyterian than that. His concern for the gospel in the
church he cherishes enough for lover's quarrels with her leadership shines
through page after page of his writings. Even in his most rambunctious
moods, he is profoundly loyal to his tradition. And he obviously knows
that the service of the gospel has its own liturgical center, whose reality
permeates the piety of every true Catholic. Therefore, he could well address
to Protestants of every stripe the question of where their center is. Where
precisely do they encounter their living Lord? This question has special

pertinence just now, when the past has lost much of its numinous quality and critical scholarship has distanced the bible's own peculiar pastness from us. Yes, the crisis of authority — whether in bishops or in books — may prompt all Christians to seek that vital presence which is eucharistic. Perhaps the Catholic is more relaxed in the face of episcopal folly and biblical criticism because his or her heart and treasure are beyond corruption. They are, according to Vatican II, in that liturgy which is "the summit toward which the activity of the Church is directed; at the same time it is the fountain from which all her power flows."[12] Such insight may recall Protestants to that promised presence of Christ in the breaking of the bread, thereby nurturing a live and embodied piety that can live through historical revolutions with equanimity and ethical engagement.

Perhaps Protestants may be granted to ask whether it is a genuine faithfulness to this eucharistic center that has allowed ecclesiastical structures to become so conspicuous as to appear ends in themselves. Why is it, for example, that it is the papacy — which could function as the servant of the servants of God — which has continued as the single most visible obstacle to unity? Should it not be troublesome, even for Catholics, that an audience with the "vicar of Christ" has become and continues to be such a precious moment in the lives of the pious that it tends to overshadow the definitive location of Christ's real presence among believers, a presence as common and sure as their gathering for the eucharist? Is it because, ultimately, the papacy still stands as the sign of a traditional authority, which is only occasionally charismatic and which seeks to be venerated and ministered to, rather than itself ministering? What has happened to the center if it is finally acknowledgement of the traditional papacy which has become the price of church unity? Yet the days may soon come when the crises of authority have become so profound that questions such as these, and others too, can be asked without rancor, without the warping burdens of the past twisting them into unfaithfulness, and with that honest candor which truly befits the gospel of one Lord.

---

1. *Authority in the Church* (New York: Sheed and Ward, 1966) 121.

2. For pointed expositions of such excesses, see several of the essays in J. L. McKenzie, *Did I Say That?* (Chicago: The Thomas More Press, 1973).

3. Irenaeus, *Adv haer* 4.26, 2. The translation used is from H. Bettenson, ed., *Documents of the Christian Church* (2nd ed.; Oxford: Oxford University, 1963). The Greek and Latin texts appear in SC 100.

4. See W. Pannenberg, *Basic Questions in Theology II* (Philadelphia: Fortress, 1971)

1-27; *TDNT* 1, 232-51; P. Friedländer, *Plato: An Introduction* (New York: Harper & Row, 1964) 221-29.

5. H. Arendt, *Between Past and Future* (New York: Viking, 1968) 91-141.

6. *Between Past and Future*, 121-22.

7. Quoted in J. B. Bury, *The Idea of Progress: An Inquiry into Its Origin and Growth* (London: Macmillan, 1920) 93-94.

8. H. Adams, *The Education of Henry Adams: an Autobiography* (Boston: Houghton Mifflin, 1918) 382, 497.

9. J. L. McKenzie, *The Roman Catholic Church* (New York: Holt, Rinehart and Winston, 1969) 215-16.

10. *Authority in the Church*, 168.

11. See *The Roman Catholic Church* and "Roman Catholicism," in *The New Encyclopaedia Britannica in 30 Volumes* (Macropaedia vol. 15; Chicago: Encyclopaedia Britannica, 1974) 985-1002. Note that in *The Roman Catholic Church* McKenzie gives 123 pages to structure in a text that runs to only 271 pages.

12. "Constitution on the Sacred Liturgy," I.10, in W. M. Abbott, ed., *The Documents of Vatican II* (New York: America Press, 1966) 142.

GREGORY BAUM

An Ecclesiological Principle

In his book, *Authority in the Church,*[1] John L. McKenzie mentions an ecclesiological principle that has very rarely been applied in theological reflection on the church. John McKenzie only alludes to this principle and makes a simple application of it; yet his approach is so important that it deserves careful analysis. The principle, as we shall see, calls for the entry of sociology into the exercise of ecclesiology.

The first and major section of *Authority in the Church* deals with the teaching of the NT on authority in the Christian community. Since Jesus himself and his followers were critical of the authority structure in the Jewish community to which they belonged, and since the early Christians in an apocalyptical mood looked upon the Roman Empire as the representative of an evil world and the symbol of all repression and injustice, there is in the NT a strong anti-authoritarian trend. Those who are first in the Christian community, Jesus said, should not be masters but servants or slaves. Jesus defined leadership in the church in terms that inverted the hierarchical order of the world. Whatever order there will be in the Christian community, it shall not be modelled after the hierarchical structures of the religious community of Israel or the Gentile secular societies. Jesus did not leave a detailed plan for the structure of authority in the church; he only provided a teaching that would enable the community to authenticate and test the manner in which the churches ordered their worship and their collective life.

John McKenzie gives an account of how the Christian communities in NT times actually dealt with their problems of authority and how they devised organizational patterns to meet their communal needs. These patterns were by no means uniform. The local congregations organized themselves in different ways. Common among them was the refusal to call their leaders by titles drawn from the Jewish hierarchy or the Roman State. Also common among them was that they understood leadership in terms of service, or even servanthood, in fidelity to the teaching of Jesus. In the later parts of the NT we find hints that a development was taking place in the

Christian communities, a development that was eventually to be found in the entire church; namely, the concentration and summation of all ministerial functions in a single person, the bishop.

After this study of the NT material, John McKenzie, in the second part of his book, turns to theological reflections on the contemporary church. He tells us that it would be methodologically improper to judge present church structures in terms of the models and ideals presented in the NT. A long historical development has taken place since the apostolic age. The church has moved through a variety of cultures and more than that — a point McKenzie does not stress enough perhaps — the church has become a very large organization and the size of a community imposes structural requirements that are not called for in smaller groups. It would be lacking in historical sense altogether if one were to evaluate the authority structure and ecclesiastical organization of the contemporary church in terms of the leadership patterns of the early church.

But if the NT cannot be applied directly to evaluate present church order, where does the theologian find principles by which to approve and criticize ecclesiastical developments? The NT, according to the Christian tradition, does exercise a normative role in the faith and life the Christian community. But how can the evangelical wisdom be translated into contemporary terms?

John McKenzie does not deal with this question in a theoretical way. He does, however, make a number of very useful moves. In particular, in an interesting chapter entitled "The Organization," he turns to thinkers who regard it as their specific task to analyze and criticize social structures and estimate the effect of these structures on the people who live within them. In other words, he turns to sociology. To be precise, John McKenzie makes use of William Whyte's sociological best-seller of the fifties, *The Organization Man*,[2] which examines how modern corporations in the United States transform their executives into an efficient, obedient, and dedicated bureaucracy and describes the effects of these measures on the personalities of these men. For the sake of efficiency, the organization tries to gain complete control over its managerial staff, and for the sake of security, the executives willingly surrender to the pressures exerted on them and cooperate in the process that increases the power of the organization over them. The successful promotion of ideals such as togetherness, belonging, loyalty and dedication, which the executives assimilate and communicate in their own ranks, helps the organization to gain total power over its members. For the sake of efficiency and good order, much more is required of the managerial class than obedience to specific commandments and administrative rules; through the recommendation of a specific set of values and style of life, an atmosphere is created in which the executives become the guardians of their own fidelity to the company's ideals. Even the private lives of these men are taken over. The organization is able to insinuate the kind of house they should inhabit, the clothes they should wear, the literature they should read and the entertainment they should enjoy. The corporation does not select their wives, but it specifies the kind of woman the wife of an executive should be. The perfect conformity to the ideals of the organization produces a curious hatred of vitality, imagination and genius. What is loved is mediocrity and compliance. William Whyte claims that what takes place in these corporations is the total de-personalization of the people involved in it. They no longer live; the organization lives in and through them.

John McKenzie regards *The Organization Man* as an important book that should be read by people involved in ecclesiastical institutions. He thinks that it will make them uncomfortable, for in this book is drawn a caricature of what actually goes on in church organization, a caricature close enough to the truth to be embarrassing. As we read the patent and subtle ways in which corporations promote togetherness, belonging, loyalty and dedication among the staff, the ecclesiastical reader becomes aware that the style of church government, the manner of treating the ordained officers, the spirituality supplied to them, the rewards promised to them, etc., are so many techniques by which the organization dominates the lives of its staff and creates an atmosphere of conformity. People no longer count; what counts is the church — which in this case means the organization, the hierarchical church. And out of the need for security, the ordained willingly cooperate in their own de-personalization. The organization assures them employment, protects their privileges, settles their doubts, and gives them a good conscience. This description of the organization is obviously a caricature of the church: it neglects those aspects of church life that protect and promote the humanity of its staff. Still, the total organization is a useful model for discerning an institutional trend within the church and for uncovering the latent function of many accepted customs and values.

At this point, John McKenzie begins his theological reflection drawn from the NT. He tries to show that to the extent that church becomes the organization, it deviates from the biblical ideal. The type of leadership described in the NT does not lead to de-personalization but to greater humanity; it does not promote the hatred of vitality and new ideas but promotes life and rejoices in the freedom of God's children; it does not promote conformity but encourages personal responsibility. The church must resist in its own life the trend to become total organization.

What theological method is McKenzie applying in this chapter? He does not turn to scripture and tradition to find principles by which to evaluate contemporary ecclesiastical life. Instead, as a first step, he turns to sociology. There are sociologists of institutions whose special field of interest is to analyze organizations and to evaluate in terms of human growth and human freedom the effect these organizations have on their staff. Could it not be that listening to sociologists arguing about their analyses and evaluations of various forms of institutional life, the theologian with sensitive ears will hear the raising of issues to which, possibly to his surprise, biblical teaching can be applied? The biblical teaching on authority and leadership cannot be directly applied to the organizational structure of the contemporary church. But listening to the divergent views of sociologists trying to understand how institutions work and affect the people who belong to them, the theologian may well hear controversies in which the concerns of the NT writers find expression, and in which the theologian, relying on the biblical teaching on leadership and authority, may actually take sides. Listening to William Whyte's analysis of the total organization, John McKenzie was able to formulate a theological principle, derived from the scriptures, by which to evaluate contemporary church structures.

This, it seems to me, is an application of Paul Tillich's method of correlation[3] to ecclesiology. The careful analysis of the present order and the discussion arising out of such an analysis allows the theologian to recognize a certain parallel or correlation between the conflictual powers operating in the present situation and those presented in the biblical books. This correlation, then, enables the theologian to let the biblical message shed light on the ambiguity of the present and disclose, present in the contemporary situation, a divine orientation towards new life. Thanks to this method, God's word in the scriptures is understood as judging the evil operative in our lives, personal and social, and as initiating us into the forces of redemption offered to us.

In the Catholic tradition Tillich's method of correlation can be understood in a theologically more adequate way. In Tillich's writings one has the impression that the critical analysis of the present situation is a purely human wisdom which measures God's revealed word. The Catholic tradition tends to be more conscious of the universality of divine grace and hence of God's presence in the conversations of people seriously wrestling with the ambiguity of their lives. God's word addresses people from within the serious discussion in which they are engaged. Hence the truthful discernment of present ambiguity, transcending blindness and self-interest, is never a purely human wisdom. It is due to a human word mediating God's call. By letting the present ambiguity of life guide our reading of the scriptures, we are not subjecting God's word to a human measure: we rather permit God to shape the ear with which we listen to the biblical message. Therefore, the method of correlation relates a question formulated in us by the Spirit to a reply present in the teaching of scripture and tradition.

From this it follows that when we listen to social thinkers arguing about the humanizing and de-humanizing effect of society upon men and women, it is likely that in the views expressed and the perspectives defined, we will eventually discern the critical presence of the divine word in human conversation. Every community, encouraging conversation among its members, generates a significant critique of itself through which the divine summons is present to them. God is present to people's history and their culture, especially as judgment on the evil operative in their midst, and it is the task of Christian theologians to discern this critical voice, to read the signs of the times, and to identify themselves with the critical movements in which the divine summons is perceived.

This means that in ecclesiology, in particular in the theology of the church as institution, the theologian should turn to the conversation of sociologists discussing the effect of organization on its members and hope that issues will be raised and viewpoints defended which provide a context for applying the biblical teaching on leadership and authority. This method, we note, outlines a rather restrictive use of sociology in the theological understanding of the church. Not every sociological theory of society nor every approach to empirical research can be applied to ecclesiology. It is only from a contact with the discussions and controversies within the field of sociology that theologians may be able to select a perspective and follow an approach that is useful in ecclesiological research.

John McKenzie turned to a well-known critic of bureaucracy. In a footnote he recommends a wider reading in the sociology of organization, in particular Max Weber's important work on bureaucratic institutions.[4] The great German sociologist is the originator of the sociology of organization, including its practical application in what is today sometimes called management science; at the same time, he is the first great critic of bureaucracy to whom all subsequent critics are greatly indebted and whose original insights even shine through a work such as *The Organization Man*.

In this article, then, following the suggestions of John McKenzie, I wish to pursue the conversation among sociologists of institutions in the hope of finding a useful perspective for a theological evaluation of ecclesiastical life.

To study the manifold organizational forms in world history in a great variety of cultures, Max Weber creates an "ideal type" of bureaucracy, i.e., he constructs a model which embodies what he regards as the most characteristic features of bureaucracy. How does he define bureaucracy? A government operates through a bureaucracy if its activities are divided into fixed and official jurisdictional areas which are ordered by law.[5] The regular and continuous activities in these areas are defined in a fixed way and assigned as official duties to administrative officers. The authority granted to these officers for the discharge of their duties is distributed in a stable way and delimited by rules concerning the coercive means at their disposal. Only those persons are employed who have qualifications determined by law.

From this basic structure of fixed and official jurisdiction flow the detailed practice of bureaucratic administration, which includes — I am following Robert Nisbet's summary here[6] — the functional priority of the office over the person occupying it, the emphasis on written and recorded communications, the sharp distinction between official and personal interests in the administration of finances, the specified training as preparation for certain offices, the stress on official attitudes rather than personal preferences, the conversion of as many activities and functions as possible to clear and specifiable rules, and the stress on official and impartial treatment of people and the consequent suppression of more personal responses.

Max Weber regards this ideal type as the pattern toward which all bureaucratic institutions inevitably move if their goal is efficiency and reliability.

> Experience tends universally to show that the purely bureaucratic type of administrative organization — that is the monocratic variety of bureaucracy (as opposed to the collegial type) — is, from a purely technical point of view, capable of attaining the highest degree of efficiency and is in this sense formally the most rational known means of carrying out imperative control over human beings. It is superior to any other form in precision, in stability, in the stringency of its discipline, and in its reliability.[7]

According to Max Weber the Catholic church has become a monocratic bureaucracy of the type described by him. He mentions in passing several reasons for this.[8] He refers to the growing centralization of power in the papacy, he speaks of the development that made the universal episcopate assume total legal competence in all matters dealing with religion, and finally he mentions the bureaucratization of the priesthood through the disappearance of the former church benefices and the total dependence of priests on their bishop for sustenance payment. Weber insists that monocratic authority structures are more efficient than collegial ones, except when the collegial structures are in fact dependent on a single person of supreme authority. He mentions specifically the collegial system of bishops which has only consultative power and is completely overshadowed by the proper legislative authority of the pope.[9] Bureaucracies in which the decisions are made on various levels by colleagues or teams are, in Weber's eyes, less efficient, less competent, and less able to deal with the purposes of the institution than monocratic organizations. For Weber, then, the Catholic church is one of the most remarkable and most successful bureaucracies of world history.

How are we to understand Weber's apparent recommendation of efficient bureaucracy? Some sociologists have been annoyed with the German sociologist. Professor Carl Friedrich complained that Weber's "very words vibrate with something of the Prussian enthusiasm for the military type of organization and [his approach] seems to bar any kind of consultative, let alone cooperative pattern."[10] Yet this accusation completely misunderstands Weber's intention. While Weber calls his definition of bureaucracy an ideal type, he in no way suggests that this sort of bureaucracy is ideal. For him, as we mentioned above, the ideal type is a heuristic model designed for the observation and systematization of complex social phenomena. He chose this particular model because it seemed to him that it was the institutional goal toward which all bureaucratic organizations move in the process of becoming more efficient and reliable. This process Weber called rationalization. To understand how the German sociologist looked upon bureaucracy we have to consider the role he assigned to rationalization in society.

Weber holds that there is an observable movement toward greater rationality in the social and cultural histories he has studied. By this he means simply that again and again, through certain significant events, people reform or restructure the social institutions in which they live and the cultural patterns out of which they operate. This is achieved by introducing greater coordination among distinct areas of activity, by elaborating a more definite hierarchy of values according to which they make public decisions, and by adopting a life style that more effectively channels their vital energies into the exercise of their social functions. Society and culture thus become more rational. Rational here does not refer to a metaphysical principle: it refers to the trend, very pronounced in modern society, to critique and reform social institutions in terms of coordination and efficiency. Through the discoveries of science, through the Puritan work ethic, through the application of technology to the processes of production and finally through the democratization of society, this rationalizing trend has become dominant and irresistible in the modern world. According to Weber this will lead to the bureaucratization of life everywhere. Coordination and efficiency will become the major values in all areas of human life. Rationalization, in Weber's eyes, acts as a kind of tragic principle of evolution. This principle operative in primitive societies brought greater freedom and the conditions of greater personal consciousness; but the same principle operative in modern society leads to the dehumanization of social life. The bureaucratization of society will produce what Weber calls "the iron cage."[11] Technology and bureaucracy will inevitably lead to "the disenchantment of the world."[12] Life will become gray, pedestrian, devoid of great passions and dreams. The young rebels of the sixties, following Weber's analysis rather than Marx's, spoke of "technocracy" as the great enemy of human growth and human freedom.

Weber's language is misunderstood when his ideal-typical definition of bureaucracy as "the most rational known means of carrying out imperative control over human beings" is taken as an enthusiastic recommendation of bureaucratic government. The truth is that Weber sees the movement of bureaucratic systems toward coordination and efficiency as the major source of dehumanization; thus he creates so negative an image of bureaucracy that it undermines all hope for significant social reform. Movements of social reform will only extend the influence of rationality in society and hence will eventually lead to greater bureaucratization of human life. For Weber, the conformity produced by "technocracy" is so powerful that he saw no significant difference in the long run between capitalist and socialist societies. The iron cage and the disenchantment of the world will define the future of human life.

Should Max Weber be believed? Sociologists have criticized Weber for exaggerating the efficiency of monocratic bureaucracies and underestimating the counter-productive components implicit in them. In a famous article entitled "Bureaucratic Structure and Personality," Robert Merton[13] significantly modifies Weber's theory of bureaucracy by paying attention to the dysfunctional elements of bureaucracies that prevent them from achieving the ends for which they were created. Merton uses the concept of "trained incapacity" or "professional deformation." He shows that the highly disciplined bureaucrat, faithful to the rules of the organization and nothing else, becomes, by this very dedication, blind to certain aspects of reality and thus unable to fulfill satisfactorily the service assigned to him. Monocratic bureaucracy is not as efficient and reliable as Weber thought; it is ambivalent, and hence there is good reason to disagree with Weber that the bureaucratic system described by him is in fact the most rational.

Robert Merton shows that the officers of a bureaucracy, under pressure to conform to the rules, easily become so attached to the operations they perform that they lose sight of the end for the sake of which the bureaucracy was created. "This very emphasis (on rules) leads to a transference of sentiments from the aims of the organization onto the particular details of behavior required by these rules. Adherence to these rules, originally conceived of as means, becomes transformed into an end-in-itself; there occurs the familiar process of displacement of goals where an instrumental value becomes a terminal value."[14] A bureaucracy is always in danger of becoming its own end. Instead of serving the goal and purpose for which it was devised it comes to be more and more concerned with its own maintenance and expansion. This trend is dysfunctional. By making fidelity to the rules the object of primary attention the officers develop blind spots of various kinds, lose touch with reality, and become unable to serve the people assigned to their competence. Far from being a rational institution (in Weber's sense), such a bureaucracy becomes under certain circumstances — especially in times of social and cultural change — quite unfitted to deal with its own tasks and purposes. But so strong is the attachment to rules that even then the bureaucrats may be unable to discover their own inefficiency. The rules have acquired symbolic power for them. They symbolize the good for the sake of which the institution exists. What follows from this is that under such circumstances bureaucrats find it almost impossible to change their ways. Even a new set of orders coming from the highest authority may be unable to change the bureaucratic process: the organization continues to run along the old lines, despite its inability to fulfill its task.

It follows from these observations that the trend toward greater rationality operating in society, according to Weber's analysis, does not necessarily lead to the kind of bureaucracy described by him. Instead it might lead to the correction of a rigid, monocratic bureaucracy. A successful bureaucracy ought to provide occasions for discussion, an open climate between various levels of jurisdiction, and a sustained opportunity for self-criticism involving all levels of the staff. Only in this way can an organization remain faithful to its aim. In Merton we find a more positive and hopeful view of bureaucracy than in Weber.

Merton's contribution has been enormously influential in the contemporary sociology of institutions. When we read the studies of scholars such as Peter F. Drucker[15] and Rensis Likert[16] we find a lively discussion of how institutions are enabled to fulfill the goals for which they were constituted. These discussions include elements not studied by Weber for the jurisdictional patterns are not the only variables that determine the working of an institution. What also counts are the climate of the organization, the interpersonal relations between staff members on all levels, the informal leadership operative in the organization, the approachability of superiors, and the provisions made for self-criticism and change. These principles apply to any kind of organization, be it hierarchical or democratic, for they deal with the style of an organization, and this style is determined by cultural ideals.

It is my contention that the conversation among sociologists of institutions is one to which theologians and churchmen could usefully listen. For here issues emerge which reflect biblical concerns. This conversation deals with matters on which the biblical teaching on leadership and authority has something to say; in particular, what kind of person an organization should create, what quality of relationship between persons belonging to the same and to different ranks an organization should encourage, what effects the institutions should have on the people whom it serves, how open it should be to adapt itself to the changing needs of these people, and what provisions it should make for self-criticism and change. On all of these issues the NT has a message.

The distinction between the *structure* and the *style* of an organization ought to find an abiding place in ecclesiology. We note, moreover, how modestly the preceding paragraph defines the influence of management science on ecclesiology. The theologian should not follow a single author in the hope of applying his management theory to an evaluation of church bureaucracy. What I have proposed, rather, is that the theologian listen to the conversation between sociologists and test whether in this context issues emerge regarding the humanization and dehumanization of life that recall the biblical message of leadership and authority. What is recommended, in other words, is the method of correlation.

While management science is concerned with the growth and freedom of persons, its ultimate criterion for evaluating organizations is their efficiency and reliability. This is the reason why the theologian cannot make a direct application of this science to the church bureaucracy. According to Talcott Parsons, religious organizations do not subject themselves to such criteria. They evaluate their organization in terms of symbolic appropriateness[17]; that is to say, they want their structure and its style to symbolize their religious self-understanding. Thus the church structures originally reflected the church's theological self-image and as this self-image changed so did the church's organizational structure. After the structure could not change any more, at least the style continued to change with the developing self-understanding. Pope and bishops at one time symbolized the transcendent Christ in the church. Today we have become more aware of the presence of this Christ in all Christians and, in fact, in the whole of history, so that we want the organizational style in the church to symbolize the servant function the leaders are called to exercise in the wider community, and the solidarity and simplicity of brothers and sisters beyond worldly divisions. While Vatican II did not change much in the church's structure, it did recommend a new style which was to symbolize more appropriately the church's contemporary self-understanding. [18] We may not be able to change the monocratic structure of the Catholic Church, but we ought to be able to change its organizational style to symbolize more appropriately the impact of the gospel on the world.

1. *Authority in the Church* (New York: Sheed and Ward, 1966).

2. *The Organization Man* (New York: Simon and Shuster, 1956).

3. P. Tillich, *Systematic Theology* (vol. 1; Chicago: University of Chicago, 1951).

4. The sections dealing with bureaucracy of Max Weber's three-volume work, *Wirtschaft and Gesellschaft* are available in English translation in *The Theory of Social and Economic Organization* (New York: Free Press, 1968) 329-40; and in *From Max Weber* (ed. Gerth and Mills; New York: Oxford University, 1958) 196-244.

5. Cf. *From Max Weber*, 196.

6. R. Nisbet, *The Sociological Tradition* (New York: Basic Books, 1966) 146.

7. *The Theory of Social and Economic Organization*, 337.

8. Ibid., 334.

9. Ibid., 398.

10. "Some Observations on Weber's Analysis of Bureaucracy," in R. Merton, et al., eds., *Reader in Bureaucracy* (New York: Free Press, 1952) 31.

11. *The Protestant Ethic and the Spirit of Capitalism* (New York: Charles Scribner's Sons, 1958) 181.

12. "Science as a Vocation," *From Max Weber*, 155.

13. *Reader in Bureaucracy*, 361-71.

14. Ibid., 365.

15. *The Practice of Management* (New York: Harper and Brothers, 1954); *Managing for Results* (New York: Harper and Row, 1964); *The Age of Discontinuity* (New York: Harper and Row, 1968).

16. *New Patterns of Management* (New York: McGraw-Hill, 1961; *The Human Organization, Its Management and Value* (New York: McGraw-Hill, 1967).

17. T. Parsons, *The Structure of Social Action* (New York: Free Press, 1968) 258.

18. J. P. McCrea, "Organizational Structure and Organizational Climate of the Roman Catholic Church as Reflected in the Documents of Vatican II" (M.A. Thesis; Toronto: Institute of Christian Thought, St. Michael's College, 1975).

P. Joseph Cahill

Myth and Meaning: Demythologizing Revisited

Introduction

In a two-part 1941 essay Bultmann thematized the problem of demythologizing the NT preaching.[1] The proposal to demythologize included affirmations and implications in three areas.

The first area of affirmation is the world of the NT. The books contain myth, expressions of other worldly reality in terms of this world.[2] The myths derive from an obsolete cosmology. This antiquated cosmology, part of the writers' cultural heritage, obscures or prohibits understanding the kerygma against the horizon of a different world view. The NT mythology, nonetheless, is still potentially meaningful.

Secondly, demythologizing leads to affirmations about interpretation. To understand the message and the meaning resident within mythology, one must interpret the text, but not in terms of literal meanings. The interpretation is made in an existential framework — the meaning that myth has for man's existence. Such understanding comprehends two spheres: the text (kerygma) and the reader (hearer). Translation accompanies and follows textual understanding. Implicit in the process of interpretation and understanding is a distinction between myth and history. Likewise implied, and not brought to conscious affirmation until a long time later, is the double intentionality of myth and its characteristic of both concealing and revealing.[3] It is this latter trait of symbolism and its assembly into the story we call myth — clearly implied in the interpretative process proposed by Bultmann — that was to generate so much theoretical reflection on biblical hermeneutics from about 1959 to the present.[4]

Thirdly, Bultmann's 1941 essay, for all the opposition it aroused, involved a very forthright view of man — be he the technical or non-technical interpreter, that is, a hearer (potential or actual) or searcher for the word. Ultimate meaning, and with it what Bultmann calls eschatological existence, is available to man only through an

275

understanding and appropriation of the religious realities signified in the NT. This is the one and only way to authentic human existence.[5] Any meaning which on principle excludes this ultimate meaning or orientation to it is sin, which, of course, is the absolutizing of the relative.[6] Such absolutizing of the relative, which Bultmann frequently calls the search for security, places man in an ineluctable tension, for all human existence is beset by the question about God. No surrogate suffices, yet substitutes consistently and invitingly challenge.[7] If myth, then, impedes potential understanding and leaves man in inauthenticity, its interpretation is a serious and urgent task.[8]

The thematic of 1941 and its attendant implications has been virtually absorbed into larger horizons, perspectives, and viewpoints. This broadening of the hermeneutic field, while being very productive in many areas, particularly that of hermeneutics as such, still involves a certain ambiguity. The clarification and resolution of this ambiguity is the point of this paper.

1. The Problematic

The ambiguity is manifest in the complexity of the interpretative effort used to extract meaning from myth, in the concession that myth seems to recede in sophisticated societies, in the uncritical contrast of myth to history, in the tenacious identification of myth with falsehood. Thus myth seems to have a tenuous relation to truth and an almost inevitable and firm association with the fanciful, the benighted, the surd, the naïve. Ambivalence and autonomy seem to result from the fact that there is no critical grounding which establishes myth as a legitimate, necessary, and permanent carrier of human meaning. Nor will any elaborate hermeneutic directed at understanding myth long survive if myth is merely some type of amorphous and transitory mode of consciousness. It does not suffice to say that myth is merely the product of a particular world view. If that is the case myth by definition is not a necessary carrier of meaning.

Stated another way, one might say the fundamental problem lies in the type of opposition the interpreter sees between mythological consciousness and its opposite — rational, scientific, historical consciousness. Is this opposition genetic so that a later form supersedes an earlier form of thought? Is the opposition dialectical so that the modes of thought must be opposed and a satisfactory resolution achieved? Or are these modes of thought complementary so that they may co-exist in one and the same person and in one and the same culture? Unless these questions are critically answered, the ambiguity that has resolutely attached itself to the study of myth will be increased.

When the problematic itself is not articulated, the interpreter remains in an ambivalent state of mind. Myth is merely asserted to be a legitimate carrier of meaning, if somewhat obsolete. And yet in common language myth is actually equated with falsehood, is commonly contrasted to the category we call history, and is certainly opposed to modern scientific thought. This obscure postulate operates as a presupposition in all discussion of myth. The ambiguity and obscurity work as a cause or principle. But the ambiguous state of mind itself is an effect or result of a prior cause, previous understandings of myth, previous efforts at the interpretation of myth throughout the history of interpretation. Before proceeding to answers to our questions it is necessary first to explore the presuppositions within the ambiguous state of mind and then to turn to the history of the development causing the ambiguity.[9] I will conclude with a resolution of the ambiguity.

2. Presuppositions

The basic problem for the student of myth in the West is the sense of unreality that accompanies the very study to uncover realities with which myth purportedly deals. It is not to our point to analyze the causes of the feeling of discomfort associated with the study of myth, particularly religious mythology, except to ask the reader to verify it for himself. Surely the obscurity of the term myth and its almost inevitable association with either falsity, with the primitive and undifferentiated consciousness, or with unreality plays a role. The myth is almost defined by its opposition to "what really happened."[10] Anthropology, sociology, psychology, and history — all the human sciences and more evidently the empirical sciences — these all seem to deal with reality. The world of myth appeals to poetic and imaginative souls who are easily capable of understanding and translating the world of fantasy.

Thus a certain malaise accompanies the interpreter, particularly when he moves into the NT. And the historical-critical method, to which we owe so much understanding of the bible, accords a certain verbal primacy to history and to criticism[11] as opposed to myth. It is further assumed that while myth plays a large role in other religions — ancient and modern — particularly those of the East, it is likewise assumed that the biblical religion is a religion of history and not of myth.

Now while it is true that one can easily find religions which emphasize myth far more than does the NT, some NT mythical presentations are of central importance. Consider, for example, the retrospective importance of the creation narratives after Paul's comparison of Jesus and Adam. Likewise turn to the four NT hymns: Phil 2:6-11; Col 1:15-20; 1 Tim 3: 1b; and Heb 1: 2-5 with their definite mythical and cosmic language. To this list one may even add the Johannine Prologue. Surely no one would say that the realities with which these passages deal are peripheral or accidental to the NT. But because the admission that there are any mythical elements has been a reluctant and labored process, it does not follow that myth is any the less important in the production and understanding of the NT. It simply means that in addition to a feeling of discomfort vis-à-vis myth, we do not have a viable hermeneutic of myth.

This situation becomes more complex when the exegete turns to the realm of theology or of faith or of religion in the concrete and finds a demythologizing taking place with a whole series of theological affirmations or beliefs of faith or practices of religion. Consider, for example, the status of the following in the communal consciousness of Western Christianity: angels, satan, places or states of punishment and reward, virgin birth, pre-existence of the logos, teaching powers of a church, sacraments and their efficacy, the supposed absolute nature of Christianity, description of Christ in terms of primal man, eschatology in general. Gradually the feeling of discomfort must inevitably change to the realization that one must have a more realistic approach to myth and the NT. This is not only important for the study of the NT but ultimately for the study of all religions.[12]

3. History of the Ambiguity

The mythopoeic mentality was found to be characteristic of early societies. The analysis provided, for example, by Frankfort[13] is well known. The characteristics of mythopoeic thought were largely constructed by their opposition to modern scientific, discursive thought. Mythic consciousness tends to be characterized by a series of contrasts. Myth is on the level of the *vécu* as opposed to the *thématique*; the *existenziell* as opposed to the *existenzial*; *exercite* as opposed to *signate*; the fragmentarily expressed as opposed to the methodically known; the fact vs. the theoretically explained; that which proceeds from fantasy vs. that which comes from rational analysis; the pre-critical vs. the post-critical; the non-discursive symbol vs. the discursive symbol; the lived relation vs. its refraction in representation; the operative vs. the altered.[14] This series of descriptive oppositions is an inheritance whose genesis may be traced back to Thales and Pythagoras. In all instances of the contrast myth seems to be an inferior and replaceable thought product.

Plato, Epicurus, and the Stoics, followed by Christians such as Eusebius and Augustine, had an historical explanation of myth, Euhemerism. The gods of myth were deified men who had actually lived on earth. Myth is then a kind of distorted history. Such a view proved congenial to early Christian apologists who could contrast their message to the distorted history of the Greeks and Romans. Some of these myths were also understood to have been taken from Jewish religion and corrupted by unholy storytellers.[15] Euhemerism was revived in the eighteenth century and modified so that myth disclosed eternal, if allegorical, truths.

The Enlightenment period was characterized by an attempt to describe myth simply as "meaningless, absurd, incomprehensible, degrading, frivolous fables."[16] The Romantics, on the other hand, adopted a sort of allegorical Euhemerism in which the heroes became types or class symbols. Schelling eliminated the allegorical interpretation for a "tautogorical interpretation" of the mythical figures who were "autonomous configurations of the human spirit."[17] However varied in detail, the Romantics agreed that the myth was an imaginative and inventive portrayal. They were, however, in no position to give a good critical grounding for the validity of myth as an carrier of meaning.

The most extended and technical study of myth, and no doubt the most influential for the study of religions, was initiated in 1856 by the man who may be considered the founder of the study of comparative religion, Max Müller, by his publication, "Comparative Mythology."[18] Müller's analysis of myth as a "disease of language," developed first by an initial misinterpretation (Dyaus, sun, becoming Zeus) and elaborated by polyonomy and homonymy, is well-known. Such a procedure originated, according to Müller, in a mythopoeic period which was, of course, the whole period antecedent to the discovery of scientific, discursive thought.[19]

However long and animated the opposition of Andrew Lang, who held that myth derived from an animistic period of history in which man personified natural forces, both he and subsequent comparative religionists, until very modern times, held myth to be what Lonergan has called a genetic horizon, one that is meant to be superseded as the child develops into maturity.[20] During these years the interpreters of myth had made preparations for its funeral.

The early views of the comparative religionist were gradually modified in the twentieth century by anthropologists, sociologists, comparatists in religion and literature, biblical scholars, and even philosophers. Most influential on the theoretical level at this point were perhaps Ernst Cassirer[21] and Suzanne K. Langer[22] both of whom contributed to the generic conclusion that myth is an autonomous and permanent feature of human consciousness, not reducible to another thought form, and in general a legitimate carrier of meaning. This elaborate development has not only not dissipated some of the ambiguities surrounding the study of myth but perhaps increased the obscurity as may appear more clearly when we turn to a study of myth from the biblical standpoint.

4. The Biblical Context

Once the literal-historical method "became the principal exegetical method of the Christian Church,"[23] the question of myth and the bible was not raised until the eighteenth century. Christian Heyne (1729-1812), classical philologist and historian of culture at Göttingen, had said that myth was "the conceptual and articulative form of the childhood of the human race,"[24] a hypothesis which his student J. G. Eichhorn (1752-1827) applied to scripture. Eichhorn described as mythical the temptation of Jesus, apparition of angels, pouring out of the Holy Spirit, and the miraculous events. However, he was careful to employ natural explanations for seemingly supernatural events only in the OT, not the NT. Johann Gabler (1753-1826), a student of Eichhorn, though emphasizing the historical character of a biblical theology, went beyond Eichhorn. Gabler proposed that the origin of mythical accounts be thoroughly investigated so that one not only could discover the factual content but also uncover the exact meaning of the text. Gabler perceived myth as a much more acceptable category for understanding than the use of the natural explanation for seemingly supernatural events.[25] We know from Gabler's attempts to answer objections against the use of the category "myth," that the term was considered unsuitable and tended to alienate people. By 1802 the theories of Eichhorn and Gabler had become firmly enough established for Georg L. Bauer (1755-1806) to publish a "Hebrew mythology of the Old and New Testaments, with parallels from the mythology of other peoples."[26]

Such was the background and the ground work for David F. Strauss (1808-1874) and the publication of his *Leben Jesu* in 1835-1836. Though Strauss over extended the application of myth, his work "marked out the ground which is now occupied by modern critical studies,"[27] that is, that direction of study which attempts to ascertain the nature of the historical claims of the NT. Moreover, Strauss established that myth is the language of religion, that Jesus is to be understood in terms of Jewish apocalypticism, that the gospels are not eyewitness accounts nor history in a crude sense, and, perhaps most importantly, that in John we encounter a highly developed form of myth. This latter not only anticipated Bultmann but also sharpened the Synoptic-Fourth Gospel contrast for all critics. Strauss' Johannine observations exercised a large influence on the effort of students of the Fourth Gospel to narrow the distance between the Fourth Gospel and the Synoptics especially in terms of an opposition between history and myth.[28]

Unfortunately, it must first be noted that Strauss *de facto* did undermine the potential credibility of the bible, as the events of his life make clear. Secondly, he accepted the evolutionist hypothesis that mythical consciousness was the consciousness of the human race in its infancy. Thus he lent weight to the conclusion that an adult civilization had created a thought form that would supersede and replace mythical thinking, though he obviously did not draw out the implications of his position.[29] Therefore Strauss could not provide any systematic foundation for eliminating the idea of myth as simply a fictitious account.

We mention only in passing how direct is the line from Strauss to the so-called History of Religions School and its well-known members: Hausrath, Pfleiderer, Heinrici, Gunkel, Dalman, Bousset (whose chair at Giessen Bultmann occupied in the autumn of 1920) and Troeltsch. With a certain inexorable logic, the concept of myth as a vehicle of expression suitable for an infantile society and in one of limited scientific and technological development, led directly to the even more complicated problem of historical relativism, especially the problem of historical relativism, vis-à-vis the absolute claims of Christianity. This general and particular historical process led to the formation of diverse understandings of myth.

5. Postures Toward Myth

Perhaps because of the inconclusive nature of the dialectic on myth in the intellectual history of the West, we still find at least five perceptible understandings of myth both in the scholarly and popular common-sense world.

The first understanding conceives myth almost at the level of early magic. Myth is a very primitive stage of expression. It is destined to be replaced by a superior thought form — usually the discursive mode of thought. Myth is to be left behind, superseded. Interpreters as diverse as the early Levy-Bruhl, Frazer, and Freud fit here. In the light of later scientific developments, myth as such is false.

The second group is formed almost in direct reaction to the first. Myths are literally true. Selectivity may be involved by saying that certain stories in Christianity are not myths but comparable stories in other religions are myths and therefore false. In a certain sense this position affirms myth to be false just as does the first group but for far different reasons. What critics would call myths are interpreted literally, e.g., the Adamic myth becomes one man, one fall, a state of pure nature, a state of fallen nature, a kind of biological transmission of sin. Strangely enough this second position, and its variations, in interpreting the myth as history has within itself the seeds of salvation if the subsequent theological explanations are themselves considered as myth.

A third position is characterized by a sort of philosophical neutrality. Myths are gathered into texts and studied. One focuses on the myth in its own milieu and simply reports on the functions of myth in a particular society. The societies, in general, tend to be primitive as, for example, in Malinowski's studies. Myth then provides an historical and sociological understanding. One may even, by a sort of archaism which is certainly productive from the standpoint of research, interpretation, and the study of history, spend most of his time virtually living in the period or culture he is studying. Such a posture bypasses any evaluative judgment upon differentiations of consciousness represented by mythical thinking and other forms of thought.

The fourth position tends to be what I shall call the nostalgic-romantic approach. And it has two divisions. The first proceeds from a certain antipathy to the modern scientific and technological world and its attendant complexities. Supporters of this view would wish that we could return to a world whose dominant thought form was myth. This view is characterized by a strong feeling of the contrast between the modern western world and a seemingly simpler but richer world. The benefits of the past are increased by distance. This romantic feeling, however, never quite overcomes the realistic sentiment and never fully stifles the question, "Is it true?" Clearly this dilemma is in part the cause for turning to religions whose dominant thought form is still the myth and even perhaps for finding refuge in the esoteric and the occult.

Within this romantic group one finds a second faction which insists that the mythological thought form must co-exist with modern discursive thought if one is to lead a full and rich human life. However there is no critical grounding for this suggestion. Some proponents from within this group find myth everywhere in the modern world, in scientific thinking itself, in advertising, in virtually every human activity. At this point, however, myth loses its technical meaning.[30] Others within this group find myth to be a necessary and complementary thought form; but myth refers exclusively to the subjective dimension of man in his effort to live peacefully and comfortably within the universe.[31]

A fifth group, usually technical scholars, accommodates itself gradually to the extension of mythical elements even into religious documents which they had hitherto accepted, for the most part, in a literal sense. In proportion to the degree of reflection on the process of accommodation there emerges another group which may be described as the group of critical realists. This group seeks to establish the meaning of myth, the scope of myth within the books that they are interpreting, and gradually moves towards some type of critical grounding for the interpretation of myth.[32] From this perspective arises the attempt to affirm the legitimacy of myth as a carrier of human meaning and a simultaneous attempt to provide a hermeneutic of mythology. The members of this school attempt to come to grips with the temporal orientation and development of consciousness pointed out by Langer. The school takes seriously the question, "Is it true?" which seems to terminate the phase of mythical consciousness. It takes seriously the hermeneutic problem presented to all religious thought by the new and irreversible differentiation of consciousness produced by the emergence of scientific discursive thought.[33] It is within the perspective of this approach that a solution to the problem of the meaning of religious mythology is to be reached.

6. Critical Realism

One of the pioneers, of course, among the group that we have chosen to call critical realists is Rudolf Bultmann. His program of demythologizing placed the problems of locating, understanding, and interpreting myth in the broad field of hermeneutics. The movement to hermeneutics slowly generated a new critical perspective one aspect of which was the attempt to ground an interpretation of religious myth. The interpretation of myth became a part of the problem of interpreting any voice at all from the past. In this sense, therefore, the two essays on demythologizing in 1941 were but the preliminary steps to the major consideration: the problem of hermeneutics. This specific motif was taken up by Bultmann himself and further developed by exegetes, historians, and philosophers. In this larger horizon one may perceive a genetic growth from Schleiermacher to Dilthey to Bultmann and to Ricoeur.

The latter, in two major works and a series of papers, turned his attention to several dominant western myths as well as the more general theme of the phenomenology of symbols.[34] He analyzed the process whereby a primal experience finds a language, assembles the language into a myth, and subsequently generates reflection on the myth. This reflection turns into a theology, usually systematized. Thus myth, secondary symbolism, emerges from primary symbolism and has developed into an elaborate tertiary symbolic system. In this process myth retains its own peculiar identity, though the tertiary symbolic process tends to be an interpretation and development of the myth. This tertiary symbolic system, as well as the differentiation of consciousness we call scientific-discursive thought, has created a chasm between the primal experience and modern man. One bridges this distance by a process Ricoeur calls second naïvete, the central act of which is a sympathetic re-enactment of the meaning of the primary symbolism. However, this sympathetic re-enactment is neither so amorphous as the re-enactment theory of Collingwood nor the principle of empathy of Schleiermacher. Rather, the second naïvete is the employment of the scientific-historical method by a developed critical consciousness. This possibility, however, is available on the basis of a clear and real distinction between myth and history. Thus Ricoeur has taken the problem and used it as a solution.

Ricoeur developed the process in which the experience of evil generates a primary symbol, in this case defilement, sin, guilt. These primary symbols, taken from the experience of participants and subsequently modified by the experiences of compilers of the tradition, are the bases from which secondary and tertiary symbolism develop. Thus Ricoeur's procedure focuses on symbols. And myth finds its place in the field of symbols. These primary and secondary symbols themselves have six characteristics, according to Ricoeur. The symbols are signs that communicate a meaning. These signs, secondly, have a double intentionality — the literal which points beyond itself to something like itself, e.g., stain is used to signify sin and guilt. Hence these primary symbols are transparently opaque which accounts for the depth of the symbol. Thirdly, the symbolic meaning, on the second level of intentionality, is constituted by the literal meaning. In this sense the primary symbol is donative. The first intentionality confers meaning on the second. Fourthly, the symbols precede hermeneutics and thus are evocative or suggestive. It is this evocative quality which means, when Ricoeur uses the term, "sympathetic re-enactment," that the interpreter will reach the meaning of the primary symbols only by a careful examination of his own experience and language. Fifthly, these symbols are the very opposite of a symbolic logic because rather than univocity, these symbols are "heavy with implicit intentionalities and anological references to something else which it (they) present enigmatically."[35] Sixthly, these symbols are genera of which myth later becomes a species. Symbol, therefore, in the sense of Ricoeur is quite different from that of Cassirer and is quite equivalent to what Wheelwright calls a "tensive symbol" as opposed to a "steno-symbol."[36] In this sense Ricoeur affirms that "symbol gives rise to thought."

7. Toward a Foundation

Ricoeur, of course, has articulated the process whereby the meaning of myth becomes available to the modern reader. He also selects certain myths whose definition really resides in the double intentionality of the symbolism. The fundamental avenue of approach is the double intentionality of the symbols and the interpretative procedure which discloses the meaning of the second intentionality.

There remains, however, a more fundamental problem. Ricoeur is dealing with what is given. Can we find any foundation or ground within man which explains the given or explains why man employs symbols which both reveal and conceal? Can we suggest any orientation of man that will indicate why man, in the first place, created myths and seems to go on doing so in spite of the presence of other seemingly more accurate thought forms? Can we further suggest any critical resolution of the real problem whereby myth has come to be equated with falsehood? Such a foundation for the generation and interpretation of myth is, I think, available.[37]

We must first of all speak of transcendence, mystery, horizon, and man's capacity for knowledge. If we describe transcendence as "the elementary matter of raising further questions,"[38] then man is orientated towards transcendence, toward "going beyond." The unknown is the mysterious. "Though the field of mystery is contracted by the advance of knowledge, it cannot be eliminated from human living."[39] Thus beyond any present horizon is transcendence and mystery. And beyond all cumulative horizons is transcendence and mystery. "The immanent source of transcendence in man is his detached, disinterested, unrestricted desire to know."[40] Thus man lives in perpetual tension characterized by an unrestricted desire to know and a very finite capacity to fulfill this desire. However full his accomplishment he always knows there is more. As history unfolds and differentiations of consciousness emerge, man's store of answers increases but new questions arise because man's horizon is all being. Particular questions, once transcendent and mysterious, receive answers. But beyond any new horizon there is still the unknown, the mysterious. In the face of the unknown and mysterious man creates myth.[41]

8. Types of Myth

A study of religions leads us to the conclusion that myths are of two types: one may be called etiological, the other existential. The etiological myth is a story that gives a cause for a particular situation or effect and in a sense becomes a pseudo-scientific explanation. It is characterized by single intentionality. Later a more developed consciousness and a more developed thought form indicates the etiology provided by the myth is false. This takes place if indeed the symbols of the myth did not have a second intentionality. At a given point the myth, formerly taken seriously, may now be described as false, as a fanciful story, though perhaps still providing the benefits of any product of fantasy. When the true etiology is provided the realm of the unknown and mysterious recedes. The prior explanation must be considered not only inadequate but now not necessary, however splendid its world of imaginative discourse. This type of myth has led to the widespread acknowledgment of myth as fiction or falsehood.[42]

A second type of myth, which we may call existential, is created so that man can live with the tension of his unlimited desire to know and his finite capacity to achieve. Thus the function of this myth is to evoke the transcendent, the unknown, the mysterious. Against the permanent horizon of mystery, transcendence, and the permanently unknown, myth provides a realistic orientation. These myths are all characterized by their existential capacity to orient man to the still mysterious. Such myths are capable of providing some realistic sense of equilibrium in the tension at the heart of all human existence. (It is precisely in this type of tension that Bultmann locates the question of God at the heart of all human existence. It is just on or beyond the horizon that other interpreters, e.g., Lonergan and Rahner, locate the question about God.) Thus, as Bultmann rightly saw, the truly existential myth must be interpreted in terms of man's existence. This is its only point. The existential myth obviously does not resolve the tension of human existence. But it is precisely a vehicle to remind man of his ultimate orientation. What it does beyond this, if our hypothesis is accepted, is a question yet to be developed. But the myth contains within itself its criterion of adequacy and truth.[43]

Hence if we pose the question of whether or not myth is a valid carrier of human meaning, the answer now becomes more nuanced. The truly etiological myth is only temporarily a valid carrier of human meaning. (In a pluralistic world, one culture cannot very easily distinguish the two types of myth as they exist in another culture. Nonetheless the affirmation still stands). The existential myth, however, is permanently a legitimate vehicle of human meaning. It is within this latter category that a hermeneutic or phenomenology of symbols will be effective. The other forms of myth are best handled by some discipline concerned primarily with historical, sociological, poetic, or other interests.

If asked to identify some of these myths in the biblical tradition, I should be much more cautious than Bultmann whose epistemological basis for the discrimination of myth — its opposition to modern thought — is entirely too haphazard. There is the creation myth, involving Adam, free choice, the emergence of consciousness and its attendant problems, the mystery of evil. There is a hint in Deutero-Isaiah of some sort of redemptive process achieved via one man or one group. There is a notion of a cosmic salvation that is in the background of the entire biblical tradition. There is the presentation of Jesus as the second Adam by Paul. There is the Johannine Prologue and its cosmic implications as well as the hymns mentioned earlier in the paper and, of course, there are the eschatological presentations in both the OT and the NT. The discovery and discrimination of mythical elements, as Bultmann has pointed out, is a long process.

Conclusion

With these distinctions we have a foundation for myth, a systematized criterion of distinguishing types of myth. One may then proceed to the interpretation of the existential myth and the interpretation which will distinguish the etiological from the existential myth. At the same time the interpreter is theoretically capable of distinguishing between true and false myths. It is the foundation within man that serves as the basis for the phenomenology of symbolism exercised in the hermeneutic of myth. Such a foundation then places mythical consciousness in a horizon complementary to scientific-discursive thought. Only in the case of the clearly etiological myth will there be dialectical opposition.[44]

Thus the answers to the questions suggested at the beginning of this essay are available. Myth is both a legitimate and necessary carrier of human meaning. The meaning of myth is derived by a phenomenology of symbols. And myth may be described as an imaginative, secondary, bi-polar (realistic and romantic) symbolic verbal attempt to evoke transcendent or unknown reality by a dramatic presentation of human origins, destiny, desires, and meaning. The definition is grounded in man's actual orientation to transcendence.

1.   R. Bultmann, *Kerygma und Mythos* (ed. Hans-Werner Bartsch; 4th ed.; Hamburg-Bergstedt: Herbert Reich, Evangelischer Verlag, 1960). This series, containing over nineteen separate volumes or items, contains the data of the ensuing development from the perspective of Bultmann's original proposal. English translation of vols. 1 and 2 by R. H. Fuller. The thematic expressed in 1941 is clearly present in Bultmann's writings from at least the mid-1920's. It is important to keep in mind not only the continuity of Bultmann's hermeneutics but also its growth within and through the historical-critical exegesis of the NT.

2.   Under challenge Bultmann modified somewhat the definition of myth. The argument about this is of minor importance for our purposes.

3.   Cf. P. Ricoeur, *The Symbolism of Evil* (New York: Harper & Row, 1967), and *Freud and Philosophy: An Essay on Interpretation* (New York: Yale University, 1970).This double intentionality had earlier been described in English literary critics. Cf. N. Frye, et al., *Myth and Symbol: Critical Approaches and Applications* (Lincoln: University of Nebraska, 1963). The editor, B. Slote, summarizes the theme: "The emphasis, first of all, is on the doubleness of literature — that what is given in language and form is only the embodiment of something more that is not, that cannot, be wholly stated. If we simplify definitions, we may say that a symbol contains both a literal reference and a much greater range of unwritten meaning, implication and emotion." Ibid., v.

4.   For a broader understanding of the term, cf. J. M. Robinson, "Hermeneutic Since Barth," *The New Hermeneutic* (New York: Harper & Row, 1964) 1-89. Cf. H. -G. Gadamer, *Wahrheit und Methode* (Tübingen: Mohr, 1965) for a broad history and a theory of hermeneutics. Because of the demanding nature of the historical-critical method, it is perhaps not surprising that as late as 1973 an eminent NT scholar recommended, in his presidential address, a three-fold hermeneutical task: establishing the historical-critical understanding of the text, examining the evocative power of the symbol, exploring "the processes of human understanding." N. Perrin, "Eschatology and Hermeneutics: Reflections on Method in the Interpretation of the New Testament," *JBL* 93 (1974) 3-14.

5.   I have deliberately been rather general — but hopefully accurate — in this phrase to keep open the very large question of how the religious realities, the event of Jesus Christ, are available outside a Christian culture. Troeltsch's question, raised with new seriousness by comparative religion and the history of religions, is more urgent now than ever before. One cannot even imagine how much further the question would have been elaborated in the past four hundred years had not the brilliant and pioneering efforts of M. Ricci and R. De Nobili been stopped.

6.   R. Bultmann, "What Does It Mean to Speak of God?" in *Faith and Understanding* (London: SCM, 1969) 53-65.

7. The problems of religionless man, a world "come of age," socialism, the church, etc., as theological problems are aspects of the four-fold division of a new collection of Bultmann's essays which attempts to show the unity of Bultmann's technical exegesis and theology or the application of the NT to concrete history. R. Bultmann, *Gesammelte Aufsätze* (ed. K. Matthiae; Berlin: Evangelische Verlaganstalt, 1973).

8. Ricoeur has made the point that a phenomenology of symbols seeks the meaning of the symbol for the interpreter himself. Thus in modern times hermeneutics is divided into two categories: the first which seeks restoration or recollection of "a meaning addressed to me"; the second, which understands hermeneutics "as a demystification, as a reduction of illusion." This latter is called "the school of suspicion." Ricoeur, *Freud*, 27. Pp. 28-31 are relevant.

9. We may put the problem in other terms. There is in the West a common general meaning to the term myth. This common, shared meaning has a history which effectively grounds the common meaning. Any critical attempt to change the common meaning always meets that same meaning as a presupposition. Any answer to the questions of this essay must deal effectively with the presuppositions and their history. In the empirical sciences and the definitions they generate, one can live with a conflict between a common sense and a technical understanding of terms. But religious literature, to achieve its purpose, must be understood in the common sense language of each culture. If myth is commonly understood as falsehood or fiction, then religious literature can hardly hope to gain serious or widespread or lasting attention. Perhaps most serious is the fact that we have no technical definition of myth to which the common sense meaning will ultimately appeal for clarification. But definitions must have foundations. It is about this foundation that we are here primarily concerned.

10. Two simple examples: "History like the drama and the novel, grew out of mythology, a primitive form of apprehension and expression. . . . " Arnold J. Toynbee, "History, Science and Fiction," *The Philosophy of History in Our Time* (ed. Hans Meyerhoff; Garden City: Doubleday, 1959) 115. "The German mark of the historians was largely a myth, corresponding to no reality." C. L. Becker, "What Are Historical Facts?" *Philosophy of History*, 124.

11. This method follows the Aristotelian search for univocity of meaning. However, any definition of myth tends to be *coincidentia oppositorum*. Myth is transparently opaque. Ricoeur, *Symbolism*, 15, 347-57.

12. This, of course, was precisely the intent of the 1941 articles. A coalescence of diverse influences was required both to alter presuppositions as well as to provide the understanding and techniques to explore the problem.

13. H. and H. A. Frankfort, et al., *Before Philosophy: The Intellectual Adventure of Ancient Man* (London: Hazell Watson & Vinney, 1963) 11-36.

14. The reader will recognize my indebtedness to Ricoeur and Lonergan for some of these distinctions.

15. R. Chase, *Quest for Myth* (Baton Rouge: Louisiana State University, 1949) 5. For this and the following paragraph I gratefully acknowledge the paper of a former student, L. Cronkhite, who did careful research of the periods in question.

16. Ibid., 20.

17. D. Bidney, "Myth, Symbolism and Truth," *Myth: A Symposium* (ed. T. A. Sebeok; Bloomington: Indiana University, 1972) 6.

18. For a full bibliography, cf. J. Waardenburg, *Classical Approaches to the Study of Religion* (2 Bibliography; The Hague: Mouton, 1974).

19. For the lunar mythologists (Ehrenreich, Sieke), the solar mythologists (Frobenius), the wind, weather and sky-color mythologists (Kuhn), cf. R. M. Dorson, "The Eclipse of Solar Mythology," *Myth: A Symposium*, 25-63; and B. Malinowski, *Magic, Science and Religion* (Garden City: Doubleday, 1954) 96-99.

20. " . . . successive stages in some process of development." B. J. F. Lonergan, *Method in Thology* (New York: Herder & Herder, 1972) 236. Freud, for diverse reasons, had drawn the inevitable conclusions suggested by people such as Sir J. Frazer, Comte, etc., and made myth a dialectical horizon standing in utter opposition to scientific thought.

21. E. Cassirer, *Philosophy of Symbolic Forms* (New Haven: Yale University, 1953-57).

22. In addition to *Philosophy in a New Key* and *Feeling and Form*, cf. Langer's magnum opus, *Mind: An Essay on Human Feeling* (Vols. 1 and 2; Baltimore Johns Hopkins, 1967, 1972).
    Developments by individual scholars were complemented by the study of folklore at universities such as Indiana, Pennsylvania, U.C.L.A., U.C. Berkeley, and North Carolina. Psychoanalysists and psychiatrists, following Freud or Jung, e.g., Rollo May, have explored the meaning of myth in terms of the unconscious. Religious Studies departments and Comparative Literature departments have included myth and symbol in their curricula. This type of interest has led to a comprehensive anthology. Cf. B. Feldman and R. D. Richardson, *The Rise of Modern Mythology, 1680-1860* (Bloomington: Indiana University, 1972).

23. R. M. Grant, *A Short History of the Interpretation of the Bible* (New York: Macmillan, 1963) 101.

24. W. G. Kümmel, *The New Testament: The History of the Investigation of Its Problems* (New York: Abingdon Press, 1970) 101.

25. C. Hartlich and W. Sachs, *Der Ursprung des Mythosbegriffes in der modernen Bibelwissenschaft* (Schriften der Studiengemeinschaft der evangelischen Akadmien, II; Tübingen: Mohr, 1952).

26. Kümmel, *New Testament*, 423.

27. A. Schweitzer, *The Quest of the Historical Jesus* (5 ed.; New York: Macmillan, 1968) 84.

28. Kümmel, *New Testament*, 124.

29. Pioneers in comparative religion made the same mistake some years later.

30. Cf. R. Patai, *Myth and Modern Man* (Englewood Cliffs: Prentice-Hall, 1972).

31. E.g., J. Campbell.

32. Bultmann, Ebeling, Fuchs, J. M. Robinson, Wilder, Lonergan and McKenzie

belong to this group, but each in his own fashion.

33. Few have done more to validate myth as a legitimate carrier of religious meaning than the scholar, teacher, and writer to whom these essays are dedicated, John L. McKenzie. He has written at least five articles (cf. *Myths and Realities*; Milwaukee: Bruce Publishing Co., 1963) directly on the subject. Perhaps only a few will remember how advanced his article, "The Literary Characteristics of Genesis 2-3," published in 1954, really was. His article. "Myth and the Old Testament," published in 1959, is among the very best and earliest articles on the subject. In addition to original contributions to the understanding of myth in the bible, he was among the first to disseminate the better aspects of German scholarship at all levels, thus breaking down artificial but rigid boundaries.

34. Cf. Ricoeur, *Symbolism of Evil.*

35. Ibid., 18.

36. Cf. J. J. Collins, "The Symbolism of Transcendence in Jewish Apocalyptic," *BR* 19 (1974) 5 and his reference to Perrin and Wheelwright.

37. The main lines I follow have been suggested by the reading of Goethe and Lonergan. From Goethe I take his idea about great ages of culture being characterized by faith. From Lonergan, despite his consistent equation of myth with the untutored desire to know, I take his carefully differentiated understanding of the process of knowing as this knowing has actually taken place.

38. B. J. F. Lonergan, *Insight, A Study of Human Understanding* (London: Longmans, Green, 1958) 635. Cf. W. Richardson, *Heidegger: Through Phenomenology to Thought* (The Hague: Martinus Nijhoff, 1967) 4-5 for "*transcendere.*"

39. Lonergan, *Insight,* 546.

40. Ibid., 636.

41. Cf. Lonergan, *Insight,* 531-34, especially his comments on the threefold distinction of image.

42. The identification of such myths is difficult though not impossible. Myths based on the Ptolemaic cosmology (widely used in the Middle Ages) and not admitting of any double intentionality, seem to fit this category. Perhaps also the attribution of mental and physical illnesses to reprehensible behavior on the part of the person or his ancestors, especially if one can attain to a certain scientific cause.

43. Developments in empirical science seem to support man's orientation to mystery.

44. If, as I suspect, ontogeny repeats phylogeny, then genetic opposition does not in every instance mean that later forms of thought must totally supersede earlier forms. Rather an integration can take place.

JAMES M. ROBINSON

The Internal Word in History

John L. McKenzie, known over the years as a colleague through the
Society of Biblical Literature, has played a significant role in my
development by providing entrée into the Roman Catholic-Protestant
dialogue — not by being directly my dialogue partner, but by being the
critical thinker from within who makes it possible for the outsider to enter
in on an already-initiated internal discussion. With McKenzie on the
inside, one is put on notice that contributors to the dialogue are expected to
make use of their critical faculties. By observing him in action, one can
catch sight of the higher loyalty and the maturity inherent in addressing
one's critical faculties to the ongoing life of the church. An invitation to
speak at the Roman Catholic-Protestant Colloquium at Harvard in 1963
provided the occasion for me to become acquainted with and appreciative
of the *sensus plenior* hermeneutic popular in Roman Catholic circles, a
trend which is in significant ways parallel to the new hermeneutic current in
the Protestant circles with which I have been associated. McKenzie drew
my attention to problems involved for the Roman Catholic situation by
this development. Hence I commented: "Of course, just as such Protestant
translation for our day poses problems of distortion, modernization, and
dogmatic prejudice, just so the criteria of *sensus plenior* are an area of
unfinished business, as the Catholic critic John L. McKenzie has pointed
out."[1] At the first Lonergan Congress in 1970 I was again brought together
with McKenzie at an ecumenical gathering, in this instance as the exegetical
minority among predominantly philosophically oriented theologians, in
which capacity we shared the platform in the closing symposium. That
meeting, which brought us together in more ways than one, triggered
parallel responses to Lonergan, his documented in his incisive review of
Method in Theology,[2] mine in the following reflections on the traditional
distinction between internal and external word recurring in Lonergan's
position.

To talk of thought as itself language is a fruitful approach. For then a basic cleft between thought and its secondary objectification as language is potentially *aufgehoben* in an overarching "word," which is internal as well as external. Now language is historic, as is man. It is therefore fruitful, in maintaining the distinction between man and God, in maintaining consistently a recognition of human finitude, to designate man's inwardness with a term associated with language and, as such, with historic conditioning and limitation. For all too often the soul is attributed unhuman traits such as the divine attribute of immortality, and in the process man's inwardness becomes, if not his god, as divine spark, *imago dei*, or religious *a priori*, then his *hybris*, his justification, his standing as *homo religiosus*, which Paul referred to as *hamartia*.

This theological point could be scored, or this theological value protected, by referring to man's reasoning, his rationality, his logicality, as a kind of word; yet the concept of internal and external word could and has cut the other way: language, word, is but a product, perhaps secondary, derivative, defective and distorting, of the innate logos, itself free from such defects of objectification, the logos which is ultimately to be apotheosized as spermatic Word or as the microcosmic correspondence to the cosmic rationality of *natura sive Deus*.

Between the two extremes of the medium becoming the message, the consciousness *of*. . . replacing that of which it is conscious, and language becoming an irrelevant, defective and interchangeable external implement, lies an area of fruitful discussion, if careful distinctions and responsible exploration prevail.

A step in this direction may lie in a recognition, in terms of the historicness of man, that verbalization, linguistic formulation, is not to be understood ultimately as a secondary objectification (which in many cases need never even occur) of a primary experience that itself is pre-linguistic. To be sure, such an invidious distinction would seem more tenable the more restricted one's definitiion of language be. For language, meant in a narrow sense, is not co-terminous with man. Infants, primitive man, and lovers live off gesture, with an occasional grunt or chirp being hardly more than an audible gesture. But once the cleft between deed and word has been transcended by the recognition that they are interlocked as eloquent action and effective word, as gesture and symbol, then language can be recognized in gesticulation as well as in verbalization. It is in such an embracive sense that the term language is here meant.

Language is not merely the secondary expression of a more primary experience, but rather an ingredient in the experiencing itself. If we are historic through and through, our inner processes are formed by the language world in which we swim, as conditioned reflexes. We live in style.

An illustration from our tradition, humorous and perhaps apocryphal though it could be, may point up the issue. Missionaries come to a simple uncultured native tribe, proclaim the gospel, tell the stories of Jesus, including the exorcisms, and thus by implication instill, together with faith and various beliefs, also the belief in demon possession. The natives not only take heart and have faith; they also appropriate ideological beliefs and practice what was thus indoctrinated. In brief, demon possession breaks out like an epidemic. And, much as modern medical missionaries, the evangelists with their *pharmakeia athanasias* just as promptly save/cure the lost/sick by exorcism in the name of the Lord. Had such missionaries however been Bultmannians (if this is not a *contradictio in adjecto*), one may well question whether the epidemic would have broken out in the first place. For their kerygma would have been built, one may fear, exclusively on Paul and John, neither of whom record any exorcisms. Without the language world of demon possession, the natives would probably not have experienced their ills as demon possession nor their rescue as exorcism.

The effect of Bultmannianism would not have been first felt in the subsequent language describing the newly converted tribe's Christian faith. To be sure this language of the subsequent witness would be free of exorcism talk. But this would not be because exorcisms had been demythologized by Bultmannian transmitters of the tradition of the tribe's faith, but because exorcisms had not even happened in the first place. Cures and/or conversions would have happened in other language worlds. To be sure medical problems would still have produced objective medical symptoms such as pain, spasm, etc. But the absence of demon-possession language does not mean they would have been experienced in a pre-linguistic form. Rather they would have been experienced in terms of some other language world (e.g., in the Pauline, as thorns in the flesh or *stigmata*). Even if they were experienced in antiseptic purity as symptoms of viral infection, they would have been experienced in a language world: our technological world.

This train of thought could be put into focus for the dogmatician more directly with reference to a problem posed by another case: Why is it that Jesus was not born again, but did rise from the dead? Perhaps because the Israelite (and hence still to some extent the Jewish) language world avoided sexual concepts in speaking of God, preferring the seemingly more worthy language of creation to that of procreation. Put in their language one might say that Mary, in distinction from pagan maidens who bore divine humans, not only did not know Joseph, she did not know God. After Jesus' time, his movement entered the language world built upon divine sexual activity. Thus regeneration became increasingly possible for Christians in a way it was not for Jesus himself. When one examines in terms of the history of ideas (better: in terms of the trajectory of language) the emergence of the doctrine of regeneration, one notes as one moves progressively through primitive Christianity, or works one's way chronologically through the NT, that Jesus' sexless metaphor of becoming like a child or Paul's doctrine of new creation subsequently becomes (with Jas 1:18 as a missing link) the Johannine doctrine of rebirth from above and then in Tit 3:5 and 1 Pet 1:23 the doctrine of regeneration.

Not only did Jesus not live in a language world in which regeneration was at home; the first precedent-setting instances of experiencing the unworldliness of his coming did not take place in such a language world. The earliest view as to when to begin his story was to begin with his baptism. The inclusion there of the descent of the Holy Spirit could readily have come to expression as regeneration, had such a language world been at hand. The fact that the legend of Jesus' baptism was not initially experienced in the language world of regeneration is negatively attested by the fact that the attachment to his baptism as his point of departure leads instead to the doctrine of adoptionism. The more orthodox rejoinder was to move further back to an infancy narrative. The doctrine of regeneration did not come to mind probably because it was not in mind as internal word. Therefore one cannot simply say that there is no doctrine of Jesus' regeneration because he did not need regeneration — for he did not need John's baptism of repentance for the remission of sins, yet received it, much to the discomfort of the Evangelists, who progressively explain it away. It is an undisputed fact, then, that he did undergo a rite which, as a phenomenon in the history of religions (*rite de passage*), is elsewhere often called regeneration. Thus if one is not thinking in terms of language one could speak of his baptismal regeneration. The only real reason he was not born again is that he did not experience baptism — and primitive Christians did not initially experience his baptismal experience — in the language world of regeneration. His baptism, or his baptism story as we have it, is a model of a regeneration narration. All the ingredients of regeneration are there — except the internal word. Thus the reason that the primitive Christian experiencing of Jesus' baptism was only inadequately brought to expression in the heretical language of adoptionism is not to be found in a tragic devolution as one moves from the purity of internal word to the fallen status of external word, but in the continuity of a language world, which, as petrified philosophy, informs internal word and hence preforms subsequent external word.

In the case of Jesus' resurrection, the situation is instructively different. To be sure, resurrection is hardly a doctrine known and believed always everywhere by everyone. The Sadducees were no doubt right in branding it an innovation not represented in Torah, and the Pharisees, in appropriating the term, were yielding to the pressures of innovative popular piety, as do the liberal theologians of every age. On the norm of always, everywhere, by everyone, resurrection is not dogma, and here Sadducees are joined, in not making use of such a modernistic concept, by Q and the Gospel of Thomas as the truly orthodox. But Jesus and those who witnessed to his resurrection came either from the classes of popular piety led by the Pharisees or from the Pharisaic class itself (Paul). Therefore their experiencing of Easter included, as an internal word within that experience, the language of resurrection. Easter was a language event not only in Bultmann's sense that Jesus rose into the kerygma; it was also a language event of the internal word. The resurrection of the dead informed the Easter experience and thus preformed the witness to that experience as the witness to Jesus' resurrection. However the historian and/or theologian may describe what happened on Easter, one ingredient in such an explanation must be the tracing of the movement from the internal word of the common belief in the resurrection to the external word of the witness to Jesus' resurrection. Perhaps source material for such a tracing of this movement is to be found in the pre-Pauline (Rom 1:4) and post-Pauline (Acts 17:32) use of the general Pharisaic idiom "resurrection of (those) dead," though in both cases what is actually meant is only Jesus' resurrection. Apparently the internal word has colored the formulation of the external word in a slightly inaccurate way.

The shift in defining what is to be believed, from believing the language of dogma to believing what that language meant, is not a move from the historically conditioned and secondarily objectified dimension of language into a purer and truer dimension of *intellectus*, whose *adaequatio* to the *res* could be more readily affirmed than could the adequacy or correspondence of distorting language. The *intellectus* is used by a language world to have that world's say; it is not timeless, rational or natural in a way language is not, but, like language, is timely, existential and historic. (E.g., in the instance given, the internal word was as Jewish as the external word was Christian.) To be sure one could approach an *adaequatio intellectus et rei* from the other end: *Res* could also be recognized as historic, as the issue at stake, much as Heidegger has shown "thing" to be not the most depersonalized, technologized irrelevancy, but rather what is worth contending over, the cause for which one stands. Then a historic *intellectus* would tend to be more adequate.

To be sure, there is a kind of *adaequatio intellectus et rei* which is of the kind traditionally intended by that phrase, and which is convincing to us all: the ability of science's technology to land on the moon on target. But before one takes science and technology as the ultimate proof of the ontological superiority of the uncontaminated truth-sphere of their intellect and reality, one should note that this rarified sphere is being increasingly purified of the human factor as its contamination. The intellect is less and less the thinker, and becomes more and more the computer, electronic recorder, the machine. And the reality of science and technology is less and less the reality we experience, and increasingly an artificial laboratory environment where things never exist in nature (a real problem for natural theology). It is a reality often beyond our five senses, involving our knowing through sense experience only to the extent that we can communicate with the machines that communicate with the experiment-reality. The reality of the black box should not be given ontological priority over our home whose maker is God (in distinction from the laboratory technician). The historicness of man is an ontological fact attested by the petrified philosophy of the language world informing the internal word, as well as by the culturally conditioned language of the external world of reality and the web of meanings in which experience (in distinction from experiment) knows of things. One might say, somewhat paradoxically, that perhaps theology will become more adequate to the reality of its subject matter, and thus more scientific, in direct proportion to the extent it increases its recognition of the linguisticality of man and of his reality.

1.   "Interpretation of Scripture in Biblical Studies Today," *Ecumenical Dialogue at Harvard: The Roman Catholic-Protestant Colloquium* (eds. S. H. Miller and G. E. Wright; Cambridge: The Belknap Press of Harvard University Press, 1964), 106, citing John L. McKenzie, "Problems of Hermeneutics in Roman Catholic Exegesis," *JBL* 77 (1958) 197-204, esp. 201-02.

2.   J. L. McKenzie, "An Exegetical Answer to Lonergan's Method in Theology," *Listening: Journal of Religion and Culture* 10 (1975) 2-12.

Donald H. Wimmer and Harry M. Culkin

A Bibliography of the Books, Articles, and Reviews of John. L. McKenzie

Works are listed according to year of publication, books first, followed by articles and book reviews. Translations and later editions are included with the original and therefore are sometimes not in chronological order. Books, scholarly articles, popular writings, and book reviews from scholarly, professional and popular journals are listed. Writings which appear in publications that are directed primarily toward the membership of an organization or an institution have, for the most part, been excluded, along with audio tapes, study aids, and materials of a similar nature.

1933

Review of

Taylor, A. E. *Socrates*. *ModSch* 11: 46-47.

West, Rebecca. *Saint Augustine*. *ModSch* 11: 21-22.

1934

"Abstraction in St. Thomas." *ModSch* 11: 75-76, 91-94.

"Horace's Lament for Quintilius." *ClassBul* 10: 12-14.

"Mr. Demos on Non-Being." *ModSch* 11: 39-41.

1935

"Aristotle on Delivery." *ClassBul* 11: 70-71.

"Wisdom Hath Built Herself a House." *ModSch* 13: 28-30.

1939

"Enuma Elis and the Hexaëmeron." *HPR* 39: 1052-60. [Editors' note: in error attributed to Michael Gruenthaner.]

1943

"Divine Sonship of the Angels." *CBQ* 5: 293-300.

1944

"Imprecations of the Psalter." *AER* 111: 81-96.

1945

"Divine Sonship and Individual Religion." *CBQ* 7: 32-47.

"Divine Sonship of Men in the Old Testament." *CBQ* 7: 326-39.

1946

"Divine Sonship of Israel and the Covenant." *CBQ* 8: 320-31.

Review of

> Lattey, Cuthbert. *The Psalter in the Westminster Version of the Sacred Scriptures. CBQ* 8: 249-51.

1947

"The Dynastic Oracle: II Samuel 7." *TS* 8: 187-218.

Review of

> Bonsirven, Joseph. *Les Enseignements de Jésus-Christ. TS* 8: 301-3.
>
> Burrows, Millar. *An Outline of Biblical Theology. TS* 8: 315-16.
>
> Frankfort, Henri, *et al. The Intellectual Adventure of Ancient Man. TS* 8: 512-15.
>
> Snaith, Norman H. *The Distinctive Ideas of the Old Testament. TS* 8: 142-44.
>
> Sutcliffe, Edmund F. *The Old Testament and the Future Life. CBQ* 9: 488.

1948

"Appellative Use of El and Elohim." *CBQ* 10: 170-81.

"Report of the Tenth General Meeting of the Catholic Biblical Association." *CBQ* 10: 87-92.

Review of

> Frankfort, Henri. *Ancient Egyptian Religion. TS* 9: 606-7.
>
> Frankfort, Henri. *Kingship and the Gods. TS* 9: 327-30.
>
> Garnot, Jean Saint Fare. *La vie religieuse dans l'ancienne Egypte. TS* 9: 606-7.
>
> Matthews, I. G. *The Religious Pilgrimage of Israel. TS* 9: 142-44.
>
> Simpson, Cuthbert A. *Revelation and Response in the Old Testament. TS* 9: 611-12.
>
> Zacharias, H. C. E. *Proto-history. TS* 9: 604-6.

1949

"A New Study of Theodore of Mopsuestia." *TS* 10: 394-408.

Review of

Daniel-Rops, Henri. *Sacred History*. *TS* 10: 459-62.

Daniélou, Jean. *Origène*. *TS* 10: 446-48.

Duncker, Petrus G. *Compendium Grammaticae Linguae Hebraicae Biblicae*. *CBQ* 11: 347-49.

Micklem, Nathaniel. *Religion*. *TS* 10: 609-11.

Prado, Iohannes. *Praelectionum Biblicarum Compendium II*. 5th ed. *CBQ* 11: 118-19.

Sellers, Ovid R. and Edwin E. Voight. *Biblical Hebrew for Beginners*. *CBQ* 11: 347-49.

Ziegler, Joseph. *Isaias*. *TS* 10: 317-19.

1950

"A Note on Psalm 73(74):13-15." *TS* 11: 275-82.

Review of

Baumgartner, Walter *et al.*, eds. *Festschrift für Alfred Bertholet*. *TS* 11: 616-20.

Bultmann, Rudolf. *Das Urchristentum im Rahmen der antiken Religionen*. *TS* 11: 438-40.

Callan, Charles J. *The New Psalter*. *CBQ* 12: 361-62.

Dupont, Jacques. *Gnosis: La Connaissance religieuse dans les épîtres de Saint Paul*. *TS* 11: 418-22.

Ferm, Vergilius, ed. *Forgotten Religions*. *TS* 11: 586-88.

Fosdick, Harry E. *The Man from Nazareth*. *Cath World* 170: 317-18.

Lewy, Immanuel. *The Birth of the Bible*. *CBQ* 12: 472-73.

van Paassen, P. *Why Jesus Died*. *Cath World* 170: 317-18.

Schrade, Hubert. *Der verborgene Gott. Gottesbild und Gottesvorstellung in Israel und im alten Orient*. *TS* 11: 588-93.

1951

"A Chapter in the History of Spiritual Exegesis: de Lubac's *Histoire et esprit*." *TS* 12: 365-81.

Review of

Bammel, Fritz. *Das heilige Mahl im Glauben der Völker*. *TS* 12: 235-36.

Cerfaux, L. *et al*. *Problèmes et méthode d'exégèse théologique*. *TS* 12: 560-62.

Dölger, Franz Joseph. *Antike und Christentum*. Vol. 6, part 4. *TS* 12: 241-43.

Herntrich, Volkmar. *Der Prophet Jesaja 1-12*. ATD 17. *TS* 12: 93-99.

Kraus, Hans-Joachim. *Die Koenigscherrschaft Gottes im Alten Testament*. *TS* 12: 565-67.

Moscati, Sabatino. *Storia e Civiltà dei Semiti. CBQ* 13: 455-56.

Ohm, Thomas. *Die Liebe zu Gott in den nichtchristlichen Religionen. TS* 12: 388-91.

Steinmann, Jean. *Le Prophèt Isaïe. TS* 12: 93-99.

1952

"God and Nature in the Old Testament." *CBQ* 14: 18-39; 124-45. Reprinted in *Myths and Realities* (Milwaukee: Bruce, 1963) 85-132.

"The Hebrew Attitude Towards Mythological Polytheism." *CBQ* 14: 323-35. Reprinted in *Myths and Realities* (Milwaukee: Bruce, 1963) 133-45.

Review of

Bertrand, Frederic. *Mystique de Jésus chez Origène. TS* 13: 447-49.

Coleman-Norton, P. R., ed. *Studies In Roman Economic and Social History. CBQ* 14: 304-05.

Dirksen, Aloys. *A Life of Christ Together with the Four Gospels. CBQ* 14: 414.

Gelin, Albert. *Jérémie.* Temoins de Dieu 13. *CBQ* 14: 409.

Gelin, Albert. *Jérémie, Les Lamentations, Baruch. CBQ* 14: 409.

Gordis, Robert, ed. *Max Leopold Margolis: Scholar and Teacher. CBQ* 14: 414.

Guillet, Jacques. *Thèmes bibliques. CBQ* 14: 195-99.

Hölscher, Gustav. *Das Buch Hiob.* 2e Aufl. *CBQ* 14: 393-96.

LeSaint, William, trans. *Tertullian: Treatises on Marriage and Remarriage.* ACW 13. *CBQ* 14: 305.

Metzger, Bruce M. *Index of Articles on the New Testament and the Early Church Published in Festschriften. CBQ* 14: 209.

Peters, N. and J. Decarreaux, trans. *Notre Bible: Source de Vie. CBQ* 14: 296-97.

Rosenkranz, Gerhard. *Evangelische Religionskunde. TS* 13: 468-69.

Smalley, Beryl. *The Study of the Bible in the Middle Ages.* 2nd ed. *CBQ* 14: 381-83.

Thiele, Edwin R. *The Mysterious Numbers of the Hebrew Kings. CBQ* 14: 298-303.

1953

"The Commentary of Theodore of Mopsuestia on John 1: 46-51." *TS* 14: 73-84.

"The Jewish World in New Testament Times." *A Catholic Commentary on Holy Scripture* (ed. Bernard Orchard *et al.*; New York: Thomas Nelson) 728-41 (sec. 584-96). Revised in *A New Catholic Commentary on Holy Scripture* (ed. Reginald C. Fuller *et al.*; New York: Thomas Nelson, 1969) 766-83 (sec. 605-18).

Review of

Browne, Laurence E. *Ezekiel and Alexander. CBQ* 15: 518.

Connolly, R. H., ed. and trans. *The Explanatio Symboli ad Initiandos. CBQ* 15: 270-71.

Kerrigan, Alexander. *St. Cyril of Alexandria: Interpreter of the Old Testament.* AnBib 2. *CBQ* 15: 492-94.

Montgomery, James A. *A Critical and Exegetical Commentary on the Book of Kings. CBQ* 15: 88-91.

Moscati, Sabatino. *L'Oriente Antico. CBQ* 15: 489-91.

Rowley, H. H. *The Servant of the Lord and other Essays on the Old Testament. CBQ* 15: 241-44.

Sparks, H. F. D. *The Formation of the New Testament. TS* 14: 467-69.

Steinmann, Jean. *Le Prophète Jérémie: Sa vie, son oeuvre et son temps.* LD 9. *CBQ* 15: 241-44.

Taylor, Vincent. *The Gospel According to St. Mark. TS* 14: 299-309.

de Vaux, Roland, *La Genèse. CBQ* 15: 244-46.

Vincent, Albert. *Le livre des Juges; le livre de Ruth. CBQ* 15: 239-41.

Zeitlin, Solomon. *The Zadokite Fragments. CBQ* 15: 128-29.

1954

"The Literary Characteristics of Genesis 2-3." *TS* 15: 541-72. Reprinted in *Myths and Realities* (Milwaukee: Bruce, 1963) 146-75. Abridged in *TD* 6 (Winter 1958) 19-23.

Review of

Baron, Salo W. and Joseph L. Blau, eds. *Judaism: Postbiblical and Talmudic Period. CBQ* 16: 502.

Block, Joshua. *On the Apocalyptic in Judaism. CBQ* 16: 98-100.

Bultmann, Rudolf. *Theologie des Neuen Testaments.* 3. (Schluss) Lieferung. *CBQ* 16: 250-53.

Dibelius, Martin. *Botschaft und Geschichte. CBQ* 16: 253-56.

George, A. Raymond. *Communion with God in the New Testament. TS* 15: 474-78.

Goodspeed, Edgar J. *The Student's New Testament. CBQ* 16: 382.

Gregorianum: Indices Generales 1920-1950. CBQ 16: 273.

Graef, Hilda C., trans. *St. Gregory of Nyssa: The Lord's Prayer; the Beatitudes.* ACW 18. *CBQ* 16: 381. [Unsigned.]

Kleist, James A., and Joseph L. Lilly, eds. and trans. *The New Testament Rendered from the Original Greek. CBQ* 16: 491-500.

Mitton, C. Leslie. *The Epistle to the Ephesians. CBQ* 16: 118-22.

Moriarty, Frederick L. *Forward to The Old Testament Books. CBQ* 16: 381.

Moscati, Sabatino. *Geschichte und Kultur der semitischen Völker. CBQ* 16: 73-76.

Schürmann, Heinz. *Der Paschamahlbericht: Luke 22, (7-14) 15-18. CBQ* 16: 262-63.

Steinmann, Jean. *Le prophète Ezéchiel et les débuts de l'exil. CBQ* 16: 480-83.

Taylor, Vincent. *The Names of Jesus. TS* 15: 120-22.

Vaganay, Léon. *Le Problème Synoptique. TS* 15: 639-44.

Vogels, Heinrich Josef. *Evangelium Colbertinum. CBQ* 16: 126-27.

1955

"Divine Passion in Osee." *CBQ* 17: 167-79 (287-99).

"Knowledge of God in Hosea." *JBL* 74: 22-27.

Review of

Asensio, Feliz. *Yahveh y su Pueblo. JBL* 74: 88-90.

The Holy Bible: Revised Standard Version. CBQ 17: 88-90.

Internationale Zeitschriftenschau für Bibelwissenschaft und Grenzgebiete, Band I (1951/1952). CBQ 17: 117-18.

Kaufmann, Yehezkel. *The Biblical Account of the Conquest of Palestine. CBQ* 17: 95-97.

Schürmann, Heinz. *Der Einsetzungsbericht: Lk 22, 19-20. CBQ* 17: 528-29.

Spodafora, Francesco. *Collettivismo e Individualismo nel Vecchio Testamento. JBL* 74: 133-34.

XXXV Congreso Eucaristico Internacional Barcelona 1952: Sesiones de Estudio. Tomo I, II. *CBQ* 17: 118.

1956

The Two Edged Sword: An Interpretation of the Old Testament. Milwaukee/London: Bruce/G. Chapman; reprint ed., Garden City: Image Books, 1966. Translations: *Geist und Welt des Alten Testamentes* (trans. Hildebrand Pfiffner; Luzern: Räber-Verlag, 1962); *Espíritu y mundo del Antiguo Testamento* (trans. A. Oltra; Estella: Verbo Divino, 1968); *La spada a doppio taglio* (ed. Fausto Salvoni; Torino: Marietti, 1968); *Os Grandes Temas do Antigo Testamento* (trans. Cácio Gomes and Therezinha Gomes; Petrópolis, Brasil: Editora Vozes, 1971). Excerpt "Israel and the Nations," in *Modern Catholic Thinkers* (ed. A. Caponigri; New York: Harper & Row, 1960) 440-53.

"Mythological Allusions in Ezek 28:12-18." *JBL* 75: 322-27. Reprinted as "Note on the Mythological Allusions in Ezekiel 28:12-18," in *Myths and Realities* (Milwaukee: Bruce, 1963) 175-81.

"Training Teachers of College Theology." *JesuitEdQ* (October 1956) 94-108.

Review of

> Bultmann, Rudolf. *Theology of the New Testament*. Vol. 2. *CBQ* 18: 219.
>
> Davies, W. D. and D. Daube, eds. *The Background of the New Testament and its Eschatology*. *TS* 17: 415-19.
>
> Fohrer, Georg. *Ezechiel*. *CBQ* 18: 324-27.
>
> Johnson, Aubrey R. *Sacral Kingship in Ancient Israel*. *TS* 17: 242-43.
>
> Williams, Walter G. *The Prophets: Pioneers to Christianity*. *CBQ* 18: 450-51.

1957

"How to Read the Bible." *Ave Maria* 85, 9: 12-15, 30.

"Royal Messianism." *CBQ* 19: 25-52. Reprinted in *Myths and Realities* (Milwaukee: Bruce, 1963) 203-31.

"The Sacrifice of Isaac (Gen 22)." *Scr* 9: 79-84.

Review of

> Mowinckel, Sigmund. *He That Cometh*. *CBQ* 19: 274-78.
>
> Ringgren, Helmer. *The Messiah in the Old Testament*. *CBQ* 19: 279-80.
>
> Vawter, Bruce. *A Path through Genesis*. *TS* 18: 104-05.

1958

"Annotations on the Christology of Theodore of Mopsuestia." *TS* 19: 345-73.

"Getting to Know Christ." *Ave Maria* 88, 8: 20-23.

"The Language of Old Testament Worship and Scripture." *North American Liturgical Week* 19: 156-58.

"Problems of Hermeneutics in Roman Catholic Exegesis." *JBL* 77: 197-204.

"Sex *is* in the Bible." *Voice of St. Jude* 24, 7: 13-16.

"Theology as an Integrating Factor in Jesuit Education." *JesuitEdQ* (June 1958) 19-26.

Review of

> Dubarle, A. -M. *Le péché originel dans l'écriture*. *TS* 19: 425-27.
>
> Fohrer, George. *Messiasfrage und Bibelverständnis*. *CBQ* 20: 560.

1959

"The Elders of the Old Testament." *Bib* 40: 522-40. Reprinted in *Scientia Biblica et Orientalia* (AnBib 10) 1: 388-406.

"Myth and the Old Testament." *CBQ* 21: 265-82. Reprinted in *Myths and Realities* (Milwaukee: Bruce, 1963) 182-200.

"Scriptural Approach to Vocations." *NCEA Bul* 56: 377-81. Revised in *Vital Concepts of the Bible* (Wilkes Barre: Dimension Books, 1967) 81-91. Condensed in *CDigest* 33, 11: 20-23.

"The Task of Biblical Theology." *The Voice of St. Mary's Seminary* 36, 7: 7-9, 26-27.

"Theology in Jesuit Education." *Thought* 34: 347-57.

Review of

Bouyer, Louis. *The Meaning of Sacred Scripture. TS* 20: 445-46.

Dibelius, Martin. *Botschaft und Geschichte.* Band 2. *CBQ* 21: 240-41.

Eltester, Friedrich-Wilhelm. *Eikon im Neuen Testament. CBQ* 21: 241-42.

Robert, A. and A. Feuillet, eds. *Introduction à la Bible 1: Introduction générale; Ancien Testament. TS* 20: 108-10.

Scharl ert, Josef. *Solidarität in Segen und Fluch im Alten Testament und in seiner Umwelt.* Band 1. BBB 14. *CBQ* 21: 90-91.

Vincent, Albert. *Le livre de Juges. Le livre de Ruth. SBJ;* 2nd rev. ed. *CBQ* 21: 223-24.

1960

"Messianism and the College Teacher of Sacred Doctrine." *Proceedings of the Society of Catholic College Teachers of Sacred Doctrine* 6: 34-53; ("Discussion Summary," 53-59). Reprinted in *Myths and Realities* (Milwaukee: Bruce, 1963) 232-50. Revised as "The Transformation of Old Testament Messianism," in *Studies in Salvation History* (ed. Luke Salm; Englewood Cliffs: Prentice-Hall, 1964) 96-133.

"A Response [to Michael Novak]." *CBQ* 22: 315-16.

"Vengeance is Mine." *Scr* 12: 33-39.

"The Word of God in the Old Testament." *TS* 21: 183-206. Reprinted in *Myths and Realities* (Milwaukee: Bruce, 1963) 37-58.

Review of

Beaucamp, Evode. *La Bible et le sens religieux de l'univers. TS* 21: 465-66.

Childs, Brevard S. *Myth and Reality in the Old Testament. CBQ* 22: 337-38.

Coppens, J. *et al.*, eds. *Sacra pagina: Miscellanea biblica Congressus Internationalis Catholici de re biblica. TS* 21: 634-35.

de Fraine, J. *Adam et son lignage: Etudes sur la notion de "personnalité corporative" dans la Bible. TS* 21: 277-78.

Gelin. A. *Jérémie. Les Lamentations. Baruch. SBJ;* 2nd rev. ed. *CBQ* 22: 360.

Gottwald, Norman K. *A Light to the Nations. TS* 21: 136-38.

Ligier, Louis. *Péché d'Adam et péché du monde.* Part 1. *TS* 21: 661-62.

Robert, A. and A. Feuillet, eds. *Introduction à la Bible 2: Nouveau Testament. TS* 21: 283-85.

Steinmann, Jean. *Le Prophétisme biblique des origines à Osée. TS* 21: 140-41.

Trinquet, J. *Habaquq. Abdias.* 2nd rev. ed. *CBQ* 22: 360.

1961

"The Bible in Contemporary Catholicism." *Cath World* 193: 225-32.

"Faith and Intellectual Freedom." *Critic* 20, 1: 8-10; 68-71. Reprinted in *Myths and Realities* (Milwaukee: Bruce, 1963) 18-34; *Cadence in Loyola Thought* 16, 1: 2-12.

"Intellectual Liberty Revisited." *HPR* 61, 4: 350-59. Reprinted as "Intellectual Liberty in the Church," in *Myths and Realities* (Milwaukee: Bruce, 1963) 3-17.

"Into the Desert." *Way* 1: 27-39. Revised in *Vital Concepts of the Bible* (Wilkes Barre: Dimension Books, 1967) 7-29.

Review of

Auzou, Georges. *The Word of God: Approaches to the Mystery of the Sacred Scriptures.* *TS* 22: 280-81.

Behler, G. -M. *Les Paroles d'adieux du Seigneur.* *TS* 22: 332.

Benoit, Pierre. *Exégèse et Théologie.* *CBQ* 23: 486-87.

Bonnard, Pierre E. *Le psautier selon Jérémie.* *TS* 22: 283-85.

Cleveland, Ray L. *The Excavation of the Conway High Place (Petra) and Soundings at Khirbet Ader.* *CBQ* 23: 65-66.

Guillet, Jacques. *Themes of the Bible.* *CBQ* 23: 520.

Isaac, Jean. *La révélation progressive des personnes divines.* *TS* 22: 331-32.

Rabanos, Ricardo. *Propedeutica Biblica. Introducción General a la Sagrada Escritura.* *CBQ* 23: 331-32.

Robert, A. and A. Tricot. *Guide to the Bible.* Vol. 1. 2nd rev. ed. *CBQ* 23: 94.

Smart, James. *Servants of the Word.* *JBL* 80: 101.

Sinclair, Lawrence A. *An Archaeological Study of Gibeah (Tell el-Ful).* *CBQ* 23: 65-66.

Steinmann, Jean. *Le livre de la consolation d'Israël et les prophètes du retour de l'exil.* *TS* 22: 462-64.

1962

Editor. *The Bible in Current Catholic Thought.* New York: Herder & Herder.

"Church Unity Through the Bible." *Pax Romana Journal* (1962, no. 4) 15-18.

"The Four Samuels." *BR* 7: 3-18.

"The Judge of All the Earth." *Way* 2: 209-18. Reprinted in *Contemporary New Testament Studies* (ed. M. Rosalie Ryan; Collegeville: Liturgical Press, 1965) 295-303. Revised in *Vital Concepts of the Bible* (Wilkes Barre: Dimension Books, 1967) 31-48.

"Le mouvement biblique." *Pax Romana Journal* (1962, no. 3) 3-5.

"Pastoral Apologetics and Modern Exegesis." *Chicago Studies* 1, 2: 158-70. Reprinted in *Myths and Realities* (Milwaukee: Bruce, 1963) 70-82.

"The Social Character of Inspiration." *CBQ* 24: 115-24. Reprinted in *CrossCurr* 12 (1962) 423-31; in *Myths and Realities* (Milwaukee: Bruce, 1963) 59-69.

Review of

    Bible Key Words 3: Faith, by Rudolf Bultmann and Artur Weiser; *Spirit of God*, by Eduard Schweizer *et al.* *TS* 23: 345.

    Frör, Kurt. *Biblische Hermeneutik.* *CBQ* 24: 314-16.

    Gnilka, Joachim. *Die Verstockung Israels: Isaias 6:9-10 in der Theologie der Synoptiker.* *TS* 23: 459-61.

    Hempel, Johannes. *Apoxysmata: Vorarbeiten zu einer Religionsgeschichte und Theologie des Alten Testaments.* BZAW 81. *CBQ* 24: 239.

    Legier [sic], Louis. *Péché d'Adam, péché du monde 2: Le Nouveau Testament.* *TS* 23: 286-87.

    Léon-Dufour, Xavier *et al.*, eds. *Vocabulaire de théologie biblique.* *TS* 23: 645-46.

    von Rad, Gerhard. *Genesis.* *CBQ* 24: 73-74.

    Rahner, Karl. *Inspiration in the Bible.* *TS* 23: 104-06.

    Schweizer, Eduard. *Church Order in the New Testament.* *TS* 23: 116-17.

    Vawter, Bruce. *The Conscience of Israel— Pre-Exilic Prophets and Prophecy.* *CBQ* 24: 76-77.

    Vincent, Albert. *Lexique biblique.* *CBQ* 24: 194-95.

    1963

Myths and Realities: Studies in Biblical Theology. Milwaukee/London: Bruce/G. Chapman. Translation: *Mito y realidad en el Antiguo Testamento* (Madrid: Morova, 1971).

"The Biblical Movement and the Laity." *CMind* 61 (April) 37-43.

"Jacob at Peniel: Gn 32, 24-32." *CBQ* 25: 71-76.

"Scripture and Tradition in Roman Catholicism." *Dialog* 2: 282-87.

"The Significance of the Old Testament for Christian Faith in Roman Catholicism." *The Old Testament and Christian Faith* (ed. B. W. Anderson; New York: Harper & Row) 102-14.

"Some Recent Books on the Bible." *New City* 1 (February 15) 4-8.

Review of

    Childs, Brevard S. *Memory and Tradition in Israel.* *TS* 24: 714-15.

    Deissler, A. and M. Delcor. *La sainte Bible 8/1: Les petits prophètes (Osée, Joël, Amos, Abdias, Jonas).* *TS* 24: 329.

    Douglas, J. D., ed. *The New Bible Dictionary.* *TS* 24: 121-22

    Grelot, Pierre. *Sens chrétien de l'Ancien Testament: Esquisse d'un traité dogmatique. TS* 24: 291-93.

Heschel, Abraham J. *The Prophets. TS* 24: 470-71.

Larcher, C. *L'Actualité chrétienne de l'Ancien Testament d'après le Nouveau Testament. TS* 24: 668-70.

Larsson, Edvin. *Christus als Vorbild. TS* 24: 678-80.

Noth, Martin. *Das dritte Buch Mose: Leviticus. CBQ* 25: 484-85.

Porteous, Norman W. *Das Danielbuch. CBQ* 25: 485-86.

Ringgren, Helmer *et al. Sprüche/ Prediger/ Das Hohe Lied/ Klagelieder/ Das Buch Esther. CBQ* 25: 216-17.

1964

"An Everlasting Love." *Way* 4: 87-99.

"Authority and Power in the New Testament." *CBQ* 26: 413-22. Reprinted in *Contemporary Spirituality* (ed. R. Gleason; New York: Macmillan, 1968) 141-51.

"Comments on George Malone's 'Mater Si! Magistra Si!' " *Chicago Studies* 3: 84-86.

"Evaluating the Deluge Myth." *Critic* 23, 3: 31-35.

"Exegete at the Manger." *Comm* 81: 439-42.

"Natural Law in the New Testament." *BR* 9: 3-13.

"One English Bible?" *Extension* 59 (May) 24-25. Abridged in *CDigest* 28, 12: 68-71.

" 'Proclamation' and 'Teaching' in the Primitive Church." *Living Light* 1, 2: 118-36.

"Roman Catholic Perspective on the Discussion with Theologians." *Criterion* 3, 2: 35-38.

"Rudolf Bultmann: A Catholic Survey." *Month* 32 (July-August) 51-62. Revised as "Rudolf Bultmann and the Bible," in *Vital Concepts of the Bible* (Wilkes Barre: Dimension Books, 1967) 93-116.

"Signs and Power: The New Testament Presentation of Miracles." *Chicago Studies* 3: 5-18.

"The State in Christian Perspective." *Critic* 22, 6: 15-21.

"Theology in the Seminary." *Perspectives* 9: 169-78. Reprinted as "Theology in the Seminary Curriculum," in *Seminary Education in Time of Change* (eds. James M. Lee and Louis J. Putz; Notre Dame: Fides, 1965) 405-28.

Review of

Albright, William Foxwell. *History, Archaeology and Christian Humanism. Critic* 22, 6: 69-70.

Bruce, F. F. *Israel and the Nations from the Exodus to the Fall of the Second Temple. TS* 25: 129-30.

Dentan, Robert C. *Preface to Old Testament Theology.* Rev. ed. *TS* 25: 306-7.

Greenslade, S. L., ed. *The Cambridge History of the Bible, 2: The West from the*

Reformation to the Present Day. TS 25: 254-55.

Gunkel, Hermann. *Genesis. CBQ* 26: 487-88.

Loretz, Oswald. *Gotteswort und menschliche Erfahrung. CBQ* 26: 377-78.

McCarthy, Dennis J. *Treaty and Covenant: A Study in Form in the Ancient Oriental Documents and in the Old Testament. TS* 25: 308.

Metzger, Bruce M. *The Text of the New Testament. Critic* 22, 6: 69-70.

Mowinckel, Sigmund. *Tetrateuch-Pentateuch-Hexateuch. CBQ* 26: 495-96.

Renckens, Henricus. *Israel's Concept of the Beginning. TS* 25: 422-24.

Shedd, Russell Philip. *Man in Community. TS* 25: 433-35.

1965

Dictionary of the Bible. Milwaukee/London: Bruce/G. Chapman; reprint ed., Milwaukee: Bruce, 1966; New York: Macmillan, 1967. Translation: *Dizionario Biblico* (trans. F. Gentiloni Silveri; Assisi: Cittadella, 1973).

The Power and the Wisdom: An Interpretation of the New Testament. Milwaukee/London: Bruce/G. Chapman; reprint ed., Milwaukee: Bruce, 1965; New York: Macmillan, 1967; Garden City: Doubleday, 1972. Translations: *El poder y la sabiduría* (trans. C. Giménez; Santander: Sal Terrae, 1967); *Die Botschaft des Neuen Testamentes* (trans. Hildebrand Pfiffner; Stuttgart: Räber, 1968); *Le scelte di Cristo* (trans. Clarisse di S. Chiara di Roma; Assisi: Cittadella, 1969); *Os Grandes Temas do Novo Testamento* (trans. Cácio Gomes and Therezinha Gomes; Petropolis, Brasil: Editôra Vozes, 1972); *Moc I Madrość* (Warsaw: Instytut Wydawniczy "Pax," 1975).

"Archaeology and Gen 1-11." *BibToday* 16: 1035-41.

"The Growth of Expectation." *Way* 5: 298-306.

"The Holy Spirit in the Church." *Living Light* 2, 1: 8-19.

Review of

Altmann, Peter. *Erwählungstheologie und Universalismus im Alten Testament. JBL* 84: 333.

Benoit, Pierre. *Aspects of Biblical Inspiration. TS* 26: 675-76.

Carlson, R. A. *David, the Chosen King: A Traditio-Historical Approach to the Second Book of Samuel. TS* 26: 110-13.

Congar, Yves. *Power and Poverty in the Church. Critic* 23, 4: 75-76.

Gottwald, Norman K. *All the Kingdoms of the Earth. TS* 26: 431-33.

Grässer, Erich. *Der Glaube im Hebräerbrief. CBQ* 27: 423-24.

Harrelson, Walter. *Interpreting the Old Testament. TS* 26: 507-8.

Otzen, Benedikt. *Studien über Deuterosacharja. CBQ* 27: 287-88.

von Rad, Gerhard. *Das fünfte Buch Mose: Deuteronomium. CBQ* 27: 72-73.

[Rahner, Karl et al.] *The Word: Readings in Theology. Critic* 23, 3: 69-70.

Renaud, B. *Structure et attaches littéraires de Michée IV-V.* *TS* 26: 109-10.

Ruppert, Lothar. *Die Josepherzählung der Genesis: Ein Beitrag zur Theologie der Pentateuchquellen.* *CBQ* 27: 434-35.

Speiser, E. A. *Genesis.* AB 1. *TS* 26: 333-34.

de Vaux, Roland. *Les sacrifices de l'Ancien Testament.* *TS* 26: 109-10.

1966

Authority in the Church. New York/London: Sheed and Ward/G. Chapman; reprint ed., Garden City: Image Books, 1971. Translations: *La autoridad en la Iglesia* (trans. Antonio González Molina; Bilbao: Mensajero, 1968); *Autorität in der Kirche* (trans. P. I. Erbes; Paderborn: Schöningh Verlag, 1968); *Het gezag in de Kerk: Naar een dimensie van gemeenschappelijkheid* (trans. Martha van den Walle; Tielt: Lannoo, 1968); *L'autorità nella Chiesa* (trans. G. Toselli; Torino: Gribaudi, 1969); *L'Evangile et le pouvoir dans l'Eglise* (trans. Luce Gérard; Paris: Editions du Centurion, 1970). Excerpt "Prestige of Authority," in *Sign* 45, 10: 24-26; "Reflections on the Church's Teaching Authority," in *Cath World* 203: 86-90.

Mastering the Meaning of the Bible. Wilkes Barre/London: Dimension Books/Burns Oates (1969).

The World of the Judges. Englewood Cliffs/London: Prentice-Hall/G. Chapman (1967). Translations: *Il mondo dei Giudici* (trans. Centro Catechismo Salesiano; Torino: Elle Di Ci, 1971); *El mundo de los Jueces* (Bilbao: Mensajero, 1972).

"Biblical Concepts of Community and State." *Church-State Relations in Ecumenical Perspective* (ed. E. Smith; Pittsburgh: Duquesne) 78-91.

"Christian Authority and Christian Obedience." *Direction* 13, 3: 5-12.

"Foreword." Ingo Hernann. *The Experience of Faith.* New York: P. J. Kenedy.

"The Freedom of the Christian." *Ampleforth Journal* 71· (1966) 143-49. Reprinted in *Religious Liberty: An End and a Beginning* (ed. John C. Murray; New York: Macmillan, 1966) 96-106; *Faith and Freedom, Essays in Contemporary Theology* (ed. Charles B. Ketcham and James Day; New York: Weybright and Tally, 1969) 59-68.

"Key Words in Scripture: Law." *Living Light* 3, 4: 93-98.

"Law in the New Testament." *Jurist* 26: 167-80.

"Q.E.D." *Critic* 25, 3: 12-14, 92, 94, 96.

"The Word of God in Church and World." *North American Liturgical Week* 27: 72-80.

Review of

Cameron, J. M. *Images of Authority.* *JES* 3: 570-71.

Eissfeldt, Otto. *The Old Testament: An Introduction.* *TS* 27: 266-67.

Gerstenberger, Erhard. *Wesen und Herkunft des "Apodiktischen Rechts."* *CBQ* 28: 500-1.

Gordis, Robert, ed. *Max Leopold Margolis: Scholar and Teacher. CBQ* 14: 414.

Myers, Jacob M. *I & II Chronicles.* AB 12, 13. *TS* 27: 267-68.

1967

Vital Concepts of the Bible. Wilkes Barre/London: Dimension Books/Burns and Oates (1968).

"Amorrites." *NCE* 1: 451-52.

"Diaspora, Jewish." *NCE* 4: 852.

"Elam." *NCE* 5: 236-37.

"Foreword." Leopold Sabourin. *The Names and Titles of Jesus.* New York: Macmillan.

"The Freedom of the Priest-Scholar." *Academic Freedom and the Catholic University* (eds. Edward Manier and John W. Houck; Notre Dame: Fides) 164-77.

"The Historical Prologue of Deuteronomy" *Fourth World Congress of Jewish Studies.* Jerusalem: World Congress of Jewish Studies. I, 95-101.

"Ivories of Palestine." *NCE* 7: 778-80.

"Key Terms in Scripture: Prudence." *Living Light* 4, 1: 94-98.

"Key Words in Scripture: Community." *Living Light* 4, 3: 106-11.

"Key Words in Scripture: Peace." *Living Light* 4, 2: 77-80.

"Key Words in Scripture: Work." *Living Light* 4, 4: 74-79.

"Q.E.D." *Critic* 25, 4: 10-11, 88.

"Q.E.D." *Critic* 25, 5: 10-12, 88.

"Q.E.D." *Critic* 25, 6: 6-8, 91-92.

"Q.E.D." *Critic* 26, 1: 6, 8, 79.

"Q.E.D." *Critic* 26, 2: 8, 10, 92.

"Q.E.D." *Critic* 26, 3: 10-11, 13, 88.

"Reflections on Wisdom." *JBL* 86: 1-9.

"Scripture and Tradition: A Roman Catholic View." *Reconsiderations* (New York: World Horizons) 13-25.

"The Son of Man Must Suffer." *Way* 7: 6-17. Reprinted in *The Mystery of Suffering and Death* (ed. M. Taylor; Staten Island: Alba House, 1973) 31-44.

"Sophisticating the Catechism." *Comm* 87: 201-2.

"Susa." *NCE* 13: 824-25.

"The Values of the Old Testament." *Concilium* 30 (New York/London: Paulist/G. Chapman) 5-32/4-17. Translations in European editions: "Les valeurs de l'Ancien Testament," *Concilium* 30: 11-33; "Los valores del Antiguo Testamento," *Concilium* 30: 536-63; "Valores do Antigo Testamento," *Concilium* 10: 7-30; "I valori dell'Antico Testamento," *Concilium* 3, 10: 19-45; "Die Werte des Alten Testaments," *Concilium* 3,

12: 774-88.

Review of

Adolfs, Robert. *The Grave of God: Has the Church a Future? Comm* 87: 415.

Dahood, Mitchell. *Psalms I: 1-50.* AB 16. *CBQ* 29: 138-40.

Davis, Charles. *A Question of Conscience. National Catholic Reporter* 4 (Supplement, December 6) 1.

Jeremias, Joachim. *Le message central du Nouveau Testament. CBQ* 29: 265-66.

Jones, A. *The Jerusalem Bible. Critic* 25, 4: 68-69.

Kuntz, J. Kenneth. *The Self-Revelation of God. TS* 28: 835-36.

Noth, Martin. *Das vierte Buch Mose: Numeri. CBQ* 29: 667-68.

Perrin, Norman. *Rediscovering the Teaching of Jesus. CBQ* 29: 671-72.

Ramsey, Paul. *Deeds and Rules in Christian Ethics. Comm* 86: 525.

Schmid, Hans Heinrich. *Wesen und Geschichte der Weisheit. JBL* 86: 220-21.

Soma, Nahum M. *Understanding Genesis: The Heritage of Biblical Literature. StAnth* 74 (June) 22.

1968

Editor [with Ovid Sellers *et al.*]. *The 1957 Excavation at Beth-Zur.* AASOR 38. Cambridge: American Schools of Oriental Research.

Second Isaiah. AB 20. Garden City: Doubleday.

"Adam and Eve." *Encyclopaedia Britannica.* 14th ed. 1: 119-21.

"Aspects of Old Testament Thought." *JBC* 2: 736-67. Translation: "Aspectos del pensamiento veterotestamentario." *Commentario Biblico "San Jeronimo."* (Madrid: Christiandad, 1972) 607-82.

"The Excavation and Structures of Fields I and III." *The 1957 Excavation at Beth-Zur* (ed. Ovid Sellers *et al.*; AASOR 38; Cambridge: American Schools of Oriental Research, 1968) 18-25.

"The Gospel According to Matthew." *JBC* 2: 62-114. Translation: "Evangelio según San Mateo." *Comentario Biblico "San Jeronimo."* (Madrid: Christiandad, 1972) 163-293.

"Hexateuch." *Encyclopaedia Britannica.* 14th ed. 11: 468.

"Israel." *Encyclopaedia Britannica.* 14th ed. 12: 696-97.

"Key Words in Scripture: Creation." *Living Light* 5, 1: 95-99.

"Key Words in Scripture: Mystery." *Living Light* 5, 2: 71-76.

"Key Words in Scripture: Obedience." *Living Light* 5, 3: 93-98.

"Key Words in Scripture: World." *Living Light* 5, 4: 93-97.

"Mizpah." *Encyclopaedia Britannica.* 14th ed. 15: 607.

"No Idle God." *Way* 8: 171-80.

"Pentateuch." *Encyclopaedia Britannica.* 14th ed. 17: 581-83.

"Q.E.D." *Critic* 26, 4: 12, 15, 87-88.

"Q.E.D." *Critic* 26, 5: 10-11, 13, 95.

"Q.E.D." *Critic* 26, 6: 6, 8.

"Q.E.D." *Critic* 27, 1: 8-9, 78.

"Q.E.D." *Critic* 27, 2: 8, 10, 102, 104.

"Q.E.D." *Critic* 27, 3: 8, 10, 93-95.

"The Sacraments in Bultmann's Theology." *Rudolf Bultmann in Catholic Thought* (eds. Thomas O'Meara and Donald M. Weiser; New York: Herder and Herder) 151-66.

"Twelve Tribes of Israel." *Encyclopaedia Britannica.* 14th ed. 22: 427-29.

"Zephania, Book of." *Encyclopaedia Britannica.* 14th ed. 23: 960-61.

"Zion." *Encyclopaedia Britannica.* 14th ed. 23: 974.

Review of

> Baum, Gregory. *The Credibility of the Church Today: A Reply to Charles Davis.* *StAnth* 76 (August) 10-13.

> Fitzmyer, Joseph A. *Pauline Theology: A Brief Sketch. CBQ* 30: 94.

> Haenchen, Ernst. *Der Weg Jesu: Eine Erklärung des Markus-Evangeliums und der kanonischen Parallelen. CBQ* 30: 615-17.

> Zimmermann, Heinrich. *Neutestamentliche Methodenlehre: Darstellung der historisch-kritischen Methode. CBQ* 30: 136-37.

1969

Editor. *The New Testament for Spiritual Reading.* 25 vols. New York/London: Herder and Herder/Burns and Oates, 1969-71. Original ed.: Wolfgang Trilling *et al.*, eds. *Geistliche Schriftlesung.* Düsseldorf: Patmos-Verlag, 1965-70.

The Roman Catholic Church. New York: Holt, Rinehart and Winston; reprint ed., New York: Holt Rinehart and Winston, 1969; London: Weidenfeld and Nicolson, 1969. *Translation:Kościół Rzymsko Katolicki* (trans. Tadeusz Szafranski; Warsaw: Instytut Wydawniczy "Pax," 1972). Excerpt and condensed "Saints," in *CDigest* 34, 1: 33-38; "Saints. Their Lives are the Best Explanation We Have of Christianity," in *Sign* 48, 11: 5-7.

"The Authority of the Word." *Preaching* 4 (October-November) 20-29.

"Key Words in Scripture: Dominion." *Living Light* 6, 3: 90-95.

"Key Words in Scripture: Meekness." *Living Light* 6, 4: 89-93.

"Key Words in Scripture: Temptation." *Living Light* 6, 2: 76-81.

"Key Words in Scripture: Truth." *Living Light* 6, 1: 65-69.

"The Newness of God." *Way* 9: 267-77.

" 'Peace': A Biblical Concept." *New Testament Themes for Contemporary Man* (ed. R. Ryan; Englewood Cliffs: Prentice-Hall) 156-60.

"Q.E.D." *Critic* 27, 4: 10, 12, 95-96.

"Q.E.D." *Critic* 27, 5: 8, 10, 93, 96.

"Q.E.D." *Critic* 27, 6: 6-7, 99-100.

"Q.E.D." *Critic* 28, 1: 8, 10, 92-94.

"Q.E.D." *Critic* 28, 2: 8, 10, 110-11.

"The Suffering of Staying In." *National Catholic Reporter* 5 (March 26) 6. Reprinted in *Creative Suffering* (Philadelphia: Pilgrim Press, 1970) 83-95.

Review of

> Dahood, Mitchell. *Psalms II: 51-100.* AB 17. *CBQ* 31:80-81.
>
> Dentan, Robert C. *The Knowledge of God in Ancient Israel. TS* 30: 115-16.
>
> Eissfeldt, Otto. *Kleine Schriften.* Vol. 4. *CBQ* 31: 426.
>
> Fohrer, Georg. *Geschichte der israelitischen Religion. CBQ* 31: 428.
>
> Lindblom, J. *Gesichte und Offenbarungen. Bib* 50: 580-82.
>
> Müller, Hans-Peter. *Ursprünge und Strukturen alttestamentlicher Eschatologie.* BZAW 109. *CBQ* 3: 594-95.
>
> Rahner, Karl *et al.*, eds. *Sacramentum Mundi.* Vol. 1, 2. *Comm* 89: 677-78.
>
> Rowley, H. H. *Dictionary of Bible Personal Names. JBL* 88: 250.
>
> Rowley, H. H. *Dictionary of Bible Themes. JBL* 88: 250.
>
> Simons, Francis. *Infallibility and the Evidence. Critic* 27, 3: 8.
>
> de Vaux, Roland. *Bible et Orient. TS* 30: 157-58.

1970

"The Institutional Church." *The Dynamic in Christian Thought* (ed. Joseph Papin; Villanova: Villanova University) 254-78.

"The Meaning of Salvation." *Way* 10: 278-87.

"Q.E.D." *Critic* 28, 3: 8, 10, 94-96.

"Q.E.D." *Critic* 28, 4: 8, 10, 86-87.

"Q.E.D." *Critic* 28, 5: 6, 87-88.

"Q.E.D." *Critic* 28, 6: 8-9, 79-80.

"Q.E.D." *Critic* 29, 1: 8-9, 93-94.

"Q.E.D." *Critic* 29, 2: 8, 94-95.

Review of

> Klatt, Werner. *Hermann Gunkel: Zu seiner Theologie der Religionsgeschichte und zur Entstehung der formgeschichtlichen Methode. CBQ* 32: 459-60.

Schulz, Hermann. *Das Todesrecht im Alten Testament: Studien zur Rechtsform der Mot-Jumat Sätze. CBQ* 32: 307-8.

1971

"Authority Crisis in Roman Catholicism." *Erosion of Authority* (ed. Clyde L. Manschreck; Nashville: Abingdon) 37-58.

"The Demythologizing of Louis Evely." *Comm* 94, 13: 307-10.

"Duchowieństwo [The Clergy], *Życie i Myśl* 21: 27-41.

"The Hebrew Community and the Old Testament." *The Interpreter's One-Volume Commentary on the Bible* (ed. Charles Laymon; Nashville: Abingdon) 1072-76.

"No Runs, No Hits, No Errors." *National Catholic Reporter* 7 (July 30) 10.

"Q.E.D." *Critic* 29, 3: 8, 95-96.

"Q.E.D." *Critic* 29, 4: 6, 8, 87-88.

"Q.E.D." *Critic* 29, 5: 10, 12-13.

"Q.E.D." *Critic* 29, 6: 8-9, 78-79.

"Q.E.D." *Critic* 30, 1: 8, 10, 86-87.

"Q.E.D." *Critic* 30, 2: 8-9, 82-84.

Review of

Boecker, Hans Jochen. *Die Beurteilung der Anfänge des Königtums in den deuteronomistischen Abschnitten des 1. Samuelbuches: Ein Beitrag zum Problem des "Deuteronomistischen Geschichtswerks." CBQ* 33: 415-16.

Dahood, Mitchell. *Psalms III: 101-50.* AB 17A. *CBQ* 33: 421-22.

Dulles, Avery R. *The Survival of Dogma. Spiritual Life* 17: 289-90.

Kornfeld, Walter. *Religion und Offenbarung in der Geschichte Israels. JBL* 90: 106, 108.

Pauritsch, Karl. *Die neue Gemeinde: Gott sammelt Ausgestossene und Arme (Jesaia 56-66). JBL* 90: 488-89.

Pohlmann, Karl-Friedrich. *Studien zum dritten Esra: Ein Beitrag zur Frage nach dem ursprünglichen Schluss des chronistischen Geschichtswerkes.* FRLANT 104. *CBQ* 33: 598-99.

Rice, Charles E. *Authority and Rebellion: The Case of Orthodoxy in the Catholic Church. National Catholic Reporter* 8 (November 19) 17.

Swidler, Leonard and Arlene, eds. and trans. *Bishops and People. JES* 8: 651.

1972

"Biblical Anthropomorphism and the Humaneness of God." *Religion and the Humanizing of Man* (ed. James M. Robinson; Waterloo, Ontario: Council on the Study of Religion) 172-86.

"God With Us." *Way* 12: 14-19.

"Ministerial Structures in the New Testament." *Concilium* 74 (New York: Paulist) 13-22. Translations in European editions: "Amtsstrukturen in Neuen Testament," *Concilium* 8: 239-45; "Les structures du ministrère dans le Nouveau Testament," *Concilium* 74: 21-29; "Strutture ministeriali nel Nuovo Testamente," *Concilium* 8, 4: 644-56.

"Q.E.D." *Critic* 30, 3: 8, 10-11, 92-93.

"Q.E.D." *Critic* 30, 4: 9-11, 95-96.

"Q.E.D." *Critic* 30, 5: 6, 8-9, 96.

"Q.E.D." *Critic* 30, 6: 6-8, 80.

Review of

Eagleson, John and Philip Scharper. *The Radical Bible. Comm* 96: 503.

Edwards, George R. *Jesus and the Politics of Violence. Comm* 96: 503.

Grønbaek, Jakob H. *Die Geschichte von Aufstieg Davids (1 Sam. 15 - 2 Sam. 5): Tradition und Komposition. CBQ* 34: 220-22.

Hesse, Franz. *Abschied von der Heilsgeschichte. CBQ* 34: 504-5.

Keet, Cuthbert C. *A Study of the Psalms of Ascents: A Critical and Exegetical Commentary upon Psalms CXX to CXXXIV. CBQ* 34: 83.

Smith, Morton. *Palestinian Parties and Politics that Shaped the Old Testament. ATR* 54: 122-24.

1973

Did I Say That? Chicago: Thomas More.

Contributing Editor. *Encyclopedia Americana.* International edition. New York: Americana Corporation.

Seek. Epistles. Contemporary Guide to the New Testament. Chicago: Thomas More.

"Justice and Justification." *Way* 13: 198-206.

"Roman Catholicism." *Encyclopaedia Britannica.* 15th ed. Macropedia 15: 985-1002.

"Samuel." *Encyclopaedia Britannica.* 15th ed. Macropedia 16: 207-8.

Review of

Fohrer, Georg. *History of Israelite Religion. CBQ* 35: 382.

Lyonnet, Stanislao. *Il Nuove Testamento alla luce dell'Antico. CBQ* 35: 251.

von Rad, Gerhard. *Das erste Buch Mose: Genesis.* 9th Aufl. *CBQ* 35: 403.

1974

Joint Author [with J. J. Wylie.] *Proclamation: Advent-Christmas.* Series A. Philadelphia: Fortress.

A Theology of the Old Testament. Garden City: Doubleday.

"Primitive History: Form Criticism." *Society of Biblical Literature 1974 Seminar Papers.* Vol. 1 (ed. George MacRae; Cambridge: Society of Biblical Literature) 87-99.

Review of

Balz, Horst and Siegfried Schulz, eds. *Das Wort und die Wörter: Festschrift Gerhard Friedrich. ATR* 56: 360-61.

Cazelles, Henri, ed. *Introduction à la Bible 2: Introduction critique à l'Ancien Testament.* 2nd ed. *TS* 35: 552-54.

Eissfeldt, Otto. *Kleine Schriften.* Vol. 5. *CBQ* 36: 103-4.

Léon-Dufour, Xavier, ed. *Dictionary of Biblical Theology. TS* 35: 400.

Maguire, Daniel C. *Death by Choice. Critic* 33, 1: 85-87.

Seybold, Klaus. *Das davidische Königtum im Zeugnis der Propheten.* FRLANT 107. *ATR* 56: 70-71.

Zenger, Erich. *Die Sinaitheophanie: Untersuchungen zum jahwistischen und elohistischen Geschichtwerk. CBQ* 36: 445.

1975

Light on the Epistles. Chicago: Thomas More.

"The Church as an Institution: An Eschatological View." *The Church and Human Society at the Threshold of the Third Millennium* (ed. Joseph Papin; Villanova: Villanova University) 177-97.

"An Exegetical Answer to Lonergan's Method in Theology." *Listening* 10: 2-12.

Review of

Hayes, John H. ed. *Old Testament Form Criticism. ATR* 57: 227-28.

Holmgren, Frederick. *With Wings as Eagles. Isaiah 40/55. ATR* 57: 226-27.

Miranda, José Porfirio. *Marx and the Bible: A Critique of the Philosophy of Oppression. JBL* 94: 280-81.

Rogerson, J. W. *Myth in Old Testament Interpretation.* BZAW 134. *CBQ* 37: 290-91.

Contributors:

Gregory G. Baum	University of Toronto
Elizabeth Bellefontaine	Mount Saint Vincent University (Halifax)
Joseph Blenkinsopp	University of Notre Dame
Raymond E. Brown, S. S.	Union Theological Seminary (New York)
John E. Burkhart	McCormick Theological Seminary
P. Joseph Cahill	University of Alberta
Bernard Cooke	University of Windsor
John Dominic Crossan	DePaul University
Harry M. Culkin	Cathedral College and Long Island University
James W. Flanagan	University of Michigan
Joseph A. Fitzmyer, S. J.	Weston College School of Theology
David Noel Freedman	University of Michigan
Robert W. Funk	University of Montana
George E. Mendenhall	University of Michigan
Thomas N. Munson	DePaul University
Roland E. Murphy, O. Carm.	Duke University Divinity School
Anita Weisbrod Robinson	University of Notre Dame
James M. Robinson	Claremont Graduate School
Gerard S. Sloyan	Temple University
Bruce Vawter, C. M.	DePaul University
Kathleen O'Brien Wicker	Scripps College
Donald H. Wimmer	Seton Hall University

Index of Scripture
and Source References

Index of Modern Authors

345

164